Naomi Ozaniec is an author and teacher. .... Kabbalah as a practical system of psycho-spiritual development and awakening since the 1970s, and has worked with Gareth Knight and Dolores Ashcroft-Nowicki, both experienced teachers and proponents of practical Kabbalah.

By the same author:

Chakras: A Beginner's Guide

Meditation: A Beginner's Guide

Teach Yourself Meditation

New Perspectives: Chakras

Thorsons First Directions: Chakras

Teach Yourself Tarot

Dowsing: A Beginner's Guide

The Illustrated Guide to Tarot

The Little Book of Egyptian Wisdom

The Elements of the Chakras

101 Essential Tips: Basic Meditation

Initiation into the Tarot

Daughters of the Goddess – The Sacred Priestess

D1425299

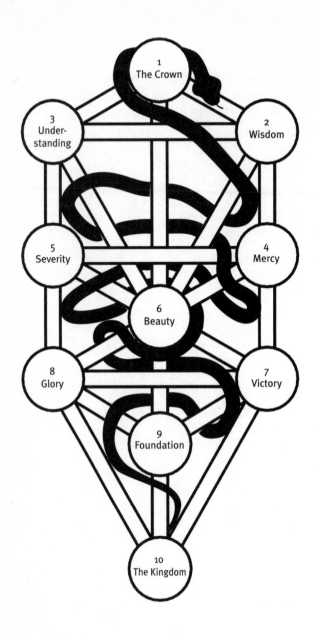

'Discover the serpent of illusion by the help of the serpent of wisdom and then will the sleeping serpent mount upwards towards the place of meeting.'

ALICE BAILEY, *A TREATISE ON WHITE MAGIC*

THE
KABBALAH
EXPERIENCE

A PRACTICAL GUIDE TO KABBALISTIC WISDOM

Naomi Ozaniec

WATKINS PUBLISHING
LONDON

This edition published in the UK in 2005 by
Watkins Publishing, Sixth Floor, Castle House, 75-76 Wells Street,
London W1T 3QH

First published in the UK in 2003 as *The Aquarian Qabalah*

© Naomi Ozaniec 2003

Designed and typeset by Jerry Goldie

Printed and bound in Great Britain

British Library Cataloguing in Publication data available

Library of Congress Cataloguing in Publication data available

ISBN 1 84293 143 1

www.watkinspublishing.com

*This book is dedicated firstly to D.F. for paving the way.
It is also dedicated to all the friends and family who have
supported me in so many ways, both great and small.
A special mention goes to my son who has come of age in
the world of computing and has been a good companion
and able assistant. Nor can I forget my father, whose
ceaseless intellectual sparring provided the grit which created
the pearl. Lastly, thanks are due to all the unsung heroes
who kept Kabbalah alive in their hearts while the world
was busy with other things.*

The Kabbalah Experience provides the core curriculum
in the House of Life, a contemporary Mystery School in
the Western Mystery tradition. For more information
on becoming part of the House of Life visit
www.thehouseoflife.co.uk

Contents

FIGURES

TAROT CARDS

Foreword

Invitations to explore pathways of wisdom come in strange and unlikely ways. Back in the late 1960s, my invitation came by means of a poster glimpsed in the London Underground. It offered a series of lectures upon the Kabbalah – a word I then didn't even know the meaning of. Impelled by some unknown necessity, I duly turned up, wondering at my temerity, and sat down to hear the lecturer give what I now recognize was a very skilful introduction to the subject. The ideas ran like wildfire through my brain, making merry synaptic leaps. It was as if the loose pile of beads that was my consciousness had been strung coherently together on a single thread. At the end of the evening, with yet more wonder, I realized that not only had I understood every word the lecturer had uttered, but I had somehow recognized and remembered the arcane concepts he'd delivered. Surely it was impossible that I should so easily have grasped such a complex tradition. Of course, that was not the end of the story. I had experienced one of those rare moments of simultaneous vision and comprehension that suddenly flare and inspire. The following 15 years were spent catching up with that moment and discovering how to turn those concepts into living principles that would pave my way through life.

Kabbalah has been one of the most instrumental teachings in the shaping of the Western esoteric tradition – that wisdom-laden river which has run beneath orthodox spiritualities and state religions. It is known as one of the most traditional of pathways, but it is also one of the most powerful. Tradition is a much traduced word in Western culture, and its true meaning has become distorted. But rather than signifying the ossification of customs and practices, tradition is about the handing over of wisdom from one to another. It can happen, however, that one generation's wisdom appears to be folly to a subsequent generation, solely because the forms that uphold it have not been sufficiently flexible. People grow impatient with old forms, especially those that keep wisdom stagnant. Wisdom relies on the essential sparkle of running water for its lore to be imbibed. Then, like a stream finding new channels, wisdom finds its way, sometimes seemingly flowing underground, sometimes emerging to surprise and delight us. In every generation, wisdom finds its way to us and we yearn to drink of its living waters. When we seek wisdom it is important that we go to the best teachers, those who have sought out the purest sources. I have been fortunate in having many great Kabbalistic teachers, both living and dead, to guide my steps along the paths of the Tree of Life. But how does anyone taking the first steps upon the road to spiritual formation today find teachers with similar insight, courage, compassion and wisdom? Fortunately, though the framework of traditions alters down the centuries, the wisdom-bearers are always known by their devotion to the lore that is passed from mouth to ear. They both speak and live their wisdom. It is thus with great confidence that I recommend this book and its writer to you, for she is one who combines all the above qualities in her dedication to the Mysteries.

Every age needs its own study of the Kabbalah. The 20th century saw the pioneering work of Dion Fortune and Gareth Knight, among others, whose books brought fresh insights to an ancient wisdom tradition. In *The Kabbalah Experience*, Naomi Ozaniec invites you to apply the wisdom of the Kabbalah to your spiritual path in the 21st century. May that journey unfold with wonder and delight as you progress along this way of wisdom!

Caitlín Matthews

Preface

This is an age in search of Wisdom; we have extraordinary technology, we have unprecedented knowledge in so many fields, we have industrial and military power, we have access to unlimited information but where is Wisdom to be found?

The quest for Wisdom is not new but ancient and every tradition has created its own interior path to this elusive citadel. Wisdom is not gained except through personal apprenticeship and willing commitment. It is forged from within the human heart and hewn from the stuff of life experience. Fortunately each new traveller is never alone on this path; others have walked this same road and left landmarks and signs for each new generation. *The Kabbalah Experience* invites the reader to journey upon one of Wisdom's many roads.

Although this particular pilgrimage is rooted within the rich Judaic mystical tradition, this presentation is a more recent Hermetic offshoot from Wisdom's mighty tree. Nonetheless worthy for being a relative newcomer, this path has an additional significance since the Tree of Life has become the backbone and modus operandi of Western Mystery Schools. In the new spirit reflecting the times in which we live, *The Kabbalah Experience,* in conjunction with *The Watkins Tarot,* offers a Mystery School curriculum freely and openly. Such openness was quite impossible a generation ago. But we are living through a spiritual renaissance when the doors of the House of Wisdom have been thrown open to all who wish to enter.

The Kabbalah Experience is not merely a book; rather, it is an opportunity to share and participate in a newly defined Mystery School. In keeping with the Mystery School tradition, this curriculum serves the needs of Wisdom by inviting its companions to the path of re-orientation, rebirth and revelation. But in the light of a new paradigm, the tools of transformation are freely offered to as wide an audience as possible. Here is a unique opportunity to enter the embrace of a Mystery School and become a lover to Wisdom.

The Mystery School has long existed; it has often been a powerful if almost invisible force in the shaping of society. Like an enzyme within the physical body, the Mystery School acts to catalyse, energize and transform both the individual and the group mind. Its potency has little to do with its size but relates instead to its inherent and unique nature; the Mystery School holds and transmits its teachings of being and becoming. This path is one of personal and practical experience, not dogma. Once called 'esoteric science', this body of wisdom teachings has been devalued, ignored and even forbidden. But times change and once-secret and arcane practices have now become culturally acceptable. Embraced as facets of holistic spirituality, the everyday practices of the Mystery School have become commonplace; meditation is considered to be a normal part of life, self-awareness is considered to be a normal personal aspiration. Those teachings once defined as esoteric have passed beyond the confines of the few, even the word 'esoteric' is passing out of current use, ousted by a newer vocabulary; holistic spirituality instead now calls to the many. However, esoteric wisdom never lost sight of a holistic understanding even when society at large had forgotten the meaning of the word. Now that holistic goals find favour with the many, the Mystery School curriculum may find a place of worth in society at large.

Despite claiming a similar territory, the domain of the Mystery School is not at all usurped by the rise of contemporary spiritual practice. Rather, the widespread spiritual resurgence makes it easier to comprehend the potency and value of a nodal point dedicated to transmitting spiritual teachings and initiating into spiritual dimensions.

The mind of the school permits participation within its own unique and unparalleled continuum. The Mystery School still holds the experience of Holy Mystery in the realm of Wisdom's embrace. This is its unique gift, the revealing moment of an awakening.

The Kabbalah Experience invites you to share in the bounty of the Mystery School curriculum: awakening of mind, opening of heart, the many gifts of spirit, dynamic creativity, unexpected inspiration, keen insight, personal empowerment and the multitude of transformations both great and small that fuel the momentum for ongoing renewal, regeneration and rebirth. The book also opens the door to the school itself if your heart reaches out for the touch of the numinous.

As a questing traveller, I am indebted to all my teachers who opened the door to another realm, and in return I hope that this work might offer the same to others.

I hope you will find stable steps on that journey of infinite becoming which is the path of Wisdom.

How to Use this Book

It must be emphasized heavily that the Tree, wonderful as it may be, is a means and not an end. It is not in itself an object for worship or some idol for superstitious reverence. The Tree is a means, a method, a map and a mechanism, for assisting the attainment of the single objective common to all Creeds, Systems, Mysteries and Religions, namely the Mystical Union of Humanity and Divinity in the Great AT-ONE-MENT.

William G. Gray, *The Ladder of Lights*

This book invites the reader to share in a gradual process of transformation and expansion; it is not simply to be read. The book offers a journey of participation and engagement. Each chapter offers a Table of Correspondences, a Commentary, an Evocation, an Internalization and further exercises (*Exercitia Spiritualia*).

The Table of Correspondences begins the work of connection and relationship through which the microcosm and the macrocosm will become reflected. As the reader will discover, the Tree of Life may be thought of as a filing system with ten major divisions which remain ever open to hold new experiences. It is this basic function which gives Kabbalah the flexibility which makes it as relevant in our century as in any other. The Commentary provides an intellectual context which frames each of the inner journeys. The Evocation feeds the intuitive mind. Its fluid style lends itself well to being read aloud. The Internalization or guided meditation synthesizes the intellectual structure with an intuitive understanding and precipitates the possibility of personal realization. The Spiritual Exercises widen and deepen the foundation of understanding which has already been established.

The Kabbalah Experience offers the reader an initiatory journey of self-discovery and personal transformation. Kabbalah cannot be conveyed through the intellect alone. An initiatory process is holistic, engaging the intellect and the imagination, the intuition and the intelligence. Engagement with the Tree of Life takes place through three approaches.

Intellectual

This level involves a deepening familiarity with the structure of the Tree and its traditional correspondences. This represents the primary level of learning which forms the vital intellectual foundation. This is a shared level of understanding which can be learned from an informed teaching source.

Intuitive

This level arises as the symbolic correspondences become absorbed, integrated and internalized. Intuitive understanding cannot arise without the fuel gained by meditation, reflection and contemplation. This is a personal level of insight which arises only from interaction with the symbolic aspects of the Tree.

Inspirational

This level arises spontaneously from the marriage of intellectual understanding and intuitive insight. Inspiration is the child of this union. Independent and irrepressible, inspiration channels both the intuition and the intellect into a single creative stream. It arises in response to the initiatory journey into the Tree. Inspiration is the fruit of the Tree of Life.

These three levels interact and overlap in a continuously mobile process of discovery and realization. Together the broadening of the intellect, the awakening of the intuition and the birth of inspiration impel the process of initiatory transformation.

The Preliminaries – Expect Change

1. Kabbalah will initiate a process of dynamic change.
2. Proceed steadily. According to an old saying, 'Make haste slowly'.

The Practicalities – Keep a Journal

1. Record your intellectual study.
2. Record your meditative experiences.
3. Record your dreams and realizations.

These sources together will cumulatively provide personal inspiration and a
dynamic momentum which will fuel your drive for self-understanding.

The Process – Participate Inwardly and Outwardly

The process of change operates both inwardly and outwardly. Inwardly the
process of change is precipitated by the meditative involvement with the
Tree. Outwardly the process of change is precipitated by relating the experiences of everyday life to the Tree, which offers itself as a filing system
holding all life experience.

Pathworking – The Journeys of Transformation

Traditionally the meditative journeys on the Tree of Life have been called
Pathworkings. Like a path, the inner journey connects two locations. To
work a Path is to engage with the processes it presents. *The Kabbalah
Experience* however has departed from tradition by employing the related
Tarot Trump directly as the vehicle for realization and transformation. The
symbolism of the 22 Tarot Trumps of the major Arcana provides the sub-
stantive experience of each Path in place of the more traditional broader
and looser constellation of symbols. This decision reflects the contemporary popularity and shared understanding of the Tarot. This new approach
builds in a positive way upon the relatively recent connection between the
22 Paths and the 22 Trumps. Such new ways of interacting with the Tree of
Life affirm its strength and adaptability. Employing the Tarot Trumps in this
specific way also dignifies and restores a potency that has been somewhat
overlooked in the myopic rush to reduce Tarot solely to a tool for divination.
This redefinition of Pathworking can be seen as a contemporary development in both Tarot and Kabbalah. *The Kabbalah Experience* describes these
inner journeys as Internalizations to stress the in-depth and participatory
nature of the process.

Inner journeys take place within the imaginative mind and may require
some individual preparation. Become familiar with the symbolism and
imagery of the relevant Tarot Trump. Read the journey first, simply as text,
and become familiar with its phases before proceeding to engage with it

imaginatively. As each Path connects two Sephiroth, become familiar with the nature and function of the Sephirah at the end of the journey before you actually undertake it.

The journeys through the Paths often have a magical and transformative quality, which is also to be found in the long tradition of imaginative literature of the West. These new journeys often take the form of brief stories with a fairy tale quality, or short vignettes using mythic themes. The purpose of the journey is to precipitate a personal response, not merely to replicate the imagery.

Each Path can be undertaken in two directions – it can be the Path of Ascent or the Path of Descent. Complete the full upward journey through its 32 phases before viewing the journey from a different perspective. Since each Path and Temple can also be experienced at four levels, the model provides plenty of scope for further personal interaction and engagement. Additionally, each of the temple settings may be used as an internal location for personal and unguided reflection where spontaneous imagery and dialogue can take place.

The journey is always one of encounter, with the power of symbol dressed as accessible image. Within the symbol lie the powers and potencies of being and becoming. A single encounter with any Path will be insufficient to engage with the in-depth dynamics present in the journey. Be prepared to revisit a single Path until its meaning has become internalized. Visualizing its landmarks brings only a surface familiarity. Every Path seeks internalization as its psychic contents are gradually ingested. The feelings evoked by the journey should be recorded straightaway. These moments of personal realization begin to express the gnosis of the Path.

In practical terms, because each journey into the Paths begins in its relevant temple (see Appendix 2), create this setting first. At the end of the journey, return to the setting of the temple and spend a little time collecting your thoughts and responses before closing the session. The doorway of the temple represents the threshold between the subjective and objective world. After you have passed through it on the journey of return, dissolve all the images that you have created as a conscious act of closure. Record the experience of each journey straightaway. It remains only to wish you fruitful and insightful travelling.

CHAPTER 1

Introduction and Overview

How and with what we identify holds tremendous power. This becomes the core around which we coalesce through life. Name, status and profession provide an immediate identity. But what remains beneath the social, cultural and economic masks? Stripping these acquired identities away reveals the private world of self-validation which has evolved in response to the accumulated interactions of all significant others in life. But this too is another mask, devised and placed in position by the opinions, judgements and values of others. Such labelling is often distorted. Living out the identity created by others is crippling and diminishing. Living by the identity of social and cultural stereotypes is superficial and inadequate. How is it possible to create an authentic, dynamic and empowering identity which transcends the limitations of upbringing and social role? Additionally, why does this really matter? What are the implications of, firstly, accepting and, secondly, transcending, socially conditioned identities as models to live by? This question lies at the heart of all psycho-spiritual initiatives. The drive towards individuation, becoming yourself, can only take root when impoverished and incomplete models have been put to one side. The transcendent identity which is open, expansive and empowering can only be created through a source which offers a means of recreating the self in a new transcendent role. The Tree of Life is such a source.

Jean Houston, a contemporary pioneering teacher in the field of holistic spirituality describes three realms of self-identity. The first draws upon factual, biographical and historical information. She calls this realm simply THIS IS ME. It is a place where we are easily identified. She calls the second realm WE ARE. This offers the possibility of a shared and mythical identity. It is the place where the individual identity is expanded by symbolic and archetypal identity. Finally, the third realm is that of transcendent identity. This is the realm of the I AM. Here personal identity is totally subsumed into the overarching identity of universal experience. The quantum leap from personal to universal identity is the métier of sacred psychology under whatever guise it is operative. This is the alchemical transformation of lead into gold, as limited view is replaced by infinite view. This is the journey through the Thirty-two Paths of Wisdom.

The Question

The quest opens with a question: Who are you? The question can be answered in many ways and from many levels of understanding. So begin by writing down the first thing that springs to mind. Your name will doubtless be among your first answers. Continue to answer the question by offering many different responses until you feel that you have exhausted the biographical and factual information about your identity. Next answer the question by moving away from factual information about your own life, to an identity which includes others. Let your answer begin with the phrase 'We are'. Finally, answer the question 'Who are you?' by replying with answers that begin 'I am'. This affirmative statement of being is intended to shift your responses away from the periphery of identity towards the core of being. The range of your answers begins the work of expanding a handed-down identity. It represents the first step on the Path of Being and Becoming. In the light of this brief exercise, examine the following propositions and reflect upon each of them in turn.

The Propositions

1. That a reconstructed transcendent identity cannot take place without the expanding and fertilizing qualities of rich symbolic vocabulary.

2. That contemporary society is symbolically impoverished.

3. That symbolism in its fullest and widest sense sustains the health of the psyche by giving expression to the depth, complexity and wholeness of the human person.

4. That without the expansive and liberating functions of transcendent symbols we are reduced to assume an impoverished identity.

5. That in the absence of a symbolically rich cultural milieu, a symbolically rich tradition offers the possibility of exploring depth, involving complexity and attaining wholeness of being.

6. That the Tree of Life is a symbolic tradition.

The Invitation

1. You are invited to participate in an exciting, revealing and challenging journey of personal development.

2. If you accept the invitation in good grace, you will step onto the path of self-realization and self-revelation.

3. If you begin the work of self-realization, you will be taking up the Great Work which lies at the heart of the Ageless Wisdom.

4. If you take up the challenge of the Great Work, your life will undergo a total revolution.

5. The decision whether to accept or decline the invitation lies in the heart not the mind, so spend some reflective time gauging the heart's desire.

The Path

The way ahead has already been mapped out by generations of spiritual pilgrims who have left adequate testament in their writing and the record of their lives. Sometimes however the language of the past has become too distant to serve our needs. We need to hear the landmarks of the journey described in the language of today. The 20th-century development of humanistic depth psychology has rendered a great and often unacknowledged service by placing the tools and techniques of both personal and transpersonal growth within reach. Humanistic psychology might be thought of as a route by which we become integrated and individuated persons. Its purpose is the emergence of the whole or holy self. Its method is one of reconciling apparent duality and opposition into a centre of unity.

The rationale of Jung's analytical psychology and its offshoot systems – such as psychosynthesis, evolved by Roberto Assagioli – provides important keys for the journey ahead. We begin with the 20th-century concept of the unconscious mind. Jung wrote, 'Analysis has given us profound insight into the importance of unconscious influences.'[1] He re-evaluated the very substratum of consciousness. Jung concluded that the demands and tensions of contemporary Western life demanded the development of a concentrated and directed conscious functioning at the expense of a more primitive and immediate awareness. This one-sided development, a long-standing feature of Western culture, has produced an imbalance between consciousness and the unconscious as complementary opposites. Instead of a fluid membrane which permits easy dialogue and two-way communication, a defensive

barrier has grown up. It serves neither mode well and does disservice to the
cause of wholeness. Yet the barrier is invisibly laid down and mostly unrecognized. The division between conscious awareness and the contents of the
unconscious becomes crystallized; the two partners forget how to speak
with one another and indeed take up arms one against the other as different
agendas are carried out. 'The answer obviously consists in getting rid of the
separation between conscious and unconscious.'[2] This barrier is the first
challenge for the traveller. In the words of Roberto Assagioli, 'We have first
to penetrate courageously into the pit of our lower unconscious in order to
discover the dark forces that ensnare and menace us, the "phantasms", the
ancestral or childish images that obsess or silently dominate us, the fears that
paralyse us, the conflicts that waste our energies.'[3] The descent into the
unconscious is the inescapable prelude to the journey of unification. But
how may this descent be accomplished? Jung's answer to this key question
is direct: by spontaneous fantasies, and free association taken under the aegis
of the creative imagination. The quest into the depths may be perilous but
the rewards are rich. 'After having discovered all these elements, we have to
take possession of them and acquire control over them.'[4] The unconscious
is the place where, 'We shall also discover the immense reserve of undifferentiated psychic energy latent in every one of us; that is, the plastic part of
our unconscious which lies at our disposal, empowering us with an
unlimited capacity to learn and create.'[5] The raw energy of the psyche
provides the fuel for the journey. It is the inexhaustible power of becoming.
This stage of the journey has its counterpart on the Tree. But the descent
into this hidden area is just the preparation for the next phase. 'The regions
of the middle and higher unconscious should likewise be explored. In that
we shall discover in ourselves hitherto unknown abilities, our true vocations,
our higher potentialities which seek to express themselves but which we
often repel and repress through lack of understanding, through prejudice or
fear.'[6] The map of consciousness expressed by Assagioli has much in common
with the journey expressed through the Tree of Life.

Assagioli provides a crucial key for the journey as a whole with the
words, 'We are dominated by everything with which our self becomes
identified. We can dominate and control everything from which we dis-
identify ourselves.'[7] This principle is applied to engagement with the Tree
over and over until the original small localized identification of self has been
completely and naturally replaced by an infinite, boundless and eternal
identity. This is not a matter of dogma but of gnosis. 'Why cannot the
unconscious be left to its own devices?' Jung asked. In answer, he observed

1. Lower Unconscious

2. Middle Unconscious

3. Higher Unconscious or
   Superconscious

4. Field of Consciousness

5. Conscious self or 'I'

6. Higher Self

7. Collective Unconscious

8. Contents of the Superconscious

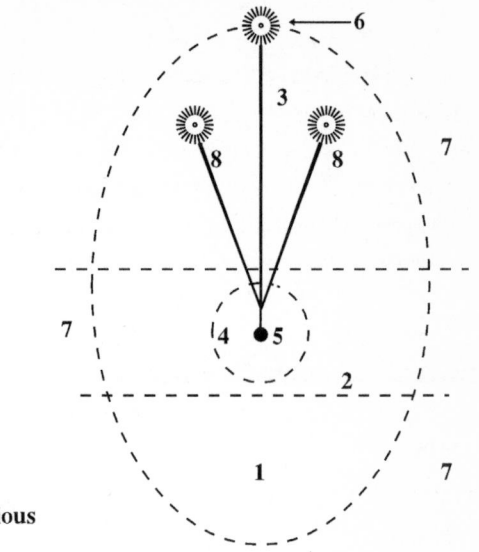

FIGURE 1 THE EGG OF CONSCIOUSNESS

that 'The psyche of civilised man is no longer a self-regulating system.'[8] In other words, the imbalance between the two parts of the one whole has become a schism, no longer even a negotiable barrier. Put at its simplest, we have need to access the deep resources of the unconscious, individually and collectively, if we are to escape the fate of becoming the cloned robots of the 21st century. Individuation – in other words, becoming yourself – cannot be effected without the fertilizing and nourishing waters of the deep.

The process of psychosynthesis can be summarized as gaining a thorough knowledge of one's personality, learning to control its various elements, discovering or creating a new centre and, finally, forming or reconstructing the personality around the new centre. The goal of the process is the achievement of 'harmonious inner integration, true Self-realization, and right relationship with others'.[9] This also describes the journey on the Tree of Life.

At the heart of this work, the reconstruction of being, lies the symbol. Its value, significance and centrality cannot and must not be diminished. 'The transformation of libido through the symbol is a process that has been going on ever since the beginnings of humanity and continues still.'[10] The symbol, like an electrical transformer, has the unique power to translate one current into another and thereby make a viable connection. This is the transcendent function, the bringing together of two opposed powers through a mediating dynamic. By stating that, 'Psychic development cannot be accomplished by intention and will alone; it needs the attraction of the symbol',[11] Jung provides a powerful endorsement for the Tree of Life, which is a metaphysical philosophy enshrined in symbols. As its symbols are plucked and ingested through the process of psychic absorption, so transformation becomes a dynamic process. The Tree of Life fulfils Jung's criteria for a source of transcendent symbols, and it utilizes the same stages suggested by Assagioli. Kabbalah, of course, was in existence long before humanistic psychology provided a validation.

Let us close these introductory insights with the words of an intrepid 20th-century traveller, Dion Fortune, who lived and loved the Tree. 'For the last ten years I have lived and moved and had my being in the Practical Qabalah; I have used its methods both subjectively and objectively till they have become a part of myself, and I know from experience what they yield in psychic and spiritual results, and their incalculable value as a method of using the mind.'[12] She understood its significance and system better than most. The Kabbalist 'formulates a concrete symbol that the eye can see, and lets it represent the abstract reality that no untrained human mind can grasp'.[13] The Kabbalist 'uses the symbol as a means of guiding thoughts into the Unseen and Incomprehensible'.[14] So with these thoughts in mind let us begin the work of using the symbol as a means of guiding us to the unseen and incomprehensible.

The Tree of Life Today

> As we grow the Tree grows. It bears a different variety
> of fruit in the twentieth century than it did in the
> fourteenth, but it still fulfils its function of producing
> sustenance for the insatiable human soul in search of its
> own meaning. What is more its fruits are literally
> inexhaustible, since they constantly renew themselves with
> fresh supplies of Inner Energies. The harder we pluck the
> Tree, the more plentifully comes its amazing fruit.
>
> **William G. Gray,** *The Ladder of Lights*

The Kabbalah Experience presents a view of Kabbalah suited to the times in which we live. It is accessible and relevant to life today. It does not purport to be a presentation of Rabbinical Kabbalah; rather, it is a new view from a Hermetic standpoint. *The Kabbalah Experience* presents a new and unorthodox view designed for the times in which we find ourselves. Just as William Gray restated Kabbalah in 20th-century terms and subtitled *The Ladder of Lights* 'Qabalah Renovata', so *The Kabbalah Experience* is a 'Kabbalah Renovata'. While acknowledging the Jewish origins of Kabbalah, at the same time it is impossible to ignore non-Jewish influences which have become incorporated into its fabric. Kabbalah is the mystical face of Judaism, but its teaching is also universal. In the words of Dion Fortune once more, 'Let it be clearly understood, therefore, that I do not say, This is the teaching of the ancient Rabbis; rather do I say, This is the practice of the modern Qabalists, and for us a much more vital matter, for it is a practical system of spiritual unfoldment; it is the Yoga of the West.'[15] Though best known for its physical component, Yoga is a complete metaphysical system. Yoga means 'to yoke' or 'to unite', and it is the means by which the self is made whole. The Yoga of the West serves the same purpose.

The Kabbalah Experience offers a redefined Kabbalah to an emergent Aquarian generation. Kabbalah is not a fixed and closed system of dogma. It is a living and dynamic system which holds true for every age. A new approach to an established tradition may offend the purists, but it is in keeping with the very essence of the tradition itself. Kabbalah has been enriched by the absorption of new material. The very ease with which current metaphysics have been integrated into the Tree of Life speaks highly for the original blueprint which encompasses growth without modification or violation. The most recent of such offshoots is the merging of Tarot and Kabbalah. This marriage is a by-product of the occult revolution of the late 19th century. Purists might indeed view this as a marriage made in hell, while others might see it as the perfect partnership. Jung lends some support to the idea that Tarot images provide tools for transformation. 'It also seems as if the set of pictures in the Tarot cards were distantly descended from the archetypes of transformation.'[16] In any event, it is a partnership that is not likely to be dissolved. The Tarot and the dynamics of the Tree have become indissoluble. As Robert Wang clearly states, 'The interlock of Tarot and Kaballah is so precise that the two systems are mutually explanatory.'[17] This is our starting point.

The Origins of Kabbalah

The Qabalah is the foundation stone of the Western
Esoteric Tradition.

Will Parfitt, *The Living Qabalah*

The word *Qbl* means 'from mouth to ear' or 'that which is received'. As an
oral tradition, the Kabbalah's precise origins are hard to locate. In recognition of its importance, its beginning has been given a supra-human status.
Accordingly, Moses received this body of esoteric teaching on Mount Sinai.
Another tradition claims that God himself taught it to some of his angels,
who after the Fall communicated it to the children of earth. From here it
was communicated to Adam, Noah and Abraham who took it to Egypt,
where Moses was initiated into its wisdom. However, it is most likely that
Kabbalah arose from the bedrock of early Jewish mysticism, fertilized by the
rich Neo-Platonic, Christian-Gnostic and Neo-Pythagorean currents.

Unlike any other mystical tradition, Kabbalah offers very few written
texts. The Sepher Yetzirah, the Book of Creation, is the cornerstone of
Kabbalistic philosophy. This is a brief and cryptic work in four versions,
ranging from a mere 240 words to a modest 2,500 words. It is attributed to
the patriarch Abraham. The work uniquely describes the process of creation
through the symbolism of letters and numbers while simultaneously serving
as an initiatory text. The Sepher Yetzirah undoubtedly set the tone for the
special strength of Kabbalah. Encoding the sacred into symbolic form created
a unique mode of transmission and protection. Whether this development
occurred through a sense of persecution or not, the method brought concealment. Where an open written tradition would have incurred danger,
encoding mystical ideas into a mnemonic system brought safety. The translation of a complete mystical philosophy into a single complex symbol, the
Tree of Life, is an extraordinary and wonderful achievement. Despite being
a Judaic system, Kabbalah was later discovered by non-Jewish minds, and
became an invigorating current during the Renaissance when ancient
sources and texts were re-evaluated with conscious spiritual intent. Cosimo
de Medici founded the Platonic Academy as a centre for Neo-Platonic
ideals, and a Christian Kabbalah emerged from a Jewish rootstock. Now, at
the beginning of the 21st century, the spirit of another renaissance can be
felt. We too live in a time of conscious spiritual quest. A grass-roots
revolution in consciousness is taking place. As we recast the Tree of Life in
the light of Aquarius, we too are renewed by the process.

The Seven Hermetic Principles

In 1912 a small book, *The Kybalion*, presented a summary of Hermetic principles. These seven principles link the ideas of the distant past to the present moment and provide the springboard from which the mind may leap into the future.

The Principle of Mentalism
The ALL is MIND, The Universe is Mental.

The Principle of Correspondence
'As Above, So Below'; 'As Below, So Above'.

The Principle of Vibration
Nothing rests; everything moves; everything vibrates.

The Principle of Polarity
Everything is Dual; everything has poles; everything has its pair of opposites; like and unlike are the same; opposites are identical in nature but different in degree; extremes meet all; all truths are half-truths; all paradoxes may be reconciled.

The Principle of Rhythm
Everything flows; out and in; everything has its tides; all things rise and fall; the pendulum-swing manifests in everything; the measure of the swing to the right is the measure of the swing to the left; rhythm compensates.

The Principle of Cause and Effect
Every Cause has its Effect; every Effect has its Cause; everything happens according to Law; chance is but a name for Law not recognized; there are many planes of causation but nothing escapes the Law.

The Principle of Gender
Gender is in everything; everything has its Masculine and its Feminine Principles; gender manifests on all planes.

The Living Tree

The Thirty-Two Mystical Paths of the Concealed Glory
are ways of life, and those who want to unravel their
secrets must tread them.

Dion Fortune, *The Mystical Qabalah*

A tree is a living system. It is long-lived, often massive, but it grows from a
tiny seed. Though the trunk, leaves and branches are visible, the real life of
the tree is hidden away underground in its roots and beneath the bark.
Growth is slow but steady as the young tree begins to reach upwards towards
the sky bridging heaven and earth. The tree offers numerous gifts: shade;
shelter; a home for insects, birds and other creatures. Its wood, fruits, bark

---

THE INNER TREE

Create the following scene in your mind. Find yourself standing outside
the gateway of a high-walled garden. A sense of curiosity and anticipation arises. You are standing in front of the gate. You reach forwards
and grasp the heavy metal handle. It turns with ease. The gate opens
and you step into the garden. Once inside, you see that the garden has
been laid out with great care. Paths lead from each gateway set in the
centre of the four walls. These flow into a circular pathway which marks
out the central area of the garden. Within it stands a tree. You walk
towards the centre and, by following the pathway, walk around the tree,
observing it from every direction. The tree grows broadly so that its
shape extends almost fully across the circle. Its branches can easily be
touched from wherever you stand. You reach out and run your hands
over its lower branches. This action seems to release a wonderful
perfume for the air is suddenly filled with a pleasant scent. Looking
more closely, you see that the tree produces fruit. Small fruits nestle in
green cups. The fruit is unfamiliar so all the more tempting. You reach
out and pluck one of the fruits. It is perfectly ripe and comes away
with ease. You eat the fruit and find it to be delicious, sweet and full
of flavour. The taste is quite new. Inside the fruit at its centre is a seed
resembling a stone. Rather than discarding it, you hold the seed for
safekeeping, and you wonder whether another tree might grow from
it. Holding that thought in your mind, you prepare to leave the garden.
Choose any of the four gates to make your departure. Once outside,
close the gate firmly. Allow the scene to fade completely. Record all
your impressions.

and leaves provide raw materials, medicinal agents, food and supplies. The deciduous tree renews itself in a cycle of regeneration; the evergreen never loses its colour. The tree naturally represents qualities of endurance, nourishment, renewal and healing. Rooted in the earth but aspiring to heaven, it symbolizes the self and its many seasons of growth and change. The tree has a long history as a symbol. It appears in myth as the World Tree, the Moon Tree and the Tree of Knowledge. It still functions in this symbolic capacity if you are prepared to engage with it.

The Structure of the Tree of Life

> The Tree of Life works in relation to consciousness just as a computer. Data is fed and stored in associative banks and then fed out on demand.

> **William G. Gray,** *The Ladder of Lights*

We commonly speak of the spiritual journey. The Tree of Life is our road map for the path ahead. It is as interactive as any contemporary computerized experience. As we incorporate the symbols presented to us, we are changed accordingly. Dion Fortune expresses this relationship succinctly.

> Each symbol upon the Tree represents a cosmic force or factor. When the mind concentrates upon it, it comes into touch with that force. In other words, a surface channel, a channel in consciousness, has been made between the conscious mind of the individual and a particular factor in the world-soul.[18]

Let us now prepare for the journey ahead. Kabbalah is a way of life; it has to be lived.

The Tree of Life is represented by a combination of circles and lines when drawn in two dimensions. But this flat representation belies an inner world composed of planes of consciousness and interconnecting pathways. The planes of consciousness – called Sephirah in the singular and Sephiroth in the plural – represent the successive Emanations of the Divine Mind as creation is unfolded. Although an eleventh Sephirah is represented, only ten are counted. The eleventh emanation carries a unique status and historically was not regarded as a full Sephirah. The linking pathways are known as Paths, less commonly as Stages or Grades. The journeys through the 10 Sephiroth and the 22 Paths make up the Thirty-two Paths of Wisdom.

Thirty-one of the Paths correspond to the 31 nerves emanating from the spinal cord. The final Path corresponds to the entire complex of 12 cranial nerves. In Hebrew the number 32 is written with the letters Lamed and Beth, which together spell out the word for heart. The Divine Mind creates the heart of mankind. This basic blueprint is our starting point.

The word *sephirah* shares a common root with the word *sepher*, meaning a book. Like a book, each of the Sephiroth holds information which can be read. The word also shares a root with *sephar*, meaning 'number'. The Sephirah is considered to be the source from which the numbers originate as creation is unfolded. As a creative power, numbers appear through these successive emanations. Finally, the word shares a root with the word *sippur*, meaning 'communication' and 'telling'. These are the three roots of the Tree of Life.

> The first Sephirah is called Kether, meaning Crown.
>
> The second Sephirah is called Chockmah, meaning Wisdom.
>
> The third Sephirah is called Binah, meaning Understanding.
>
> The fourth Sephirah is called Chesed (also called Gedulah), meaning Mercy.
>
> The fifth Sephirah is called Geburah (also called Pachad), meaning Severity.
>
> The sixth Sephirah is called Tiphareth, meaning Beauty.
>
> The seventh Sephirah is called Netzach, meaning Victory.
>
> The eighth Sephirah is called Hod, meaning Glory.
>
> The ninth Sephirah is called Yesod, meaning Foundation.
>
> The tenth Sephirah is called Malkuth, meaning Kingdom.
>
> The eleventh Sephirah is called Daath, meaning Knowledge.

The Sephiroth are arranged in a particular pattern which establishes the interrelationships between the Sephiroth as pairs of opposites, as trinities, and ultimately in relation to each other as parts of a whole. This structure sets up a number of fundamental dynamics which define the nature of each Sephirah in the Macrocosm and in the Microcosm. These complex and multi-dimensional relationships will become clear as the journey into the Tree takes shape.

The Sephiroth are viewed as Divine Emanations. Each proceeds from the previous one as overflowing water seeks to fill another container.

FIGURE 2 THE TREE OF LIFE

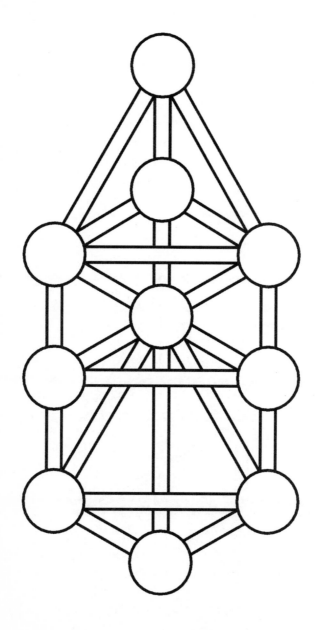

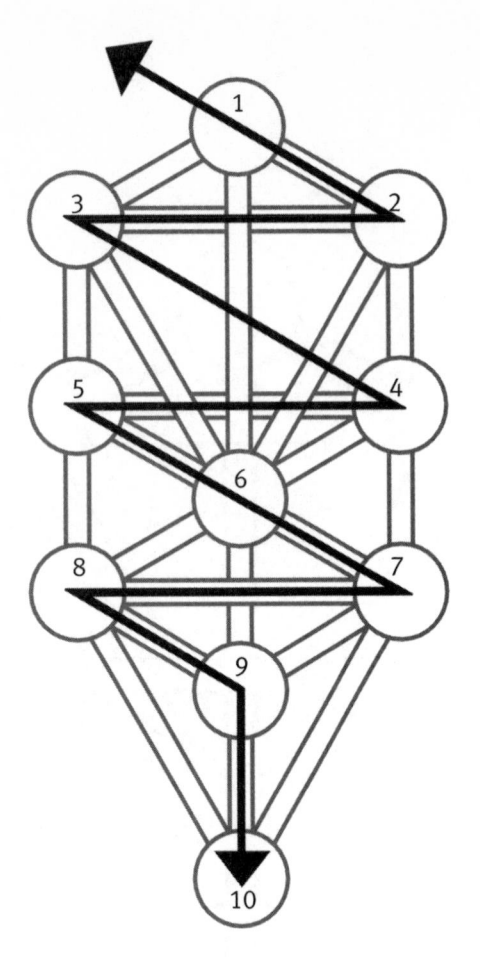

FIGURE 3 THE LIGHTNING FLASH

The Sephiroth are indeed called Vessels of Light. As each is also positive or negative in relation to its neighbours, a series of dynamic tensions, almost like magnetic or gravitational fields, defines the ensuing structure. The first Sephirah, Kether, gives rise to the remainder of the Tree. All the remaining Sephiroth therefore partake of its nature in some way, despite a separate identity and function. The pattern of unfoldment follows a particular pattern known as *The Lightning Flash*, or *The Descent of Power* or *The Path of the Flaming Sword*.

The basic blueprint throws up a number of clearly defined internal structures. Firstly, it is clear that the second, fourth and seventh Sephiroth form one boundary while the third, fifth, and eighth form a second. These

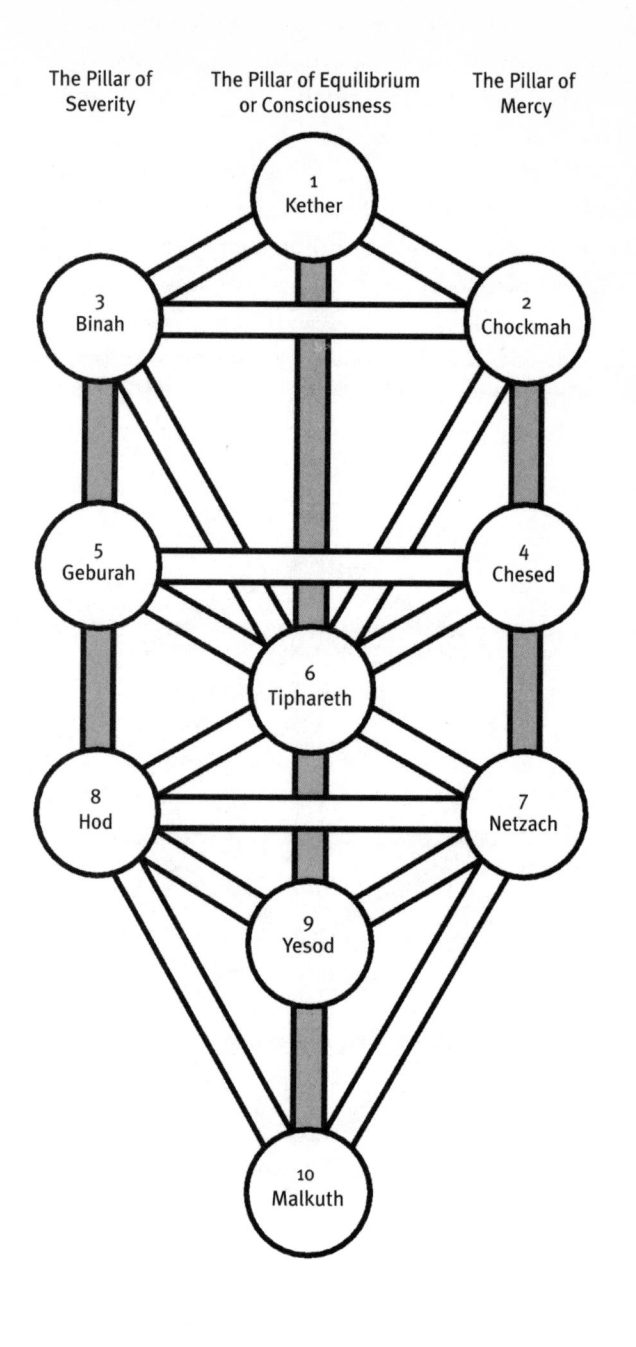

The Pillar of
Severity

The Pillar of Equilibrium
or Consciousness

The Pillar of
Mercy

1
Kether

3
Binah

2
Chockmah

5
Geburah

4
Chesed

6
Tiphareth

8
Hod

7
Netzach

9
Yesod

10
Malkuth

FIGURE 4 THE THREE PILLARS

twin dynamics are referred to as the Pillars of Manifestation. The Pillar of Severity is formed by the Sephiroth Binah, Geburah and Hod. The Pillar of Mercy is formed by the Sephiroth Chockmah, Chesed and Netzach. The Pillar of Severity is formed by the three Sephiroth which bestow the quality of form. The Pillar of Mercy is formed by three Sephiroth which bestow the quality of force. The polarity between the Sephiroth of Force and those of Form brings a constant interplay and exchange, much like the interplay of yin and yang represented in the Tao. It is also clear that a central alignment has come into being. This Middle Pillar of Equilibrium or Consciousness is formed by the Sephiroth Kether, Tiphareth, Yesod and Malkuth. Additionally, the veiled Sephira Daath rests behind this pillar, above Tiphareth but below Kether.

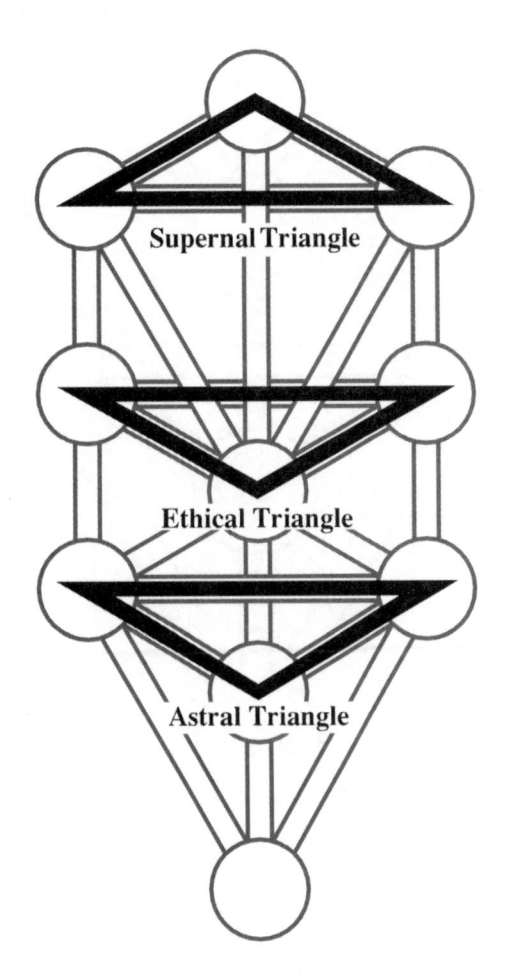

FIGURE 5 THE THREE TRIANGLES

Within the overall structure further relationships can be seen. Three triangular dynamics are apparent. Starting at the top of the Tree, the first, second and third Sephiroth – Kether, Chockmah and Binah – are in a triune relationship, known as the Supernal or Archetypal Triangle. The second triangle consists of the fourth, fifth and sixth Sephiroth – Chesed, Geburah an Tiphareth. This is known as the Moral or Ethical Triangle. A third triangle is formed by the seventh, eighth and ninth Sephiroth – Hod, Netzach and Yesod. This is known as the Astral or Psychological Triangle. The tenth Sephirah, Malkuth, forms the entry point. As the journey through the Tree of Life unfolds, we will come to experience the significance of the three trinities. This division has particular practical significance as the personal journey into the Tree commences. Malkuth represents the starting point. The journey through the Sephiroth Yesod, Hod and Netzach via the relevant Paths forms the substance of the Lesser Mysteries. Engagement with the Sephiroth Tiphareth, Chesed, Geburah and the attendant Paths forms the substance of the Greater Mysteries. Finally, the journey into Binah, Chockmah and Kether through the related Paths forms the work of the Supreme Mysteries.

The ten Sephiroth permit other overlays. Together Kether, Chockmah and Binah form the Vast Countenance, *Arik Anpin*. The next six Sephiroth form the Lesser Countenance, *Zaur Anpin*. Malkuth is called the Bride. The complexity of Kabbalistic thinking begins to surface already. Its richness confounds the linear process of rational thought and expands all definitions into multi-dimensional relationships which are not fixed but fluid. This symbolic architecture fosters an organic and open-ended response as further keys are put in place.

Kabbalah envisages four levels of reality, the Archetypal World, the Creative World, the Formative World and the Active World. When these abstract ideas are applied to the Tree, the resulting fusion yields another rich vein for meditative thought. The Archetypal World or Atziluth is attributed to Kether alone. The Creative World, called Briah, includes the Sephiroth Chockmah and Binah. The Formative World, or Yetzirah, includes the Sephiroth Chesed, Geburah, Tiphareth, Hod, Netzach and Yesod. Assiah, the Active World, includes Malkuth alone. This fourfold perspective can also be applied in other ways which continue to expand our thinking dramatically. As we can already see, the Tree offers a complex model. Like playing a three-dimensional chess game, we have to adopt a multi-dimensional perspective in order to view the inner dynamics from many viewpoints simultaneously. If we do not possess a multi-faceted mind at the outset, engaging with the Tree will certainly develop one.

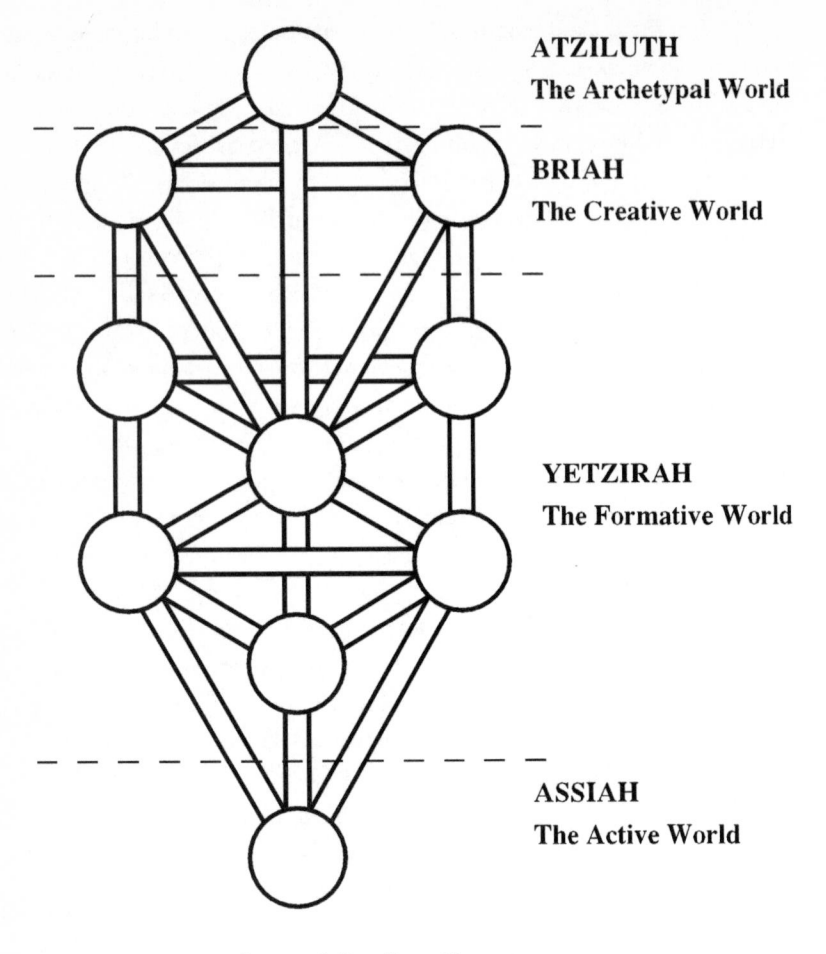

ATZILUTH
The Archetypal World

BRIAH
The Creative World

YETZIRAH
The Formative World

ASSIAH
The Active World

FIGURE 6 THE FOUR WORLDS

The framework that has been outlined provides only the bare skeleton. Now we can begin to embellish it by looking in more detail at both the Sephiroth and the Paths. The Sephiroth represent objective states of being. Each one has its own characteristics, functions and qualities. These are described in detail through a number of attributions which make it possible to compare the Sephiroth one with another. We might think of the Sephiroth as a series of chambers. Each contains the same range of items, but each range is unique to its own chamber. This simplistic analogy will help us to understand how to decode the various attributes. As each Sephirah we enter is an imagined chamber or temple held in the creative imagination, the analogy is quite practical. Each Sephirah is assigned a number of attributions or correspondences. These state its qualities, functions and powers. Each Sephirah is attributed a God-Name, an Angelic Power, a Magical Image, a Spiritual Experience, a range of Symbols, a Vice and a Virtue, a Title, a Mundane Chakra, Colours and Tarot Correspondences.

The God-Name: This represents the most spiritual aspect of each Sephirah.

The Angelic Power: Together the archangel and the angelic order represent the organizing intelligence of the Sephirah.

The Magical Image: This is the visual representation of the powers of the Sephirah.

The Spiritual Experience: This describes the nature of the experience which accompanies the realization of the powers of the Sephirah.

The Symbols: These are subsidiary images which throw further light on the nature and characteristics of the Sephirah.

The Vice and Virtue: These are the reactions of the human psyche to the powers of the Sephirah.

The Title: This is the root idea behind the Sephirah. It symbolizes how the Sephirah functions in the world.

The Mundane Chakra: This is the cosmic exteriorization of the powers of the Sephirah.

The Personal Chakra: This is the energy centre related to the Sephirah. This is a recent correspondence.

The Colours: These are the symbolic colour codes used to visualize various aspects of the Tree. One colour scale is attributed to each of the Four Worlds. The Colour Scale attributed to the Briatic World is most commonly used to represents the dynamic of the Creative World.

The Tarot Correspondences: The various components of the Tarot are aligned to the Tree in particular ways. The cards of the Minor Arcana are assigned to the Sephiroth.

The meaning assigned to each Sephirah is encapsulated in symbolic code, which is decoded through study and meditation. As the relevant symbols become absorbed and integrated, the cumulative effect precipitates initiation into the full potency of the Sephirah. In this way life is changed and enriched by contact with Kabbalistic symbols.

The Paths of the Tree

Each Path is said to represent the equilibrium of the two
Sephiroth it connects.

Dion Fortune, *The Mystical Qabalah*

The Sephiroth are connected by 22 Paths, Stages or Grades. Like the
Sephiroth, the Paths are also accorded a number of attributions which reveal
the function assigned there. According to Dion Fortune, 'The Sephiroth
may justly be considered macrocosmic, and the Paths microcosmic.'[19] This
understanding is the starting point of the journey which will serve to unite
the Microcosm with the Macrocosm.

The Paths are described through:

Tarot Correspondences: The Trumps of the Major Arcana are
assigned to the Paths and represent the subjective experience of the
Path.

Hebrew Letters: These represent the key to the Path.

Astrological Symbols: These represent the spiritual significance of
the journey.

Text: This describes the nature and function of the Path.

Colours: These represent the vibration of the Path in the appropriate
world.

Relating the nature and purpose of the Paths to Tarot and astrological
symbols which belong to independent symbol systems, brings another
complex and rich symbolic language to bear. The Hebrew language is a
third symbol system in which every letter carries its own symbolic value.
The Hebrew word for the letters is *Autiot* – in the singular, *Aut*. This denotes
not only a letter but also a sign, proof, a symbol and even a miracle. The 22
letters are divided into groups of three Mother Letters, seven Double Letters
and 12 Simple Letters. The three Mother Letters – *Aleph, Mem* and *Shin* –
represent elemental creative power. The Double Letters – *Beth, Gimel, Daleth,
Kaph, Pe, Resh* and *Tau* – are related to particular qualities in polarized pairs.
To mark the difference between the two qualities these letters may be
pronounced with either a soft or hard sound. The 12 Simple Letters – *Heh,
Vau, Zain, Cheth, Teth, Yod, Lamed, Nun, Samekh, Ayn, Tzaddi* and *Qoph* – are

related to a month of the year, a sign of the zodiac, an internal organ, a direction and a human function. In this way every letter, like a gate, opens a new realm of symbols and ideas for meditative consideration. The merger between abstract systems old and new provides a rich source of images, ideas and transcendent perspectives which both describe and initiate the nature of the journey. The Sephiroth represent objective states; the Paths represent the subjective means of relating to these states. Together the Sephiroth and the Paths form a map of being. As its experiences are integrated, so identity shifts from the local to the transpersonal. As the journey into the inner realms of the Tree of Life deepens, change both subjective and objective is precipitated. In *The Ladder of Lights*, William. G. Gray states that:

> By presenting the Tree as a Qabalistic puzzle of mental and spiritual magnitude, an opportunity is afforded for the genuine progress of mind and spirit to whomsoever has the wits and endurance to attempt its solution.[20]

The Tree of Life is truly the Great Adventure. Welcome to the Otz Chiim, The Tree that is Life.

EXERCITIA SPIRITUALIA

Draw the Tree of Life (see Appendix 1):
Label the Sephiroth, the Lightning Flash, the Three Triangles, the Three Pillars, the Four Worlds.

Take the Following Themes as Subjects for Meditation:

- The Lightning Flash
- The Three Triangles
- The Four Worlds
- The Three Pillars

CHAPTER 2

Malkuth
– The Kingdom

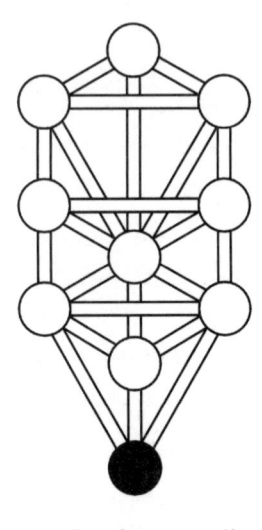

FIGURE 7 THE SEPHIRAH MALKUTH

TABLE OF CORRESPONDENCES

God-Name: Adonai Malekh or Adonai ha Aretz – Lord of Earth

Archangel: Sandalphon

Order of Angels: The Ashim – Souls of Fire

Magical Image: A young woman crowned and throned

Spiritual Experience: Vision of the Holy Guardian Angel

Symbols: Altar of the Double Cube, the Equal-Armed Cross, the Magic Circle, the Triangle of Evocation

Virtue: Discrimination

Vice: Avarice, Inertia

Titles: The Gate, The Gate of Death, Gate of the Shadow of Death, Gate of Tears, Gate of Justice, Gate of Prayer, Gate of the Daughter of the Mighty Ones, Gate of the Garden of Eden, The Inferior Mother, Malkah the Queen, Kallah, the Bride, the Virgin

Mundane Chakra: Cholem ha Yesodeth – The Sphere of the Elements

Personal Chakra: Muladhara – the Root Chakra

Text: The Resplendent Intelligence

Colour in Atziluth: Yellow

Colour in Briah: Citrine, Olive, Russet and Black

Colour in Yetzirah: Citrine, Olive, Russet and Black flecked with Gold

Colour in Assia : Black rayed with Yellow

Tarot Cards: The Four Tens

Ten of Wands: Oppression

Ten of Cups: Perfected Success

Ten of Swords: Ruin

Ten of Pentacles: Wealth

COMMENTARY

The Tenth Path is called the Resplendent Intelligence because it is exalted above every head and sits upon the Throne of Binah. It illuminates the splendours of all the Lights, and causes an influence to emanate from the Prince of Countenances, the Angel of Kether.

Malkuth, the Kingdom, is the tenth Sephirah. It is found at the base of the Tree of Life where it receives influences from each of the Three Pillars of Force, Form and Equilibrium or Consciousness. Its nature expresses the end result of a process. Malkuth is the world of effect, not of cause. Malkuth holds a unique position. It is the only Sephirah not to be part of the triangular structure of the Tree and it is also the only Sephirah to be cross-quartered into four segments. Malkuth receives influences from the whole of the Tree of Life. Placed in the direct line of descending power from Kether, via the invisible Sephirah Daath, the Sephirah Tiphareth and the Sephirah Yesod, Malkuth contains and expresses the descending influences of the Central Pillar in addition to the influences generated by the two Pillars of Manifestation. Malkuth expresses force, form and consciousness in combination. It is the place of incarnation. Dion Fortune describes Malkuth as 'the, nadir of evolution, the outermost point on the outgoing arc, through which all life must pass before returning whence it came'.[1] Malkuth is the Kingdom.

The Four Elements

Neither earth, nor fire, nor air, nor water, came from each other. These four elements must be the Godhead.

Marcus Manillus, Roman poet

At Malkuth we first encounter a theme which will become increasingly familiar on the journey, namely the fourfold symbolism of the elements. Malkuth is called *Cholem ha Yesodeth*, meaning the Sphere of the Elements. Earth, air, fire and water – these are the elements which make up the Kingdom which is Malkuth. The elements are represented by the primary

colours – blue for water, red for fire, yellow for air. The element of earth is
symbolized by black, which is deliberately reminiscent of a dark and fertile
loam. The colours assigned to Malkuth however are citrine, olive, russet
and black. These are the colours of the sub-elements – water of earth, fire
of earth, air of earth and earth of earth. Citrine shows a predominance of
yellow, the colour attributed to the element of Air. Olive shows a predominance of blue, the colour attributed to the element of Water. Russet displays
a predominance of red, the colour attributed to the element of Fire. Black
remains unchanged.

The four elements are not merely the physical qualities of the everyday
world but express a wider symbolism which includes qualities and characteristics of being. Which qualities of being would you describe as being
earthy, watery, fiery and airy in nature? Symbolism draws its effectiveness
from analogy. A well-fitting analogy gives life to the symbol. The element
of Water well represents the emotional life, the element of Air well represents
the mental life, the element of Earth well represents the physical life and
the element of Fire well represents the spiritual life. In this way the element
is but another symbol for a constellation of qualities, characteristics and states
of being. This is the way of Kabbalah, to lay symbol upon symbol in an
infinite multi-dimensional assembly. It is a work of immense subtlety. As
we become caught up in the process of decoding the message and following
the clues ever deeper, we are changed from within as the symbols take root
and come to form both the structure and the vocabulary of an interior life.
Internalizing the increasing subtlety of this symbolism creates a mental flexibility which precipitates insight and intuition.

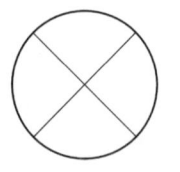

FIGURE 8 THE ELEMENTAL MANDALA

Malkuth is represented by a cross-quartered circle divided into four segments
giving an elemental mandala. The circle is a universal symbol of wholeness
and completion. It represents the cycle of the year, the passage of life, and
it is the blueprint for all magical circles. The subdivided circle becomes the
year divided into its seasons, the manifest world divided into its elemental
components, unity rendered into diversity. The cross-quartered circle or

elemental mandala provides an effective model on which to place a fourfold correspondence. Malkuth is also symbolized by the equal-armed cross of the elements. Here is a symbol of balance and equilibrium. Imagine if one or other of the arms were disproportionate; the image would signify a fundamental disharmony. The four equal arms represent a balance of forces within the self. The balanced cross speaks of a unity between mind, body, heart and soul. Jung popularized four functions of the self as sensation, feeling, intuition and intellect. These equate well with elemental qualities: sensation relates to the element of earth, feeling relates to water, intellect to air and intuition to fire. When the four cardinal directions are combined with the four elements, a multi-dimensional symbolic model instantly takes shape. The East becomes the place of sunrise, the place of the first breath of the day, the natural quarter for the element of Air, representative of the capacity for awareness through thought, the place of beginnings, the season of spring and the time of youthful exuberance. The South becomes the place of noon, the place of the hot breath of the day, the natural quarter for the element of Fire, the capacity for intuitive understanding which arises suddenly like a flame, the place of summer and the time of steady growth. The West becomes the place of sunset, the place of cooling dusk, the natural quarter for the element of Water, the capacity for emotional depth, the season of autumn and the time of full maturity. The North becomes the place of midnight, the place of blackness, the natural quarter for the element of Earth, the capacity for physical form, the season of winter and the time of old age.

This fourfold symbolism has the capacity to embrace simultaneously a description of the individual and the cosmic round of cyclic time. 'As Above, So Below' says the maxim, and we will come to see its veracity time and time again. Describing the cycles of the day and the year, the ages of life and the qualities of being through a single symbolic code, begins the work of connecting the individual and the cosmos; the Great Above is rejoined to the Great Below. The fourfold rhythm discloses the annual pattern of the solstices and equinoctial markers. These natural rhythms underpin the seasonal rise and fall of light. Attunement to these landmarks begins the work of reconnecting the personal life to the greater pattern of earth, sun and moon. The great cosmic patterns are reflected in manifestation; the four equal arms of the cross radiate outwards from a central point exemplifying the Kabbalistic view of creation – 'Light in Extension'. Spirit and matter are eternally united in sacred marriage in the realm of the Virgin, who is also the Queen and the Bride.

THE CROSS OF THE ELEMENTS

Become centred in yourself and imagine that a seed of light dwells in the heart. As you watch the heart space, the seed begins to send out rays of light equally to the four directions. To the front, a shaft of light reaches out to the eastern horizon. To your right, a second shaft of light extends into the far distance of the southern horizon. Behind, a shaft of light extends back into the far reaches of the western horizon. To your left, a shaft of light extends to the northern horizon. Hold the image steadily in your mind. See that the four shafts of light are equally balanced. Now, from the farthest point of the eastern horizon, imagine that the light begins to extend itself, moving first towards the south on your right. Feel the light sweeping around you in a vast movement until the current has created a complete circle at the level of the heart.

Use this image as a focus for meditation. Dissolve the circle by allowing the image of light to fade in an anti-clockwise direction. Next draw in the four shafts of light equally and together until each is dissolved into the heart-seed. Finally, dissolve this too and return to ordinary consciousness.

Malkuth is symbolized by the quartered circle and the point extended into a cross. Both speak of elemental balance in silent eloquence. Malkuth has a third image with elemental meaning: the Altar of the Double Cube. In totality, the six faces of the cube represent the six directions: the four cardinal directions plus the infinite sky above and the infinite earth below, which are represented by the upper and lower faces. When placed one on top of the other, the double cube shows only ten faces, the number of the tenth Sephirah, Malkuth. Here is yet another image of the Hermetic truth 'As Above, So Below'.

The Spiritual Journey

> I think the starting point of the spiritual path is the
> understanding that we can transform ourselves.
>
> Ringu Tulku, *The Lazy Lama Looks at Bodhicitta*

The first steps towards an inner orientation are taken at Malkuth. In the Western Mystery Tradition the path to self-realization begins with the elements of the psyche. The elements may be seen externally in the world, but also in the elemental balance of the psyche. This is the first seed from which the Great Work of inner alchemy begins. It is also the way of psychosynthesis mapped out by Roberto Assagioli. This is the starting point of the inner journey. By combining the traditional four elements with the four Jungian qualities of being, a preliminary model of self can be established. Time spent in reflection will show the current balance of personal energy. Reflect on the following. Do you react and express yourself primarily through:

- The Element of Earth and the quality of sensation?
- The Element of Air and the quality of intellect?
- The Element of Fire and the quality of intuition?
- The Element of Water and the quality of emotion?

Identify which is your strongest and most often used quality? Which is your weakest and least used quality? Express this understanding symbolically by drawing an elemental mandala to describe this. Place your strongest and weakest qualities opposite one another. Shade the segments to reflect your strengths and weaknesses. Now express the same information through the Cross of the Elements. Let a strong quality be expressed as a full arm of the cross and a weak quality be expressed as a partial image. An imbalance between the elements is probable but with time and change, harmony will prevail.

The path of self-realization begins in the simple observation of everyday life; it takes root through the detached watching of self. The Virtue of Malkuth is Discrimination, which is conscious choice. Applying the Virtue of Malkuth kick-starts the process of self-realization which begins with aspiration and ends with liberation. Discrimination demands an objective honesty, a deep evaluation, and necessitates a watching awareness. On the other hand, the Vice of Malkuth, Avarice or Inertia speaks of the slumber of sloth, the laziness of mediocrity and the emptiness of materialism. The avaricious heart has no space for anything other than possession. Inertia is the inability to enter the fullness of life. It brings a passivity which denies our ability to create and live dynamically. These are the options presented by the Sephirah Malkuth. The process of dynamic change commences with Malkuth. This process is not linear but multi-dimensional, moving forward on various fronts with differing momentum and power. As the view of self shifts, so too does the view of the wider world.

Malkuth is aptly named The Gate. A gate is opened or closed, to bar or admit. It cannot be opened from the outside, only from within. When the gate is opened the traveller is free to step upon the path beyond. The spiritual journey is commonly described as a path. Buddhism speaks of the *Lam Rim*, the graduated path towards enlightenment. Yoga speaks of the *Marga*, the Path or Way. In the Western Mystery Tradition, the Path is to be found in the 22 byways and the 10 Sephiroth of the Tree of Life. How may the gate be opened? Where is the key? There is but one key: 'Know Thyself'. This is the single key to admittance. Take time to reflect on this theme.

The Resplendent World

> To see the world in a grain of sand,
>
> And a Heaven in a wild flower.
>
> Hold Infinity in the palm of your hand.
>
> And Eternity in an hour.

William Blake, *Auguries of Innocence*

Malkuth is assigned the Resplendent Intelligence, an evocative title which raises our view of the world from the ordinary to the extraordinary. The world is indeed physical, yet it is solid only in appearance. This is now the age of quantum physics. Its ramifications have not percolated into everyday awareness. The world appears as solid as it has ever done, yet this is only an appearance. Beneath, behind and within the world of form is another level of reality. Veiled from ordinary view, a subatomic energy substratum dazzles and dances in the continuous motion of an altogether different order of creation. The world of energy and the world of substance co-exist continuously; we are immersed in both simultaneously. Newtonian physics has been superseded by the quantum revolution.

Malkuth needs to be appreciated in relation to not only the whole Tree of Life but also the neighbouring Sephirah, Yesod. Malkuth represents the world of physical creation; its neighbour Yesod represents, among other things, the substratum of universal energy. It is no longer possible to view the external world as a series of separate objects. Recognizing the mysterious relationship between the subatomic energy substratum and the emergence of matter changes our understanding of the world in which we live. This is an extraordinary time. Contemporary physics supports the Kabbalistic perspective and lends empirical weight to mystical notions and concepts. Modern physics unwittingly redefines the role of consciousness in creation. We are not merely detached observers watching a fixed creation from behind a protective window. Every act of observation is an act of participation. This rarefied concept hardly touches everyday life, but it lies at the heart of all magical and spiritual encounters, which are always participatory. This participatory quality has always been recognized by those who have walked far upon the path of self-realization. The transformation of consciousness brings engagement with a universal energy and invariably elicits a responsive and seemingly reciprocal dimension to life experience. Synchronicity or coincidence becomes a characteristic of a life engaged in a self-conscious participatory mode, through the application of a holistic model of reality. Coincidences which seem purposive, helpful, even highly personal, strengthen an interactive and participatory view of reality. We are currently shaking off the legacy of a mechanistic and reductionist model of reality. The Virtue of Malkuth is Discrimination, simply the power to make a choice. Choosing a model of reality is the most fundamental choice of all. Kabbalah offers a holistic and participatory model. This view begins by endowing each aspect of the Tree with a responsive intelligence. By assigning God-Names and Angelic Orders to each of the Sephiroth, Kabbalah places an immanent intelligence within matter. This is not a backward superstition but a psycho-spiritual technique which serves as a means of exploring our own consciousness. According to Dion Fortune, 'The esotericist... points out that matter and mind are two sides of the same coin... There comes a point in one's investigation when it is profitable to change over one's terminology and talk of force and form in terms of psychology, as if they were conscious and purposive.' This is deliberate use of the analogy. Dealing with subtle forces 'as if they were intelligent' enables us to discover that we each have a subtle aspect of consciousness 'which responds to them and to which we fondly believe they respond. At any rate, whether the response is mutual or not, our powers of dealing with them are, by this means greatly extended.'[2] In other words, the personification of subtle forces as intelligences, conscious and purposeful, is a chosen approach which is to be judged by its effect within our own consciousness. *The Kabbalah Experience* adopts this approach fully and all travellers upon the Tree of Life will have every opportunity to apply this proposition for themselves through the broad range of correspondences aligned to each part of the Tree. The angelic Ashim, or Souls of Fire, are assigned to Malkuth. These are best visualized as sparks of energy, like the short-lived inhabitants of the particle world.

The Spiritual Experience assigned to Malkuth, the tenth Sephirah, is the Vision of the Holy Guardian Angel. This is a meditative encounter with an internally rooted source of personal wisdom. This relationship develops as the journey unfolds. The spiritual experience of Tiphareth, the sixth Sephirah, is the Knowledge and Conversation of the Holy Guardian Angel. The brief vision at Malkuth becomes the ongoing dialogue of Tiphareth.

At a time of ecological and environmental concerns, the way in which we view the world we inhabit may prove to be crucial. Materialism, the philosophy of plunder, has driven us into a collective cul-de-sac. Nature has become forgotten in today's high-tech world. Contemporary life has done much to insulate us from the land, the seasons, the cyclic moon, patterns of growth and the whole panoply of nature's tapestry. Yet we forget this relationship only at our peril. The now dated but still prevalent model of reality is shifting towards a quantum and holistic view; this is a participatory model without boundaries. Kabbalah provides the modus operandi for discovering a new holistic model of reality. The Magical Image ascribed to Malkuth, that of a young woman crowned and enthroned, provides a timely antidote to a deep sense of alienation. This is an image of nature, Natura. She carries no single name for she embodies all the archetypal figures that have sat upon the same throne to receive homage and thanks for a full harvest and bountiful existence. She embodies all the goddesses of corn and harvest, all the virgin May queens, all the images of bounty and fruitful abundance. She is here called The Inferior Mother. Mother Nature at Malkuth is considered to be an outer reflection of the Superior Mother attributed to the Sephirah Binah. Malkuth is also called the Queen, the Bride and the Virgin.

Meditations and reflections upon Malkuth are infinite. Each has the power to bring a new perspective and deepen understanding. Malkuth is assigned to the Archangel, Sandalphon, who is traditionally visualized swathed in robes coloured citrine, olive, russet and black. Sandalphon may be approached in meditation for wise counsel, especially in matters which relate directly to the care of the earth. The name Sandalphon comes from the Greek *syndelphos*, meaning a brother. This introduces Sandalphon in familial and comfortable terms, rather than as a lofty and unapproachable presence. Sandalphon is sometimes described as the dark angel who presides over the karma played out through Malkuth as the Gate of Justice and the Gate of Tears. He is said to be another form of Metatron, the bright angel who is attributed to Kether. This relationship emphasizes the connection between the source and the created world. The physical world is seen as a sanctified place, the final emanation of the creative impulse. It is stated that Malkuth 'causes an influence to emanate from the Prince of Countenances, the Angel of Kether'. The Archangelic intelligence of Sandalphon is seen as another living quality of the Sephirah. In a participatory universe of bizarre and paradoxical qualities, the impact of consciousness upon energy is an untestable proposition. Is it even possible that an aspect of the subatomic substratum might not respond to intensive consciousness through the mechanism of a synchronous event with all the qualities suggestive of high intelligence and wise counsel!

The Resplendent Intelligence assigned to Malkuth has an inner resonance which has the power to awaken, vivify and recharge the whole person. Surely creation is indeed resplendent, from the awesome and vast events of interstellar space to the minute lives of cells. Yet how often is this acknowledged or celebrated? If a participatory model urges engagement, then become engaged with the Resplendent Kingdom.

EVOCATION

Welcome to my kingdom. Behold the world of form. Is it not beautiful to behold? Have you become so blinded that you do not see the magical resplendence in everything? Your world is full of colour, texture, sound and delight. It is never still but constantly changing according to patterns that are hidden from you. Earth, air, fire and water are here but do you see them? Have you ever been thankful for the gifts and bounty at your fingertips? Or do you take without remembrance? Here is the world of effects, the end result of a subtle interplay of forces and powers unseen. You too have your part to play for my kingdom is not complete without you. Your thoughts and intentions, choices and decisions each leave a mark like a track carved into the future. Mine is the world of illusion. I wear the veil of Maya and you are dazzled by it, caught up with your own dreams of separateness and solidity. Yet you are part of me as I am part of you. Behold the path which beckons. Have you the courage to find yourself? Dare you lift the veil of Maya? Do you wish to *know* what lies beyond my kingdom? What is your true will? Can you be *silent* about the mysteries that you find? Will you awaken to wonder even though others remain entrapped in the Great Illusion and do not choose to awaken yet? I have many names. I am called the Gate, for none may find the Path without the gate. I am called the Gate of Tears. None may pass this way without tasting sorrow. I am called the Gate of Death. None may pass this way without tasting death. Yet I am also called the Bride and the Queen for I am ever in a sacred marriage with an unseen beloved. You have arrived at my gate, but will you enter my kingdom?

INTERNALIZATION – THE TEMPLE
OF MALKUTH

Construct the Temple of Malkuth in the creative imagination. When you have established this inner space, first stand between the two pillars. Let this become the eastern quarter. From here proceed towards the altar. A single central candle burns brightly. It is surrounded by four unlit candles, one for each of the cardinal points. Stand in front of the altar and light the first candle from the central flame. Turn outwards to face the East, upraise the light with the words 'I bring light to Air in the East.' Turn and replace the candle on the altar. Contemplate the meaning of this action.

Now walk clockwise and stand at the southern face of the altar. Light the second candle from the central flame. Turn outwards to face the South, upraise the light with the words 'I bring light to Fire in the South.' Turn and replace the candle on the altar. Contemplate the meaning of this action.

Now walk clockwise and proceed to the western face of the altar. Light the third candle from the central flame. Turn outwards to face the West with the words 'I bring light to Water in the West.' Turn and replace the candle on the altar. Contemplate the meaning of this action.

Now walk clockwise and proceed to the northern face of the altar. Light the fourth candle from the central flame. Turn outwards to face the North with the words 'I bring light to Earth in the North.' Turn and replace the candle on the altar. Contemplate the meaning of this action.

You have created a circle by your walking and your intent. Watch the five lights now burning. Reflect on your actions. You have created both the Cross and the elemental mandala in light here in the Temple of Malkuth.

Now a soft and gentle voice calls your name. You turn to see a young woman seated upon a throne. She is crowned with flowers and sheaves of wheat have been placed at her feet. Her robe is embroidered with fruit and flowers and with creatures of the earth, sea and sky. In your mind it seems that she speaks directly to you. 'Welcome to my inner kingdom which is our shared home. What service are you willing to give to this realm?' Give your answer when you are ready. But when you look again, her image has vanished.

When you are ready, leave through the door. Finally, dissolve all images and return to ordinary consciousness.

Exercitia Spiritualia

Take the Following as Subjects for Meditation:

- Adonai ha Aretz – Lord of Earth
- The Archangel Sandalphon
- The Ashim
- The image of a young woman crowned and enthroned
- The Holy Guardian Angel
- The Sphere of the Elements
- The Resplendent Intelligence

Contemplate the Following Questions and Record your Responses:

- How does the function of Discrimination operate in your life?
- How does the function of Inertia operate in your life?
- How does the nature of Malkuth relate to the Root or Base Chakra?
- Which additional correspondences can you relate to the Sephirah Malkuth?
- How do the four Tarot cards relate to Malkuth?

Visualize the Following and Record your Experiences:

- An image of an Earth Goddess from a sacred tradition of your choice
- The Temple of Malkuth including the Archangel Sandalphon
- The Journey to the Temple of Malkuth

CHAPTER 3

The Thirty-Second Path: Malkuth–Yesod

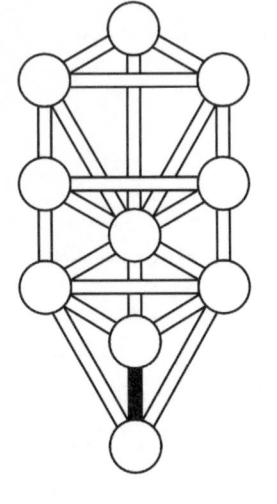

FIGURE 9 THE 32ND PATH:

MALKUTH–YESOD

TAROT TRUMP XXI:

THE WORLD

TABLE OF CORRESPONDENCES

The Journey: Tarot Trump XXI, The World,
  The Great One of the Night of Time
Key: The Letter Tau, meaning a cross
Double Letter: Power – Servitude
Spiritual Significance: Saturn
Text: The Administrative Intelligence
Colour in Atziluth: Indigo
Colour in Briah: Black
Colour in Yetzirah: Blue-black
Colour in Assiah: Black rayed Blue

COMMENTARY

The Thirty-second Path is the Administrative Intelligence, and it is so called because it directs and associates the motions of the seven planets, directing all of them in their proper courses.

Here is our first journey on the Path of Ascent. The 32nd Path joins Malkuth, the Kingdom, with Yesod, the Foundation. This Path takes us from the everyday world of appearance and the senses into the invisible hinterland that shapes all that we recognize. The 32nd journey will take us from the known to the unknown, from the physical to the immaterial, from the conscious to the unconscious, from the Kingdom to the Foundation.

The Transforming Power of Symbol

The psychological mechanism that transforms energy is the symbol.

C.G. Jung, *The Structure and Dynamics of the Psyche*

The 32nd Path connects the experience of the objective shared world with the experience of the subjective personal world. By linking the Kingdom with the Foundation, this Path connects the outer physical world with the inner world of the psyche. In other words, it provides the first opportunity to 'penetrate into the pit of our lower unconscious', as Assagioli describes the first foray into self-awareness. This journey can only take place in the light of understanding about the relationship between consciousness and the unconscious. The two aspects exhibit a compensatory and complementary function towards each other. Like the Tao image which demonstrates both yin and yang in complementary flow, consciousness and the unconscious together form a whole. To deny one at the expense of the other is to inflict self-injury. However, these two poles of mind seldom agree: they speak a different language, follow different agendas and fulfil different though complementary functions. When two parties are at odds with each other, a third mediating party is needed to act as go-between, peacemaker and bridge builder. In life, this is the office of the arbitrator who has the best interests of both parties at heart. In psychoanalysis this role falls to the symbol. Its transcendent function arises at the union of conscious and unconscious. Like a bridge, the symbol facilitates movement which would otherwise not take place.

The Path from Malkuth to Yesod leads from conscious awareness towards awareness of the unconscious. It is a journey that demands a particular guide – conceptual language can no longer serve in this new realm. We will need to move from a literal to a symbolic vocabulary. A word carries a literal meaning; it denotes a particular concept. A symbol carries a metaphorical meaning; it denotes a wide range of associations, ideas and possibilities. Like a seed, the symbol is rich with potential. A concept has limits and boundaries. It functions through precision and definition. A symbol crosses boundaries and loosens definitions. It functions through suggestion and the evocation of ideas. The symbol holds the power to brainstorm the mind. The word holds the power of description and prescription. The word addresses the intellect and reason. The symbol addresses the imagination and the intuition. The word provides the language of the conscious mind. The symbol provides the language of the unconscious mind. Now we must learn to read the language of symbols.

It was Jung who alerted the 20th century to the significance of the symbol as a vital factor in the journey towards wholeness and integration. The substance of his work makes it quite clear that reason and intelligence alone are insufficient as tools with which to plumb the psyche and heal its warring parts. His validation of the symbol has provided tremendous insight into the value of traditional psychic environments rich in symbol, such as myth, sacred enactment and sacred philosophy. The symbolic image or metaphor succeeds in facilitating a genuine shift in consciousness where reason and intelligence fail; the inherent potency of multi-faceted meaning and deep resonance has the power to tap into, release and transform the dynamic energy of the psyche. Symbolism is a universal language: tree, river, sun, moon and star express a common range of meanings and will generate a broadly similar series of associations from any group. It is a language derived from life and from the distillation of experience. This is the inner language of the dream and the outer language of metaphysics.

Since the Sephiroth represent objective states and the Paths represent a subjective means travelling between them, the symbolism attributed to each Path becomes the means of forward momentum. Each symbol so carefully placed, hovers at the boundary between conscious and unconscious under- standing. By integrating, internalizing and ingesting the relevant symbolism, the qualities and potencies of the Path are absorbed in their own right and as a stage of preparation for encountering the next Sephirah and beyond that the further reaches of the Tree. The relationship between the symbol and the energy of the psyche lies at the heart of dynamic change. It is the single key to the Tree of Life, to the process of psychoanalysis, to the model of psychosynthesis and to the holistic healing and re-integration of the Self.

The everyday physical world, Malkuth, is familiar to us through the five senses of touch, taste, smell, hearing and seeing. But these senses are insufficient guides if we are to move awareness beyond the appearance of things. Buddhism symbolizes the five senses by a mirror, some fruit, a conch shell, perfume and a piece of cloth. Far from being reliable interpreters of experience, the five senses 'cause us to waste a great deal of time'. Hindu practice also closes the gates of the senses through the practice of Yoga and turns the attention inwards. Turning towards the Sephirah Yesod through the experience of the 32nd Path represents the same process.

In the place of the separated five senses we now need to call upon a single unified and holistic sense, that of the creative imagination. Relegated to the realm of children, the imagination is undervalued in Western culture. Yet it is a key component within all meditation systems. It enables particular images to be inwardly generated, internalized and integrated. Complex interior landscapes are created through the imagination, and images spontaneously generated from far reaches of mind can be observed. Moreover, the imagination as a whole state brings an affective and empathic quality into play. In common parlance, 'imagining yourself in somebody else's shoes' is the quickest route to rapport and empathy. Intellectual understanding always lacks this vital component. Developing the creative imagination is no mere esoteric indulgence – it will pay handsome dividends in all areas of ordinary life. It begins the work of unifying heart and mind.

The imaginative mind is the natural milieu for children: a child's mind is playful and inquisitive, alive and vivid. The imagination creates a new world, changes identity, transforms surroundings and suspends disbelief. Adults may like to believe that such childish pastimes have long gone but the imagination still exerts a powerful fascination. The imaginary world still has the power to capture the adult mind. The enduring appeal of Tolkein's world, Roddenberry's *Star Trek* and the *Star Wars Odyssey* among many others, provides eloquent proof of our love affair with enchantment. Formal education leaves the world of story far behind and we exchange the acquisition of information for the development of the imagination. It is a poor trade however since all creativity stems from an ability to imagine or envision something new. Writers, artists, creative thinkers, inventors, scientists,

---

THE WELL OF MEMORY

Imagine yourself standing beside a well. A spindle set across the top holds a rope and a bucket. You begin to turn the handle and the bucket begins to descend. You continue turning until the entire rope is played out.

Now it is time to bring the bucket to the surface. Winding up the winch is more difficult. The bucket is heavy and you have to exert continuous effort. At last the bucket comes into view and you reach out and set it on the wall. Within the bucket a small silver goblet lies in the water. You take it out and drink deeply. The water has a strong taste. It is not unpleasant but earthy and rich with minerals and salts. As you drink you allow the mind to open to all the hidden richness of this underground nourishment. When you have drunk your fill, empty the bucket and place the silver cup back within it for another thirsty traveller to find. Be patient for the memory to find your surface consciousness, but be pleased when it does so.

---

musicians, poets, designers and architects, all use the imagination as a springboard for the creation of something new. Here the creative imagination is used to give birth to selfhood.

Apply the creative imagination to stimulate your memory of a time or place that might now have a new relevance for you. Awaken a forgotten hope or a lost aspiration and allow these memories to live again.

The Creative Imagination

> The creative imagination in itself is an incredibly
> powerful force. If you channel it in the right way it can
> reach deep levels of mind which can't be accessed
> through verbal means or mere analysis. This is because
> on a very deep level we think in pictures.
>
> **Tenzin Palmo,** *Cave in the Snow*

Jung recognized the value of the creative imagination, which he described as, 'a sequence of fantasies produced by deliberate concentration'.[1] This is a sequence of planned intent. Though it stems from the same source as the daydream, reverie and our ability to enter the temporary reality of a brilliant novel or a gripping drama, the creative imagination is a willed application of this ability. The image-making facility of the mind provides the modus operandi through which the symbolic innerworld landscape of the Tree is created. The active imagination is a major key in the process of radical transformation which takes place through the journey upon the Tree. It is through the creative imagination that symbolic material is planted in the mind; it is therefore a technique of great value and significance.

The 32nd Path takes us away from Malkuth towards Yesod. In other words, the focus of our attention needs to be shifted through the development of the creative imagination. However, this is but a primary tool. Where the creative imagination is in current Western usage, it is often referred to as 'visualization'. This term, though not inaccurate, presents only a partial truth. The creative imagination is not wholly visual but has auditory, kinaesthetic and even olfactory components. Not everyone naturally visualizes with the same ease – tactile and auditory keys can also take the mind into a subjective awareness. The creative imagination holds a fullness and completeness which the term visualization diminishes. Creating a scene – no matter how complex – in the mind's eye is a method, not the end result. It serves no other purpose than to place particular material within the view of the subjective mind. Visualization without inner reflection serves no purpose whatsoever; it is no better than idle reverie. Rather, visualization is the means whereby particular images, usually of a symbolic nature, are placed in the mind in order to generate a response. Precipitating a personal response is the purpose of the exercise, visualization is but the tool. In the East, which has a long history of visualized meditations, visualization has been described as 'grabbing a tiger by its tail'. This conveys a degree of power – even danger – in the technique. The West still tends to underestimate the potential of visualization.

The rational reasoning mind serves well at Malkuth. It does not serve at Yesod. Another guide is needed for this different realm. Spiritual hunger is assuaged not by indigestible intellectual information but by interaction. Our obsession with information represents the first imbalance that we need to address. This strident passion has overpowered the imaginative facility which, like a flickering ember in a dying fire, needs to be brought back to life. Here on the 32nd Path we can at last begin to breathe life into the creative imagination.

The Inner World

> The Tree provides the means of receiving Innerworld
> contacts with types of consciousness normally
> inaccessible to the ordinary human mind. It is from and
> through these sources that the teaching comes.

W.G. Gray, *The Ladder of Lights*

Between Malkuth and Yesod, the Kingdom and the Foundation, the 32nd Path takes us beyond appearance towards the forces implicit in manifest life. It shows us the forces of mind as both the personal and collective unconscious, while simultaneously revealing the forces of nature as the subatomic maelstrom. The Tarot Trump assigned to this Path is Trump XXI, The World, nowadays more often called The Universe. The Trump shows a figure dancing within an ovoid of laurel. Each corner of the Trump displays one of the four elements (Earth, Air, Fire and Water) as one of the four fixed signs of the zodiac (Scorpio, Leo, Taurus and Aquarius). These elemental forces are the Four Holy Kerubs assigned to Yesod. They represent the hidden energies that give rise to the four elements of the physical world. Curiously, the most basic laws of physics are also four in number: the strong and weak nuclear forces, electromagnetism and gravity. In the Tarot Trump, the four are directed by a dancing figure representing a fifth directing power – *akasa*, or spirit. This is an image of the world within the world, the veiled inner world of energy implicit within appearance. The veiled dancer is a fitting metaphor. In his book *The World of Elementary Particles*, Kenneth Ford even uses the phrase, 'the dance of creation and destruction' to describe the flow of energy patterns of the particle world. Twenty-first-century physics has for the first time in history lifted the veil of nature and seen straight into the subatomic heart of the world. What lies beneath the appearance of stability and solidity is a dynamic, ceaseless flow of energy manifesting itself as a dynamic interplay in which particles are created and destroyed without end in a continual variation of energy patterns. At the subatomic level unity prevails; subatomic particles exist not as isolated entities but as an integral part of an inseparable whole. The image of the world dancer is not new.

The Hindu god Shiva is also known as the Lord of the Dance. In this aspect he is called *nataraja*, from *natya* (dance) and *nataka* (theatre). Creation is the theatre in which Shiva displays five aspects: creation, preservation, destruction, oblivion and grace. 'He is a mystery waiting to be unfathomed, just like life. To understand him is to understand the ultimate reality that governs the cosmos, the eternal, absolute truth.'[2] Shiva, the world dancer, is traditionally depicted poised with one foot on the wheel of birth and rebirth. His four arms display the elements of creation. The upper right hand holds a drum, representing the primal creative power of sound. The upper left hand holds a tongue of flames, representing destruction. The lower right hand makes the gesture of dispelling fear while the lower left hand points down to the uplifted foot to symbolize release from Maya or illusion. The planted foot meanwhile subdues the demon of ignorance which has to be overcome. As Fritjof Capra has said, 'Shiva's dance is the dance of subatomic matter.'[3]

Tarot Trump XXI opens the journey into the Tree on the Path of Ascent and closes it on the Path of Descent. It is therefore a Trump which signifies both beginnings and endings simultaneously. Like its polar companion, the Fool of Tarot Trump 0, the figure of The World is depicted as being androgynous. Shiva too has an androgynous aspect as Ardhanarishivar, 'the Lord who is half woman'. Duality and unity are reconciled. What Heinrich Zimmer has said of Shiva may also be said of the figure on Tarot Trump XXI:

> His gestures wild and full of grace precipitate the cosmic illusion;
> his flying arms and legs and the swaying of his torso produce,
> indeed they are, the continuous creation-destruction of the
> universe, death exactly balancing birth, annihilation at the end of
> every coming forth.[4]

This Path is assigned to the Administrative Intelligence; 'it is so called because it directs and associates the motions of the seven planets, directing all of them in their proper courses'. The seven planets referred to are the planets of classical astrology. It is therefore an image of wholeness as perceived by the minds of the past. This astrological reference draws in a further system of correspondences and symbols. Astrology is another holistic discipline which unfolds the Hermetic maxim 'As Above, So Below'. The Administrative Intelligence, embodied by the dancing and directing figure, is that which upholds the created universe, not as a static system but as a dynamic, constantly changing, continuously moving interplay of forces. To comprehend this intelligence is to realize the mobile and fluid nature of all that exists. This insight pierces the illusion which binds the mind. It is a step towards liberation.

The 32nd Path directs our attention towards the unseen energies that shape life. Shiva as Lord of the Dance directs our attention towards the subatomic reality within physical form; the four fixed signs of the zodiac as emissaries of a holistic philosophy direct our attention to the elements within consciousness from the personal to the collective. Finally, Saturn draws our attention to a third unseen but potent force – *karma*. Connecting Malkuth and Yesod, the 32nd Path connects the physical world to the collective pool of emotional and instinctive drives and memories. It acts as a conduit for karmic forces which indelibly imprint incarnate life. Saturn is known as the Lord of Karma. Malkuth is the field of action and events where karma is played out. This Path is the means by which this storehouse is mediated into manifestation.

Saturn is often depicted as a figure much like contemporary images of Father Time. Invariably aged, Saturn is most often clad in sombre clothing with a hood, wielding a scythe and carrying an hourglass. This image is of course close to another familiar one, that of Death himself wielding the scythe. The image of Saturn as Time is a deeply karmic representation. The hooded face reminds us that karmic factors are impersonal. The aged figure reminds us that karmic factors take time to mature and formulate as events and circumstances. The scythe is an implement of harvest, a reminder of the adage 'You reap what you sow'. Saturn brings purposeful boundary and restriction. Saturn's lessons are patience, endurance, continuing application, self-discipline, self-control and, eventually, self-mastery. His province is time, his task is karmic adjustment. Currently the cult of youth is worshipped, maturity is sidelined. Yet age brings the wisdom of experience and the maturity of the years. Saturn's gifts are time and wisdom. Time is the great teacher showing us how to turn pain into process. On the greater transpersonal stage Saturn is called The Great One of the Night of Time. He represents the passage of the aeons, the forward march of the millennia and the continuing evolution of all life's myriad forms. In the *Bhagavad Gita*, Krishna speaks the following words when talking of the continuous round of creation:

> At the end of the night of time all things return to my nature; and when the new day of time begins, I bring them again into light.

The dance goes on. Matter and spirit have not become separate but are conjoined in a divine marriage of opposites.

EVOCATION

Travel my path and discover for yourself that matter is not dead. Everything lives. You see earth, air, fire and water, but look beyond to the hidden world of energies to atoms and molecules and then to another world of dancing particles. All is interchange and movement. All is in constant flux. I am the One in Four and the Four in One. I am unity. I am duality. I am the energy of life.

I am energy becoming form, thought becoming appearance, intent taking shape. I am the reappearance of the hidden storehouse of the invisible past, for I am Saturn, the master of karma both great and small. Reflect if you will on the power of mind to create form.

The dance never ceases. Stability and permanence are no more than mere appearance. Acknowledge this and begin to see through the veil. Liberate yourself from the imprisonment of illusion. Look behind form. Search beneath appearance. Everything moves and lives. Everything changes. You will change. Every idea permits change. Examine your imprisonment in the cage of mental matter handed down to you by your forebears and speakers from times past. Instead seek out what is real, let this become your pattern. Examine the thought forms that imprison and deny, diminish and demean. Understand the power of thought and begin the work of creating your own liberation from the tyranny of ignorance.

Remember, the dance never ceases. I am the world dancer. I weave together stars and planets, galaxies and possibilities beyond your wildest imaginings. I dance in worlds unseen and unknown by you. But I also dance around and about, above and below. So come take my hand. Enter the dance and step joyfully. Join me and become a dancer in the dance of never-ending creation.

INTERNALIZATION – THE 32ND PATH: MALKUTH–YESOD

Construct the Temple of Malkuth in the creative imagination. Find yourself standing before the door of the World. The Archangel Sandalphon draws back the tapestry curtain so that you may pass.

You realize that you have entered a tunnel. You take a few moments to adjust to your new surroundings. Ahead of you there is a luminescent glow. You walk on, attracted by the strangeness of the light. Now you are approaching the far end of the tunnel, which opens out into a great cave. You pass from the tunnel into the vast expanse of the cavern itself.

Here in the centre of the cave you see a raised dais. On it spins a figure, naked except for a swathe of purple cloth passing from shoulder to thigh. In the strange glow within the chamber, tiny bursts of light flash and hang in the air for but a moment. As your eyes adjust, you see that the air is full of moving lights, darting and shimmering. Some even seem to pass through your body, causing you to wonder about your own physical reality. Holding out your hand, you watch as dancing lights pass through you. Forgetting about yourself and your own amazement, you turn your attention to the spinning figure within the chamber. The dancer holds a baton in each hand and with these, seems to direct the flow of lights within the chamber. As you watch, it seems that lights are drawn into patterns and directed into moving forms. Streams of shimmering light spin outwards to the four directions. Each moving path of light spirals away from the turning figure out towards the periphery, towards four pillars or centres of sparkling energy. Your attention is magnetized. As you watch these too seem to change form, moving from one appearance to another continuously. Now you see four pillars of light rising upwards and disappearing from view. In a split second the pillars of light have become four spinning spheres, but they change again even as you watch. Now it seems that a shape is forming from within each vortex. Momentarily, you seem to glimpse the shining forms of Ox, Lion, Eagle and a human face. But as soon as you have recognized the familiar, everything changes once more, flowing into a new and different assembly.

Now you hear a voice. It seems to come from nowhere and everywhere at the same time: 'I am the Great One of the Night of Time. You have seen my dance and you are a part of it.' Suddenly you feel freed from any inhibitions. You begin to dance too, circling and stepping, turning and leaping with a sense of absolute freedom. As you dance, you see that every step leaves a brief trail of shimmering light. Your hands leave sparking patterns that hang but briefly. Plumes of light swirl around your head. Looking now at yourself, see that you dance in your energy form. Your dense physical body seems to have no place here. Instead you are translucent with light and transparent with a scintillating brilliance. Every move and step leaves a trail or shower of white light. This is a dance of joy.

From the depths of your mind, a thought reminds you that you will have to leave and take up a solid form once more. Gradually your dance diminishes. As it does so, physicality slowly returns.

When you are ready, return the way you came to the temple. When you are ready, leave through the doorway. Finally, dissolve all images and return to ordinary consciousness.

EXERCITIA SPIRITUALIA

Take the Following as Subjects for Meditation:

- The Great One of the Night of Time
- The letter Tau
- Power – Servitude
- Saturn
- The Administrative Intelligence
- Earth, Air, Fire, Water and *akasa*, or Spirit

Make Notes on:

- Tarot Trump XXI, The World
- Shiva, from the Hindu tradition

Visualize the Following and Record your Experiences:

- The Temple of Malkuth including the Archangel Sandalphon
- The Journey of the 32nd Path

CHAPTER 4

Yesod
– The Foundation

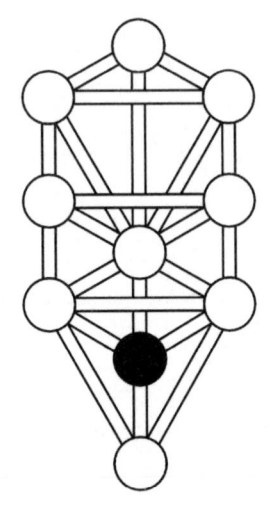

FIGURE 10 THE SEPHIRAH YESOD

TABLE OF CORRESPONDENCES

God-Name: Shaddai el Chai – The Almighty Living God
Archangel: Gabriel
Order of Angels: The Holy Kerubs
Magical Image: A naked man, very strong
Spiritual Experience: Vision of the Machinery of the Universe
Symbols: Perfumes and Sandals
Virtue: Independence
Vice: Idleness
Titles: The Treasure House of Images
Mundane Chakra: The Moon

Personal Chakra: Swadistana – the Sacral Chakra
Text: The Pure Intelligence
Colour in Atziluth: Indigo
Colour in Briah: Violet
Colour in Yetzirah: Very dark Purple
Colour in Assiah: Citrine flecked Azure
Tarot Cards: The Four Nines
Nine of Wands: Great Strength
Nine of Cups: Material Happiness
Nine of Swords: Despair and Cruelty
Nine of Pentacles: Material Gain

Commentary

*The Ninth Path is called the Pure Intelligence because it
purifies the Emanations. It proves and corrects the designing
of their representations and disposes the unity with which
they are designed without diminution or division.*

The ninth Sephirah, Yesod, is found on the Pillar of Equilibrium or
Consciousness. It is related closely to Malkuth and Tiphareth on the Middle
Pillar and to Hod and Netzach on the twin Pillars of Severity and Mercy.
Yesod, the Foundation, is encountered directly beyond Malkuth. It is
therefore the first Sephirah on the Path of Ascent and the final Sephirah on
the Path of Descent. Malkuth is the place of form. Yesod is the realm of
force. Malkuth is the place of appearance. Yesod is the place of energy.
Malkuth is the sphere of consciousness and physical matter. Yesod is the
sphere of the subconscious and non-physical energy. Dion Fortune says,
'Yesod, then must be conceived of as the receptacle of the emanations of all
other Sephiroth and as the immediate, and only, transmitter of these
emanations to Malkuth, the physical plane.'[1] Makuth is the Kingdom but
Yesod is the Foundation.

The Hidden Depths

The movement to meet our transpersonal selves is not
so much a raising of unconscious life to consciousness
but more of a descent or deepening to unconscious life.

Alan Bleakley, *Fruits of the Moon Tree*

Western psychology has familiarized recent generations with the idea of
subconscious or unconscious forces. At the time of its development early
in the 20th century, this concept met much resistance and hostility. Jung,
the great pioneer in this field, saw the concept as a corrective to the symbolic
and thereby spiritual poverty of the times. He wrote, 'This is why we have
a psychology today and why we speak of the unconscious. All this would be
quite superfluous in an age and culture that possesses symbols.'[2] In other
words, a richly symbolic culture feeds the totality of consciousness. We have
lost, even destroyed, our symbolic legacy and at the dawn of the 21st century

we are now faced with the challenge of reinstating a meaningful inner vocabulary. We have walked en masse into the blind alley of the intellect and indoctrinated ourselves into an inadequate and insubstantial perception of life. 'Our intellect has achieved the most tremendous things, but in the meantime our spiritual dwelling has fallen into disrepair.'[3] Why is it that we cannot become whole people through reasoned intellect and rational processes alone, unaided by symbols and signs of the numinous? The intellect is a fine tool. Its deductive and reductive purpose can be put to good use. But it lacks the affective quality which builds relationships, makes connections and assigns meaning. Without meaning, both personal and collective life is a fragmented series of unconnected empty events. This emptiness of soul, the ability to relate to others and life itself is the void at the heart of our materially affluent and technologically astounding culture. So we must listen to a different voice and follow a new path if we are to find wholeness, meaning and purpose in life. This path begins in earnest with Yesod, the realm of the invisible and the unseen.

Malkuth and Yesod are intimately connected. Where Malkuth can be likened to the visible area of the iceberg, Yesod can be likened to its hidden bulk beneath the surface. The content of waking consciousness is made visible when the light of awareness throws thought processes into sharp relief like a moving stream passing beneath a spotlight. But this sample is highlighted only briefly and the depths beneath the surface remain unknown. Yet surface and depth are as one, inseparable and indivisible. This metaphor is no empty allusion. Writing from a wide analytical experience of symbols both personal and collective, Jung was able to state with confidence, 'Water is the commonest symbol for the unconscious.'[4] He also made it clear that accessing the depths of consciousness was of great redemptive value. 'Whoever looks into the mirror of the water will see first of all his own face. Whoever goes to himself risks a confrontation with himself. The mirror does not flatter, it faithfully shows whatever looks into it; namely, the face we never show to the world because we cover it with the *persona*, the mask of the actor. But the mirror lies behind the mask and shows the true face.'[5] He concludes, 'This confrontation is the first test of courage on the inner way.' Yesod is the first testing place on the Path because it holds the mirror of the unconscious and asks that we find the courage to gaze within and not be afraid.

The unconscious cannot be ignored except at the peril of division. It is the substratum upon which daily life is built. Like the iceberg, choices and day-to-day behaviour rest upon the bulk of forgotten experiences

---

THE MIRROR OF SELF

Sit in front of a mirror in a meditative state of mind. Observe all the thoughts that arise as you see the face that you show to the world. Observe your face and look deeply into your own eyes. Watch your own reflection deeply and allow it to lead your thoughts. Record all that transpires.

---

and patterns of parenting – in fact, upon the totality of past events. 'We call the unconscious "nothing", and yet it is a reality *in potentia*. The thought we shall think, the deed we shall do, even the fate we shall lament tomorrow, all lie unconscious in our today.'[6] This is the realm of Yesod, the Foundation. 'Know Thyself', says the inescapable dictum. 'Know Thyself', exhorts the voice of Jung in the name of an analytical psychology, the modern relation to the rich spiritual traditions of the past. The Tree of Life provides the very nourishment that Jung recognized by its absence. It is a rich symbolic innerworld culture of relationships and connections. It offers a journey of reconnection and expansion. By providing the unconscious with a vocabulary and means of expression, the Tree of Life offers a living fruit to the starved mind and empty soul. Here is a journey which will beyond doubt prove to be healing, therapeutic and illuminating. The Virtue of Yesod is Independence. This is the Path towards Individuation and the way of self-realization. The Vice of Yesod is Idleness, a laziness of being which is content to be one of the crowd, partial, incomplete and unfulfilled.

The Energies of Life

All of creation is energy and it is our energetic blocks which entrap us in patterns of imbalance and ill health. Bringing awareness to this flow, whether through body-work, diet, exercise or counselling, starts to free our energies and increase our vitality. It gives us more room to manoeuvre in, more space to explore ourselves.

Franklyn Stills, *The Polarity Process*

The Sephirah Yesod is called the Foundation. This is the foundation upon which the material world arises. Malkuth represents the familiar physical world, the foundation on which it rests is neither solid nor familiar. As Malkuth receives influences directly from Yesod, the preceding ninth Sephirah, so Yesod in turn receives influences from the eighth Sephirah, Hod, which is a sphere of mind. Hod represents the directing power of the awakened mind. Yesod represents a dynamic and malleable life force: 'Energy follows thought', says the maxim. Malkuth represents the arena of outcome. Yesod is the realm of living energy. It is assigned to the God-Name, Shaddai el Chai, meaning the Almighty Living God.

At the turning of this century, many bio-energetic systems have undergone a revival. In the East, the universal life energy is known as *prana* or *chi*. The West has no word for such a concept. Willhelm Reich offered the concept of *orgone* energy. Previously, Karl Von Reichenbach had applied the term *od* or *odic* to a universal life energy. None of these terms has passed into common use. The concept of a universal life force has never taken deep root in Western spirituality – now we have to borrow terminology from elsewhere. Shiatzu, acupuncture, Jin Shin Jyutsu, Tai Chi and Chi Gong all originated in the East. Such systems integrate mind and body and the vital life force which infuses both. Redirecting life energies through skilful intervention can rebalance and rejuvenate health. These systems have much in common. Each expresses the interconnectedness of emotion, energy and the body/mind. This same relationship is expressed by the connections between Hod, Netzach, Yesod and Malkuth. The applied mind redirects a life energy which in turn produces a physical effect. The thought is conceived in Hod. It is given shape by the creative imagination in Netzach. The created thought is received by the etheric substance of Yesod which underpins the world of material effect and physical consequence. We may describe this same relationship through an older esoteric language of mental, astral and physical influences. The term 'astral' remains an esoteric one and has little place in current healing or therapeutic arts, but it emphasizes the fluidity and, ultimately, malleability of a life force which reflects emotion and is shaped by the mind. The subtle energies are immensely impressionable to both thought and feelings. Prana or chi can be circulated through the body by thought in visual form. It can be stimulated and directed by the conscious breath. *Pranayama* is the ancient science of breath control.

The Treasure House of Images

> There exists a second psychic system of a collective,
> universal and impersonal nature which is identical in all
> individuals. This collective unconscious does not
> develop individually but is inherited.

> C.G. Jung, *The Archetypes and the Collective Unconscious*

The revival of these ancient healing arts has made us familiar and comfort-able with the idea of a living energy. The concept of 'astral' energy is a little more elusive to grasp. This is the province of magicians and shamans, of healers and practitioners of the ancient arts and all those who have learned to walk between the two worlds – by whatever name they are known. If living energy can be moulded by individual thought and is impressionable to the emotions of an individual, what effect can the massed thoughts of communities and nations have on a level of reality which acts as a bridge between thought and matter? Collective thoughts, deeply moulded by centuries of repetition, shape energy currents into recollections of earthly images. The Summerland, beloved of psychics and spiritualists, is an aspect of the astral light. Though real upon its own plane, it is at the same time also illusory. Dion Fortune says that, 'Yesod is the sphere of that peculiar substance, partaking of the nature of both mind and matter, which is called the Aeyther of the Wise, the Akasha, or the Astral Light according to the ter-minology that is being used.'[7] Etheric energies are themselves dynamic, constantly moving, subject to human consciousness. Imagine for a moment that the massed energies of every human desire and expression could take visible form. Imagine how feelings of massed anger, guilt, rage, despair, joy, compassion and love might appear if such a transformation were possible. Yesod is a realm where the massed thoughts, feelings, desires and expres-sions of the human heart and mind find expression as living energy. This is the Treasure House of Images, the realm of the unconscious, both personal and collective. Within this Treasure House the human imagination is without limit. Here is a deep pool of human history in all its forms. Here also are the dark collective memories of an entire evolutionary history. Some have called this the *akashic* record, others have referred to it as holotrophic memory. This is the realm of Yesod. It is the foundation upon which we all stand.

Energy follows thought in a constantly reflecting dance of mirrors. The group mind is itself highly malleable – it is the raw material of both political manipulators and the media industry. The importance of subtle energies should not be underestimated at either a group or personal level. The subtle energies provide the blueprint – physical effects will follow. The angelic powers attributed here are the Kerubim, the Strong. The group mind at a fluid astral level has always been the concern of those trained to see into it as a reflecting mirror. Those who walk between the worlds have existed in every culture. Malkuth provides the image of the Gate onto the Path, Yesod provides the image of sandals. The meaning is clear: the Path is to be trodden, not merely contemplated from afar. It is the way which asks to be walked.

The Magical Image attributed to Yesod is that of a naked man, very strong, upholding the world. Like the Kerubim, this is an image of the strength immanent in the subtle, etheric, astral or energy template. Workers in magical dimensions seek to effect a change upon the inner levels by planting a powerful mental seed in the astral-etheric energy level, from where it may later take form in the physical world. This route employs the Hod–Yesod–Malkuth relationship with good effect; the mind deliberately imprints energy as the template for physical result.

The realm of Yesod is not bound to a single form of energy. It describes the subatomic stratum recognized by physics, the unconscious – both personal and collective – recognized by psychology, and the etheric or astral energies recognized by esotericists. Yesod embraces the widest concept of those forces and factors that lie just beneath the surface of appearance.

The subtle potency of perfume is one of the symbols attributed to Yesod. Like the subtle energies which are central to the nature of this Sephirah, perfume is both invisible yet detectable through the appropriate sense. The sense of smell is highly developed and sophisticated. Scents are mood changing and have soothing and healing qualities. It is perhaps even noteworthy that along with the appearance of the many healing arts which are themselves related to Yesod, aromatherapy has established itself as a healing vehicle. It too can be attributed to Yesod, combining both the perfumes and the subtle energies assigned to this Sephirah. Incense too has acquired an everyday popularity. It has moved beyond the sacred circle and the temple.

The Sephirah Yesod embraces all those invisible, implicit and imbedded forces which affect not just the single individual but the whole. The spiritual experience of Yesod is the Vision of the Machinery of the Universe. Such glimpses are life changing and radical, destroying and invalidating a partial understanding at the instant as a window briefly opens to another wider, broader and richer comprehension. The Archangel assigned here is Gabriel, called The Strong One of God. As the Archangel of the Annunciation, Gabriel is the giver of the Power of Vision. Clairvoyance, the ability to see clearly, begins to awaken as the qualities and gifts of Yesod become integrated. Contemplation of Yesod takes us from the world of appearances and fragmented events to an understanding of the rhythms, cycles and life energies which give rise to the world in which we live. The functions of Yesod are said to mirror those of Daath but upon a lower arc. The relationship is an important one. Yesod represents the creativity of sexual generation. Daath, represented by the Throat Chakra, symbolizes the creativity of artistic generation as a vital expression at the inmost core of being. These two levels of expression are intimately connected. We first tread the unfamiliar landscape of Yesod before attempting to comprehend the even less familiar setting of Daath, the veiled Sephirah.

The Rainbow Bridge

> Building the Antakarana as a spiritual endeavour may be
> another way of saying that we must work at our minds
> until they cease to be an impediment to cosmic
> consciousness.

> **Mary Scott,** *Kundalini in the Physical World*

Yesod is the realm of the subtle energies of life. Western spirituality has recently been energized by an influx of Eastern teaching relating especially to the subtle bodies and its energy centres or *chakras*. These subtle centres provide a blueprint for self-realization and personal transformation which has much in common with the Tree of Life. As the Sephiroth represent objective states which are attained and integrated, so the chakras also represent different levels of consciousness. The model of being presented as *Sat-Cakra-Nirupana*, Description or Knowledge of the Chakras, meshes with the model of being presented as The Tree of Life.[8] The full model of the chakras is to be found on the 28th Path between Yesod and Netzach, where the seven chakras are represented by the seven stars in the sky on the Tarot Trump of The Star. The Sephirah Yesod matches the symbolism and meaning assigned to the Swadistana or Sacral Chakra. Both Yesod and the Sacral Chakra are related to sexuality, reproduction and personal relationships. Both Yesod and the awakened Sacral Chakra bring psychic abilities, including clairvoyance. Both Yesod and the Swadistana Chakra represent the role of unconscious or subconscious feelings in human development. Both Yesod and the Sacral Chakra are represented by images of the moon and water. This equivalence has emerged despite two entirely different cultural backgrounds; symbolic language is universal, natural and spontaneously generated. Yesod is assigned to the moon, the Swadistana Chakra is assigned specifically to the crescent moon. The lunar powers have been an important influence in the development of culture, specifically in the development of notation and the calendar. The province of the moon has acquired a sacred and numinous quality; its domain of cyclic change and light stands under the aegis of a moon goddess. The many names given to the goddesses of the moon speak of a wide and long-lived appreciation. Her names may vary but her realm is unchanging. The moon claims the realm of ebbing waters and changing shapes, burgeoning life and nocturnal rhythms. Its waxing and waning brings a cosmic timepiece, its regular disappearance brings a sense of unease. The changing moon has become linked to the feminine principle as the unchanging sun has become linked to the masculine principle. The soft light of the night has come to represent the dimly experienced realm of the subconscious mind, the private world of dreams and the mysterious realm of possible magic. The sun has come to represent the bright light of day where all is made plain and visible. This is the light of the rational mind, clear and constant.

The diffuse energies of Yesod are represented by the natural mirrors of moon and water. The moon, having no light of its own, reflects the light of the sun. Still water serves as a mirror. Traditionally scrying is performed by gazing into a dark reflective surface or upon the surface of still water. The mirror-like surface merely symbolizes the process within the mind. Images arise when the outer five senses have been stilled and the sixth sense is used to look into the reflecting mirror of the mind. The multi-dimensional aura is the true mirror of individual being. The collective unconscious serves as the mirror of the human family.

The work of constructing the Rainbow Bridge, the *Antakarana*, is seeded in Malkuth but it takes root in the realm of Yesod. The Rainbow Bridge is the refined vehicle of consciousness which mirrors the transformative journey of self-realization. A changed level of mind creates changes in the etheric structure. The emotional vehicle is stilled through observing all desires and motives from a detached viewpoint. Regular periods of quiet meditation will bring both calmness and insight. When the emotional vehicle becomes still and clear, like a mirror, this level of consciousness will begin to reflect impressions and inspiration from mental levels. The path of self-realization unifies, aligns and transforms the subtle energies of the living aura into a pillar of light rooted in Malkuth but stretching towards Kether. This is the Rainbow Bridge. It is a vehicle of increasingly subtle refinement and sensitivity. Dr Valerie Hunt, Professor of Kinesiology, has discovered a correlation between the measured electrical activity of the muscles and the use of mind. An approximate output of 250 cycles per second is associated with plain biological function and with individuals who focus on the material world. Psychics or healers reveal electrical activity in the range of 400–800 cycles per second. Individuals working through trance or as channellers reveal readings of 800–900 cycles per second. Mystical personalities who are, 'aware of the cosmic interrelatedness of all things and are in touch with every level of human experience', show readings of 900 cycles and above.[9]

Kirlian photography has shown us that all living forms radiate an energy field, a bioplasma which extends slightly beyond the physical form. Physicists have glimpsed the subatomic sea which underpins all matter. Jung has shown us the collective unconscious. The sphere of Yesod represents all these unseen forces which nonetheless exert a shaping force on the world that we recognize.

EVOCATION

Welcome to my kingdom which is the world behind the world. All here is as insubstantial as moonlight. This is the world of energies in motion. Look between your fingers in a gentle light and you will see my silvery web flowing from hand to hand. Sensitize yourself to the bright radiance of clear energies. Open your eyes and discover that my light shines about every living thing. You live and move in a sea of living light. I am the Foundation. My strength is unseen yet I support all worlds. I hold up your world. This is the Treasure House of Images, the box of delights for the unwary. I have so much to offer that you may spend an eternity mesmerized by my magic mirror, lulled into a stupor of idleness by patterns and pictures. The independent traveller acknowledges my world, and having seen the reflected self passes on to search for the source. All human desires pass across the mirror of Yesod, creating forms upon this plane. Do not mistake the fleeting forms that shimmer and fade for substantial form. Here is the place where thoughts take a shape and hang in the air before they are gone. Here your thoughts are real. What will you create in my world? I am to be found through the veil of appearances. Our worlds are very close. I support your world of manifest form as the foundation must support the structure. I reflect back what you reveal to me. Your hatreds and greed like prowling monsters will come to life again. All that has been created in the mind may be found somewhere here. I offer bright landscapes and unspeakable darkness. For I am the mirror. I can only reflect what you have already built. I give a home to the newly departed as I have always done. I am the Elysian Fields, the Halls of Valhalla, the Gardens of Paradise. I am Summerland and I am hell, both hot and cold. I am the mirror of your creation. My sign is the Moon, the great reflector. I am seen in all who wear the lunar crown and proclaim the natural powers of ebb and flow. Here lies the seed of your creative powers. Then truly create and join in the work of creation.

INTERNALIZATION – JOURNEY TO THE TEMPLE OF YESOD

Construct the Temple of Yesod in the creative imagination. Find yourself standing in the mirrored space of Yesod. This is complex space where it is difficult to separate reality from illusion. Every movement is multiplied endlessly. Flickering lights shine all around, yet there is but a single flame upon the altar. Recognizing that this is a place of subtle distortion and confusion, you seek to gain an inner composure. You approach the altar. You see both the statuette of the naked figure upholding the world and its refection in the mirror. Now you look into the mirror itself. Expecting to see your own face you are surprised to see shapes and colours instead. Watching these reflections, you see that these images are in constant movement, shifting and reforming constantly. This is the reflected image of your own inner space.

Now you stand quietly composing yourself. As your thoughts become more centred you become aware of a column of blue-green light coalescing beside you. Silver flashes and peacock tints appear as if from nowhere. The lights settle. You hold the mind steady and do not allow your emotions to unbalance your equilibrium. A figure coalesces from the swirling light. Here is Gabriel, Archangel of this place. He holds an upraised silver horn and at once sounds a note which is pure and clear. In response all reflections stabilize. You look into the mirror again. Now you see your own face. Clarity replaces confusion; clear sight replaces doubt. At last you see yourself. Spend some time in reflective contemplation.

When you are ready to depart, leave through the doorway. Finally, dissolve all images and return to ordinary consciousness.

EXERCITIA SPIRITUALIA

Take the Following as Subjects for Meditation:

- Shaddai el Chai – The Almighty Living God
- The Archangel Gabriel
- The Kerubim
- A naked man, very strong, upholding the world
- The Machinery of the Universe
- The Pure Intelligence
- The Moon

Contemplate the Following Questions and Record your Responses:

- How does the quality of Independence function in your life?
- How does the quality of Idleness function in your life?
- How does the nature of Yesod relate to the Sacral Chakra?
- What other correspondences can you relate to the Sephirah Yesod?
- How do the four Tarot cards relate to Yesod?

Visualize the Following and Record your Experiences:

- An image of a lunar goddess from a sacred tradition of your choice
- The Temple of Yesod including the Archangel Gabriel
- The Journey to the Temple of Yesod

CHAPTER 5

The Thirty-First Path: Malkuth–Hod

FIGURE 11 THE 31ST PATH:
MALKUTH–HOD

TAROT TRUMP XX,
JUDGEMENT

TABLE OF CORRESPONDENCES

Journey: Tarot Trump XX, Judgement,
The Spirit of Primal Fire
Key: The Letter Shin, meaning a tooth
Mother Letter: The Element of Fire
Spiritual Significance: The Elemental Powers
of Fire
Text: The Perpetual Intelligence
Colour in Atziluth: Glowing Orange Scarlet
Colour in Briah: Vermilion
Colour in Yetzirah: Scarlet flecked Gold
Colour in Assiah: Vermilion flecked Crimson
and Emerald

COMMENTARY

The Thirty-first Path is called the Perpetual Intelligence, but why is it so called? Because it regulates the motions of the Sun and Moon in their proper order, each in the orbit convenient for them.

The 31st Path connects the tenth Sephirah, Malkuth, the Kingdom, with the eighth Sephirah, Hod, meaning Glory. Malkuth represents the realm of the physical world, Hod represents a realm of mind. This Path connects the Pillar of Equilibrium or Consciousness with the Pillar of Severity within the Astral or Psychological Triangle. The 31st Path is concerned with the use of the mind as a positive factor in development and unfoldment. It relates to those factors in human development and behaviour which today appear under the umbrella of psychology. Previously, theories of mind were derived entirely from a religious model. Now the study of mind has moved away from this single base to be embraced by both the humanities and the sciences, as psychology and the new field of the neurosciences. Even now the most fundamental question still remains: how does consciousness arise from the structure of the brain?

A Model of Mind

> The psyche is the greatest of all cosmic wonders and the *sine qua non* of the world as an object. It is in the highest degree odd that Western man, with but few, very few exceptions, apparently pays so little regard to this fact.

C.G. Jung, *The Structure and Dynamics of the Psyche*

In the West psychology is still a young discipline. It is the youngest of the empirical sciences. The need for an empirical approach to mind was voiced as part of the general growth of the 17th-century scientific thrust. Christian Von Wolf (1679–1754) was the first to speak of 'empirical' or 'experimental' psychology. But more than another century was to pass before psychology took the irrevocable step away from religious philosophy towards an empirical base. At the turn of the 19th century, psychology was still in the thrall of philosophy and had no independent status. The time was ripe for a revolution. When the revolution came, spearheaded by Freud, Jung and Pierre Janet, it was most unwelcome.

The emergence of Western psychology from a theological rootstock has now produced an independent line of development. Psychology and its twin partner psychiatry have together broadened and deepened an understanding of mind, but the West still has no single comprehensive model of being which encompasses both psychological and spiritual terrain. The benefits of a Western empirical basis need to be weighed against the holism of an Eastern philosophical model. Where the West has separated the mind from a total model of being, the East has maintained a unified model. Eastern psychology remains imbedded in a wider theory of being which encompasses both personal and transpersonal levels. Western investigative instincts do not mesh comfortably with Eastern metaphysics. But the techniques of division, analysis, observation, deduction, measurement, assessment and hypothesis have not yet answered the nature of consciousness. The nature of mind remains the unsolved enigma. The West can offer no single theory of consciousness – only a range of contending models. At one extreme certain schools claim that there is nothing other than the brain and its functions. At the other extreme it is suggested that mind and matter are two sides of the same coin, with matter having a double aspect which is both physical and non-physical simultaneously. The middle view suggests that consciousness arises from the structure and function of neurones. In the 1960s the neuroscientist Karl Pribram suggested a holographic theory of consciousness. This had more in common with an Eastern metaphysical view than with the traditional Western explanations, but the weakness of the holographic theory lay in the fact that there were no neural equivalents to the laser beams necessary to generate the hologram. However, in the 30 years since the inception of the original idea, it has been discovered that large groups of neurones often fire repeatedly and in step like waves of light. This discovery adds some weight to a holographic theory of mind. Recently a new factor has intruded into the debate with all the potential to shake current perspectives to the core. This is the Quantum factor. Just as physics has been redefined by the incorporation of a Quantum understanding, so neuroscience too is yielding in the face of an inexorable power. Danah Zohar has put forward a radical view. She brings a multi-disciplinary approach to her work, being well qualified in both science and religion. She studied both physics and philosophy at the Massachusetts Institute of Technology before studying psychology and theology at Harvard. She suggests that both matter and mind stem from a deeper source, 'the quantum'. She is not alone in her view. Roger Penrose, a mathematical physicist with an impeccable reputation gained for his joint work with Stephen Hawkins on black holes and other gravitational phenomena, suggests that the human mind will only be explained by a still-undiscovered theory which must incorporate both quantum mechanics and relativity theory. He concludes that no rule-based model – whether from classical physics, neuroscience, mathematics or computer science – can ever provide the key to consciousness. His argument offers more than a passing nod in the direction of an Eastern mystical explanation. Currently there is a renewed Western drive to understand the nature of consciousness. The debate is multi-disciplined and open-ended. What is emerging beyond doubt, however, is the Quantum factor. This is creating a more receptive enquiry into the Eastern view of mind, which has always maintained an inherent holism.

The tenets of spiritual belief ring with a new truth in the light of a quantum theory. The universal mind common to both Buddhist and Hindu thought shares much in common with the Quantum ground state. The mystical element which characterizes the Eastern view is an older statement of a holistic philosophy. The relationship between the two levels is exemplified now by fractal geometry which also gives new meaning to the Hermetic axiom 'As Above, So Below'. The Western science of consciousness is moving a step closer to the metaphysics of the East. When East and West really meet face to face, the cross-fertilization of traditions can only be of mutual benefit. Such a deep dialogue has the possibility of creating an entirely new synthesis of philosophy and science. It may confirm what Jung intuitively felt to be true:

> Since psyche and matter are contained in one and the same world, and moreover are in continuous contact with one another, and ultimately rest on irrepresentable, transcendental factors, it is not only possible but fairly probable, even, that psyche and matter are two different aspects of one and the same thing.[1]

The prospect is exciting.

Awakening the Mind

In all actions I will learn to search into my mind

And as soon as an afflictive emotion arises

Endangering myself and others

Will firmly face and avert it.

The Eighth Stanza for Training the Mind

The model of mind that we choose to employ is fundamental. An inadequate model brings inadequacy. The Tree of Life presents a model of mind which is practical and personally applicable. Western psychology, even at its fullest and most holistic, relates only to a relatively small aspect of the Tree through the Astral and Psychological Triangle of the Tree formed by Hod, Netzach and Yesod. The remainder of the Tree is unrelated to present psychology. It is, however, well matched to the teachings of Buddhism in general and Tibetan Buddhism in particular which focus clearly on the transition between the personal and the transpersonal. The Tree of Life presents a holistic and unified philosophy of being which, like its Eastern counterparts, embraces both personal and transpersonal areas. The 31st Path, which represents the first awakening of mind, leads to the Sephirah Hod. Hod in turn takes its root from the higher more abstracted reaches of the Tree. It is related directly to the Sephirah Chesed, the realm of universal wisdom.

This journey on the 31st Path is symbolized by Tarot Trump XX, Judgement. It shows open coffins floating upon a sea. In the sky an angel blows a trumpet. The awakened rise with outstretched arms to greet the sound. It is tempting to interpret this as a scene of awakening to an idyllic afterlife at the sound of the trumpet. But this is not an after-death awakening; rather, it is an image of an awakening which takes place in life itself. The seas are the deep waters of the unconscious upon which the sleepers float and drift in grey coffins. The angelic presence is the Archangel Michael who brings the opportunity to awaken from the sleep-like state of automatic existence. In life this call may come in various guises: an inborn and inner sense of a spiritual dimension, a life crisis, trauma, loss, or the stagnation of success itself. The angelic note is ever being sounded. Some hear it, others search for it. Many sleep on. This is not the Last Judgement but the first awakening.

Tarot Trump XX, Judgement, is also called the Spirit of Primal Fire.

This is a path of spiritual awakening precipitated through the application of judgement, not a path of judgement upon the spiritual journey. Judgement is an active mental process which balances two or more options and evaluates the consequences. It can only take place through a detached self-awareness. The 31st Path connects Malkuth with Hod and thereby connects the Virtue of Malkuth, Discrimination, with the Virtue of Hod, which is Truthfulness. The 31st Path brings these two qualities into active and daily use. Without Truthfulness and Discrimination the journey cannot proceed. The meaning of self-judgement is not the generation of a judgmental attitude but the development of its exact opposite: a non-judgmental watchfulness, a detached observation and a silent inner witnessing. In essence, the quality of judgement assigned to the 31st Path serves the same function as the practice of mindfulness in the Buddhist tradition: it is the Perpetual Intelligence.

The Perpetual Intelligence is the mindful intelligence which brings conscious awareness to mind, body, speech, thought and feeling. This Path calls for a watching awareness of the contents of the mind. The Buddhist practice of mental mindfulness with its emphasis on watching the mind at work brings an integrated self-awareness which forms a solid foundation for the greater work of total mental transformation. 'Every day and every hour, one should practice mindfulness. That is easy to say, but to carry it out in practice is not,' says the Vietnamese Buddhist monk Thich Nhat Hanh.[2] He suggests planting the seeds of mindfulness by setting aside a day for gentle self-observation and awareness. 'The day of mindfulness will begin to penetrate the other days of the week, enabling you to live seven days a week in mindfulness.'

MINDFULNESS

'To set up a day of mindfulness', figure out a way to remind yourself at the moment of waking that this is your day of mindfulness. You might hang something on the ceiling or on the wall, a paper with the word "mindfulness" or a pine branch – anything that will suggest to you as you open your eyes and see it that today is your day of mindfulness. Today is your day. Remembering that, perhaps you can feel a smile which affirms that you are in complete mindfulness, a smile that nourishes that perfect mindfulness.'[3]

Thich Nhat Hanh, *The Miracle of Mindfulness*

This watching awareness, perpetually awake, has the power to transfer choice from unconscious to conscious process, to shift action from meaningless to meaningful choice, to transform automatic response into autonomous decision. Additionally, becoming aware of the contents of the mind, including the range and type of thoughts, begins the process of training the mental body or sheath of consciousness. The goal of thinking clearly, 'on all matters affecting the race' is not easily achieved. But this is the transforming work called for on the 31st Path as a preparation for engagement with the Sephirah Hod.

The Perpetual Intelligence is said to regulate, 'the motions of the Sun and Moon in their proper order'. The sun represents the bright constant light of consciousness. The moon represents the pale light of the unconscious. The sun is the light of the personality, the moon is the light of the private interior depths. The one light is yin, the other yang. Both are ruled by the Perpetual Intelligence as a constant and abiding presence. Opposites are united and reconciled by a third transcendent function. The Path of the Moon is to be found between Yesod and Netzach. The Path of the Sun is to be found between Yesod and Hod.

Today the tools for self-awareness are laid out in every manual and self-help workbook. The active imagination, the dream state, positive affirmations, symbol incubation, inner dialogue and much more besides have become the stock-in-trade of the New Age kitbag. These have become the mainstays of a new psychology. Mental techniques have become popularized, and exercises in self-exploration are no longer seen as arcane or esoteric but helpful and ordinary.

The popularizing of Western psychology may not please the academics and clinicians but it pleases the general public who have an unquenchable appetite for means of self-development, self-improvement and self-awareness. Psychology has become a popular subject of huge general interest. The locus has shifted from the consulting room to everyday life. The emphasis has moved from the remedial to the preventative. The mood has changed in tone from one of empirical enquiry to one of healing. The power holders are no longer clinical experts but voices of authority and experience validated and recognized by popular consent. Popular psychology is providing a new generation with the tools of self-awareness. This upsurge in its many diverse forms is but an exploration of a single theme – namely, the power of the mind to effect positive, desired change in daily life. This is the essence of the 31st Path.

This popular contemporary psychology owes much to approaches and concepts taken directly from the great spiritual traditions of the world. Its exponents may speak in a contemporary language through the medium of the video, the book or even the internet, but the message is timeless. These rightly popular and populist teachers of the West have served long apprenticeships as students of the East. For instance, John Gray, author of the best-selling *Mars and Venus* series, was a Hindu monk for nine years. He is not unique in having served a long and gruelling apprenticeship before fulfilling the role of a contemporary Western guru.

Drawing upon the holistic philosophy of Eastern spirituality which offers both technique and explanation, the new psychology is bridging the gap between a personal and a transpersonal psychology. The panoply of such techniques, whether taken directly from the ancient Eastern sources or indirectly through modern forms, are all relevant to this path.

The Fire of the Mind

> When, through occult unfoldment and esoteric
> knowledge, the relation between the personality and the
> soul is established, there is a midway spot in the centre
> of the head in the magnetic field which is called the
> 'light in the head'.

Alice Bailey, *A Treatise on White Magic*

The 31st Path carries the symbolism of fire. Tarot Trump XX is known as The Spirit of Primal Fire, and the letter Shin assigned to this Path represents elemental fire. The discovery of fire-making acted as a catalyst in human development and initiated a cycle of social and cultural development. For the Greeks, fire originated in heaven with the gods. It was Prometheus who stole the first fire from heaven in order to give it to mankind. He was punished by Zeus, who condemned him to perpetual torment – his liver was torn out by day and replenished by night. Prometheus was eventually allowed to die peacefully when the wise centaur Chiron took his place. The name Prometheus means 'forethought'. The coming of fire lights a social and cultural revolution, but the coming of forethought seeds a revolution of mind.

Fire is a universal symbol. It represents a cohesive and unifying socializing force. It signifies the warmth and security of the hearth fire and the many social and cultural factors which create shared life and a domestic environment. Domestic fire is under the aegis of the goddess Vesta. Fire also represents an undying spiritual dimension within human life. A single flame lights many others and in the darkness a light shines out as a beacon and signpost. It is the sacred flame of the altar and the vestal flame of the city. Light signifies the possibility of enlightenment. Without light, darkness is impenetrable and frightening. It signifies the state of ignorance and bondage. Fire also represents the primeval power of nature herself. It is the devastating fire of the volcano and the raging firestorm which each destroy and recreate the landscape. The mythical phoenix, the firebird, arises from its own ashes. The underworld fire belongs to Vulcan, or Hyphaestus, the archetypal smithy. Fire purges, consumes and destroys. It is the fire of the cremation ground, the destructive force of the forest fire and the terrible power of mass destruction. Intense and applied heat brings transformation. It is the furnace, the kiln and the oven. It is the inner fire of alchemical transformation and the secret inner fire of serpent power. This Path is one of evolutionary history. It points to both the past and the future. By connecting Malkuth, the Kingdom, with Hod, the sphere of mind, this Path anticipates evolutionary changes that are still to come.

> He made Shin king over fire
> And He bound a crown to it
> And He combined one with another
> And with them He formed
> Heaven in the Universe
> Hot in the year
> And the head the Soul

The Sepher Yetzirah

The Key to this Path is the letter Shin, which represents elemental fire. As one of the three Mother Letters, it represents elemental fire as a force of creative potency. The letter signifies a tooth. The tooth is virtually indestructible. It can survive in the ground for thousands of years and can even survive fire. The letter Shin is composed from the letter Yod repeated three times. With tapering bases the letter even resembles both the tooth and the flame in shape. The letter Yod is itself representative of the powers of primal creation as the first letter of the *Tetragrammaton*, the Holy Name of God. The tripling of the letter Yod to form Shin triples the impact of its meaning. This tightly packed constellation of images expands the meditative mind. The letter Yod represents primal fire; the triple Yod forms the letter Shin which is the fire of the enduring spirit. The attribution of elemental fire to this Path may also have a more literal meaning as the powers of the mind awaken.

Mystical traditions speak literally, not metaphorically, of a fire in the mind. The mystical artist and poet George Russell (who wrote as Æ) knew this. He wrote of his experiences with, 'a steady light in the brain, and it was revealed in ecstasy of thought or power in speech and in a continuous welling up from within myself of intellectual energy, vision or imagination'. He called it, 'the candle upon the forehead', and elsewhere even referred to it as, 'the Promethian fire'. He recorded his experiences with the detached eye of an observer. He spoke of, 'a growing luminescence in my brain as if I have unsealed in the body a fountain of interior light'.[4] Alice Bailey speaks of this light in the mind too. 'The personality hides within itself as a casket hides the jewel, that point of soul light which we call the light in the head. This is found within the brain and is only discovered and later used when the highest aspect of the personality, the mind, is developed and functioning.'[5] This is the fire of the mind, not metaphorical but literal.

This wonderful and extraordinary interior illumination begins simply with the development of the Perpetual Intelligence through the process of watching the mind, which is here on the 31st Path called Judgement. This light begins here in the lower reaches of the Astral, Psychological Triangle of the Lesser Mysteries and comes to fruition on the higher ground of the Supernal Triangle and the Supreme Mysteries.

EVOCATION

Welcome to my kingdom. Travel my path to discover the powers of your own mind. What is Mind? This question has puzzled the great philosophers of the ages. Is Mind not a great mystery? I am the Angel of the Awakening and it is my task to awaken. Do not think that my lessons are dull. Only the sleeping mind is dull. The awakened mind scintillates with an inner brilliance. It lives. Do not confuse the plain tasks of remembering with the learning that I offer. I offer the delight of understanding and the satisfaction of true comprehension. I will not bore you with meaningless puzzles and absurd tasks. I will enable you to find the meaning of your own life. I will enable you to discover who you are. I will show you how the awakened mind creates change. I will show you how the awakened mind pierces illusion. I will show you how the awakened mind lives. But first you must awaken. How will you recognize me? My voice is often muted by the sounds of the world. Yet be assured, you will find me in the word for it is from here that awakening proceeds. The trumpet call is sounded all about you continuously. Look into the eyes of the world. Can you sleep when the world calls you to service? I call you to awaken. Exercise judgement. Discover your own mental powers and you will be surprised. Unlike those who mistake the deductive powers of the reasoning mind for the mind itself, you are prepared to discover otherwise. The rational mind, so valued by your peers and contemporaries, is but one reflection of the Great Mind. When the personal mind is aligned to the higher mind, you will awaken to new realities and possibilities. You will know how to awaken others. When your mind wakes, its waking sets up a ripple which in time brings the abstract mind to life. So be patient, exercise self-judgement in all matters and Primal Fire will awaken within you. Welcome to the life of the mind.

INTERNALIZATION – THE 31ST PATH: MALKUTH–HOD

Construct the Temple of Malkuth in the creative imagination. Find yourself standing beside the door of Judgement. The Archangel Sandalphon draws back the tapestry curtain so that you may pass.

You find yourself passing through a light mist. When you emerge you find that you stand at the foot of a steep slope. You begin to climb the bank. It is quite a climb and there are times when you think about stopping. At last you reach the top. From your vantage point you see that a vast ocean stretches out in front of you. You begin to run down the hill. You are eager to reach the waters.

You arrive at a quay. There is a row of boats there and you decide to board one. You choose a boat with the Hebrew letter Shin painted on its side. You recall that this sign means both a tooth and Elemental Fire. As you muse on the meaning of this, your boat begins to move as if driven by an unseen motive force. Time passes and along with many other boats you ride upon the ocean. Suddenly and without warning the calm of the day is rent by a sound which has no obvious source. It seems to come from everywhere at once. The sound is powerful and intense. It reminds you of a Tibetan horn. Its low and deep vibration sets up a resonance. Even the structure of the boat begins to vibrate. Your body is shaking with a resonant sound. You stand up in the boat so that you can scan the horizon for its source. The trumpet continues to sound its long resonating note. Even the surface of the water seems to shake. Now the occupants of other boats are standing too. Everyone is searching for the source of the sound. A bright ray of sunlight bursts though the clouds and for a moment it seems that you see a great angelic figure sounding a trumpet in the heavens. This vision hovers briefly before the clouds close again. Is this some trick of the light? You have no way of knowing. Now you look to the sky again and there is nothing to see but blinding sunlight. From the depths of your mind comes the single word, 'Awake'. At last the sound ceases and there is nothing to be heard but the gentle lapping of water against the side of the boat. The boat returns to shore and you disembark.

When you are ready, return the way you came to the Temple. When you are ready, leave through the doorway. Finally, dissolve all images and return to ordinary consciousness.

EXERCITIA SPIRITUALIA

Take the Following as Subjects for Meditation:

- The Spirit of Primal Fire
- The Letter Shin
- The significance of Elemental Fire
- The Perpetual Intelligence

Make Notes on:

- Tarot Trump XX, Judgement

Visualize the Following and Record your Experiences:

- The Temple of Malkuth including the Archangel Sandalphon
- The Journey of the 31st Path

CHAPTER 6

The Thirtieth Path: Yesod–Hod

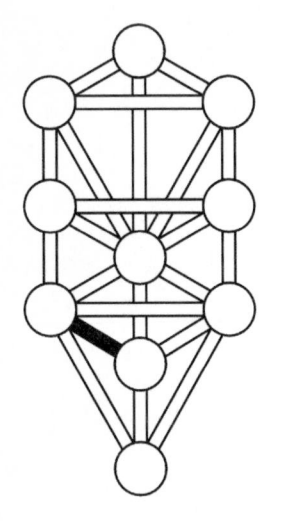

FIGURE 12 THE 30TH PATH:

YESOD–HOD

TAROT TRUMP XIX,

THE SUN

TABLE OF CORRESPONDENCES

Journey: Tarot Trump XIX, the Sun, Lord of the
Fire of the World

Key: The letter Resh, meaning the Head

Double Letter: Fertility – Barrenness

Spiritual Significance: The Sun

Text: The Collecting Intelligence

Colour in Atziluth: Orange

Colour in Briah: Gold Yellow

Colour in Yetzirah: Rich Amber

Colour in Assiah: Amber rayed Red

COMMENTARY

The Thirtieth Path is called the Collecting Intelligence and it is so called because Astrologers deduce from it the judgement of the Stars, and of the celestial signs, and the perfections of their science, according to the rules of their resolutions.

The 30th Path connects the ninth Sephirah, Yesod, with the eighth Sephira, Hod. It thereby joins the realm of the unconscious with that of rational consciousness. It is a Path which deals with the use of mind. This Path is the polar opposite to the 28th Path which links Yesod to Netzach and links the realm of the unconscious with that of instinct and imagination. The 30th Path shares certain similarities with the 31st Path, which connects Malkuth with Hod. Both Paths connect the Central Pillar of Consciousness with the side Pillar of Severity. Both Paths reach Hod and therefore each is related to practices which awaken and expand mental horizons and powers as part of the Astral or Psychological Triangle. This journey is represented by Tarot Trump XIX, The Sun, which is also called Lord of the Fire of the World.

The Collecting Intelligence

> Wonder is the beginning of philosophy.

Aristotle

This Path is assigned to the Collecting Intelligence.[1] This title is reminiscent of the Victorian passion for collecting specimens and samples. It is the modus operandi of museums and laboratories, and the delight of small children. It is the founding experience of specialized knowledge. Collecting provides the basis for naming, cataloguing, describing, differentiating and defining. Collecting develops the key skills of observation, comparison and analysis, which form the basis of scientific method. Collecting samples brings a direct interaction and unique engagement with the natural world. The initiative to explore knows no boundaries, from the depths to the heights, from the hidden interior to the infinite horizon of space, from deserts to the Arctic, from ocean to mountain top, this is the quest to know the world in which we live. This urge is an elaboration and modification of the higher instincts – the drive to activity, the need to be reflective and the power to express creativity. Innate curiosity powers the Collecting Intelligence. This is the first key to the experience of the 30th Path.

The 30th Path is one of mental expansion and the joyful empowerment that this brings. It is a Path of increasing light and mental illumination as new ideas take hold in the mind. Knowledge brings the power to act with practical effect. Understanding the properties and functions of plants, animals and raw materials leads to the many fields of human mastery: medicine, architecture, engineering, agriculture, navigation and many more. This Path demonstrates the power of discovery and its application. Archimedes expressed the essence of this Path with the cry 'Eureka!' It is the moment of realization, the sudden breakthrough, a spontaneous seeing into the workings of nature. It is driven by the intense and creative brooding which characterizes deep enquiry and sustained curiosity. The Collecting Intelligence is the drive to know and understand. This is a passion as great as any artistic force. The Collecting Intelligence by virtue of its innate mental intensity can suddenly and unexpectedly cross the boundaries from information into insight, generating a momentary flash of pure illumination. The steam-powered revolution took on new momentum when George Stephenson idly watched a kettle boil with the open eye of awareness. Isaac Newton suddenly glimpsed the Law of Gravity as he saw an apple fall from a tree. Such realizations catalyse chain reactions which continue in perpetuity, and society shifts gear with each successive revolution – from the Bronze Age to the Iron Age, from the agricultural revolution to the Industrial Revolution, from the technological revolution to the space revolution. The wonders of nature are infinite. The applied power of the human mind is awesome. Who can deny the wonder of the Hubble Telescope and the refined and precise skills which made it possible? Such wonders begin in the realm of the idea and are made real in the world.

The 30th Path connects the experience of Yesod with that of Hod. It unites the Vision of the Machinery of the Universe assigned to Yesod with the Vision of Splendour assigned to Hod. In other words, the drive to understand the workings of the universe naturally generates the Collecting Intelligence and brings its own reward, the Vision of its Splendour. The Collecting Intelligence is the basis of the scientific imagination. The scientific vision of reality is no less passionate or intense than the artistic view. The lifetime of study and endeavour seen in the work of many great scientists is very often motivated by early childhood experiences, when the desire to explore is brought to life by the power of the imagination. Einstein himself was fascinated by magnets as a young child of about four. It was a fascination that became a driving force to understand the forces of creation. Seeing beneath nature's veil – whether through a microscope, telescope or particle accelerator – is indeed a Vision of Splendour. This is an infinite vision.

The Art of Memory

> Few people know that the Greeks, who invented many arts, invented an art of memory which like their other arts was passed on to Rome, whence it descended in the European tradition.
>
> **Francis A. Yates**, *The Art of Memory*

How good is your memory? A poor memory is an irritant, a very poor memory is an obstacle to learning and even to social interaction. It has been noted that schizophrenics suffer from 'thought derailment', when memory does not serve to keep consciousness on track. The quality of memory is implicit to all personal and cultural development. To remember is to re-member and to collect the scattered fragments into a whole. It is central to the Collecting Intelligence.

Today a specialized memory has little special value. But in an earlier age where oratory and rhetoric were prized abilities, memory had a real and practical significance. Seneca the Elder, a teacher of rhetoric, could repeat two thousand names in the order in which they were given. Simplicius, a friend to Augustine, himself trained in rhetoric, could recite Virgil backwards. Such extraordinary feats were undoubtedly the result of training in memory.

The Greek poet, Simonides of Ceos, is regarded as the founder of a system which far outlived him. The principles of his memory system went on to become indelibly but invisibly imprinted in the cultural fabric of Western civilization. The Greek performing arts borrowed the techniques suggested by Simonides. The great orators of Rome employed and developed the same principles. Later, in complete contrast to the powerful words of oratory and public speaking, unworldly Christian monks sermonized upon a mnemonic framework, and in a final incarnation, Hermetic, Kabbalistic and Neo-Platonic principles were placed upon the same structure.

The basic rules were simple and have continued to form the basis of all memory systems ever since. In principle, what needs to be remembered is allied to something memorable, most probably with pictorial representations. The classical work on memory, *Ad Herrenium*, suggests a series of *loci*, ideally buildings, and a series of images chosen for especially memorable qualities. To align the easily forgotten with the never forgotten lends the charged energy of the intense to the low energy of the mundane and the forgotten becomes memorable:

> Nature herself teaches us what we should do. When we see in everyday life things that are pretty, ordinary and banal, we generally fail to remember them because the mind is not stirred by anything novel or marvellous, but if we see something exceptionally base, dishonourable, unusual, great, unbelievable or ridiculous that we are likely to remember for a long time... We ought then to set up images of a kind that can adhere longest in memory and we shall do so if we establish similitudes as striking as possible.[2]

From Greece and Rome *ars memorativia* passed to a new tradition of learning in the age of scholasticism. The skills of oratory were now redirected towards memorizing sermons and to moral and devotional purposes. The Christian Vices and Virtues appeared in personified forms as Wisdom, Prudence and Knowledge as part of an extended family or an *aide-mémoire*. This method of mind became the mainstay of medieval scholasticism. It proved to be a creative impetus for imagery both real and imagined. Evidence reveals that within the monastic community specific inner pictures were called to mind as part of a mnemonic training for recalling lengthy texts or points of a sermon. The creation of interior landscapes is in many ways not surprising; it is in perfect accord with the practices of the great mystical traditions and it was in the monastic lineage that mystical Christianity arose. What is surprising, perhaps even astonishing, is that such *aides-mémoire* now included undoubted pagan imagery carried over from Greece and Rome: Juno, Neptune, Pluto and the family of the pagan gods stowed away, neatly concealed within the bowels of the good ship, The Scholastic Mnemonic System. They were, however, not destined to be stowaways indefinitely. These unlikely passengers were released and restored to full vigour by the exponents of a new Renaissance philosophy. 'Through Renaissance Neo-Platonism with its Hermetic core, the art of memory was once more transformed, this time into a Hermetic or occult art, and in this form it continued to occupy a central place in European tradition.'[3]

THE PALACE OF MEMORY

This is a memory exercise in the classical tradition. First decide that you are going to visualize a palace. Take each of its elements in turn and create each of them with as much or as little detail as you wish. Create the doorway, entrance hall, circular staircase, mirrored ballroom and balcony in your mind. Add other features too if you wish. Having constructed your location, place anything you wish to remember in the various rooms. Be experimental and see if you can make this system work for you. The wilder and more bizarre the connection, the more likely you are to stimulate the ability to remember.

The Sephirah Hod, the destination of the 30th Path, is first point of contact with Hermetic Wisdom. Both the Tarot and the Kabbalah are systems of symbolic encodement. Both individually and together Tarot and Kabbalah clearly stand in the tradition of the mnemonic system, the art of memory. This tradition may even shed light on the origins of Tarot, which are not shrouded in the mists of time but clearly discernible. The Tarot may even have emerged as one facet in the art of memory. As a series of *loci* and images the Tarot is certainly in keeping with this tradition. The Art of Memory was transformed by the hermetic impetus of the Renaissance. It was no longer in the service of Christian monasticism. Now it was the new and secret exposition of a Neo-Platonic philosophy strongly infused by the Kabbalah of the time. 'Into the old bottles of the art of memory there had been poured the heady wine of the currents of Renaissance, "occult philosophy", running fresh and strong into sixteenth-century Venice from its springs in the movement inaugurated by Ficinio in Florence in the late fifteenth century.'[4]

The Apollonian Light

The art of memory has become an occult art,

a Hermetic secret.

Francis A. Yates, *The Art of Memory*

The 30th Path is assigned to Tarot Trump XIX, The Sun, which is also known as Lord of the Fire of the World. As the centre of our solar system, the sun is the literal fire of the world. Metaphorically, the ideas whose time has come can set the world afire with a tide of enthusiasm and new energy.

Revolutions both practical and intellectual stem from a new idea. The right idea changes both the Vision of the Machinery of the Universe and the Vision of Splendour. It is the idea which ultimately changes the world. The Renaissance was fired by a new Vision of the Machinery of the Universe; it resulted in a new Vision of Splendour.

The 30th Path is symbolized by the letter Resh which represents the head – more specifically, the front of the head. It refers to a consciousness which is distinctly human, the power of abstract thought. This immensely sophisticated development creates all symbolic representations. Sounds represent meaning, shapes represent sounds, concepts represent abstracted qualities, ideas represent abstracted concepts, abstracted forms stand for experiences; symbolic communication, symbolic thought and symbolic expression are born. These are the very qualities which the art of memory developed to such a high level, achieved by the continuous invention of the varied symbolic systems which played such a big part in the spiritual life of the Renaissance.

Tarot Trump XIX features a rayed sun and a single naked child riding on a white horse before a wall topped by four sunflowers. This is the infant Apollo. Related to healing, music and prophecy, Apollo's gifts seem more closely related to the emotional and artistic bounty related to the Pillar of Mercy. But Apollo as a solar image represents a willed use of the conscious mind exemplified by the art of memory. This journey brings the Apollonian Light to birth. It is a light which shines into the development of the sciences as well as the arts. The Hermetic impulse seeks to know without limit.

From our perspective it is perhaps difficult to understand the power released and made visible by so innocuous a device as a memory training system. But we should not underestimate the significance of this method of mind training. Internal imagery unlocks the deeper powers of the mind by providing a holistic framework which breaks into the tyranny of linear thinking. In other words, the restructuring of memory is transformative. 'Many people say "Memory? Why should I bother to develop my memory?" One excellent reason is that memory is our *integration in time*. It is memory that supplies the connecting link between the chronologically separate parts of the self.'[5] Rabbi Areyh Kaplan links memory directly to the non-verbal consciousness assigned to Chockmah. 'Memory is not verbal, but is stored in the mind in a non-verbal mode. It is only when one brings memory to the surface that it becomes verbalized. Since memory is completely non-verbal, it is in the category of Wisdom.'[6] The *ars memorativia* were far more than mere mental callisthenics, and when combined with a holistic Hermetic philosophy provided the fuel of cultural revolution. Yates has referred to the centrality played by this art of memory in the making of the Hermetic Mage. The Renaissance use of the memorizing arts shares much in common with the higher reaches of psychosynthesis through its use of transpersonal symbolism as a dynamic medium. When applied in this way the training of memory becomes so much more; it becomes the awakening of the truly creative imagination.

Creativity, as the truly creative know, moves in with the power of a possessing force; surrender must take place to accommodate the unfolding inner process which lives by its own momentum. This possessing power is the Muse. 'Almost every poet has a personal muse... and even if an occasional poet divines the Muse's existence from other poetic works and from natural surroundings traditionally associated with her immanence – such as mountains, woods and seas – his sense of possession by her is real enough.'[7] The number nine is related to Yesod, the reservoir of unconscious potency. The Nine Muses dwell in latency to be made potent by the awakening of Mnemosyne, the tenth figure. Ten is the number of Malkuth, physical manifestation. The nine daughters of memory are Clio, Euterpe, Thalia, Melpomene, Terpischore, Polyhymnia, Erato, Calliope and Urania. Each of the nine daughters presides over a specialized realm and carries the traditional insignia related to it.

For the Greeks, Memory was personified in the figure of Mnemosyne, Mother of the Muses. This description is fascinating and represents memory as the source of culture and in close relationship to each of the arts. Tending to Mnemosyne awakens her children, who are the Nine Muses. This in-depth involvement with symbolic archetypal forms brings entry into the realm of sacred psychology defined by Jean Houston: 'Sacred psychology is the process and practice of soul making.'[8] But memory itself awaits instruction as a dancer awaits a choreographer. Within the Greek mindset, Apollo is the dance leader of the Muses. It is the Apollonian Light which orchestrates and choreographs the dance. Jean Houston speaks of the personal effects and results of undertaking the work of sacred psychology. The impact is not abstract but leads to physical changes:

> Part of the work of sacred psychology seems to re-educate the brain and nervous system... Doing the work of sacred psychology you will move from lacklustre passivity into conscious orchestration of your life. You stop living what Keats referred to as a posthumous existence... You may begin to notice occasional flashing states of

unusual intenseness and aliveness, which in turn begin to extend themselves in time as your nervous system gets used to them.[9]

The results of the art of memory stand historically as the multi-faceted Renaissance achievement. The results of sacred psychology are seen in the empowering and transformative process of private lives. Francis Yates speaks of a huge shift of vision rendered by new use of the art of memory:

> It represents a new Renaissance plan of the psyche, a change which has happened within memory, whence outward changes derived their impetus. Medieval man was allowed to use his lowly faculty of imagination to form corporeal similitudes to help memory; it was a concession to his weakness. Renaissance Hermetic man believes that he has divine powers; he can form magic memory through which he can grasp the world, reflecting the divine macrocosm in the microcosm of his divine *mens*.[10]

The Double Letter Resh, which signifies the head and thereby the mind, offers two meanings – Barrenness and Fertility. These qualities describe the results of educating the mind (from *educare*, meaning 'to lead out'). The first of these qualities, Barrenness, is the result of rote learning and an excessively dry cerebral method which relies upon memory alone to remember the unmemorable. This approach starves the well of memory while at the same time paying lip service to it. A fertility of mind follows only from an approach which feeds the springs of memory and pays homage to Mnemosyne, Mother of the Muses. The 30th Path is one of mental expansion and the joyful empowerment of the awakening mind. The classical textbook on memory, *Ad Herrenium*, closes with advice to the student:

> In every discipline, artistic theory is of little avail without unremitting exercise, but especially in mnemonics. Theory is almost valueless unless made good by industry, devotion, toil and care.[11]

Despite the passing of the centuries, this advice still stands.

EVOCATION

Welcome to my kingdom. I am the central sun. I am the light which permits self-reflection. I am the light which brings life to the mind. I am rooted in memory but crowned with glory. My light and fire awakens and transforms the latent power of mind. I am the Lord of the Fire of the World. I can set you ablaze with a passion for learning. I can show you the power of the idea. I enable you to contemplate the whole world and all that it is in it by giving you entry into the world of symbolic forms. This is my secret and my gift. It is your inheritance to mentally manipulate, explore and realize, invent, create and discover. It is your birthright to plan, anticipate and envision, express, share and symbolize. It is your destiny to create within creation.

How do you use my gifts? Do you squander the gift of mind in idle and thoughtless pursuits? I can free you from the tyranny of the present moment, liberate you from the drudgery of the concrete and the limitations of the immediate. I can liberate you from the monotony of repeated experience. Instead, through the art of memory you may learn from every action, from everyone, from the distant past or even the anticipation of the future.

I show you how to train the mind, how to awaken Memory the Mother and her gifted children. I will shine a light on your Path as you climb towards the full coming of light. I am the sun within; I am obscured in the shade until you seek out my brilliance. Receive the Apollonian Light. Awaken to memory and be transformed. I am the light of the mind.

INTERNALIZATION – THE 30TH PATH: YESOD–HOD

Construct the Temple of Yesod in the creative imagination. Find yourself standing beside the door of the Sun. The Archangel Gabriel draws back the tapestry curtain so that you may pass.

As you step out you instantly feel the warmth of the sun on your skin. You find yourself standing on the lowers slopes of a mountain. The sky is blue and clear. The ground is reddish in colour, warmed by long acquaintance with a hot sun. As you look you see that these slopes are dotted with olive trees gnarled through the fullness of time. Everywhere you hear the sound of cicadas. But now another sound reaches you. It is the sound of a child's laughter, as liquid as water and as pure as sunlight.

Somewhere close by a horse whinnies. Now a white horse comes into view carrying a young boy, naked and bronzed by the sun. He sees you and breaks into laughter. The horse stops only momentarily, then the boy kicks his heels and the two begin to move off towards the higher slopes. You set off too, following the sun-kissed boy and the white horse. The path leads up through olive groves. The view over the land below becomes more spectacular. The horse and boy are moving faster than you. They are almost out of sight now so you continue to make your own way gently upwards.

The walk is hard, you are feeling hot and thirsty now. You walk on hoping that you might find water. As if in answer to your unspoken thought, ahead you see water descending over rocks. You approach and drink from it, washing your hands and face too. There is something familiar about this classical landscape of mountain and stream. You allow the mind to roam. You wonder if this might be Mount Helicon, the Greek home to the Muses.

Having refreshed yourself you continue upwards. At last you reach a plateau with spectacular views. Here is a circle of shrines, each shrine with a figure of one of the Muses and her insignia. You walk from one to the next, stopping to enter into a state of mental awareness. Which of these Muses will take you as apprentice? First pay your respects to Mnemosyne, Mother of the Muses, and then begin to walk from shrine to shrine in a contemplative frame of mind. Clio, the Muse of History, is shown unfolding a scroll. Euterpe, the Muse of Lyric Poetry, carries a lyre. Thalia, Muse of Pastoral Poetry, carries the mask of Comedy and a shepherd's staff. Melpomene, the Muse of Tragedy, carries the mask of Tragedy and a sword. Terpischore, the Muse of Dance, holds a lyre and a plectrum. Polyhmnia, the Muse of Sacred Song, carries a small portable organ and a garland of roses. Erato, the Muse of Love Poetry, carries a tambourine. Calliope, the Muse of Epic Poetry and Eloquence, carries a tablet and a stylus. Urania, the Muse of Astronomy, carries a compass and a celestial globe.

Time passes as you pay your respects to each of the traditions represented by the statues. You see gifts left by others – flowers dried by the hot sun and tiny pottery shapes. But you have brought no gift and you wonder what you can give. Now you hear the sound of adult laughter. A young man dressed in a short white kilt and carrying a lyre emerges as if from nowhere. Now he stands in front of you and laughs. He closely resembles the young boy on the white horse who has led you here. He picks up his lyre and begins to play. Instantly you know what your gift shall be. His music is so insistent and lyrical that you begin to dance. This is your gift. You dance among the statues, allowing yourself absolute openness of mind. To which of the Muses shall you make a gesture of dedication and hopefulness? Your dance continues until at last you come to rest before the shrine of your hearts desire. When it is finished you make a deep obeisance in a final closing gesture. You hope to find favour with the Muse of your heart. The music ceases. As you rise you find that you are quite alone. When you are ready, return the way you came to the temple. When you are ready, leave through the doorway. Finally, dissolve all images and return to ordinary consciousness.

EXERCITIA SPIRITUALIA

Take the Following as Subjects for Meditation:

- Lord of the Fire of the World
- The Letter Resh
- Fertility – Barrenness
- The Sun
- The Collecting Intelligence

Make Notes on:

- The Tarot Trump XIX, The Sun
- Apollo from the Greek tradition

Visualize the Following and Record your Experiences:

- Apollo from the Greek tradition
- Mnemosyne and the Muses from the Greek tradition
- The Temple of Yesod including the Archangel Gabriel
- The Journey of the 30th Path

CHAPTER 7

Hod – Glory

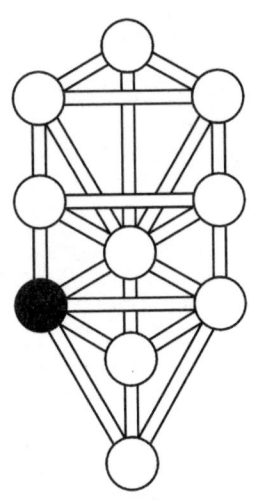

FIGURE 13 THE SEPHIRAH HOD

TABLE OF CORRESPONDENCES

God-Name: Elohim Tzabaoth – God of Hosts

Archangel: Michael

Order of Angels: Beni Elohim – Children of the Gods and Goddesses

Magical Image: A Hermaphrodite

Spiritual Experience: Vision of Splendour

Symbols: Names and Versicles, The Apron

Virtue: Truthfulness

Vice: Falsehood

Titles: None

Mundane Chakra: Mercury

Personal Chakra: Manipura – the Solar Plexus Chakra

Text: The Absolute or Perfect Intelligence

Colour in Atziluth: Violet-Purple

Colour in Briah: Orange

Colour in Yetzirah: Red-Russet

Colour in Assiah: Yellowish Black flecked White

Tarot Cards: The Four Eights

Eight of Wands: Swiftness

Eight of Cups: Abandoned Success

Eight of Swords: Shortened Force

Eight of Pentacles: Prudence

COMMENTARY

The Eighth Path is called Absolute or Perfect Intelligence
because it is the mean of the Primordial, which has no root
by which it can cleave or rest, save in the hidden places of
Gedulah, from which emanates its proper essence.

Hod is the eighth Sephirah. It stands in polarity to Netzach, the seventh
Sephirah. Taken together these two Sephiroth constitute the powers of Force
and Form within the Astral Triangle. Hod is to be found on the Pillar of
Severity; Netzach is to be found on the Pillar of Mercy. Hod and Netzach
each contribute an opposing but complementary influence to Tiphareth,
Yesod and Malkuth. As each of the lower Sephiroth receive and mirror
influences from the higher reaches of the Tree, Hod reflects certain aspects
from the fourth Sephirah, Chesed (Gedulah). This relationship is crucial to
understanding the functions of Hod. Chesed holds the archetypal blueprints
for Wisdom. Hod offers the first encounter with the nature of wisdom. In
Hod the mind is turned towards wisdom. Through Hod the mind begins to
awaken to the possibility of its own nature. At Chesed the mind is awakened,
wisdom is a living reality, no longer the object of an elusive quest. The quest
for wisdom begins at Hod.

The Path to Wisdom

> With Wisdom a house is built, with Understanding it is
> established, and with Knowledge its rooms are filled.

Proverbs 24: 3, 4

The quest for wisdom is eternal and universal. Wisdom is the pearl of
revelation within all spiritual traditions. Wisdom is the mystical heart of
every living faith tradition. But wisdom is neither doctrine nor dogma,
knowledge nor faith. Wisdom must be sought, it cannot be given. It must
be nurtured from within, as a seed which in time comes to fruition. The
mystical journey upon the Tree of Life is a quest for wisdom. This is a
journey into the heart of being.

The Thirty-two Paths of Wisdom are called *Netivot*, an uncommon term
meaning path, in contrast to the common word *Derekh*, meaning a public

road or route used by all people. A *Nativ* is a personal route, blazed by the individual for personal use. The word used to describe the hidden paths without signposts or markers is *Peliyot*, which means mystical. This comes from the root *Pala*, which carries the additional meaning of something hidden and separated from the world at large. It is also closely related to the word *Peleh*, meaning a miracle. These terms unequivocally describe the nature of the journey towards wisdom. The path is uncommon, the route is hidden and without signposts, the journey is separated from the everyday world and the individual must blaze the trail. But within the implications of trial and tribulation, a miracle is possible.

The journey begins at Malkuth with the application of the Virtue of Discrimination. Mental transformation begins on the 30th and 31st Paths, which together lead to Hod. The Path of Judgement and the Sun, represented by the letters Shin and Resh, bring the qualities of memory and mindfulness into conscious awareness. The Perpetual Intelligence of the 31st Path and the Collecting Intelligence of the 30th Path lead into the Absolute or Perfect Intelligence assigned to Hod. The Archangel assigned here is Michael. He is called 'the perfect one of God'. He wields a rod or spear and is considered to be the leader of the heavenly host. His strengths are protection, power and perfection. Each of these qualities is an aspect of the Virtue of Hod, which is Truthfulness. This quest for truth is the quest for the ultimate nature of reality. It cannot be undertaken through the limited view of the rational mind, only through the gestation of wisdom which begins here. The journey through the Thirty-two Stages of Wisdom precipitates the birth of a new mind. Hod represents the first turning towards wisdom and the first glimmerings of the transforming mind.

The Absolute or Perfect Intelligence assigned to Hod is described as, 'the mean of the Primordial, which has no root by which it can cleave or rest, save in the hidden places of Gedulah, from which emanates its proper essence'. In other words, the essential nature of Hod is derived from Chesed, which is also known as Gedulah. Hod serves as a reflecting surface, equilibriating the ineffable into the accessible. Hod is described through the imagery of a water temple where primordial forms from higher, more abstracted, realms are projected into conceivable images. Chesed is said to, 'contain all the Holy Powers, and from it emanate all the spiritual virtues'. The Perfect Intelligence assigned to Hod is a reflection of the Receptive Intelligence of Chesed. Although Chockmah is the Sephiroth, Wisdom, it is through Chesed that Wisdom teachings emanate, and it is in Hod that the seed of wisdom is first planted.

The Sepher Yetzirah provides instruction in how to approach the Sephiroth. Wisdom itself must be gestated from within. It is the only means of reaching the Sephiroth:

Understand with Wisdom
Be Wise with Understanding
Examine with them
And probe from them

The word for 'probe' here is *Chakar*. It implies attaining the ultimate knowledge of a thing. The word used to translate the concept 'examine with' is Bachan. It means to test things for their intrinsic quality as they are in the moment. This is very close to the idea that enlightenment springs simply from the 'is-ness' of things. Seeking an intrinsic quality implies seeing through illusion, moving beyond projection, and a freeing from partial perception. It is the exhortation to see reality directly. The Names and Versicles also assigned to Hod speak of the meditative tradition of contemplating Divine Names. This is a rich mystical vein since Kabbalah takes much delight in letters, their permutation, significance and symbolism. Such meditations deconstruct the literal and linear mind, constructing instead the basis of a unified mystical consciousness which is the consciousness of Wisdom. It is here through Hod that the mind becomes apprenticed to its long task of mental transformation. The symbolism of the Apron speaks of the workman apprenticed to a craft under the tutelage of the master craftsman. Our teacher and guide as we take up the work of transforming the mind will be the triune power Mercury-Hermes-Thoth.

The Thrice Great God

The god who occupies the position between light and dark, upper world and underworld, ego and shadow is Hermes, who represents our communications and commerce between conscious and unconscious life.

Alan Bleakley, *Fruits of the Moon Tree*

The Sephirah Hod is assigned to Mercury. Mercury is the fastest moving planet, orbiting the sun in 88 days. As the swift messenger of the gods, Mercury represents Hod's ability to receive impressions from more subtle levels and provide concrete forms through which such concepts may be encapsulated. An abstract idea is hard to grasp until it is expanded by analogy or embodied through a concept. Moving upwards into the higher reaches of the Tree, highly abstract ideas begin to predominate and, in the absence of a common conceptual framework, understanding becomes increasingly difficult. Words alone, without support from experiential references, convey little meaning and the mind begins to reel and struggle with pure abstraction. Astrologically, Mercury represents the quality of mental agility, the ability to analyse, and the power to reason.

The Roman god Mercury is also the Greek god Hermes. As winged messenger, Hermes represents an ability to travel between heaven and earth, the conscious and the unconscious, the known and the unknown. This mediating role places Hermes-Mercury in the office of psychopomp or leader into the realm of the unconscious. As quicksilver, Mercury forms and reforms, moving from part to whole, breaking boundaries with seamless ease. This is the power of the transcendent function – namely, to create synthesis from opposition. Hermes is traditionally seen with the caduceus, a staff encircled by solar and lunar serpents. Curiously, this ancient image has passed into current usage, where its power has been reduced from that of symbol to mere sign. It currently indicates medicine and the healing arts. This ancient staff displays the full significance of healing which extends beyond the body into the depths of the psyche. 'The staff of Hermes is an emblem of healing and medicine because the process of separation and synthesis of the two major forces in life is the healing work. In depth psychology, it is the process of coming to gain a creative attitude to shadow, to the unconscious, from the perspective of our conscious, waking lives.'[1] Ironically, the staff of Hermes so fondly displayed in medical environments is also the Tree of Life.

Behind these Greek and Roman forms stands another wisdom figure of mature gravitas and authority – Thoth, the archetypal Guardian and Initiator into the Egyptian tradition of wisdom. Having none of the playful and trickster aspects of Mercury, Thoth is the Lord of Wisdom, not just the promulgator of insight. Thoth is the Egyptian patron of learning. His realm encompasses medicine, writing, the measurement of time and all the scribal and priestly arts and sciences. He is portrayed as an ibis-headed figure carrying the scribal palette. Thoth is an important figure in Egyptian mythology. He is peacemaker to the warring brothers Horus and Set. He is teacher to Isis, herself a wisdom goddess. He presides in the Judgement Hall with another personification of wisdom, Maat, the goddess of truth. In his capacity as a god of time, Thoth wins the five additional days needed to balance the calendar with the solar year.

This triplicity represents the dynamic movement which takes place within the mind as the seeds of wisdom take root. Mercury acts in the role of guide to a domain under the aegis of Hermes where Thoth as the most ancient embodiment of cosmic wisdom is to be found.

The Hermetic Wisdom

> The Hermetic Philosophy brought a much needed breath of fresh air into the stagnant atmosphere of late medieval Europe.
>
> **A.G. Gilbert, *The Hermetica***

Hod introduces the Hermetic Wisdom which takes its name from the fabled Thrice-Great Hermes, Hermes Trismegistus. The term 'thrice great' is an accolade, an appellation of honour and esteem which emulates the high epithets of the Egyptian tradition. Stranded from its cultural context it has become a curio in a world devoid of metaphorical and poetic language. The Hermetic Wisdom is not a religion but a mystical philosophy. It speaks of origins and purpose, destiny and meaning. Sharing much of the same territory as that claimed by traditional Western religious teachings, the Hermetic Wisdom has often found itself outside the boundaries of orthodoxy. This mystical philosophy is also called the Perennial Wisdom, the Ageless Wisdom or simply Natural Philosophy. It has over time become synonymous with a secret teaching. This is a misunderstanding. There is no secret teaching to be found. Understanding does not arise from dogma or doctrine but from the application and internalization of a mere handful of basic time-honoured principles. There is no single holy book and no human figurehead. It prescribes neither forms nor places of worship. This is a path of self-revelation. Hermetic precepts serve to teach, reveal and initiate heart, body, mind and soul. This is a holistic and mystical philosophy of self-revelation and self-initiation. Its silver thread is visibly interwoven with the history and development of Western culture and values. The Hermetic Wisdom has survived chameleon-like through time, always changing yet always the same.

The *Corpus Hermeticum* created a wave of intense excitement when first discovered. Appearing during a time of passionate spiritual questing, the collection at first seemed to represent the wisdom of the ancient world. It is no wonder that Cosimo de Medici, who was approaching the end of his life, ordered the scholar Marsilio Ficino to commence translation straight-away in place of the Platonic scripts he was already working on. The Hermetica was originally thought to be the ancient Greek and Latin writings of a real teacher, Hermes Trismegistus. It was only later that a more accurate picture of the texts was established. Dated to a post-Christian era, the Hermetica was proven to be the work of not a single mind but of a collection of diverse minds assembled under the aegis of Hermes. It was most probably written in Egypt under the Roman empire, by men

> who had received some instruction in Greek philosophy, and
> especially in Platonism of the period, but who were not content with
> merely accepting and repeating the cut and dried dogmas of the
> orthodox philosophic schools and sought to build up, on the basis of
> Platonic doctrine, a philosophic religion that would better satisfy
> their needs. The teaching in these little groups must have been
> mainly oral. Now and then the teacher would set down in writing
> the gist of some talk... once written it would then be passed from
> hand to hand within the group, and from one group to another.[2]

The words of these unknown writers penned in the 1st century AD planted the seeds which changed the culture of Europe. 'It was the manifesto which shocked Europe out of the middle ages, paving the way for the Renaissance and the Enlightenment which was to follow two centuries later.'[3]

The Hermetic Wisdom is the underground stream of Western civiliz-ation. Though its historical source is impossible to define or confine, its impact and effect is still discernible. The most notable and stunning Hermetic achievement is the European Renaissance itself, with all its glory and new vision. This was a holistic revolution in the human spirit. Like the Egyptian philosophy which Pythagoras also carried to a Greek environ-ment, the Renaissance mindset sought to embrace every branch of knowledge within a unified wisdom. In an age familiar with the separation and specialization of knowledge, the value of a sense of unity within the various fields of learning seems difficult to grasp. Yet Renaissance culture blossomed as a result of the rediscovery and redefinition of the idea.

The Hermetic or Ageless Wisdom has flowed through the centuries accruing new influences on its ever-widening course. Carrying Egyptian and Greek influences from the pre-Christian world, it reached Europe, where it broke out from its confines and spilled out as an invigorating force for complete cultural renewal. In complete contrast to the deferential, dogmatic and stultifying mentality of religious piety, this current carried a passion for learning, investigation, enquiry and the application of the human mind. As the Hermetic current began to flow, cautiously at first from the pages of forgotten manuscripts, it brought the life-giving waters of a new vision of reality to men who valued learning as the basis for belief. This new view of creation and humanity's role within it supported the birth of a Western scientific ethos that included a spiritual dimension. The Hermetic vision offered a sense of unity between the material and the spiritual. Discoveries about the natural world were no longer seen to be intrusive and diminishing to the role of a creator God, but reaffirmed the extraordinary nature of creation. Learning about the world was no longer considered a threat to religious belief but was instead its ally.

The Virtue of Hod is Truthfulness. This is not only a personal virtue but a fundamental belief that the truth of nature, ultimate reality, can be discerned through the powers given to the human being. The Hermetic view was an empowering one which authorized the individual spiritual quest. This is a stream of wisdom that never fails. It is the Ageless Wisdom, the Perennial Philosophy, the Natural Philosophy. Like a magnet it calls out to the questioning mind, the restless spirit and the yearning soul. Its implacable enemies have always been the traditional, the conservative, the authoritarian, the dogmatic and the entrenched. Scientific enquiry was stunted by a mindset that found curiosity unacceptable, but the Hermetic impulse towards enquiry did much to establish the relation to the sciences as its counterpart Netzach is related to the arts. Together these twin branches create a cultural embrace which reaches out to both eulogize and explain the world. Together Glory and Victory, Hod and Netzach, span the innate human need to respond in the world with question, engagement and deep involvement. The Spiritual Experience assigned to Hod is the Vision of Splendour. It is a glimpse of fulfilled potential and the realization that the full scope of human nature takes it to transpersonal or divine heights. It is a realization that to be human is also to be a splendid microcosm of the macrocosm. This is the potency of the Sephirah Hod.

THE GIFT OF HERMES

Find yourself in a study belonging to an earlier era. A leather-bound book is lying open on an oak table. You go over to it to glance through it. Curious and unfamiliar images fill its pages. The room holds an unusual smell which blends the aroma of incense and the sharpness of chemicals. This room has the air of a private sanctuary. A wooden chair, much gentled by age, stands by the desk. You sit and open yourself to the unique atmosphere of the place. Allow your eyelids to close as the inner mind begins to stir.

Let this scene dissolve and instead find yourself at the entrance to a large cavern set into a hillside. Its centre is filled by a broad staircase cut into the rock. Light streams from the very top of the staircase as if it were lit from inside by an interior brilliance. Looking towards this source of light, you see that a figure has appeared and stands framed by the light. You immediately stop and wait as the figure begins to descend the staircase. The figure glides effortlessly down the staircase on winged feet and stops in front of you. This is quicksilver Mercury shining with a silvered light. He holds out his hand and opens his palm to reveal a small caduceus, the staff entwined with twin serpents. You recognize the symbol and see that this caduceus is made from a dark and heavy metal. You gaze upon it, committing its details to memory. Finally he departs.

You set out again but soon a second figure has emerged from the opening of light at the head of the staircase. You wait once more as this figure draws closer. Watching carefully you see no youthful joviality in the approaching step. Like an older brother of the first figure, there is a recognizable similarity between the two. He wears a short cloak and, throwing it back, he too opens a closed palm to reveal a second caduceus, clearly made from silver. Being cast from a purer metal you can see more detail and refinement in the work. He allows you to look at it for a long as you wish, then he too is gone.

You begin your ascent once more but soon a third figure approaches you. He is entirely cloaked. But as he reaches you he draws back his hood and with something of a shock you discover him to be the ibis-headed god Thoth. He extends a closed palm and opening it you see a third caduceus, cast from gold. You know that this is the most prized metal, representing perfection and immortality, for it does not corrode or corrupt. You know this is a symbol of the perfected intelligence.

He too departs. You remain in a meditative frame of mind holding closely all that you have inwardly experienced. You turn to face the world once more. You can see the cave mouth below. The pale light of the exterior world becomes your guide. Every step takes you closer to the moment of return. Soon you stand at the mouth of the cavern, the threshold between the exterior world of men and the interior world of nature. As you cross from one place to another you feel the pull of the senses. And you return to the waking consciousness of the everyday world.

EVOCATION

Welcome to my kingdom, which is the realm of the mind. My door is always open but I am rarely called upon. My gift is great but it is often ignored. My blessing is bountiful but it is rarely requested. I hold open the door to all who would seek Wisdom for I know where she dwells and in what manner she will reveal herself. I am her gatekeeper and guardian. Seek her with diligence for she will not be found except by effort and labour.

I have much to teach to those wishing to learn. My lessons are not for the frivolous but for those who quest for Wisdom's treasure. I seek your commitment and dedication for my work is without end. My work will change all that exists in your mind. In truth, wisdom is already everywhere dancing in front of you in every moment. But your eyes do not see and your ears do not hear, for your mind is filled to overflowing with thoughts that leave no room for the quest.

I will show you how to prepare a space where Wisdom's seed may be planted. I will show you how to transform the mind itself. Mine is the kingdom of mind. I offer an apprenticeship to truthfulness in its many appearances and forms. My work changes and transforms, refines and restores. That which is false will fall away, that which is untrue shall dissolve. If you truly seek yourself, you will find your way into my domain with ease and you will travel in my kingdom seeking Wisdom until she comes to dwell in your heart and mind.

INTERNALIZATION – THE TEMPLE OF HOD

Construct the Temple of Hod in the creative imagination. Find yourself standing beneath the dome. Looking upwards, you wonder what lies beyond. Walking around the central pool, you run your fingers over the signs and symbols carved and find yourself wondering about this hidden language. You sense that every single shape has great meaning and depth.

High above, rays of sunlight begin to pour in through coloured glass in the domed roof. An orange glow fills the air. It plays upon the water, forming patterns and shapes. You see yourself reflected upon its surface too. As you watch the water, a light breeze springs up as if from nowhere. The surface of the pool begins to ripple and move. Patterns and shapes begin to form upon its surface. You watch intently, using all the powers of your mind to discern the patterns that are forming before your very eyes.

You look up towards the dome. It seems to you that shapes are forming in the bright sunlight. But the light is too bright and your eyes are straining to see. Instead you look to the surface of the pool which is now perfectly still. Letters and whole words seem to float across the surface.

You watch as the letters R, O, A and T glide and move as if floated by some unseen projectionist. You see the words TARO, ROTA and TORA forming and dissolving. As your concentration begins to waiver, the letters seem to fade from view, slipping beneath the surface of your mind.

You draw your thoughts together in a determined effort to focus your mind. As you watch, on the surface of the waters an image begins to form. You know that if your attention fades the image will also fade. Your mind remains razor sharp. A face begins to form. The eyes are sharp and piercing. Above the head, twin plumes and a solar disc appear. A human body coalesces. One arm is outstretched holding a sceptre.

You drop to your knees at the waterside as the full face of ibis-headed Thoth clarifies upon the surface. Use this opportunity to ask for a blessing if you will. When you stand again and look into the pool, the waters are clear. The vision has gone completely.

When you are ready, leave through the doorway. Finally, dissolve all images and return to ordinary consciousness.

EXERCITIA SPIRITUALIA

Take the Following as Subjects for Meditation:

- Elohim Tzaboath, God of Hosts
- The Archangel Michael
- The Beni Elohim, The Sons of God
- A hermaphrodite figure
- The Absolute or Perfect Intelligence
- Mercury
- The Vision of Splendour
- Wisdom

Contemplate the Following Questions and Record your Responses:

- How does the function of Truthfulness operate in your life?
- How does the function of Falsehood operate in your life?
- How does the nature of Hod relate to the Solar Plexus Chakra?
- What other correspondences can you relate to the Sephirah Hod?
- How do the four Tarot cards relate to Hod?

Visualize the Following and Record your Experiences:

- Thoth, from the ancient Egyptian tradition
- The Temple of Hod including the Archangel Michael
- The Journey to the Temple of Hod

CHAPTER 8

The Twenty-Ninth Path: Malkuth–Netzach

FIGURE 14 THE 29TH PATH:

MALKUTH–NETZACH

TAROT TRUMP XVIII,

THE MOON

TABLE OF CORRESPONDENCES

The Journey: Tarot Trump XVIII, The Moon,
Ruler of Flux and Reflux

Key: The Letter Qoph, meaning the back of
the head

Simple Letter: Sleep

Spiritual Significance: Pisces

Text: The Corporeal Intelligence

Colour in Atziluth: Crimson

Colour in Briah: Buff flecked Silver-White

Colour in Yetzirah: Light translucent Pinkish-
Brown

Colour in Assiah: Stone

COMMENTARY

The Twenty-ninth Path is called the Corporeal Intelligence,
so called because it forms every body which is formed in all
the worlds, and the reproduction of them.

The 29th Path connects the tenth Sephirah, Malkuth, with the seventh
Sephirah, Netzach. It connects the central Pillar of Equilibrium or
Consciousness with the Pillar of Mercy. As part of the Astral or Psychological
Triangle, the 29th Path connects the physical realm of Malkuth with the
realm of instinct, feeling, intuition and imagination represented by Netzach.
It connects the Resplendent Intelligence assigned to Malkuth with the
Occult Intelligence assigned to Netzach, and thereby brings the hidden
powers of instinct and innate need into physical actuality. This is the Path
of the Corporeal Intelligence. The 29th Path is one of biological inheritance, physical instinct and sexual urge. This aspect of human life has long
proved troublesome for the godly. The instinctive workings of the body are
seen to be problematical if immaterial spirit is elevated while material
substance is devalued. The Corporeal Intelligence can only be honoured in
a holistic philosophy which does not separate the spiritual from the material.

The Question of Sex

The Tantric Path teaches us to embrace and unify the
ordinary, the erotic and the sacred dimensions of life,
which all have their roots in spirit.

Margot Anand, *The Art of Everyday Ecstasy*

The 29th Path is one of evolution, both biological and cultural. The Path
relates the instincts of Netzach to the development of culture which is
assigned to Malkuth. The motivating drive of instinct, both personally and
collectively, cannot be underestimated. 'Among the psychological factors
determining human behaviour, the instincts are the chief motivating forces
of psychic events.'[1] Satisfying hunger ensures survival, satisfying the sex drive
ensures reproduction of the species. In the animal kingdom sexuality and
reproduction have remained divorced from emotional development;
breeding takes place in short, defined seasons. But in the human family,

sexuality has become a complex social and personal area. 'The sexual instinct enters into combination with many different feelings, emotions; affects, with spiritual and material interests, to such a degree that, as is well known, the attempt has been made to trace the whole of culture to these combinations.'[2] This is the Path of the Corporeal Intelligence. It is assigned to the creation of, 'every body which is formed in all the worlds, and the reproduction of them'. This Path undeniably raises the question of sex.

The sex drive has been seen as a great problem for many religions, which have spent much energy devising theological controls to overcome and bind sexual energy. The biological facts of life are straightforward enough, yet the area of human sexuality has proven to be dark and disturbed, ripe for prejudice, fear and ignorance. How is it that the Corporal Intelligence, the intelligence of the body, has become distorted, disavowed and rendered ugly?

In the slowly evolving ideology which separated matter and spirit with the precision of a surgeon and the self-righteousness of the convinced, the body and its domain fared very poorly. The Corporeal Intelligence, the body's own wisdom, was dismissed. The body became instead a source of corruption, taint and sexual temptation. As the inferior manifestation, the body could offer no redeeming qualities. Human biology became a tortured area for those seeking God in the pure, unsullied and untarnished realm of the spiritual, safely located somewhere outside nature. Mortification practices, once widespread, speak of a hatred of the body and reveal the desire to punish the flesh for imprisoning the spirit. Historically, revealed religions have regarded the human biological inheritance as a great stumbling block on the path towards God. Far from accepting a biological inheritance, theological doctrine has sought to separate the inferior body from the superior spirit. In this mindset there was no room for the joy of sex or pleasure of the body. Body and spirit had been set apart, irreconcilable opposites in a dualized creation schema. The stage was set for denial, manipulation, social control, fear and abuse.

The legacy of Western theology – the Fall, the Virgin Birth and Original Sin – has weighed heavily upon Western morality. The resulting inheritance – the sinfulness of the sex drive and the demonization of the body – has been difficult to dissolve. Such oppressive and quite unnatural fabrications still haunt the present time. In many places women are still subject to artificial and absurd constraints. Sexuality is still a matter for social control and will always be so until the schism at its root is healed.

The denial of nature, and of the Corporeal Intelligence which is the wisdom of the natural body, has resulted in absurd theological contortions.

All reproductive stages, from menstruation to intercourse, from conception to childbirth, have in the past been matters for extended theological debate and policy. The problem of reconciling the purity of the spirit with the gross habit of the body gripped the Church for centuries. Sexual reproduction produced a protracted angst which was the subject of many an edict and learned council. When Augustine, the most acclaimed of all the Church Fathers, succeeded in tying the concept of Original Sin to sexual pleasure, the stage was set for organizational misogyny on a grand scale. Sexual pleasure has long been anathema to the Church. As a consequence of the Fall from the idyllic state of paradise, sexual pleasure became the carrier for infection of original sin from generation to generation. The resulting litany still lingers. Menstruation, nature's simple way of providing a lengthy and continuous fertility in the human family, has been turned into a weapon for the disempowerment of women. Widespread menstrual taboos speak of a deep fear of the natural body. Such control is now being overthrown by women reclaiming their own power, but this cry for freedom is far from universal.

As this Path relates instinct with culture, so a new cultural view may still emerge. Freed from medieval guilt and the dead weight of theological doctrine, it is possible to rejoice in the sacramental body and its gifts, innate wisdom and natural powers. The spiritual and the sexual can be conjoined as the sacred; this is the way of Tantra.

At the dawn of an age in desperate need of integrating models, Tantra has much to offer as a holistic, life-affirming philosophy which embraces sexuality but is not dominated by it. Imported Tantra is unfortunately suffering at the hands of Western exponents who stand ill-versed in its philosophical breadth and depth. Sexuality has been divorced from the sacred for so long in the West that Tantra offers a welcome reunion. But Tantra is a holistic life philosophy, not a licence for sexuality activity. 'Tantra is a spiritual path to enlightenment. But unlike most mystical paths Tantra includes sexuality as a doorway to ecstasy and enlightenment.'[3] In this respect Tantra is probably alone in celebrating sexuality as a power to be harnessed in a spiritual philosophy. Margot Anand's work has done a great deal to broaden the Western conception of Tantra. In her book, *The Art of Everyday Ecstasy*, she offers seven keys to Tantric awakening:

1. Say yes to life in all its erotic passion.

2. Go with the flow of the life force within and all around you.

3. Trust yourself and allow your personal power to manifest in life.

4. Open your heart in loving compassion to the self and others.

5. Authentically express your creativity and your truth.

6. Look within to achieve clarity and insight into your life.

7. Surrender to your source and know gratitude, spiritual peace and a new capacity to live at your maximum potential in every moment.[4]

We now stand at the beginning of a new era. It is possible to review the damage caused by the philosophy of schism and to begin the work of healing the great divide at its root. In a new age of integration let spirit and matter, body and soul, dwell inseparably one with the other in whole and holy partnership. Change is taking place, perhaps invisibly and at a grass-roots level as an organic revolution in values with the power to create a new culture from the same biological inheritance. The researcher Paul Ray has studied more than 100,000 Americans and has identified a rising subculture of about 44 million people whom he calls 'cultural creatives'. He speaks of this group as spiritual pioneers on the road of self-realization and cultural change and places some significance on this group as agents of real change:

> We are at a tipping point in civilization, a great divide in history.
> If the ranks of cultural creatives harness their collective energies and
> carry them into public arenas, we can forge a new kind of 'integral'
> culture; one that merges the best of modernism and traditionalism,
> embraces both East and West and ushers in a new form of
> renaissance.[5]

Together the 29th and 28th Paths represent an area of life which is being reclaimed and honoured. The Sephirah Netzach represents the natural, instinctive inheritance. The 29th Path is the Corporeal Intelligence, the 28th Path is the Natural Intelligence. These two Paths represent the areas of life most undervalued and susceptible to social control and manipulation. Within an integrated and holistic philosophy, the body and its natural functions are accorded a proper regard and given an intrinsic value. Today the body is bearing the brunt of a new and more subtle level of manipulation. Eating disorders and disorders of body image represent the dangerous power of false projection. Both the 29th and 28th Paths honour the body and rejoice in a natural corporeal intelligence.

ACCEPTING THE BODY

Sit in meditation and slowly cast your inner eye over the body. Go over the body slowly and gently. Hold a body image in your mind and bring to mind how you feel about each part in turn. Allow yourself to recall projections from other people, and where these arise try to ascertain the reasons for this. Different body areas carry different messages. If you recognize that you are unhappy about aspects of your body, try to follow these ideas through to their source.

This simple exercise can be healing and insightful.

The Light of the Moon

The ancient religion of the moon goddess represents the education of the emotional life as taking place, not through a course of study, not even as the result of a system though both these things entered in, but through an initiation.

Esther Harding, *Woman's Mysteries*

The 29th Path is assigned to the Tarot Trump XVIII, The Moon. The face of the moon dominates all as the single most significant image, portraying an eerie and dream-like atmosphere in a surreal and strange landscape. The symbolism of the moon is a powerful and long-lived image in the history of the human family. But the moon is far more than merely a symbol – it has a real physical impact upon life on earth. The power of the moon is an active force in nature. Many water creatures spawn by the lunar calendar. Moonlight is deeply imbedded into the cycles of the natural kingdom. Bamboo knots at the full moon. The moon pulls up the tides in a daily and seasonal rhythm. It is no surprise that in the moon lore of myth and tradition, the moon, agriculture and fertility are intermingled. Unlike the constant sun, the moon waxes and wanes in a continuous cycle of appearance and disappearance. This Trump is also called the Ruler of Flux and Reflux. The moon is assigned to the rhythms of nature, most especially to the rhythms, both physical and emotional, of women. 'In the myths and religions relating to the moon is to be found a mine of information about the nature of the Eros and the laws which govern its functioning.'[6] The realm of Eros, in contrast to the realm of Logos, stands for all that might be described as yin in a yin-yang metaphor and all that might be described as female in a male-female paradigm. As the archetypal feminine symbol, the moon represents the undiluted powers of nature, the world of women and the realm of the goddess. It symbolizes all that has been repressed, ignored, devalued and outcast by the organized imposition of solar values. Suppressing the con-stellation of human experiences represented under the symbolism of the moon has resulted in a one-sided, unbalanced cultural development which favours the mind but is suspicious of the heart, and which values the rational but fears the imaginative. Casting out lunar values disempowers women individually and collectively. It silences female voices and female authority and amplifies the male perspective ad infinitum. It denies the place of nature and biology, replacing a philosophy rooted in the natural world with one of artifice and cerebral values. It has created the separation between mind and body which has plagued the West. It is time to heal this rift, address the imbalance and embrace lunar once again. Esther Harding is in no doubt as to the significance of this act:

> In order to gain a new vantage point from which a fresh world philosophy may perhaps be built up, a renewed contact with the deeper levels of human nature is needed so that a really vital relation may be established with the laws or principles which activate humanity. Only through such a renewing experience can we hope to be able to bridge the chasm which has opened up before our Western civilization.[7]

Like Paul Ray, Esther Harding places significance on a value-led revolution. It is in many ways a hidden revolution, the revolution of moonlight. 'The moon stands for a strange kind of thinking which comes and goes apparently with complete autonomy... Thinking of this kind is despised among us, but it has been esteemed in many ages and civilizations.'[8]

The letter Qoph, meaning the back of the head, is assigned to this Path. The letter itself is shaped rather like the hind part of the cranium and it directs our attention to the back of the head, where we find both the medulla oblongata and the cerebellum. These centres are responsible for automatic physical functions such as the maintenance of balance, steady movement and equilibrium of the body. In contrast to the letter Resh, which represents the front of the head and the powers of the cortex, Qoph speaks of the autonomic system and the older parts of the brain, as also represented by the symbolism of the moon. The back of the head is the place of the primitive non-rational brain. The functions symbolized by the letter Qoph are intimately related to the Corporeal Intelligence, 'so called because it forms every body which is formed in all the worlds and the reproduction of them'. The letter Qoph is assigned to the function of sleep, which brings dreams that form the vocabulary of the interior life. The mode of consciousness represented by the letter Qoph is most often suspect. This is the intuitive hunch, the instinctive knowing and the gut response. Reasoned argument or logical deduction does not arise here. This is the realm of dream and vision.

As we enter a new great age, the natural powers of imagination, instinct and emotion, so long repressed as unreliable, are now being valued as genuine, authentic and spontaneous expression of the human heart. More importantly, current holistic, psychological and therapeutic theories of well-being and human happiness have embraced the subjective and the non-rational as key factors for healthy development. Since all parts of the Tree of Life are equally holy, the 29th Path restores a dignity and value to the ordinary functions and instincts of the body. As the path of the Corporeal Intelligence, this Path embraces the body and biological imperatives. This vital link brings the quality of inspired imagination, heightened sensitivity and the instinctive and emotional life. Without the depth qualities bestowed by the experiences of Netzach, the mind seeks only rational and logical solutions. Cold analysis can be quite inhuman and amoral. The qualities of Hod alone are inadequate for the development of a balanced and depth vision. Esther Harding finds a sign of hope in the reappearance of Luna's realm. This compensatory power is much needed today:

> The symbols which appear today, and their development, show that
> a movement is taking place beneath the surface of consciousness
> which resembles in a fundamental way the movements which have
> immortalized in the teachings of the past. They tell of a path of
> renewal which is new in our day but old in actual fact. A path
> of redemption through the things that are lowest, which is the
> fundamental teaching of the moon religions and of the worship
> of the feminine principle.[9]

The meeting place of the solar and lunar forces, Eros and Logos, is upon the 27th Path between Hod and Netzach, which is a path of great readjustment.

The Evolutionary Path

Evolution is continuous, and our task is to carry forward
and foster this great evolutionary impulse.

Roberto Assagioli, *Psychosynthesis*

Tarot Trump XVIII, shows a path leading from a pool in the foreground
towards distant mountains in the background. A primitive crayfish emerges
from the waters, perhaps making its first landfall. Two dogs sit either side of
the path like sentinels. The animals resemble wild dogs, ancestors of the
domestic pet and the forefathers of the species. The warm-blooded dog and
the cold-blooded crayfish are separated by a huge step in developmental
evolution and in time. Beyond the dogs are two towers, clearly the work of
human builders and therefore representative of the higher function
of planning, abstraction and social organization. This is the path of evolution.
The creature emerging from the pool is a cold-blooded creature, a crustacean,
representative of a primitive developmental phase. The dogs as mammals are
representatives of a more complex mammalian development. The appearance
of early mammals some 200 million years ago produced an evolutionary
impetus. The small and often nocturnal mammal required a more sophisticated processing system which could provide temporal and spatial clues from
sensory data. The resulting cerebral cortex, a uniquely mammalian development, remained relatively simple until another evolutionary leap some
65 million years ago, when the appearance of the modern mammals resulted
in a fourfold increase in brain size. The cerebral cortex constructs mental
maps. In the average mammal it forms some 40 per cent of the whole. The
complex needs of warm-blooded, lactating mammals are reflected not only
in brain size but in complexity of function and specialization. The cold-
blooded egg-laying reptilians have developed no higher centres. The
mammalian brain has evolved a complex assembly of structures responsible
for drives and emotions combined. Instincts such as survival and sexuality
are linked to feelings and memories. Instincts provide an evolutionary
stimulus, not just as determinants of culture but also within the slowly
evolving brain and its complex features. The hypothalamus and pituitary act
to link instinctive states such as hunger and sexual arousal to emotional states.
The amygdala links sensory memories with emotional responses.
Biologically, humankind may be defined as a higher mammal. Yet we remain
linked to the primitive biological past through the very structure of the

brain. The human brain recapitulates the evolutionary past. The human brain contains the primitive brain stem, the limbic system and the unique cerebral cortex which permits the higher functions of abstraction, symbolic map-making and representation. If evolutionary need produces a physical response, will the conscious use of the higher centres in time create new brain structures? Is it possible that the human brain of the distant future will have evolved again?

EVOCATION

Welcome to my kingdom. Travel my path to trace your own physical evolution. See the path from the Pool of Life which passes into the future. This is your path. You are a part of nature too. This should not be despised but honoured. Do not forget the past. The letter Qoph reminds you of distant beginnings. You cannot escape your inheritance. Find your place within the natural kingdom and acknowledge that which you share with other living creatures.

I am Pisces. I am the age that is passing away. My evolutionary work is done. My power is spent in this cycle. As the fish gives way to higher forms of life, so the Age of the Fishes will give way to an evolutionary leap in consciousness. Will you help to carry this new wave forwards or will you be dragged along unconsciously in its wake?

As the moon, I have seen all births among species. I have watched mutation and evolution, transformation and adaptation, even extinction. I preside now over a new birth. I have power over the waters. I draw up the tides in a great and overwhelming momentum. I preside over the hidden and subtle tides in the evolutionary current. Feel the incoming tide as it approaches. Ride the crest of the wave and I will carry you forwards into the future. Aeons pass and my light will still shine. I bring a myriad of life forms into being. Diversity is my delight. Life evolves. Journey under the light of the moon and honour the Corporal Intelligence which is of the natural world.

INTERNALIZATION – THE 29TH PATH: MALKUTH–NETZACH

Construct the Temple of Malkuth in the creative imagination. Find yourself standing by the door of the Moon. The Archangel Sandalphon draws back the tapestry curtain so that you may pass.

You emerge into a mist and make your way forwards in a hazy light. You can already hear the sounds of a different world. Strange animal noises fill the air. You walk on and emerge into a primitive landscape. The sky here gives a greenish light. You push your way through giant ferns. The air is full of croaking and chattering. The sounds come from everywhere.

You stop and look carefully around. You find yourself in shallow water. Suddenly you realize that your view of the world has shifted completely. You see the ground just in front of you. You can smell the soil and taste the damp air. You identify with the body of a primitive and simple creature hauling itself up on dry land. You have a hard shell and a cumbersome body that is ill equipped to be away from water for long. Yet the desire to move forwards is compelling.

In the sky the moon sheds an eerie light. Its light seems to be calling you on like an irresistible beacon. The moon seems to be calling as you take your first lumbering steps on the long path which stretches far into the future.

Tucked beneath your protective shell you carry tiny hatchlings. As you scuttle forwards, these drop into the damp grass. The next generation is secured. You fall into the deep sleep of forgetting.

Time passes, you awaken in a new form. You now identify with warm-blooded and intelligent wild dogs. Now you are empowered by muscle, you have freedom in movement and a sharpness in the senses. You have an instinctive power to protect your offspring and secure the future generation. You sit beside the path watching less-evolved creatures scuttle by. In the sky, the moon sheds a silvery light. You see its face and howl into its light. You lie down and pass into the sleep of forgetting. Time passes. The moon continues to shine, unchanged and unchanging.

You awaken to find that you identify with the human form again. Looking ahead along the path into the distance you see two towers. These are the constructed work of minds able to plan, envision and create. These are the work of capable hands and determined minds. A huge moon, golden yellow, hangs suspended in the space between the mountains. Light and shade conspire to play tricks on you. The moon seems to have a face which is full and feminine. She seems to whisper to you of the future of possibilities and wonders. Her voice is soft and low.

You become mesmerized by the distant view and the future. Meanwhile the moon continues to shine as it has done for millions of years. Its light illuminates the landscape. In the darkness of the grass, a shining gem catches your eye. You reach for it to discover that it is a dewdrop caught in the light of the moon. You wet a finger by putting it in the tiny pool, and then place the mark of the moon on your brow.

When you are ready, return the way you came to the Temple. When you are ready, leave through the doorway. Finally, dissolve all images and return to ordinary consciousness.

EXERCITIA SPIRITUALIA

Take the Following as Subjects for Meditation:

- The Ruler of Flux and Reflux
- The letter Qoph
- Sleep
- The Moon
- The Corporeal Intelligence

Make Notes on:

- Tarot Trump XVIII, The Moon

Visualize the Following and Record your Experiences:

- The Temple of Malkuth including the Archangel Sandalphon
- The Journey of the 29th Path

CHAPTER 9

The Twenty–Eighth Path: Yesod–Netzach

FIGURE 15 THE 28TH PATH:
YESOD–NETZACH

TAROT TRUMP XVII,
THE STAR

TABLE OF CORRESPONDENCES

Journey: Tarot Trump XVII, The Star, Daughter of the Firmament, Dweller between the Waters
Key: The letter Tzaddi, meaning a fish-hook
Simple Letter: Imagination
Spiritual Significance: Aquarius
Text: The Natural Intelligence
Colour in Atziluth: Violet
Colour in Briah: Sky-Blue
Colour in Yetzirah: Bluish-Mauve
Colour in Assiah: White tinged Purple

COMMENTARY

The Twenty-eighth Path is called the Natural Intelligence; by it is completed and perfected the nature of all that exists beneath the Sun.

The 28th Path connects the ninth Sephirah, Yesod, with the seventh Sephirah, Netzach. It links the realm of subtle energies represented at Yesod with the creative world of Netzach characterized by emotion, intuition and imagination. The 28th Path links the central Pillar of Equilibrium or Consciousness with the Pillar of Mercy as part of the Astral or Psychological Triangle. It shows the significance of emotional and imaginative qualities as developmental powers. All bio-energetic therapies stress the dynamic relationship between emotional thought patterns and the invisible but vital energy system. The 28th Path highlights nature's own inheritance which is twofold, being simultaneously of material substance and living energy. It connects Yesod, where systems such as acupuncture or shiatsu may be represented, with Netzach, which represents the instinctive and imaginative inheritance. Together these forces combine to reveal the Natural Intelligence.

Natura

I have also often personified the word nature; for I have found it difficult to avoid this ambiguity.

Charles Darwin

The Magical Image assigned to Netzach is that of a beautiful naked woman. The Magical Image assigned to Yesod is that of a beautiful naked man. The 28th Path represents the evolutionary force of the interplay and dynamic exchange between opposites, energy and matter, consciousness and form. These polarities are in some utterly mysterious way conjoined and co-existent throughout the natural world. The Corporal Intelligence assigned to the 29th Path is related to the Natural Intelligence of the 28th Path. Both Paths call for a return to Nature and the release from artifice.

Nature has so often been thought of as feminine. Indeed, it is the magnetic core around which all other feminine values gather. The word 'nature' comes from the Latin *natura*, meaning 'birth'. This is a realm of birth where a feminine metaphor is most appropriate. Nature gives birth to herself quite unaided. Every season brings birth and change, increase and growth. This concept is an everyday reality for all peoples still living in proximity to the land. For city dwellers and urban civilization, it is a novel experience. We have generally lost touch with nature's power and potency and we have mistaken our ability to harness natural resources for an ability to control nature herself. Nature shows us time and again that we cannot control such elemental forces.

In the long history of religion and religious expression, adherence to a male god is relatively recent. Before worship and belief in the God, there was worship and belief in the Goddess. The Great Mother held sway for many thousands of years. Like nature, she has many forms and faces. Dethroning the Goddess and her value system has brought inevitable consequences. Living in a conscious symbiotic relationship with nature maintains a sense of harmony and co-relationship. But once the relationship is forgotten, robbing nature's plentiful storehouse becomes easy. When plunder exceeds nature's ability to self-renew, both humanity and the natural world are impoverished. From disappearing peat bogs to the rainforests, from future oil supplies to natural habitat for wildlife, concerns over natural resources are contemporary issues. The rise of ecological awareness and the entire envi-ronmental movement has arisen in the face of a mass forgetting of the Natural Intelligence. Beyond the issues related to resources, threats to species and habitat, there still lies the residue of an idea that an eternal, heavenly and immaterial afterlife outweighs the present earthly life in importance. Two quite different ideologies are represented by the realm of the Goddess as mother, immanent in nature, and the realm of the God as father, tran-scendent in an immaterial heaven. Principles, concerns and ideas constellated around the feminine pole in any value system have been relegated in favour of values and experiences which might be described as masculine. It is only recently that the pendulum of approbation has begun to waiver and move back towards a feminine pole. The imbalance, so long the model for Western society, is deeply etched on the collective psyche. The natural body, its normal processes and subjective feelings, even the land itself, have become the subject of a controlling rationale designed to overcome nature as the inferior partner in a relationship with the Almighty.

Both the 28th and the 29th Paths highlight need to reconnect what is natural – the instincts, our biological inheritance, the physical body – and the innate creative qualities of being and becoming. Both Paths draw upon the energy pool of Netzach. Awakening to the potency of the 29th Path spontaneously generates artistic and creative outpouring in praise of nature and life itself. Here the unconscious mind of Yesod is connected with the enlivening powers of the artistic imagination and creative inspiration from Netzach. The experience of the 28th Path brings a personal relationship with nature's own blueprints, whether physical and biological or subtle and based in the vital energies.

Together the 28th and 29th Paths offer the restoration of feminine values which culminates in the initiatory experience of Netzach. The restoration of these values addresses a deep wounding that many instinctively feel. The Goddess belongs not to the historical past but to the eternal present:

> In our own time, in our own culture, the Goddess once again is becoming a symbol of empowerment for women, a catalyst for an emerging spirituality that is earth-centred, a metaphor for the earth as a living organism, an archetype for feminine consciousness, a mentor for healers; the emblem of a new political movement, an inspiration for artists and a model for resacralizing woman's body and the mystery of human sexuality.[1]

The Natural Intelligence in its many manifestations exerts a powerful appeal in the face of a cultural model derived in so many ways from an unnatural intelligence. The Natural Intelligence speaks of a genuine, honest and authentic approach to life. It is the innocent simplicity of the genuine response without the artifice of social custom. It is the value of the heart, not the created value of a social group. It is an intelligence without pretence, social overlay or false embellishment. It is the antidote to the false, the unnecessary and the wasteful. Organic natural food, simpler natural clothing, green architecture and the spread of ethical and green values into the unlikely arena of business, all reflect the Natural Intelligence as a key to a new value system.

The 28th Path connects Yesod with Netzach, nature's own realm. Netzach is assigned to the Occult Intelligence – 'occult' simply means 'hidden'. The imbedded laws of nature are indeed hidden from view. Theories about the natural world and our place in it have formed an important aspect of our cultural and spiritual heritage. The view we take of this relationship is always bound with a religious belief and code of ethics. Breakthroughs into nature's private world have the power to shake prevailing beliefs to the very core. Darwin knew this. His theory of natural selection shocked the God-fearing Victorians. He had taken a power away from the Godhead and handed it back to nature. We see this again today, perhaps more sharply than ever, in the key issues flowing from genetic research. The debate about stem-cell research and cloned life rages currently. Pandora's box has been opened and it will not be closed again. Uncovering nature's own code, decoding the Occult Intelligence, directly changes our own Natural Intelligence, which is also our Intelligence of Nature. This Path relates to all activities and pursuits which seek to unveil the laws of nature.

The Star Goddess

My mother Nut,

stretch your wings over me.

Let me become like the imperishable stars,

like the indefatigable stars.

Pyramid Text

Tarot Trump XVII, The Star, is assigned to this Path. It shows a naked woman kneeling by a pool. She holds two jugs and pours water onto the earth from one while taking water from the pool with the other. Five streams spread out as the waters divide upon the ground. In the background, an ibis sits high in a tree. In the sky seven white or silver stars surround an eighth central golden star.

The naked figure on the Trump is an embodiment of the Goddess, nature herself unveiled. Images of nakedness on the Tree represent the naked truth stripped of our projections; revealed reality is laid bare. The figure on Tarot Trump XVII, embodies the Egyptian star goddess Nut, or Nuit, whose arched body forms the vault of the heavens. The presence of a star goddess on this Path places earth and humanity in the greater cosmological setting of the infinite creation. Without the stars the planets would not exist, for the matter of earth is the stuff of stars recycled through time. The stars are ever-present signs of a greater world and greater creation. In her cosmic capacity the Goddess looks out upon succeeding aeons and whispers of eternity and immortality. The goddess matrix encompasses the entire cosmological round, not merely the earthly realm of nature and its seasonal cycles. She raises vision towards the eternal round and unimaginable stretches of time. Whether as Isis, Hathor or Nuit, this goddess of the heavens conveys our relationship to the starry realm and the great cosmic cycles of time. The passage of time on earth is determined by the greater cosmic backdrop of sun and moon which defines days, months and years, but other far greater cycles are set ticking in the heavens too. The precession of the equinox is a 26,000-year cycle. Its discovery is attributed to the Greeks, but it was most certainly known to the Egyptians prior to that. This is this Great Cycle which carries us from one age to another. We are at a time of transition as the Age of Pisces gives way to the Age of Aquarius.

The Spiritual Significance of this Path is assigned to Aquarius. The sign for Aquarius is drawn as two identical zigzag lines, one above another. Here is an image of unity and duality in balance. It might even be thought to represent the Hermetic axiom 'As Above, So Below'. As an Air sign, Aquarius represents the realm of the mind, the life of the mind and the power of ideas. As the Water Bearer, the image for Aquarius represents the pouring of new waters, bringing a baptism of mind. This Trump is also called Daughter of the Firmament and Dweller between the Waters. Nuit, Daughter of the Firmament, Dweller between the Waters, pours the life-giving waters upon the land. In hieroglyphic script, the name Nuit is a vessel and the sign for water. She pours out a blessing for all to receive. The ancient Egyptian star goddess is the perfect embodiment of the Water Bearer. This is the Natural Intelligence at work, for the cosmos has its own rhythm and cycles in which we are immersed. This is the sign of the Age now establishing its roots. The incoming waters of Aquarius are already being experienced through the rippling effect of new ideas, hopes, aspirations and the rediscovery of Ancient Wisdom. This Path has the potency to inspire many forms of personal creativity. As waters from the pool nourish the land, so the reservoir of the unconscious is filled with inspirational ideas, dreams, hopes, possibilities and visions. Creativity draws from this deep well. The current Western thirst for spirituality is a measure of the cultural desert which has desiccated the human spirit for so long. Confined on all sides by the vestiges of religious and cultural conditioning, a new spirit is now emerging. Nuit pours out the life-giving waters which quench spiritual thirst and revitalize the land. This is an outpouring of Natural Intelligence: 'by it is completed and perfected the nature of all that exists beneath the Sun'. The incoming Aquarian current is the handiwork of nature, a natural movement from one cycle to another. The Aquarian symbol itself is insightful. Resembling a stylized wave, an electrical current and a movement of air, the glyph highlights where change can be expected. Ruled by Uranus, Aquarius will bring radical technology and development based on currents, waves of energy, oscillating frequencies and all things electrical. As a social sign represented by a human figure, Aquarius will bring humanizing concepts and high ideals. New ideas will replace old ones as fresh air replaces the stale air of a closed room. The incoming wave of Aquarius will build gradually like a wave taking shape far out to sea. It will not arrive in fullness until another century or more has passed. Nevertheless, we feel the ripple of the Aquarian current already. If the Aquarian initiation is to be found in any single aspect of the Tree of Life, it is here on this Path, through the aegis of Nuit as the water-bearer of the New Age. She represents the future. She carries the Aquarian Initiation.

In the background, the ibis sits high in a tree. This signifies the presence of ibis-headed Thoth, Lord of the Wisdom, who took the role of teacher and initiator to Isis herself. Thoth represents the arts of medicine, knowledge and writing. He is the Egyptian embodiment of wisdom, the overseer of all scribes and the oversoul of the Egyptian priesthood. The ibis feeds by stabbing its beak sharply beneath the waters. It stands motionless while it takes aim. The Hebrew letter attributed to this card is Tzaddi, meaning a fish-hook. The bill of the ibis and the fish-hook serve the same purpose. Both penetrate the underwater world for nourishment. Here is a metaphor for the process of meditation. Daily, the mind dips into the waters of the unconscious to fish for nourishment. Like the ibis out fishing, the mind is first paused and then directed with sure aim to its goal. As a Simple Letter, Tzaddi is assigned to the quality of Imagination. The creative imagination is of course the key to vitalizing meditative practice and to constructing a new holistic mode of thinking. Its importance should not be underestimated. Interacting with symbolically charged images through the active or creative imagination brings a response which is direct, authentic, spontaneous and often emotional. It is this depth involvement which provides the fuel for transformation and the insight this brings. The active imagination enters the drama of the interior landscape as a player, posing questions, creating dialogue, revealing feelings and pressing towards solutions. When employed in the service of self-realization, the active imagination is a tremendous force for healing and connection.

Netzach is the sphere of the emotions and the imagination. The two are intertwined and both are distrusted in today's climate. The Age of Reason has passed but rationality still rules, the irrational response still carries a certain stigma. Netzach empowers the irrational because it is a voice that must be heard. It is the natural complement to the reasonable. Either voice alone is unbalanced. The rational process offers analysis; emotional sensitivity brings empathy. Together the two opposing but complementary modes bring synthesis. But without the vital ingredient that is the imagination, both reason and emotion are no more than a stagnant well. The 28th Path leads to Netzach, where imagination and creativity find full expression in praise of and interaction with nature and the Natural Intelligence. Einstein said that imagination was more important than knowledge. He recommended daydreaming or creative reverie to his students. He used to imagine himself travelling from our sun at the speed of light to the ends of the universe, exploring as he went – with, of course, good effect. All creative thinkers – whether artists, poets, writers, scientists or planners – have discovered and naturally used the creative imagination. It is the deep well of inspiration.

The Stars Within

Spirituality is the awakening of divinity in consciousness. It is the *summum bonum* of consciousness in human incarnation which frees consciousness from the mind-body trap. This freedom is obtained by a gradual process of the transformation of sense consciousness.

Harish Johari, *Chakras – Energy Centres of Transformation*

It is ironic that while the Natural Intelligence offers itself up continuously, history shows a drive in the opposite direction, towards an authority vested almost anywhere except in the Natural Intelligence. The conflict between revealed and natural religion is an old one. The distrust in nature as a teacher is part of the same schism that renders the material world inferior, lowly and untrustworthy. Yet this is the path of the Natural Intelligence and it offers a glimpse into the Perennial or Natural Wisdom which is based on what is real and arises from it.

It is noteworthy that the natural inheritance represented by this path has been forced through historical circumstance to become a secret inheritance. The Kabbalah itself has been shrouded in secrecy. Its path, which unifies the material and the spiritual, has been a hidden one. Knowledge of the chakras, now so easily available, was once absolutely secret. Sir John Woodroffe, who finally brought key texts to the West, devoted a lifetime to the search for them. A knowledge of the subtle anatomy is as necessary for health, well-being and personal growth as a knowledge of the physical anatomy. But the Natural Intelligence, the Intelligence of Nature, has so often been resisted in favour of a philosophy not derived from nature at all.

The seven stars seen on the Tarot Trump represent the chakras or wheels of living energy within the subtle bodies. These seven interior lights form the blueprint for being at microcosmic and macrocosmic levels in accordance with the Hermetic maxim 'As Above, So Below'. Each chakra, wheel or vortex of energy signifies a level of being, a vehicle of consciousness and a plane of being simultaneously. The seven centres correspond to the Sephiroth. Malkuth is represented by the Muladhara or Root Chakra, which corresponds to the physical world. Yesod is represented by the Swadistana Chakra, which signifies the emotional and astral realm. Hod and Netzach together are represented by the Manipura Chakra, which signifies the solar plexus and the personal will. Chesed, Geburah and Tiphareth together are represented by the Anahata or Heart Chakra. Daath is represented by Vishuddi or the Throat Chakra. Binah and Chokmah are represented together by the Ajna Chakra at the brow centre. Finally, the Crown Chakra corresponds with Kether, the Crown. Like the journey presented by the Tree of Life, awakening consciousness through the seven chakras is another journey of self-realization. Yet it also the same journey from root to crown, from Malkuth towards Kether. The model for this journey is laid out here on the 28th Path as an element of the Natural Intelligence. The subtle bodies assume an increasing importance as the journey rises into the higher reaches of the Tree. The chakras as nodal points of energy each have a potential for transformation. As the bridge between material form and immaterial consciousness, the chakras are responsive to changes in either state. The vibrational nature of each chakra can be transformed by the focused thought of meditation, the circulation of life force, through the conscious breath, and the application of *Sat-Cakra-Nirupana*, the Knowledge of the Chakras. Like Kabbalah, this knowledge has been preserved in time through a narrow lineage. Like Kabbalah its teachings are enshrined in a symbolic language; the potencies of the chakras, like the potencies of the Sephiroth, are described through a symbolic language awaiting decryption. The Eastern teachings concerning the chakras complement the teachings and method of Kabbalah. It is the nature of Kabbalah to evoke and incorporate other holistic systems of spiritual awakening with comfort. Knowledge of the chakras has been grafted onto a knowledge of the Sephiroth and the two systems work well together.

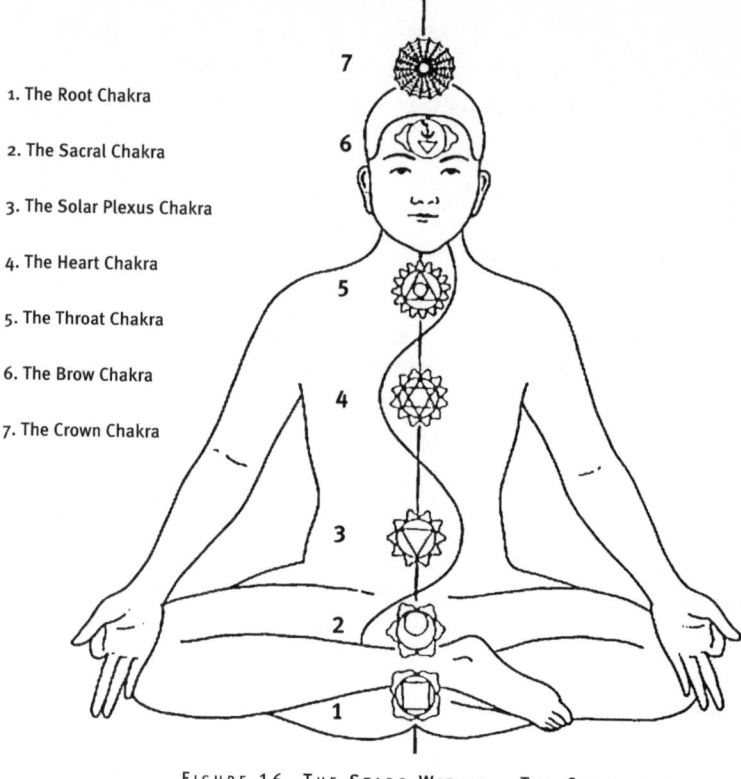

1. The Root Chakra

2. The Sacral Chakra

3. The Solar Plexus Chakra

4. The Heart Chakra

5. The Throat Chakra

6. The Brow Chakra

7. The Crown Chakra

FIGURE 16 THE STARS WITHIN – THE CHAKRAS

THE WATERFALL

Sit in meditation. Place your awareness at the base of the spine and visualize there a light or shining star. Lift your awareness upwards to the sacral or sex centre and visualize a star here too. In turn place your awareness at the solar plexus in the centre of the abdomen, at the heart, at the throat, at the brow and finally at the top of the head. At each location visualize a centre of energy as a star or a sphere of light. When you have completed this column, harmonize your in-breath with your visualization and imagine a current of white light rising up from the base of the spine. As you breathe in draw it upwards through the centres until it reaches the top of the head. On an out-breath see the white light cascading over and around the whole body. Repeat this three times. At the close of the session dissolve each of the images in turn, beginning at the crown of the head.

This meditation can be performed daily. It invigorates and begins to circulate living energy through the physical body.

The 28th Path shows us the sevenfold personal spiritual blueprint and the transpersonal blueprint as Great Age follows Great Age. It asks that we understand both the greater and the lesser cycles and live within them. These are great spiritual truths, hidden yet ever revealed for those with eyes to see.

EVOCATION

Welcome to my kingdom. I am the Age which is to come. I am drawing closer as time passes. My light is rising. Yet I come to birth only through your heart and mind. My nature is of both water and air and I will bring you both. I bring the life-giving waters of renewal and rebirth. I bring initiation into the way of the future. I offer service to all through inspiration and vision. I will help heal all that has been sundered. I speak for the Natural Intelligence. I am Nature. See how I pour out the waters of the future upon the parched land. I am of the heavens. For the heavens and the earth are not divided but united in rhythm and cycle. Expand your mental horizons. Step out from the limitations imposed by others. Look instead to the stars. See the connection between all things – the near and the far, the great and the small, the past and the present.

I have much to offer and much to teach for my waters are without end and I shall pour them endlessly. Travel my path to find the stars within. Seek your own true nature. Look for the Natural Intelligence, it is Wisdom's garment. Let all be done under the aegis of Wisdom. Seek the natural patterns and blueprints engraved in the Great Above and the Great Below. Take these as your guide. Let us become workers upon the path to the stars. Let us build the future together.

INTERNALIZATION – THE 28TH PATH: YESOD–NETZACH

Construct the Temple of Yesod in the creative imagination. Find yourself standing beside the door of the Star. The Archangel Gabriel draws back the tapestry curtain so that you may pass.

You find yourself emerging into a green haze. You walk on with steady stride and find yourself walking towards woodland hazed with the blush of early spring. Your path takes you through the wood and finally into an opening. Ahead of you in the distance is a small pool. Beside it kneels a naked woman holding two vessels.

As you watch, she takes water from the pool and pours it upon the earth. All the while she sings gently to herself.

You feel a sense of nervousness at intruding upon this private moment. Her nakedness tells you that she feels comfortable and safe here. You do not want her to feel otherwise. Yet you do not want to turn back. You feel a compulsion to speak with her, so you begin to approach. She is immersed in her private thoughts so that she does not see you until you reach the poolside, at which point she stops what she is doing and stands up in front of you.

Now your eyes meet in a long deep gaze and in that moment you know that this woman is like no other you have met. She steps into the pool and instinctively you do the same. You now stand close in front of her. She reaches down and fills both vessels, then lifts one above your head and begins to pour water gently over you in a cascade. It is not cold but slightly warm to the touch. As she pours, she begins to sing again. Water runs over you from head to foot as she now pours from the second vessel. As you stand together, you feel yourself entering an intensified state of awareness. The water now seems not merely to wash over you, but to pour through you like an interior waterfall flowing down from the very centre of your head. She continues to pour more water, drenching every particle of your being in the waters of the pool. You turn your attention outwards momentarily and look at the woman who stepped into the pool with you. Now her naked body has become a body of light filled with the colours of the rainbow. She is clothed with light. She is veiled in a pillar of light showing all the colours of the spectrum from red to violet. Looking down at yourself you see the same colours sparkling. As she continues to pour, the lights of your being seem to shine even more brightly. She sings again but this time she is singing to you. Her words sing of the Waters of Aquarius.

Then everything stops. There is silence, the waters of the pool are stilled. At last you open your eyes. You are quite alone. You body no longer shines with inner light. The Water Bearer has vanished, leaving no sign of her presence. You step from the pool.

When you are ready, return the way you came to the temple. When you are ready, leave through the doorway. Finally, dissolve all images and return to ordinary consciousness.

EXERCITIA SPIRITUALIA

Take the Following as Subjects for Meditation:

- Daughter of the Firmament, Dweller between the Waters
- The letter Tzaddi
- Aquarius
- Imagination
- The Natural Intelligence
- The Age of Aquarius

Make Notes on:

- The Tarot Trump, XVII, The Star

Visualize the Following and Record your Experiences:

- The Temple of Yesod including the Archangel Gabriel
- The Journey of the 28th Path

CHAPTER 10

Netzach – Victory

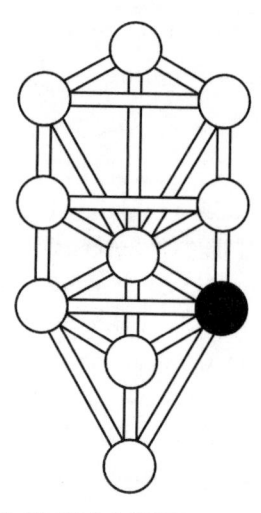

FIGURE 17 THE SEPHIRAH NETZACH

TABLE OF CORRESPONDENCES

God-Name: Jehovah Tzabaoth – Lord of Hosts

Archangel: Haniel

Order of Angels: Elohim, Gods and Goddesses

Magical Image: A beautiful naked woman

Spiritual Experience: The Vision of Beauty Triumphant

Symbols: The Lamp, The Girdle, The Rose

Virtue: Unselfishness

Vice: Lust

Titles: None

Mundane Chakra: Venus

Personal Chakra: Manipura – the Solar Plexus Chakra

Text: The Occult Intelligence

Colour in Atziluth: Amber

Colour in Briah: Emerald

Colour in Yetzirah: Bright Yellow Green

Colour in Assiah: Olive flecked Gold

Tarot Cards: The Four Sevens

Seven of Wands: Valour

Seven of Cups: Illusory Success

Seven of Swords: Unstable Effort

Seven of Pentacles: Success Unfulfilled

COMMENTARY

The Seventh Path is called the Occult Intelligence because
it is the refulgent splendour of the intellectual virtues which
are perceived by the eyes of the intellect and the
contemplations of faith.

The seventh Sephirah, Netzach, is located at the base of the Pillar of Mercy. It stands in direct polarity with Hod, the eighth Sephirah, which is to be found at the base of the Pillar of Severity. Here force and form are in dynamic tension as the two linchpins of the Astral Triangle. Netzach represents a natural inheritance. Hod represents the elaboration, development and application of the innate, the instinctive and the natural. The 29th Path leading from Malkuth to Netzach is assigned to the Natural Intelligence. Netzach itself is assigned to the Occult Intelligence, indicating that the qualities attributed here are mostly hidden – that is, implicit, not explicit.

The Inheritance of Instinct

Among the psychological factors determining
behaviour, the instincts are the chief forces of psychic
events.

C.G. Jung, *The Structure and Dynamics of the Psyche*

The seventh Sephirah, Netzach, represents the natural and innate inheritance of instinct. Though the primal drives of hunger and sex are self-evident as instinctive drives, Jung also defined 'the drive to activity' as an instinct. He defined this to include the urge to travel, a love of change, restlessness and the need to play. Beyond this he identified the reflective instinct. These two drives together lift the instinctive inheritance from the biological to the social and cultural sphere. The reflective instinct in particular carries a strong social and cultural impetus. It is the cultural instinct *par excellence*. Jung places great importance on the reflective instinct. 'The richness of the human psyche and its essential character are probably determined by this reflective instinct.'[1] The primal biological instincts are common to all species and ensure survival, but the higher instincts become a springboard for cultural and social development. The ability for reflection is a specifically human attribute. It brings a turning inwards which serves to modify the biological drives by creating a reflective pause. The ability to be reflective is a powerful modifying and refining force which holds the seeds of will and self-awareness. It provides the spur for reflective indulgence through replay, re-enactment and even rehearsal, as outer events and experiences enter the psychic structure as seeds in their own right. The instinctive need to reflect on an event or experience leads directly to those representation systems which form the basis of culture – speech and story-telling, dance and drama, art and science. Jung even placed creativity in the category of the instincts, though he qualified the definition a little: 'I do not know if instinct is the correct word. We use the term because this factor behaves at least dynamically like an instinct. Like an instinct it is compulsive but it is not common.'[2]

With self-reflection comes catharsis, meditative focus and, most importantly, the creative imagination. Imagination opens the door to emotional empathy and intellectual vision. Like an invisible enzyme, the imagination acts as a catalyst for action and forward momentum. Without the potency to imagine, experience becomes freeze-dried, captured in the moment without hope of adaptation. It is the imagination which brings originality and invention, both scientific and artistic. It is the imagination which creates and envisions. Imagination is the root of compassion. Without empathy there can be no compassionate action. Without imagination there can be no empathy. Without empathy there can be no sense of a shared identity, only a self-centred separation. Netzach is the sphere of the imagination. Awakening and applying the imagination brings a vitalizing and liberating creativity which can stimulate both directed thinking and artistic expression.

Jung's hierarchy of instincts has much in common with Maslow's Hierarchy of Needs. It is obvious that survival needs must be first met before more rarefied abstracted needs can be fulfilled. Maslow places transpersonal drives at the pinnacle of his pyramid structure, making it the least common and yet highest human need. This drive for transcendence might even be described as the highest drive of all. If so, it is the one most rarely pursued.

This instinctive inheritance provides a powerful range of force for survival and cultural elaboration. If the need for reflection or creativity were widely appreciated to be instinctive, a demand as insistent as the primal drives for survival and reproduction, self-expression might be more valued and less thwarted. It is timely to recall that the performing arts were once in sacred service. Long before dour sermonizing and moral lecture became the norm in a Western model of religious service, exuberant festival, joyous song, ecstatic dance and splendid celebrations were the natural creative and spiritual

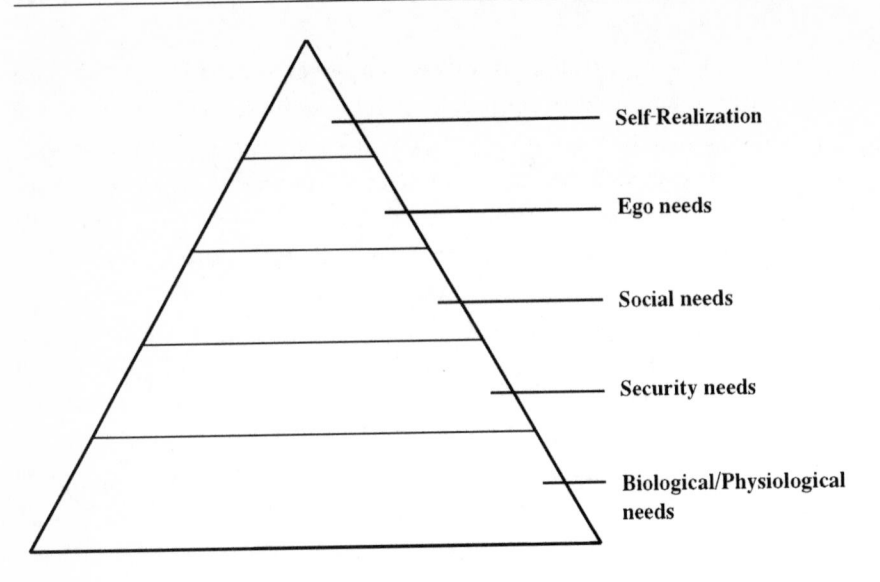

FIGURE 18 MASLOW'S HIERARCHY OF NEEDS

response to life. As Dion Fortune states, 'it's by means of dance and sound and colour that the Netzach angels are contacted and evoked'.[3]

This instinctive realm is assigned to Netzach, rightly called Victory. Netzach offers the triumph of creativity and a victory of being. Creativity is the most immediate and true expression of human life. Creativity is an awesome and immense force when unfettered by social constraints. So often the genius dies unrecognized and impoverished while the mediocre live out comfortable and comforted lives. The rational mind is exalted, the non-rational mind is misunderstood. William Blake, the English mystical poet, visionary, illustrator and engraver, clearly understood the tension between the rational and non-rational mind. He expressed this in the relationship between the two characters of Urizen and Orc. Urizen measures the globe with a pair of compasses, in keeping with the questions always posed by the rational mind. Orc on the other hand represents the raw and primal energy of creative life. Blake instinctively sought to redress the balance of power between the two. 'Energy is eternal delight,' Blake wrote. He knew this to be true, being awakened to a different order of reality at a young age. As a child he saw a London tree swarming with angels. For him the sunrise was 'an innumerable company of the heavenly host crying Holy, Holy, Holy is the Lord God Almighty'. Such perception is either mystical vision or deluded madness. It is not the common perception in which we all share but a heightened and intensified awareness. Time distinguishes the visionary from the deluded. Time has found William Blake to be both a mystic and a genius. Perhaps such rare perception is more real than the common vision, for the open eye sees more than the closed. Netzach is indeed the realm of the heavenly host. This is the realm of Jehovah Tzabaoth, the Lord of Hosts. The order of angels assigned to Netzach is the Elohim. This is the sphere where the One takes shape as the many. Its archangel is Haniel, who is visualized as a shining being of green and gold with a rose-coloured halo of shimmering light.

In Love with Nature

When we turn from books to living nature we begin to understand the ancient wisdom, and it is no longer an abstraction, for the great spirit whose home is in the vast becomes for us a moving glamour in the heavens, a dropping tenderness in the twilight, a visionary light in the hills, a voice in the heart. The earth underfoot becomes sacred and the air we breathe is like wine poured out for us by some heavenly cupbearer.

Æ, The Candle of Vision

This is nature's own realm, and Mother Nature has played the part of Muse to many an artist whose passion borders on worship. The relationship between the natural world and the artist arises spontaneously from observation which engages feelings of awe and wonder. These are the roots of spiritual and mystical sensibilities. Indigenous peoples who have lived immersed in the being of the natural world, retain and indeed develop an empathic rapport with the entire natural realm of plant, place and beast. A spiritual life spontaneously develops, bonding the community to Mother Earth through ritual and ceremony. The mode of consciousness which embraces the unity and wholeness of the natural cycle has been called *participation mystique*. It is the consciousness of Netzach, a life lived through the instincts, the emotions and the mystical imagination. Our cultural development has slowly but inexorably subtracted such sensitivities from all but the few. Nature has become a source of raw materials for a consumer society. The artist alone continues to keep faith with nature by expressing and revealing her realm as it is. Mother Nature is never a cliché or an empty label for those living within her embrace. She lives. Her epiphanies are multitudinous and manifold. Barriers disappear between the world of people, the lives of animals, and the natural world itself, as communities live within the cycle of the year and the abundance of the land. A single unified life emerges, a sensitivity to place develops, an awareness of the power of all nature remains constant. It is this identification with nature which appears so distasteful to more cerebral religions who, having removed themselves from nature's embrace, distrust the body, the instincts, the emotions and even nature herself.

In an age denuded of spiritual presence, some few still discover the numinous without the traditional signposts and landmarks. George Russell (Æ) was an author, artist and poet whose exterior life was an expression of his constant inner vision:

> When I look through the windows I see a living nature and
> landscapes not painted by hands. So too when I meditate I feel in the
> images and thoughts which throng about me, the reflections of
> personality, but there are also windows in the soul through which can
> be seen images vested not by human but by the divine imagination.
> I have tried according to my capacity to report about the divine
> order and to discriminate between that which was self-begotten
> fantasy and that which came from a higher sphere.[4]

Æ was a traveller in the world of the imagination. He was a natural mystic in love with Nature herself. By his own account his romance began at about the age of 17:

> I began to be astonished with myself, for walking along a country
> road, intense and passionate imaginations of another world seized
> me… The visible world became like a tapestry blown and stirred
> by the winds behind it. If it would but raise for an instant I knew
> I would be in paradise. Every form on that tapestry appeared to
> be the work of gods. Every flower was a word, a thought. The
> grass was speech; the trees were speech; the waters were speech;
> the winds were speech. They were the Army of the Voice
> marching on to conquest and dominion over the spirit.[5]

This inner perception never left. It remained an inspiration for his creative and spiritual life, which were utterly intertwined. For him, nature was the feminine garment of the divine: 'I think of the earth as the floor of a cathedral where altar and presence are everywhere. This reverence came to me as a boy, listening to the voice of the birds one coloured evening in summer.' He spoke using the analogy of the lover and the beloved, nature herself coyly lifting her veil to reveal herself. 'So the lover of Earth obtains his reward, and little by little the veil is lifted of an inexhaustible beauty and majesty.' For him, as for so many other creative artists, nature was his living Muse:

> So gradually the earth lover realises the golden world is all about him in imperishable beauty, and he may pass from the vision to the profounder beauty of being, and know an eternal love is within and around him, pressing upon him and sustaining with infinite tenderness his body, his soul and his spirit.[6]

His rare vision is the embodiment of the Spiritual Experience of Netzach.

Nature's secrets have inspired human creativity through the generations; wonder gives rise to creative endeavour as adoration, inspiration, exploration and celebration. Often a still small voice arises at a time when nature is forgotten, abused and violated. As the forces for industrialization gathered in momentum, William Wordsworth and his sister escaped to the Lake District and without knowing it seeded another revolution, that of the Romantic movement. He stood firm upon the ground of the 29th Path, gazing towards the beautiful naked goddess of nature, while all around society was discovering the power of the 31st Path, which is the Collecting Intelligence and the potency of scientific application. In America, Ralph Waldo Emerson spoke up for nature in a land also undergoing a frantic revolution in the push westwards. His essay on nature in 1837 sounded a note unheard in the rush to claim territory:

> In the woods is perpetual youth. Within this plantation of God a decorum and a sanctity reigns, a perennial festival is dressed and the guest sees not how he should tire of them in thousands of years. Standing on bare ground … the currents of the universal being circulate through me; I am part or parcel of God.[7]

Emerson spoke of the sanctity of woodland while others saw only timber. But Emerson's vision did not fall upon stony ground. He too seeded a small but vital revolution of spirit which can with pride claim the preservation of wilderness through the foundation of the national parks as its lasting achievement. It is a mistake to see artistic sensitivities as lacking in potency. Poetry can awaken what has been forgotten. Art can recall what has been lost. Inspiration can become action, vision can become reality.

The 28th Path is a conduit between the inner sanctum of unconscious energy and the natural world.

Hail to the Divine Feminine

> The love I had for nature as the garment of deity
> grew deeper.

Æ, *The Candle of Vision*

Nature's own realm is that ascribed to Venus, the goddess of love. For the Greeks she was Aphrodite. For the Egyptians she was Hathor. For the Sumerians she was Inanna. This realm is welcomed by all who willingly receive the gifts of the Divine Feminine, but feared by those who seek to control the uncontrollable. Netzach is assigned to the power of the feminine as muse, goddess, complementary cosmic power and creatrix. Her domain is that of the senses, of sensuality, sexuality, instinct and emotion. Her realm is love, her coinage is desire, her message is to awaken. She has the power to open the heart and call forth the soul. By whatever name she is called, the Divine Feminine is the great initiator into the depths and meaning of life. She is the Eros principle. 'The Eros is a spiritual or psychological principle, or, in the older term, it is a divinity. To be related to this principle means to be orientated to that which transcends personal aims and ambitions, it means gaining a relation to a non-personal value.'[8] The magical image for Netzach is that of a beautiful naked woman, the goddess herself, nature unveiled.

The 17th-century spiritual allegory, *The Chymical Wedding*, centres upon the discovery of the tomb of one Christian Rosencreutz, who at the climax of his journey enters the bedchamber of the Naked Lady Venus. He uncovers her sleeping form; he uncovers what has been hidden. With her usual keen insight, Esther Harding explains the significance of this moment:

> To raise the veil of Isis must mean to see nature as she really is, to understand what it is that underlies the manifestation of this world and of the emotions which so move us, to see them in their ultimate reality, not veiled by rationalization or illusion. He who is able to do that and so face reality, becomes consciously immortal, or perhaps it should read 'conscious of immortality', for he has released his mind himself from the conditioning of time and space, and especially from the distortions of facts brought about by his own ego orientation. His centre of consciousness has shifted from the personal 'I' of his

ego, to a more disinterested focal point which embraces in its outlook a larger range and has in consequence a more detached attitude.[9]

This is the Path of the Occult Intelligence – occult simply means 'hidden'. The term carries no sinister connotations. The teachings of the Eternal Wisdom have been purposefully hidden in symbol and allegory as a means of both protection and transmission. Uncovering the Lady Venus as she sleeps is a powerful rendering of the encounter with the Divine Feminine which lies at the heart of the experience of Netzach. Moreover, it was a bold statement of intent at a time when nature was not thought to be a proper subject for study and observation.

Netzach represents our instinctual inheritance and drives, raised to sublime heights. In Netzach we encounter Venus. She is the muse of creators and lovers alike for she brings inspiration and a dramatic awakening to the power of beauty. Her presence indirectly touches consciousness – for how else is great poetry, literature, art and creativity established except through inspiration? As the ruler of Taurus, Venus is another octave of the fertile earth goddess who is the bountiful and abundant mother. In times long past, nature's ability to replenish and reproduce was itself an epiphany. The beautiful naked woman of Netzach is Aphrodite or Venus and all goddesses of love and desire, ecstasy and mystery. Botticelli's painting of Venus captures this exquisite mystery. All sexploitation defiles this mystery. It is yet another separation of matter and spirit, the logical conclusion of a morality which set out to part the flesh from the life of the soul. The mystery of sexuality lies in its sacramental nature. Matter and spirit are ever conjoined. The Victory of Netzach is the recognition that nature itself is a manifestation of spirit; it is not to be despised but honoured. As body and spirit represent a unity, so all divisions are artificial perceptions. The Vice of this Sephirah is Lust which seeks to own, control and use. Lust functions and acts as if body and spirit are separate. The Virtue of the Sephirah is Unselfishness. This is the desire to share, to disseminate and to distribute. There is no desire to hold or grasp; instead the impetus is to give unceasingly.

The quality of Unselfishness is a forerunner of the character of the sixth Sephirah, Tiphareth. Tiphareth bestows a mystical consciousness which dissolves all boundaries and barriers. The symbol for unfolding conscious-ness in Netzach is the lamp which brings light to the dark. The light of the soul brings enlightenment in the place of ignorance. The remaining symbols assigned to Netzach are the undeniably feminine images of the rose and the girdle. The low-slung, loose-knotted girdle is a statement of feminine sexuality. Dante Gabriel Rossetti, who also lived under the aegis of Netzach, painted Astarte and thereby brought the goddess and her girdle to an astonished Victorian audience at a time when piano legs were covered to preserve modesty. The rose has a long identification with the goddess. An eight-petalled florette was among Inanna's symbols. Roses were sacred to the goddess Isis. The Virgin Mary is still called the Rose of Heaven and the Rose of Sharon. The rose signifies love, both earthly and divine. It is the gift of the lover and the passion of the poet. Its brief life and cruel thorns only make it a more perfect statement of human love. Transient beauty raises the rose to a mystical symbol comparable to the Eastern lotus. The *rosa mystica* symbolizes the flowering of the soul. When the mystic rose and the cross combine, the resulting rose-cross gives birth to a new spiritual impetus, the Rosicrucian current.

Netzach evokes our response to the beautiful. The encounter with true beauty has the power to evoke deep and private emotions: awe, humility and adoration. Such emotions enrich the human being. Such emotions are too infrequently felt. A lack of beauty stultifies sensitivities and emotional expression. Those who have been blessed with the eye of vision discover that such experiences have the power to nourish the psyche. This was the vision and the driving desire that sustained Æ throughout his life: 'I was bare of all but desire for the eternal. I was once more the child close to the Mother. She rewarded me by lifting for me a little veil which hides her true face. To those high souls who know their kinship her veil is lifted, her face is revealed, and her face is like a bride's.'[10] This is indeed the Vision of Beauty Triumphant.

NAMING THE BEAUTIFUL

Name seven works of art which express the essence of beauty for you. If you can, find representations of these and use them as focus points for meditation.

EVOCATION

Welcome to my kingdom. I have many delights to share with you. I offer you infinite expressions of the human spirit, countless reflections of the human nature. I offer you the opportunity to respond as a human being. Pity the soul who has never been enraptured by sweet music or moved by words. Pity the soul who has not been awakened by beauty. Pity the soul who knows only the ugly and the dark. To live without the touch of the beautiful is truly to dwell in darkness. I am the Muse who drives you to create beautiful works. I am the Muse who drives you to worship what is beautiful and true. I am the Muse to the human spirit. You can never possess me but your aching for me brings forth the child of your passion, which is the expression of our love. You may never see me yet I am always present. You cannot touch me but you will feel my presence.

Rejoice at our love. Together we will bring beauty into the world. Delight in colour, shape, and form. Celebrate the meaning of life with enactment and dance. Share the joy of life through sound and song. Find the wonder in the everyday and the mundane. Become a creator. Establish the beautiful in the world so that others may be awakened to my kingdom.

Beauty has the power to stir the soul. Philosophy feeds the mind but I nourish the senses. My language is unspoken. My language is universal. I speak the language of the human spirit. I speak of joy and delight, awe and wonder, rapture and bliss. These are my gifts. If you value them for yourself you will preserve them for others. Let the blessings of Venus alight upon all those who seek my face.

INTERNALIZATION – THE TEMPLE OF NETZACH

Construct the Temple of Netzach in the creative imagination. Your most favoured works of art fill the walls. You may spend as much time as you wish in contemplation of them. When you are ready to proceed, move to the altar. In front of it you see a small door covered with copper set flat into the pavement. Words are inscribed on it. 'Here lies buried Lady Venus, the fair woman who hath undone many a great man.' You reach out and pull up the door by its handle. You see a dimly lit staircase and, overcome by curiosity, you descend. It leads to another door. Beside the door hangs a bell rope of green cord. You pull upon it and a clear note chimes out.

The door is opened by a figure dressed in the livery of a page. He admits you into the room, where you immediately see a bed hung with cloth of green, gold, emerald and olive. The foot of the bed is inscribed with the sign for Venus. Soft drapes enclose the bed. The page invites you to draw closer and he pulls back one of the drapes, revealing a sleeping figure. Long copper hair spreads out across the white pillow. Her face holds an extraordinary and unworldly beauty. Her skin is pale and without blemish. She sleeps naked, her shoulders and arms are exposed above the covers. You see that she breathes in her sleep. You are reminded of Botticelli's painting *Prima Verra, Venus*. You stand in silence, gazing down at her sleeping form. Who is this woman? What is this place? You have come to the bedchamber of the Lady Venus. If you wish, ask for her blessing in your life. What will you do to ensure that Beauty continues to live in the world?

When you are ready to depart, the page will close the drapes once more. He escorts you to the door and leads the way back to the upper chamber. As you stand contemplating what you have seen, without warning the page reaches forward and pricks your hand with a tiny dart. With this you know that your page is certainly Venus's own servant, and that through this act you have now been admitted into her service. Now he turns and goes back to his underground vigil, leaving you in the temple. When you are ready to depart, leave the way you came in. Finally, dissolve all images and return to ordinary consciousness.

EXERCITIA SPIRITUALIA

Take the Following as Subjects for Meditation:

- Jehovah Tzabaoth, Lord of Hosts
- The Elohim
- A beautiful naked woman
- The Vision of Beauty Triumphant
- The Occult Intelligence
- The Lamp
- The Girdle
- The Rose

Contemplate the Following Questions and Record your Responses:

- How may I serve Beauty?
- How does the function of Unselfishness operate in your life?
- How does the function of Lust operate in your life?
- How does the nature of Netzach relate to the Solar Plexus Chakra?
- What other correspondences can you relate to the Sephirah Netzach?
- How do the four Tarot cards relate to Netzach?

Visualize the Following and Record your Experiences:

- The Temple of Netzach including the Archangel Haniel
- The Journey to the Temple of Netzach

CHAPTER 11

The Twenty-Seventh Path: Hod–Netzach

FIGURE 19 THE 27TH PATH:

HOD–NETZACH

TAROT TRUMP XVI,

THE TOWER

TABLE OF CORRESPONDENCES

Journey: Tarot Trump XVI, Lord of the Hosts of
the Mighty, The Tower, The House of God,
The Lightning-Struck Tower

Key: The Letter Peh, meaning a mouth

Double Letter: Grace – Indignation

Spiritual Significance: Mars

Text: The Active or Exciting Intelligence

Colours in Atziluth: Scarlet

Colour in Briah: Red

Colour in Yetzirah: Venetian Red

Colour in Assiah: Bright Red rayed Azure and
Emerald

COMMENTARY

The Twenty-seventh Path is the Active or Exciting Intelligence and it is so called because through it every existent being receives its spirit and motion.

The 27th Path connects the eighth Sephirah, Hod, with the seventh Sephirah, Netzach. By doing so, it spans the Tree and like a bridge connects the two opposing Pillars of Manifestation, that of Severity and that of Mercy. It is, like all the lateral Paths, one of dynamic potency and significance which serves to connect forces normally viewed as opposing one another. It is a Path of adjustment and rebalance as the forces of Hod and Netzach meet and find a new equilibrium. As a component of the Astral or Psychological Triangle, this Path represents the process which completes the personal work undertaken through this first triad of Hod, Netzach and Yesod. Journeying through the Psychological Triangle is both diagnostic and therapeutic in effect. Yesod represents the storehouse of unconscious contents. Hod represents the powers of the conscious mind. Netzach represents the instinctive drives. This trinity provides the basis for a rounded and stable personality. Until the forces represented by Hod and Netzach have been brought into an effective working harmony, entry into the Ethical or Moral Triangle cannot proceed. Personal engagement in the Greater Mysteries of the next triangle brings entirely new dynamics of being to bear.

Balancing the Opposites

> The psyche is made up of processes whose energy
> springs from the equilibration of all kinds of opposites.

C.G. Jung, *The Structure and Dynamics of the Psyche*

The 27th Path balances a number of oppositions as represented by Hod and Netzach, among them thinking and feeling, science and art, imagination and intellect. It is therefore a Path of radical change. Currently the functions attributed to both Netzach and Yesod are undervalued while those assigned to Hod are overvalued. The regrettable drive to separate spirit from body, intellect from emotion, instinct from mind, has warped our value system. The emotions have become identified with irrational, feminine forces. Lofty and worthy spiritual pursuits have been attributed to the masculine and to reason. This insidious legacy has become invisibly woven into the fabric of our society. It pervades institutions large and small, attitudes both personal and corporate. We have become so deeply wedded to the intellect, mistaking it for consciousness itself. There has been a slow but inexorable shift in values from those represented by the moon to those represented by the sun, from the connective power of Eros to the separating quality of Logos. But living through the word alone brings a desiccation and sterility to life. 'The sterility of this arid life can only be cured by the life-giving waters of Eros of the emotions which have been repressed.'[1] The excessive emphasis of one function at the expense of the other merely powers up the repressed function to a dangerous point. This applies both individually and collectively. 'The rational attitude to life, with its attempt to control nature in the fullness of her creation, has resulted in a one-sidedness which threatens to fall over into its opposite.'[2] In other words, the more tightly rationality is applied, the more likelihood there is of a spontaneous eruption of repressed energies.

The marriage of reason and imagination, intellect and vision, is a powerful and creative combination. This journey most often brings a destructive energy to bear as imbalances in lifestyle and personality undergo adjustment. It is the place where tensions between the two opposing types of expression are harmonized through breakdown and reconstruction. Gareth Knight notes that, 'The treading of this Path then, may be rough going unless the personality is well balanced and open to the Descending Fire.'[3] The connecting Paths permit integration between conscious awareness, instinctive drive and unconscious contents. When the bridge between these two polarities has finally been forged, immense creative energy is released as complementary but different energies are brought into relationship.

This new equilibrium serves to bring healing to the schism between the rational and the non-rational which has become such a fundamental divide in the Western psyche. When the higher instincts of Netzach are consciously given priority and expressed in conjunction with the applied will of a focused consciousness, a reservoir of potential energy is liberated. This Path is assigned to the Lord of the Hosts of the Mighty, a title formed from Lord of Hosts, assigned to Hod, and God of Hosts, assigned to Netzach. Once again this path is seen to be the conjunction between oppositions.

The nature of the relationship between Hod and Netzach is much like that between the conscious and the unconscious. Although the two appear opposed, in fact together they form a complementary and compensatory whole. Netzach, much like the reservoir of unconscious energy at Yesod, provides a pool of instinctive energy which waits upon the summons to conscious expression through Hod. It is also possible to see reflections of the hemispherical brain differences in the Hod-Netzach polarity. The functions assigned to the left hemisphere accord closely with the characteristics assigned to Hod, while the functions assigned to the right hemisphere accord closely with the characteristics assigned to Netzach. Medical research begun in the 1950s discovered that the human brain has two hemispheres bridged by the corpus callosum. This specialization has permitted evolutionary advantage. Human beings can process two streams of information at once. Each hemisphere has the capacity to processes information independently before co-operating with the second brain. 'Each hemisphere of the human brain has its own private sensations, perceptions, thoughts and ideas, all of which are cut off from the corresponding experiences in the opposite hemisphere. In many respects, each disconnected hemisphere appears to have a separate mind of its own.'[4]

Research amply demonstrates how external reality is shaped by brain function. Split-brain patients provide bizarre and eccentric responses in test situations. Though such extremes are caused entirely by the physical separation of the two hemispheres, it is salutary to consider whether to a greater or lesser degree we all suffer from an impairment which is not physical but culturally derived. It is also salutary, if not a little frightening, to realize that we utilize only about 3 per cent of the brain's capacity. The work of Dr Roger Sperry, the leading pioneer in this field, has made it possible for individuals to retrain and awaken the capabilities of the apparently weaker hemisphere. Is it possible that the holistic mental exercises which form the backbone of meditative technique have the potential to open up new areas of the brain's capacity?

The left side of the brain excels at analysis, successive or sequential thinking, logic, quantifiable knowledge, mathematical calculation, intellectually based tasks, verbal intelligence, linguistic and symbolic skills, much like the qualities assigned to Hod. It provides a tendency towards science and mathematics and uses a direct and unfanciful expression. It is also responsible for a sense of time and is aggressive or outgoing in mode. The right side of the brain excels at holistic comprehension, is simultaneous, metaphorical, configurational, perceives patterns and is present minded, much like the qualities assigned to Netzach. This hemisphere is also responsible for synthesis, practical intelligence and sensuousness. It provides a tendency towards music, art and dance and is playful, fanciful and complex. It is also passive and receptive in mode. Western society and its education system have favoured the development of functions associated with the left brain. Eastern culture has favoured the development of the qualities ascribed to the right brain. It is unusual to find developed intellect and awakened intuition together. Perhaps this time is still to come.

Technological wizardry has made it possible to view the brain in action and thereby correlate brain function with specialized activity. Maxwell Cade's work with the Mind Mirror literally provided a visual read-out for each hemisphere by registering the range of brain waves via light-emitting diodes arranged in two banks. Cade and his co-workers were able to correlate particular displays with specific mental activity, particular types of meditation, reverie, sleep and guided imagery.

Perhaps of most interest was the correlation of a particular display, elliptical in shape, extending from low theta to moderately high beta with its peak in the alpha region. Cade related this pattern to a creative mind: 'Those who do attain this pattern often have an innate sense of the ineffable with accompanying emotions of being part of them, whether of a directly spiritual nature or simply in some nameless response.'[5] The balance between the qualities of Hod and Netzach can be physically observed when it is translated into the functions of the brain. Harmony and balance bring creativity.

The letter Peh attributed to this Trump signifies the mouth and points to the power of communication as an expression of either unity or discord. As a Double Letter, Peh is assigned to the qualities of Grace and Indignation. Words used mindfully carry a graciousness which brings inclusion, expresses generosity and enables dialogue. Indignant words set up barriers, state resistance and divide co-operation. In a world of easy words, media-hype, empty talk and the seductive information of the superhighway, it is easy to mistake sound for substance. When the intellect and the intuition speak with one voice, the word becomes effective, honest and focused and carries both authority and truth.

The Lightning-Struck Tower

Winds, floods, fire, are symbols of emotion, which is essentially a movement of energy.

Esther Harding, *Woman's Mysteries*

The 27th Path is assigned to Tarot Trump XVI, the Tower. This Trump is also called The Lightning-Struck Tower or the House of God. The self often appears in a dream as a house or other building. Architectural symbolism perfectly represents the work of the self. Edifice, basement, foundation, structure and style can all be taken as analogies for aspects of the personality. The tower represents a particular formation. Unlike the familiarity of a house and its domestic implications, the tower is unusual. It therefore represents a rarity rather than the norm. The tower reaches upwards from the earth towards the heavens and represents the self on the path towards self-realization. The shape and structure of the tower implies a series of levels or chambers one above another in series. This image can be related to models representing the psyche. The unconscious corresponds to the basement or underground area while the supraconsciousness level is symbolized by the heights. The model presented by the multi-levelled blueprint for the chakras also corresponds well to the symbolism of the tower. The spiritual journey represented in 17th-century allegory of *The Chymical Wedding* also features a tower signifying the upward ascent of the soul.

The Tarot Trump shows a scene of destruction as a tower is struck by lightning. Flames issue from the top of the tower and from its three windows. Two figures – one male, the other female – are falling to the ground. Yet within this scene of apparent chaos and destruction, there are spiritual forces at work. Lightning is a powerful and frightening natural force. As a spiritual symbol it represents elemental fire descending from the heavens. It cannot be controlled but strikes where it will with terrifying impact. Tibetan Buddhism has taken the lightning bolt as a key image. The *vajra* or *dorje* is a sacred weapon in the form of a thunderbolt. Enlightenment can strike with all the power of thunder and lightning. Kabbalah too takes the symbolism of lightning as a creative force. As the Lightning Flash descends through the planes, zigzagging between Force and Form, so the Tree takes its shape and structure.

The 27th Path is assigned to the Active or Exciting Intelligence which expresses the intense dynamic of this journey. The qualities of Hod and

Netzach can only be brought together when the boundaries between them are dismantled. Spiritual exercise brings great pressure to bear as the work of realignment gathers momentum. Dynamic work on the psyche brings dynamic results. Seeking to become more closely aligned with the blueprint for our own being inevitably means a process of radical change. As heat causes particles within a substance to become excited and thereby transformed, so the psyche has the raw energy to effect a transformation of being. The Tarot Trump assigned to this Path reveals an image of destruction. So the psyche also has the power to strip away false ideals, redefine aspirations and set new and perhaps surprising goals. In other words, the rebalancing process related to this Path often brings radical change, turmoil and a sense of inner pressure. The dynamic energy of this journey is clearly visible in outer life when people make drastic life changes and quite literally start again in new relationships or circumstances.

This Path is assigned to the planetary sign of Mars, which represents the power of physical energy, courage and action. Mars is the planetary ruler of Scorpio, which itself signifies transformation. The key to this path, the two symbols of Scorpio – the scorpion and the eagle – express the process of transformation as the earthbound and dangerous scorpion becomes the airborne and powerful eagle. But before the vertical and horizontal transformation of height, depth and polar opposition, the constituent parts must be freed in order to recombine in a new way. This involves the breaking down of what has previously been created. Mars brings a purging power of considerable movement and dynamic change. The falling figures in blue and red represent the potencies of Hod and Netzach being propelled into a new relationship. The elemental powers of thunder and lightning signify dramatic and potent powers which have the force to bring instant destruction. The top of the Tower has been blasted open. This renders the interior of the tower vulnerable – as it must be if change is to occur. Representing both Kether and the Crown Chakra, the golden crown at the top of the Tower has been dynamically shaken. The Tower will fall but its foundations will survive. A new edifice will arise, suitably strong to stand in the world yet sensitive enough to function in conjunction with higher vibrations.

Spiritual Fire

> The awakening of kundalini is the greatest enterprise
> and the most wonderful achievement in front of man.

Gopi Krishna, *Kundalini*

The scene at the Tower is clearly one of destruction, with the Tower at the mercy of the elemental forces of nature – thunder, lightning and fire. Yet the scene might also be interpreted as one of reconstruction, with the Tower at the mercy of elemental spiritual forces – the same thunder, lightning and fire. Spiritual fire is not a poetic metaphor but a living experience. As the journey proceeds, the living energies of being come into sharp focus. Spiritual exercises, *exercitia spiritualia*, serve as agents of change, deeply probing and changing areas of mind, body and psyche. Far from being mind games or self-indulgent exercises in introspection, effective spiritual exercises initiate a process of radical change and have the potential to precipitate the awakening of spiritual fire. This Path introduces a concept and power which is not psychological but mystical. It appears on this Path not only as the culminating experience to the Astral Triangle but also as the point of entry into the next triad, where it plays a more direct role in shaping the reconstructed self. As we move beyond the Lesser Mysteries where contemporary psychology has been a useful guide, we will have to rely more upon a different guide in new realms. The reality of descending spiritual fire is quite outside the world defined by psychological disciplines. This is an experience which belongs to the world of spiritual encounter and to those intrepid travellers who have known this experience. Æ has left ample testament for us:

> Once at the apex of intense meditation I awoke that fire in myself which the ancients have written, and it ran like lightning along the spinal cord and my body rocked with the power of it and I seemed to be standing in a fountain of flame and there were fiery pulsations as of wings about my head and a musical sound not unlike clashing cymbals with every pulsation.[6]

Spiritual fire is a reality, not an artistic metaphor but a physical, mental, emotional and spiritual experience of tremendous intensity and power. This inner fire has the power to burn away old patterns and ways of being with a transformative fiery energy. There is tremendous intensity and power. The tongues of flame licking the three windows and rising from the top of the tower are aspects of this spiritual fire.

THE BRIDGE

Find yourself in a curious castle composed of two towers linked by a bridge. You stand in one of the towers and look out through a window towards the other. It seems you have spent all of your life in this tower. It has been your home for many years. But you have a deep curiosity about the second tower. You have seen it daily from your window but you have no memory of visiting it. In fact, you recall that you have been turned back by the guardian at the bridge on several occasions. Nevertheless your desire to explore has been so strong that you fully believe you have visited it in your dream life. Today the urge to visit feels exceptionally strong. So you make your way to the level which has access to the bridge. The gatekeeper explains that you will be allowed to cross only if you are willing to be in an environment that is quite different from your usual mindset. So first reflect on your natural strengths:

- If you are normally analytical you will find a space in which to daydream.
- If you have a holistic awareness, you will be given a task requiring precision.
- If you use lists to plan and organize, you will encounter a situation where organization has no place, such as dancing.
- If you love to daydream, you might need to create a list.

When you are ready, visualize yourself crossing over the bridge to undertake an exploration of the new tower. Try to discover the types of rooms it houses and the kinds of people who work in it. Allow yourself to be receptive to any images that arise spontaneously. Record your journey.

Hod and Netzach are united through the journey of the 27th Path, where the process of integration is represented by the symbolism of the falling tower. It is the meeting place of two different modes of being, two different ways of processing the world – in fact, it is the meeting and marriage of two different brains. The 27th Path, like the corpus callosum, bridges the chasm in outlook and permits interchange. The twin forces of Hod and Netzach are equally valued and weighted in a complementary relationship. Together Hod and Netzach express a unity. There is a growing impetus to provide a means of redress to this most fundamental imbalance. The noticeable appearance of books providing a range of specific mental tasks for this purpose suggests that the public at large are prepared to engage in a personal brain revolution.

At the turn of the 21st century we seem to be returning to a holistic philosophy. The marriage of Hod and Netzach brings vision to science, altruism to invention and inspiration to technology. It is rare and wonderful to find such qualities in harmony in a single mind. Perhaps Leonardo da Vinci stands out as the supreme exemplar of the possible. His legacy remains astonishing. He said that there were four things that he had done that others might do to release creativity: he had developed the senses, studied both the art of science and the science of art, and realized the connectedness of everything. His advice on science and art might be interpreted as a need to balance the powers of Hod and Netzach. He apparently considered that people look without seeing, listen without hearing, touch without feeling, eat without tasting, move without physical awareness, inhale without awareness of odour or fragrance and talk without thinking! This is the surely a wake-up call from a master of creative living. In *Workout for a Balanced Brain*, P. Carter and K. Russell present seven goals based on da Vinci's thinking. These are:

1. To develop curiosity.
2. To be willing to learn from mistakes and experiences.
3. To continually refine the senses.
4. To be willing to embrace ambiguity and paradox.
5. To develop whole-brain thinking.
6. To cultivate grace and dexterity, fitness and poise.
7. To discover how everything connects to everything else.

Finally, the authors conclude that, 'we are once again beginning to take a more holistic approach to our own lives, and to our planet in general, and there is a now a swing back to the Renaissance man as typified by the 15th-century scientific genius Leonardo da Vinci'.[7] It is worth restating that the Renaissance which produced da Vinci was born from a rediscovery of pagan roots, Hermetic philosophy and a Kabbalistic model.

EVOCATION

Welcome to my kingdom. Travel my Path when you are ready to take up the responsibilities of the inner Path. I unite feeling with thinking through the purgative action of Mars. I will slough off your old skin, rendering you naked and vulnerable in your own eyes. I will destroy that which is outworn. I will consume that which is unnecessary. I will test every structure that you have lived by. I will test all that you have created and what is now dead will fall. Do not fear me for I will temper you with my fires and render you stronger. I am the purging fire of Mars. My Intelligence is Active – how could it be otherwise! Do not look away as I approach. I too am part of the sacred process of becoming. You will meet me many times. I am the alchemical crucible.

But in my destruction there is construction, in my breaking there is healing. I join what has become separated. I connect what has been disconnected. When the two have become one, harmonious and balanced, a third shall arise and carry you forward with the strength of purposeful vision, grounded creativity, meaningful action and practical inspiration. You will rise on the twin wings of becoming to heights never imagined, for my Path will become a sure foundation on which to set out again.

INTERNALIZATION – THE 27TH PATH: HOD–NETZACH

Construct the Temple of Hod in the creative imagination. Find yourself standing beside the door of the Tower. The Archangel Michael lifts the tapestry curtain so that you may pass.

You enter through the doorway and find yourself plunged into the darkness of a night without moon. You walk on but time seems to pass slowly. The ground beneath your feet is rocky and hard. You feel the land rise and know that you are walking up a slope. Suddenly a flash of lightning illuminates the sky. In a moment you see that you are in a barren landscape, walking up a steep incline. Directly ahead of you, lit up against the night sky, you see a tall tower. It seems very vulnerable here in such a high place. Another flash of lightning forks across the sky. In that moment you seem to see terrified faces peering from upper windows. You feel a sharp stab of fear in your heart.

The sky is now torn by a bolt of lightning so intense that it wracks the darkness with a cold brilliance. It crackles with electrical power. With a violent outburst of power, another fork of lightning seems to stab at the tower itself. Again you see faces at the upper windows as flames begin to lick the tower. Before you can move another step, two figures leap out into the black sky. You watch them transfixed. They seem to fall in slow motion and then you lose sight of them altogether. You run forward to help but you cannot see them in the darkness and confusion. The storm does not abate but seems to increase in ferocity. The lightning is terrifying. The tower burns, illuminating the sky. Now you hear the sound of falling masonry and the crash of falling timbers. You can only watch. There is no help that you can give. You fall to the ground as flying sparks and hot stones explode close to you. You seem to lose consciousness. Your senses return. All is silent. You look up. The tower is gone from its rocky promontory, as if it had never been. There is no trace of rubble or timber, bricks or stone. You rush over to the site where you had expected to find devastation and death. All trace of the tower is gone. Perhaps it was no more than mere illusion. You search the ground for a sign. Something glints against the grey stones. You go over and pick it up. It is a nugget of gold. You put it in a pocket for safekeeping.

When you are ready, return the way you came to the Temple. When you are ready, leave through the doorway. Finally, dissolve all images and return to ordinary consciousness.

EXERCITIA SPIRITUALIA

Take the Following as Subjects for Meditation:

- The House of God, Lord of the Hosts of the Mighty, The Lightning-Struck Tower
- The letter Peh
- Grace – Indignation
- Mars
- The Active or Exciting Intelligence

Make Notes on:

- Tarot Trump XVI, The Tower

Visualize the Following and Record your Experiences:

- Either the Temple of Hod or the Temple of Netzach, including the appropriate Archangel
- The Journey of the 27th Path

CHAPTER 12

The Twenty-Sixth Path: Hod–Tiphareth

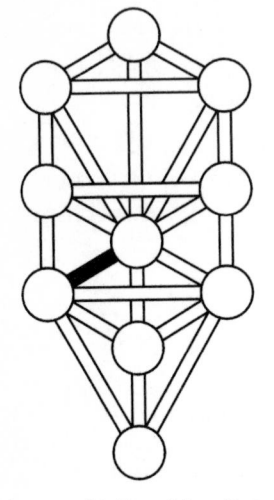

FIGURE 20 THE 26TH PATH:

HOD–TIPHARETH

TAROT TRUMP XV,

THE DEVIL

TABLE OF CORRESPONDENCES

The Journey: Tarot Trump XV, Lord of the Gates of Matter, Child of the Forces of Time

Key: The letter Ayin, meaning the eye

Simple Letter: Mirth

Spiritual Significance: Capricorn

Text: The Renewing Intelligence

Colour in Atziluth: Indigo

Colour in Briah: Black

Colour in Yetzirah: Blue-black

Colour in Assiah: Cold Very Dark Grey

COMMENTARY

The Twenty-sixth Path is the Renewing Intelligence,
because the Holy God renews by it all the changing things
which are renewed by the creation of the world.

The 26th Path connects the eighth Sephirah, Hod, with sixth Sephirah, Tiphareth, and thereby connects the Pillar of Severity with the central Pillar of Consciousness. It joins Hod, the sphere of rational mind within the Psychological Triangle, with Tiphareth, the sphere of the mystical mind within the Ethical Triangle. This path forges links across the gulf separating Tiphareth from the rest of the Tree and connects the personality to the Individuality. Tiphareth is the place of rebirth. The 24th, 25th and 26th Paths each contribute to the gestation of a reborn consciousness. The 26th Path is a journey of preparation. Its challenge is to face the obstacle which stands in the way of a universalized mystical consciousness – namely, the old fear of the devil.

The Shadow

> The shadow is a moral problem that challenges the
> whole ego personality for no one can become conscious
> of the shadow without considerable moral effort.

C.G. Jung, *Aion*

Images of demonic forces are universal. These speak of the shadow side of human nature. The shadow is the partner to the light. There cannot be one without the other. We each possess a shadow side which cannot be refused by neglect, tamed by good behaviour or silenced by the voice of piety, but instead is integrated into wholeness. However embracing, the unloved is painful and challenging:

> We seek to present a beautiful, innocent face to the world; a kind,
> courteous demeanour; a youthful intelligent image. And so,
> unknowingly but inevitably we push away those qualities that do not
> fit the image, that do not enhance our self-esteem and make us stand
> proud, but instead bring us shame and make us feel small. We shove

into the dark cavern of the unconscious those feelings that make us uneasy – hatred, rage, jealousy, greed, competition, lust, shame – and those behaviours that are deemed wrong by the culture – addiction, laziness, dependency – thereby creating what could be called shadow content.[1]

This 'invisible twin that lives just behind our life or just beside it', is the shadow, the dark twin of fairy tale and myth and the archetypal devil as the tempter of the good and pure. The split in the self is another rift waiting to be healed.

The 26th Path is assigned to Tarot Trump XV, The Devil. Like the Tarot Trump representing Death, this Trump is also commonly feared. The figure of the devil and the inevitability of death represent old and universal fears. The 24th and 26th Paths provide the opportunity to face, understand and dissolve the grip that such fears exert. The Trump shows a demonic hybrid figure perched upon a block of stone. With leathery wings, horned head, clawed feet and goat legs, the devil figure stares implacably forwards with empty eyes. Two naked figures are chained to the block. They are beginning to take on demonic forms; tails and horns have already appeared. The figure of the devil summarizes all that we fear in ourselves and others. Any brief overview of history reveals the depths and, conversely, the heights of human nature. It is impossible to ignore that the savage side of humanity is capable of cruelty, murder and depravity. It is the central dichotomy of the human condition. Both 'good' and 'evil' reside here. The battle between the two principles is perhaps the most fundamental of all themes. It takes shape as myth, legend, folk tale, epic saga and contemporary science fiction. It is the inescapable impact of a history riven by war, crime and despicable acts, yet these are paradoxically matched by heroism, generosity and altruism. Jung provides a psychological key to this conundrum through the concept of the shadow, the unwanted, despised and destructive possibilities within the self. 'To become conscious of it involves recognizing the dark aspects of the personality as present and real. The act is the essential condition for any kind of self-knowledge, and it therefore as a rule meets with considerable resistance.'[2] Meeting the shadow in the self demands personal courage, honesty and truthfulness. For those ready to seek the shadow, the authors Connie Zweig and Stephen Wolf point out its hiding places in their book *Romancing the Shadow*:

The shadow hides in secret shames.

The shadow disguises itself in our projections.

The shadow lurks in our addictions.

The shadow blurts out in slips of the tongue.

The shadow erupts in humour, especially cruel jokes at another's expense.

The shadow wears the camouflage of physical symptoms.

The shadow rears its head at mid-life.

The shadow dances through our dreams.[3]

There is much to be gained and nothing to be lost by engaging in the quest for the shadow self. It cannot be ignored except at the risk of schism. The shadow self has much to offer. It is a forgotten reservoir of dark water which can be tapped and drawn up into the light of awareness. When faced, the shadow brings the voice of authenticity. It 'reveals its gold in creative works' where struggle and pain find expression through transmutation. Embracing the shadow brings the forces of light and darkness together. It is not possible to reach the unified consciousness of Tiphareth as a leggy seedling growing too fast in the light. 'In a compassionate embrace of the dark side of reality we become like Lucifers. As bearers of the light, we open to the Other, the stranger, the weak, the rejected, the unloved, and simply through including it, we transmute it. In doing so we awaken to the larger life.'[4]

Integrating the shadow is difficult. Projecting the shadow elsewhere onto others is easy. Tarot Trump XV depicts the collective Western shadow, that most fearful creation of Christianity, the Devil. Medieval iconography reels with demons, devils, incubi and succubi waiting to lure the unwary into a pit of eternal damnation. How else might lust, greed, violence and the whole gamut of human vices be explained? Projecting the unacceptable by naming scapegoats has a long tradition. At one time, driving the scapegoat from the community with the sins of the group upon its back was a literal act, now it is only a metaphorical one. Driving out the unwanted from the confines of communal life begins the process of demonization. Bearing away the ills and accumulated failures of the tribal group brings a temporary feeling of relief, but all that is unwanted eventually haunts and threatens the stability of communal life by its excluded existence. Good and evil become polarized projections of the group mind. Certain behaviours and actions become identified as 'good', others as 'evil'. Polarization, not integration, commences. But dualized thinking cannot cross the gulf to Tiphareth. The dual mind cannot pierce the Veil of Paroketh. Dual thinking maintains a polarity between God and the Devil. But a dual mind cannot comprehend the unbounded realm of Tiphareth consciousness. Tarot Trump XV shows the demonic mind divided against itself. It is symbolized by the two horns, representing not only dualism but rigid and inflexible thinking, dogmatic views and hardened attitudes. The 26th Path between Hod and Tiphareth is a rite of challenge through which dualized thinking is understood to be false and illusory. The full realization of this is the essential preparation for the major shift into the universalized awareness of Tiphareth.

The work of the 26th Path is to break down the numerous false barriers that arise in the mind and commence the task of separations both great and small. It is on this Path that duality is challenged by the most fundamental of all schisms, that between God and the Devil, spirit and matter. Religious history has seen the enactment of this primal separation in so many ways. Orthodox religion accrued the authority to define those things considered to be of God and those things considered to be of the Devil. Moreover, orthodoxy has defended such boundaries with the force of its punitive law. The sweep of history highlights the nature of so-called heretical infringements and the realm attributed to the Devil slides on the shifting sands of social and cultural change. The fear of Devil worship never quite left the European mind; the scapegoat returned to haunt its owners as the burdens placed on its back became increasingly numerous. The doctrine of Original Sin created sexual sin and placed woman in the role of the original Eve as the archetypal temptress and destroyer of a supposed idyll. Temptation, the lure of the Devil, lurked in the unlikeliest places – in sex, in childbirth and in women's bodies. The accusation of Devil worship summoned the wrath and fire of the Church as an instrument of salvation. Heretical groups such as the Templars and the Cathars of France were burned to a man. Outcast groups, most often the Jews, were tainted by rumours of Devil worship. There were witch burnings in Europe, and the notorious events of Salem proved that this same fear travelled to the New World along with high hopes and the pioneering spirit.

This Path recounts the depth of suffering inflicted upon the scapegoated groups of humanity: heretics, Jews, women, outcasts, followers of a different religion, free thinkers. In the name of God, terror has been unleashed on the supposed ungodly through edict, decree, punishment, self-righteous counsel, religious zeal, puritanical denial, organized exclusion and sanctioned death. This is the only outcome of a dual philosophy. When belief in God simultaneously gives rise to belief in a Devil, the battle lines are implicitly drawn and will be played out wherever one group invokes the name of good against the forces of evil. Tiphareth represents the sphere of unity. It transcends conceptions of both good and evil which are no more than mental projections. The initiation of Tiphareth cannot be attained by a mind divided against itself.

The Renewing Earth

To live we must daily break and shed the blood of creation. When we do this knowingly, lovingly, skilfully and reverentially it is a sacrament. When we do it ignorantly, clumsily, greedily and destructively it is a desecration. In such desecration we condemn ourselves to spiritual and moral loneliness and others to want.

Wendell Berry, *The Gift of Good Land*

The 26th Path is assigned to the Renewing Intelligence, 'because the Holy God renews by it all the changing things which are renewed by the creation of the world'. This is clearly a Path of renewal and hope. Nature's ability to renew and regenerate is a continuous source of wonder in a material world which is constantly changing. Tarot Trump XV, though commonly known as The Devil, is also known as Lord of the Gates of Matter and Child of the Forces of Time. Tarot Trump XV is attributed to the sign of Capricorn, symbolized by the goat. Capricorn is the ruler of the tenth sign of the zodiac, which is an earth sign in its cardinal quality. This expands the meaning of the Trump. It is no longer just a picture of our distorted group projections, but also a statement about the material world. Here is a presentation of reality, stripped away from collective projections, self-justifying philosophies and false beliefs. It is a statement of the reality of physical manifestation represented by Capricorn. The goat-footed god Pan, the pipe-playing god of wild places, is a much more authentic representation of raw nature than the Devil. Pan is by tradition elusive and rarely seen, unwilling to mix with mortals. His goat nature is lusty but without guile. He is playful and joyous, enjoying the simple pleasure of music in a woodland glade. Pan hides from the civilizing instincts of the civil, having no wish to be changed, improved or refined by abstracted principles. Pan is the uncomplicated power of things just as they are.

The astrological sign of Capricorn is one of active practicality. Its positive qualities are ambition, responsibility, efficiency, practicality and patience. Its negative qualities are worry, retaliation, stubbornness, suspicion and intolerance. The positive qualities provide the basis for a healthy stewardship of physical resources. The negative qualities provide the impetus for employing controlling and manipulative strategies. We see the positive qualities in the well-adjusted psyche; we see the negative qualities in our projections and fears.

The 26th Path is one of test, and the demonic figure fulfils the role of the challenger and initiator. This hybrid creation, consisting of a goat-headed man with the leathery wings of a bird and the claws of an eagle, wielding a burning brand, presents an image of the four elements as an unbalanced whole. Instead of the balanced harmony of the equal-armed cross and the enigmatic sphinx, the Devil portrays the effects of imbalance. The element of Fire is not internalized as a source of raw energy but used to wield power over others. Elemental Water, symbolized by the scorpion-like eagle claws, is misplaced as a support in the world which is the function of elemental Earth. Elemental Air, symbolized by the wings, belongs to the mind, not to the body. When applied to the body, elemental Air implies escapism from life. This pentagram normally represents the four elements, balanced and vivified by a fifth element, *akasa*, which is spirit. But here the pentagram is inverted. The demonic figure of Tarot Trump XV states the result of misused and unbalanced elemental qualities. This figure is a travesty of the human form. Distorted and twisted by lack of balance, the devil figure portrays human qualities in destructive combination. The figure represents the negative qualities of Capricorn: an intolerance of others, the need to retaliate to overcome imagined threats, the suspicion of difference, a stubbornness of view, the worry of the unsettled mind. These are the qualities which drive the witch-hunt, the pogrom, ethnic cleansing and racial hatred. These are the qualities which drive the wedge of separation into the seamless garment of the human family.

Legend has it that the Devil is but a fallen angel. Ironically, the name Lucifer means 'light bringer'. It has no demonic or dark connotations, though it has certainly acquired them over the passage of the centuries. Perhaps we have made a Devil from the world of matter. The insatiable appetite for consumption, aggrandizement, conquest and ownership is the history of both nations and individuals. This is the wheel of karma set spinning by the energy of unrequited desire. Its momentum projects life after life.

Seeking Clearly

Why do you see the speck in your neighbour's eye...

Matthew 7:3

The letter Ayin attributed to this Path signifies the eye. The eye sees only appearance. It is easily tricked by sleight of hand and illusion. However, with the dawning of mental clarity comes the development of insight which sees beyond appearance and illusion. This Path reflects the massed illusions of past and present. History testifies to the horrible reality of a separatist illusion. All discrimination, whether racial, sexual, religious or gender-based, feeds on the belief that the other, in whatever form or by whatever name represents a difference that is so extreme as to be demonic. Beliefs have the power to enslave or liberate. Though only a mental construction, belief lies at the heart of all culture and influences choices and actions. Compare Buddhist belief with Aztec belief, the guiding beliefs of ancient Rome or Nazi Germany. Beliefs have the power to influence and determine action.

Many beliefs are no more than shallow constructs drawn from prejudice and fear. Other beliefs are incorrect conclusions, drawn from inadequate information and poor observation. The earth is not flat, nor is it at the centre of the universe. Yet these beliefs once dominated thought and action. Such shared ideas were so powerful that to question them meant risking life and limb. Standing against the predominating cultural beliefs of the majority is a lonely and dangerous place to be. This represents the most extreme test that this path can invoke, as the pioneers of the physical sciences discovered. The discoveries of Copernicus, Galileo and Darwin, among others, shattered the illusions by which men lived. Such revelations were received as affronts to God and attacks upon the entire fabric of reality.

Ordinary folk face lesser challenges on this Path. Shattering the illusions which enslave and limit action is task enough. This Path is a necessary preparation for the birth of enlightened consciousness. The experience of enlightenment is most often documented by Eastern spiritual traditions but it is a universal landmark on the spiritual journey. The process of enlightenment is punctuated by enlightening experiences, both great and small. Far from being the comfortable and cosy highlights of a personal journey, these experiences are most often described as shattering and traumatic openings of vision onto naked and unadorned reality.

> ## SHATTERING THE ILLUSIONS
> Watch your mind as you respond to events both great and small. Observe especially where your own fears lie and how these might be projected onto particular groups of people. The daily news with its global content offers the opportunity to watch your own responses to other places, cultures and people. Watch your mind and observe what fills your thoughts. What do you think about most often? Discover how much mental energy is expended on your own behalf and how much is related to the well-being of others? Be non-judgmental in this process; simply watch the mind with the detached eye of an observer.

The essence of the enlightened mindset is simple. Enlightenment comes from seeing things just as they are. This injunction appears simplistically naïve. If it were so easy to follow, the streets of the world would be filled with the enlightened. But this is clearly not the case. Clarity of vision is constantly obscured by the never-ending stream of mental projections, labels and conceptual thought that makes up the entire panoply of the dualized mind. Watching the mind is the first step to transforming it. The encumbered mind brings ready-made preconceptions to each experience, imposes a pre-existing value system on fresh encounters and destroys the immediacy of the moment by spurious expectations. Put at its simplest, the encumbered mind shapes the experience of reality by the constant imposition of a value-loaded system. The adult mind projects the values of home and school, education and socialization continuously. These are the lenses of acquired cultural values, not the open eye of direct perception. The young child, free from the inhibitions of a mental straightjacket, is curious, fascinated, intrigued, puzzled and delighted by the discovery of the world. The childlike mind is closer to the enlightened state than the mind honed by education and socialized into the mores of a single social group. Unencumbered by value judgements and expectation, the child sees directly and appreciates with spontaneous expression. This is the essence of the Renewing Intelligence, the lively, opened and awakened mind which creates no false barriers but interacts with each experience as a fresh opportunity. How different this is from the stultified and contorted philosophy which once demonized the day-to-day experience of the world.

The 26th Path is concerned with the shattering of the many illusions that hold us prisoner either individually or as a group. In Tarot Trump XV, the demonic form has enslaved two figures who are in the process of coming to resemble his likeness. Yet they are chained to him only by loose fetters which might easily be lifted. Freedom is only a decision away. Of all the many illusions that plague the mind and destroy the spirit, one alone is central. Matter and spirit are integrated and united, not separate and opposed. This is the root illusion that spawns a host of fears which in turn breed a demonic brood of mental constructions, false beliefs and dehumanizing practices.

Awakening to the enormity of our shared illusions and their repercussions in the world is an act of freedom and personal liberation. As the shackles fall away, so vision clears with a smile of relief and recognition. The letter Ayin, which signifies the eye, also carries the meaning of mirth, the irrepressible expression of contained joy. With liberation comes mirth, so much healthier than the mocking laughter of an imaginary Devil.

EVOCATION

Welcome to my kingdom. Are you afraid? Even my name strikes fear into the heart of the unenlightened. I bear the fears and hatreds of everyone. You are all so afraid of life itself. I am Lord of The Gates of Matter. Do you hate the world and all that is in it? Do you dread the bonds of matter? How foolish is the mind that replaces wonder with fear. Yet it is not my task to enlighten you. You must enlighten yourself. I do not ask that you chain yourself to me in slavish adoration – yet so many choose this path. When you only seek endless idle pursuits, gratification of your physical senses and material pleasure, then you chain yourself to me. It is not my task to release you. You must release yourself. I do not demand your adoration, yet you give it so freely, so greedy are you to own and possess.

My path is that of the Renewing Intelligence. You cannot own this great power. I offer only the appearance of stability and form, yet in truth all is change. I renew myself constantly. How can you own that which is constantly changing? It is not my task to show you these things, you must see them for yourself. Behold the letter Ayin, the eye of wisdom which sees things as they really are and brooks no deception. How many of you view the world through insight?

I am Capricorn, the sea-goat; I am the principle of fixed earth. As such my halter hangs heavy on your shoulders for my domain appears to be fixed and inert. Yet this is my greatest deception. It is the trap that yawns at your feet and waits to consume you with the same desire that you consume the kingdom of form. Though you consume with a frenzy close to madness, you are never satisfied. You are ever hungry. I cannot be owned for I am the Renewing Intelligence. You cannot possess me, though many have tried.

The desire to own and possess is so strong that it turns against you with a great demonic power. In your ignorance you attribute this power to me but in truth it lies within you. It is not my task to show you this, for as long as you wish to be a slave of goods and chattels then I shall accept you. Come into my kingdom; all is not as you think.

INTERNALIZATION – THE 26TH PATH: HOD–TIPHARETH

Construct the Temple of Hod in the creative imagination. Find yourself standing beside the door of the Devil. The Archangel Michael lifts the tapestry curtain so that you may pass.

You emerge into a darkened chamber. It is difficult to make out quite where you are, there is so little light. From the darkness beyond your view there comes the sound of a mocking and sinister laugh. A lighted torch of burning rushes moves in the darkness. You draw closer to it as it seems to be the only source of illumination here. By its light you can make out the shape of a bulky form seated on a raised dais. As if to ensure your attention, the creature holds the burning brand aloft in order to be revealed to you. Now you see that this figure exhibits the upper body of a man but the lower body of a goat. Clawed feet grip the edge of the block-like perch. The face holds human features, yet it is curiously shaped like a great wedge. Curling horns sweep down from the top of his head. Leathery wings slowly flap at his back, moving together in a slow rhythm.

Before the block stand two naked figures. Each wears a chain around the neck which stretches to a metal ring set into the block. These two prisoners – one male, one female – are beginning to resemble the demon into whose kingdom they have come. Each has developed horns and a tail. Time seems to stand still. Not a word is spoken. You find yourself wondering about these prisoners. How long have they stood in the darkness of this place? What holds them here – perhaps fear? As you gaze at them you notice how loosely and inadequately they are chained. You wonder what might happen to you if you make a move on their behalf. You step forward and in one movement simply lift the chain from the neck of each prisoner in turn. Now that you have effected this, you wonder why this pair could not simply help each other. In an instant the great block and its demonic incumbent revolves, turning completely on its axis. The prisoners are quite vanished. The dark and miserable hall has vanished too. In the place of the dark and barren block, there is now a throne decorated with the fruits of the earth. Seated on the throne is no longer the demonic incumbent but a radiant being who appears to be composed of moving particles of light. The hall is now irradiated by brilliance and suffused with a soft glow.

You take in all the details of this extraordinary revolution. The face is now gentle and expresses openness. The hardened features of the mask-like face have entirely gone. The twin horns have vanished, replaced by plumes of iridescent and scintillating fire. The leathery wings have vanished, replaced now by folded wings of matter unknown. You both burst into the spontaneous laughter which comes only from a shared moment of truth and total marvel. With outstretched hand, you are offered a green stone as token of your trial. The figure speaks at last, 'I am a light bringer too. Welcome to my kingdom.'

When you are ready, return the way you came to the temple. When you are ready, leave through the doorway. Finally, dissolve all images and return to ordinary consciousness.

EXERCITIA SPIRITUALIA

Take the Following as Subjects for Meditation:

- Lord of the Gates of Matter
- The letter Ayin
- Mirth
- Capricorn
- The Renewing Intelligence
- The Devil
- The Shadow

Make Notes on:

- Tarot Trump XVI, The Devil

Visualize the Following and Record your Experiences:

- The Temple of Hod including the Archangel Michael
- The Journey of the 26th Path

CHAPTER 13

The Twenty-Fifth Path: Yesod–Tiphareth

FIGURE 21 THE 25TH PATH:
YESOD–TIPHARETH

TAROT TRUMP XIV,
TEMPERANCE

TABLE OF CORRESPONDENCES

The Journey: Tarot Trump. XIV, Temperance,
Daughter of the Reconcilers, Bringer
Forth of Life
Key: The Letter Samech, meaning a prop
Simple Letter: Anger
Spiritual Significance: Sagittarius
Text: The Intelligence of Probation
Colour in Atziluth: Blue
Colour in Briah: Yellow
Colour in Yetzirah: Green
Colour in Assiah: Dark vivid Blue

COMMENTARY

*The Twenty-fifth Path is the Intelligence of Probation or
Temptation, and it is so called because it is the primary
temptation by which the creator trieth all righteous persons.*

The 25th Path connects Yesod, the ninth Sephirah, with Tiphareth, the sixth
Sephirah. Its route moves upwards to the heart of the Tree of Life via the
Central Pillar. This Path forges a direct line of contact between the personality and another level of being, sometimes referred to as the Individuality.
The 24th, 25th and 26th Paths together forge the link which transfers the
centre of consciousness from the Astral or Psychological Triangle to the
Ethical or Moral Triangle. This transfer is not completed until the experience
of each of these three Paths has been internalized. Tiphareth represents the
birthplace of an entirely different form of consciousness. The 25th Path rises
on the Central Pillar, which is also the Pillar of Equilibrium, the place where
oppositions are brought into harmony. This journey balances the oppositions represented as the qualities Hod and Netzach. This Path is one of
vertical and horizontal realignment.

Mysterium Coniunctionis

The world of alchemical symbols definitely does not
belong to the rubbish heap of the past but stands in a
very real and living relationship to our most recent
discoveries concerning the psychology of the
unconscious.

C.G. Jung, *Mysterium Coniunctionis*

It was Jung who rediscovered the psychological and spiritual basis of the
alchemical tradition. The popular conception of the alchemist feverishly
working on the transformation of lead into gold is not a scientific superstition but a metaphorical description of the recreation of self from the leaden
to the golden. It therefore presents a parallel process to other psycho-spiritual
paradigms. Its symbols may appear unfamiliar and bizarre but as Jung has
pointed out, 'However abstruse and strange the language and imagery of

the alchemists may seem to the uninitiated, they become vivid and alive as soon as comparative research reveals the relationship of the symbol to processes in the unconscious.'[1] The *Mysterium Coniunctionis*, or reconciliation of the opposites, is a central alchemical theme. The symbolism implicit in the external processes of extraction and recombination provides an appropriate vehicle for metaphors of dynamic inner change. The alchemical intention *solve et coagula* (dissolve and coagulate) summarizes the modus operandi as being one of separation and analysis followed by synthesis and consolidation. Every plateau where a state of harmony has been achieved gives rise to a new process of separation because the seeds for a higher level of synthesis are already present. This pattern mirrors the dynamics of the Tree of Life which present the stages for both separation (in the twin pillars) and reunification (in the central pillar). The dynamic of polarized opposition followed by harmonious reconciliation, succeeded by another level of duality and so on, is the exact way in which the Tree is climbed. Malkuth represents a unified state, but it also looks towards the polarity of Hod and Netzach which is implicit through Yesod. The separation into the different spheres of Hod and Netzach precedes the unity attainable at Tiphareth. From Tiphareth two further levels of separation are indicated. The first of these is the polarity of the Greater Mysteries represented by Chesed and Geburah. The second is the polarity of the Supreme Mysteries represented by Binah and Chockmah, even though this level is beyond the arena of conscious self-realization. The lateral paths of the Tree – the 27th, 19th and 14th – each serve to bring dynamic oppositions to resolution. The Paths of the Central Pillar serve to carry the resolved opposites forward towards the next level of separation. The phrase *solve et coagula* aptly describes the inner process of the Tree through which the self is recreated. The goal of alchemy expressed through the symbolism of the Philosopher's Stone – namely, permanence, immortality, incorruptibility and androgyny – symbolically describes the same goal as that expressed in current psychotherapeutics: an integrated wholeness.

The alchemical journey and that represented upon the Tree proceeds through drawing out oppositions in order to effect a later recombination. Bearing in mind that these opposed qualities simultaneously hold imbedded patterns of unity, any symbolic representations must convey both precision and ambiguity, infinite openness and specific relationship. In other words, such symbols must pinpoint the paradoxical nature implicit in the process. The symbols of alchemy have much in common with the symbols of the Kabbalah, and in many instances prove to be identical. The primal masculine-feminine duality is expressed through the symbolism of king and queen, emperor and empress, Sol and Luna, or simply as the red and the white.

Tarot Trump XIV which is assigned to this path, depicts an alchemical process of balancing opposing qualities of being. A winged angelic figure pours water from one chalice to another. The figure stands with one foot in a pool while the other rests at the edge. Irises frame the near side of the pool. On the far side, a path leads from the water's edge to a distant mountain range where it passes between two peaks. A sun shines from between the two mountains. This is a Kabbalistic landscape. The twin peaks are representations of Binah and Chockmah, with the rising light of Kether set between them. The pool represents the astral waters of the Sephirah Yesod, the source of the 25th Path. Speaking of the symbolism of water, Jung says, 'Water in all its forms – sea, lake, river, spring – is one of the commonest typifications of the unconscious.'[2] Not only is water present here as a source or reservoir, but it is being poured from vessel to vessel by the angelic figure. The opposition represented by the two vessels is emphasized most clearly when one chalice is gold and the other silver. But two golden vessels express the unity immanent within both partners of the relationship. The act of pouring from one chalice to another, continuously combining and recombining elements, is suggestive of a process of dynamic change and reformation until a new state of equilibrium is reached.

The process of realignment between the potencies of Hod and Netzach is one of preparation for the intended outcome: rebirth at the Tiphareth centre. Each of the three paths reaching Tiphareth represents a process which precedes the birth of this new level of consciousness. The work of the 25th Path is accomplished by the transcendent function represented by the angelic being as a power of higher consciousness. Angelic figures convey an undivided consciousness. As winged figures from a non-human realm, angels symbolize the flight of spiritual liberation and the power to rise above any present dualism. Tarot Trump XIV, is called Temperance, which suggests a moderating or mediating influence between two parties, but the Trump is also called the Daughter of the Reconcilers and Bringer Forth of Life. Both these titles point to the dynamic function of this Trump. By crossing the 27th Path, which breaks down all false boundaries between the seventh and eighth Sephirah, the 25th Path draws horizontally on the new conjunction between Hod and Netzach and carries this forward into a vertical thrust towards Tiphareth. In terms of ordinary life, when the forces of intellect and imagination have been separately developed and then jointly synthesized, the journey towards a mystical consciousness becomes a possibility.

THE TWO CHALICES

Imagine yourself holding two chalices, one of silver and one of gold. One contains a red liquid and the other a white. Your task is to mix and blend the contents of the two chalices so that they become identical. You begin to pour a little from one container into the other, observing the continuously changing colour. This action will need to be repeated many times before the work is achieved. Use this process as a focus for meditative reflection.

Initiation

> The initiate who ritually enacts the slaying,
> dismemberment and scattering of Osiris and afterwards
> his resurrection in the green wheat, experiences in this
> way the permanence and continuity of life, which
> outlasts all changes of form and phoenix-like rises anew
> from its own ashes.

C.G. Jung, *The Archetypes and the Collective Unconscious*

As the dynamic pattern through the Tree of Life becomes clearer, certain themes begin to stand out. This is a movement of separation and synthesis, but it is also a movement of successive and continuous death and rebirth. Marking these significant moments is in essence the purpose of all initiatory events, whether through the Mysteries and its offshoots or though more traditional religious avenues. The Church has used adult baptism and communion as rites of entry into the body spiritual, but the Mysteries and all systems preserving a graded and longer journey mark each and every turning point through initiatory ritual. The purpose of such rites is to effect and mark the transition from one level of awareness to its successive entry point. Like more general rites of passage, initiation demarcates one phase from another and serves to indelibly imprint the unconscious component of psyche with the relevant symbols for the next phase. Successful initiation brings a multi-levelled potency to bear. Marking the moment releases the past and empowers the future. Failed initiation is no more than empty theatre rendered impotent with an inappropriate symbolic content or else thwarted by the inner unpreparedness of the candidate. Much glamour has surrounded the whole issue of occult initiation. This false view has most probably been engendered by the secrecy surrounding such events. The Eleusinian Mysteries of Greece, however, preserved the nature of their central epiphany through a strictly enforced policy of absolute secrecy. This enabled the mystique and numen attached to the moment of supreme revelation to remain intact. It is most probable that an ear of wheat was displayed as the central epiphany; disclosure would have rendered it to be an ordinary and mundane object. Sundered from its rich symbolic connotations, an ear of wheat is just that. The power of an epiphany lies in its symbolic impact. Theatrical ritual, carefully chosen words, symbolic actions and purposive atmosphere all serve to separate mundane use from symbolic resonance and implant the vitalizing influence of a chosen epiphany. In this way wheat becomes a symbol of the part and the whole, of the process of transform-ation and of rebirth itself. Bread remains a sacramental object for these same reasons.

Though it may seem to contradict the whole history of initatory processes, self-initiation is not without significance. Although it lacks the witnessing company of others – which always serves to reinforce the import of the moment – and the surprise element often found in rites of initiation, self-initiation can motivate and serve as a statement of intent and purpose. If supported by relevant symbols, self-initiation can still effect the movement from one phase to another. This remains the *raison d'être* of the solitary walker on the spiritual path.

The 25th Path prepares the way for the coming of the initiation of Tiphareth. Together, the three journeys taken on the 25th, 24th and 26th Paths culminate in the experience of Tiphareth, the place where mystical consciousness comes to birth. This is the work of the Bringer Forth of Life. It is not until these three paths have been negotiated that the consciousness of Tiphareth can become stabilized. In order to reach Tiphareth, the Veil of Paroketh has to be negotiated. This first abyss can only be crossed when the initiations of Hod, Netzach and Yesod have been internalized.

The Tree of Life provides a very clear initiatory structure through its detailed analysis of the Path of Being and Becoming. Its rich symbolic vocabulary provides the ready-made framework for a graded path of psycho-spiritual development. The opportunity to develop such a system was not lost upon those involved in the esoteric movement at the turning of the 20th century in England and, to a lesser degree, France. The Hermetic Order of the Golden Dawn turned Thirty-two Paths of Wisdom into an initiatory sequence as an ongoing process of separation and synthesis through the three levels of the Tree.

The Dark Night of the Soul

> The highest state of the mystic life can only be reached
> when there has been a complete death of the selfhood,
> when all images and intermediaries have been
> abandoned, and when a man has entered that Dark
> Silence, that Nothingness, that Wayless Way, where the
> sons of God lose and at the same time find themselves.

F.C. Happold, *Mysticism*

The 25th Path is one of deep and radical transformation. It is assigned to the
Intelligence of Probation with all the implications of test and trial. The
Tibetan, writing through the mind of Alice Bailey, also speaks of the Path
of Probation as an inevitable and primary developmental phase of inner
growth. Accordingly, 'The Probationary Path precedes The Path of Initiation
and marks that period of life when the Individual chooses to assist the forces
of evolution by consciously working at character building.'[3] This schema
can be usefully applied to the journey represented by the Tree of Life. It
commences in Malkuth with the injunction 'Know Thyself', which continues to serve as a guiding light at every stage of the Path. Conscious
character building begins in Malkuth through the application of discrimination, which is the Virtue of Malkuth. Character building grows from
self-knowledge and self-awareness. Conscious choice effects a selection of
activities, opportunities and experiences which begin the work of shaping
aspiration, motivation and dedication. Such lowly beginnings may seem to
be an uninteresting presage to the birth of mystical consciousness – yet this
is the foundation that cannot be ignored. Character and personality are the
rootstock upon which higher consciousness may eventually bloom.
Conscious character building represents the first attempt at seeking internal
balance and equilibrium. Gaining control over elements within the personality represents the first move towards self-mastery. The clarion call
'Know Thyself' assumes an increasingly greater significance in daily life and
becomes the first ground of transformation. Its full significance is yet to be
unveiled through the further reaches of the Tree, but at the commencement
of the journey it serves as a pointer to the injunction 'To Know in Order to
Serve'. This paraphrases the words of the Tibetan since it expresses the same
desire – namely, to 'assist the forces of evolution'. These elements form the

backdrop to the 25th Path, which directly continues the work of the 32nd Path from Malkuth to Yesod.

The 25th Path cannot be undertaken until the transformational processes of the 32nd Path are established. This journey brings a refining and reformulation of the same precepts which initially propelled the inner journey. Self-knowledge now focuses on balancing the oppositions represented by Hod and Netzach. Assisting the forces of evolution in the name of service acquires a meaning and significance unavailable from the perspective of Malkuth. The 25th Path is one of test and trial which recapitulates earlier processes but with greater intensity and ferocious purpose.

The spiritual journey represented upon the 25th Path is a familiar one in religious traditions holding mystical byways. Destined for the mystical Sephirah Tiphareth, this path is one of preparation for the birth of mystical consciousness. The threefold model of selfhood is so frequent as to be the most common pattern. Catholic theology divides the mystical path into three phases: the Way of Purgation, the Way of Illumination and the Way of Union:

> The Way of Purgation has two main objectives: first of all a complete detachment from and renunciation of the things of the sense, and the death of the egocentric life, so that divine life may be born in the soul and union with the Godhead attained; and secondly, a continuous cleansing of the perceptions and a scouring of the windows of the soul, so that the light of a new reality may stream in and completely illuminate and transform it.[4]

The Indian mystic Radhakrishnan also speaks of three stages of Purification, Concentration and Identification:

> The way of growth lies through a gradual increase in impersonality by an ever deeper and more intense unifying of the self with a greater reality than itself. In this process prayer, worship, meditation, philosophy, art and literature all play their part, since all help in purifying the inner being, disposing it more and more for contact with the divine.[5]

All mystical literature speaks uncompromisingly of a surrender of the small self in order to make way for the birth of a greater self which is paradoxically no self at all.

The trials presented on this path have been summarized as an experience known in Western literature as the Dark Night of the Soul. Personal testimonies speak of the anguish and suffering of this period: 'I am plunged in such spiritual darkness that I think myself utterly lost in falsehood and illusion, deceiving both myself and others. This temptation is the most terrible of all.'[6] This is a period of fatigue and lassitude which contrasts painfully with the sustained growth of mystical awareness. It is often marked by ill-heath, a depressive mental state, intellectual disinterest, failure in relationships and an abiding and terrible sense of loss. It is, as Evelyn Underhill has said, 'a deeply human process'. It is 'the sorting-house of the spiritual life'. 'Here we part from the nature mystics, the mystical poets and all those who shared in and were contented with the illuminated vision of reality. Those who go on are the great and strong spirits, who do not seek to *know* but are driven to *be*.'[7]

This Path leads to realization of mystical Beauty represented as Tiphareth, but entry here is marked by a gulf known as the Veil of Paroketh. This first lesser abyss is a reflection of a second and greater abyss lying before Daath. Living out this Path brings turmoil and intense difficulty. Old identity must fall away in order to cross or pass through the veil which separates the common dualized consciousness from a rare, unified and mystical consciousness. This Path represents the passing away of the personality in favour of the greater interests and perspective encompassed by a new centre of consciousness termed the Individuality. This Path is one of transition between the fading needs of the small self and the nascent aspirations of the different paradigm of selfhood. The veil cannot be penetrated until the immense shift of motivation, intention and dedication has been fully internalized.

The values of the little ego which seek to own, demarcate and possess must give way to the values of the Higher Self which are universalized and seek nothing for the separate self. The very foundations of the small personal life must dissolve completely. The values and aspirations of the personality must fall away. The personal work completed through the psychological triangle culminates in ego-death, which makes way for soul-birth. The 25th Path carries the awakening impulse from the Psychological Triangle to Tiphareth, where the Individuality becomes self-conscious. This transfer is not an intellectual process. Personal testaments speak of an agonizing inner turmoil of trust and faith. This is the Intelligence of Probation or Temptation. It is called, 'the primary temptation by which the creator trieth all righteous persons'. St John of the Cross was the first to describe this inner journey in the terminology of the Dark Night. He speaks through a mystical language which has much in common with the vocabulary of alchemical symbolism and its Eastern counterpart, Taoist philosophy. Such language defies common sense, rational thought and everyday logic.

This Path is attributed to Sagittarius, which is both the archer and the centaur, half-man and half-beast. This dual nature of the centaur well represents the competing interests between the universal and the particularized self, between the higher and lower drives. But the bow of the centaur symbolizes spiritual aspiration. When the arrow flies ahead marking out a target for the future, the goal of the journey is kept perpetually in mind. It is sincere aspiration and steadfast intent which makes it possible to move forward into uncharted territory when the journey becomes a trial. Despite the testing nature of this path, the journey itself offers support, symbolized by the letter Samech, meaning a prop. The rounded shape of the letter symbolizes a rough-hewn rock set on end. It is a much needed symbol of stability at a time of great instability and change. The rainbow Qesheth is also associated with this path. It is a symbol of hope and of promise.

EVOCATION

Welcome to my kingdom. I have watched you from afar. I have seen all your trials and tribulations. I watched you awaken to the inner realities of the greater life with joy. Now I who love you must also become your tester and challenger, for I seek those who will bear the tasks of the great work willingly. I grant admission to a new realm of beauty and harmony where unity prevails. If you seek my realm with the passion of your whole being then be prepared to enter the crucible of alchemical fire. Be prepared for trial and test. Be prepared for the time of desolation and despair. Be prepared to walk unaided and alone in the wilderness of your being. All that is unbalanced, disproportionate, excessive and inharmonious will pass away. You will be tempted by the glamour of psychic gift. You will be tempted by the potency of intellectual ability. You will be tempted by the power of imaginative creation. But if you seek my kingdom, offer these gifts in the service of what you do not yet know and they will be returned to you, replenished a thousand times over. I stand at the gateway to the greater life. I am called the Bringer Forth of Life. But the personality which you know so well and wear so keenly cannot walk with you except as servant to a new master of your own making. I ask that you lose the lesser to gain the greater. This is the gift I offer.

INTERNALIZATION – THE 25TH
PATH: YESOD–TIPHARETH

Construct the Temple of Yesod in the creative imagination. Find yourself standing before the door of Temperance. The Archangel Gabriel lifts the tapestry curtain so that you may pass.

You emerge into a dry and arid landscape. You see a blazing sun in the sky. It beats down on you as you walk. Soon your mouth is parched and dry. You crave water. You carry a bow and arrow over your shoulder. You wonder if you are alone in this landscape. You take out an arrow from the quiver and make ready to shoot it into the air. Perhaps it might be spotted and taken as a distress sign. More in hope than certainty you draw back the bow. As the arrow is loosed, every thought of your being is focused on your intent. You wait but nothing changes. You must continue alone. You walk on, not even knowing which way you are going. The skies unexpectedly darken and clouds roll in. The air becomes cooler. It is a welcome relief to you. Droplets of rain begin to fall, then it begins to rain steadily. You dance in the falling rain and feel refreshed. As you look up you see that a rainbow has formed in the sky. You delight in the rainbow overhead; it forms an arch in the heavens.

You continue on with hope renewed. In the far distance you make out the shape of a clump of trees rising in the landscape. You quicken your step and come to a desert oasis. What joy, here is shade and water. You rush to the pool and fling yourself in total abandonment into the water. With some surprise you hear the sound of deep laughter close by. From beneath the shade of a tree a figure steps forward, swathed in desert garb. You can make out only a deep penetrating gaze above a linen cloth wrapped around the lower face. A hand extends a golden tray set with fruits, sweetmeats and a goblet of deep-red wine. You are sorely tempted by the prospect of food and shade and plentiful water. Yet something deep inside will not let you rest. You gather all your inner strength and decline the offer. You take your leave. You walk on and turn back for a last glance. But there is nothing to see, the landscape is quite empty. Ahead of you the rainbow still fills the sky.

When you are ready, return the way you came to the temple. When you are ready, leave through the doorway. Finally, dissolve all images and return to ordinary consciousness.

EXERCITIA SPIRITUALIA

Take the Following as Subjects for Meditation:

- Daughter of The Reconcilers, Bringer Forth of Life
- The letter Samech
- Anger
- Sagittarius
- The Intelligence of Probation
- The rainbow

Make Notes on:

- Tarot Trump XIV, Temperance

Visualize the Following and Record your Experiences:

- The Temple of Yesod including the Archangel Gabriel
- The Journey of the 25th Path

CHAPTER 14

The Twenty-Fourth Path: Netzach–Tiphareth

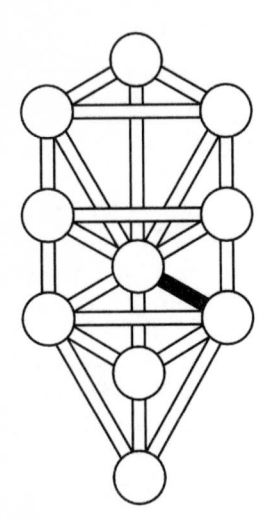

FIGURE 22 THE 24TH PATH:

NETZACH–TIPHARETH

TAROT TRUMP XIII,

DEATH

TABLE OF CORRESPONDENCES

The Journey: Tarot Trump. XIII, Death, Child of the Great Transformers, Lord of the Gates of Death

Key: The Letter Nun, meaning a fish

Simple Letter: Movement

Spiritual Significance: Scorpio

Text: The Imaginative Intelligence

Colour in Atziluth: Green Blue

Colour in Yetzirah: Dull Brown

Colour in Briah: Very dark Brown

Colour in Assiah: Livid Indigo Brown

COMMENTARY

The Twenty-fourth Path is the Imaginative Intelligence, and it is so called because it gives a likeness to all the similitudes which are created in like manner similar to its harmonious elegancies.

The 24th Path connects the seventh Sephirah, Netzach, with the sixth Sephirah, Tiphareth. It connects the Pillar of Mercy with the central Pillar of Consciousness or Equilibrium. Netzach is part of the Psychological Triangle but Tiphareth is part of the Ethical Triangle. This is one of three Paths which forge links to Tiphareth and lay the foundation for a new level of consciousness. It is one of the three Paths connecting the personality to the Individuality. The 25th, 26th and 24th journeys together represent a single process of reorientation. The 25th Path brings the opportunity to face the death of the ego or small self. The 24th Path brings the opportunity to face the death of limiting belief. The 26th Path brings the opportunity to face the death of purely material values. Fear is a limiting emotion. It has the power to paralyse action, dismantle autonomy and shrink all perspectives to the most rudimentary. These three paths taken together represent the overcoming of deep-seated human fears. On the 24th Path the fear of death is confronted. On the 26th Path the fear of the devil is confronted. On the 25th Path, the fear of losing self-identity is confronted. Only when these three fears have been conquered does it become possible to move forward. The 24th Path follows upon the Path of the Lightning Flash. It is therefore a path of particular potency.

Death, Rebirth and Renewal

Rebirth is an affirmation that must be counted among the primordial affirmations of mankind.

C.G. Jung, *The Archetypes and the Collective Unconscious*

Death and life are intermingled and intertwined. The body develops by renewal. Cells die daily but life continues. There are also parallel processes in the life of the psyche as stages emerge and then die away. Individuation or self-becoming is a process of natural transformation based upon death and rebirth. This is an ongoing process of growth and development in which the old dies away as the new comes to birth. This psychic process of self-renewal happens spontaneously and organically. 'Natural transformation processes announce themselves mainly in dreams,' Jung notes.[1] These dreams speak with a powerful voice and lodge in the mind. The rebirth symbolism is always evident even if not understood. Jung's observation – namely, that the natural process of transformation announces itself through a particular range of dream symbols – provides the key to the modus operandi of all effective psycho-spiritual systems. If individuation proceeds naturally accompanied by symbols which arise spontaneously, then might the same process be cultivated and precipitated through the application of the appropriate symbology? In this way this natural model of the individuation process becomes the pattern for what Jung calls 'technical transformation', such as the exercises of Yoga and in the West the tradition of *excercitia spiritualia*:

> These exercises represent special techniques prescribed in advance
> and intended to achieve a definite psychic effect, or at least
> promote it. ... They are, therefore, technical procedures in the
> fullest sense of the word; elaborations of the originally natural
> process of transformation. The natural or spontaneous
> transformations that occurred earlier, before there were any
> historical examples to follow, were thus replaced by techniques
> designed to induce transformation by imitating the same sequence
> of events.[2]

This is the way of Kabbalah too. It reanimates the substance of the renewing process by offering the range of symbols which precipitate rebirth, thereby seeking to induce transformation by imitating the same sequence. The same naturally occurring process of renewal and its related symbolism can also be brought vividly to life through ritualized drama in which the individual participates as a fully engaged player. As such, the player becomes a candidate for initiation, since engagement with the symbols of transformation at such a deep level of involvement brings transformation itself. The Egyptian rites of Osiris revealed the renewing power inherent in the symbolism of seed and corn. The famous Mysteries of Eleusis too centred upon the symbolism of grain. These ancient mystery dramas effected a radical transformation of being by engaging full attention in highly concentrated experiences which condensed and compressed the same elements that would naturally and organically arise within the psyche over a period of time. By engaging in the dramatized experience of life and death, most often through the life cycle of a divinity as a transpersonal mirror, the candidate comes to know the 'perpetual continuation of life through transformation and renewal'.[3] The twin poles of life and death are resolved through the single and greater encompassing cycle of life and death which transcends both polarities. A dualized consciousness belongs to the Lesser Mysteries and the ongoing work of the Astral or Psychological Triangle. A unified consciousness belongs to the Greater Mysteries and the Ethical and Moral Triangle. The shift from the one to the other necessitates a death and a rebirth.

The Inevitable Journey

> Now I see that if one doesn't know how to die, one can
> hardly know how to live.

Thich Nhat Hanh, *The Miracle of Mindfulness*

It is jokingly said that the only two certainties in life are death and taxes. It is also quite certain that you have had more conversations about your taxes than your death. The subject of death still remains a taboo.

In the long history of humanity, three perspectives on death have prevailed. The materialist, atheist or humanist sees the death of the body as the end of life. Religious teachings offer the hope of an afterlife in some form. Those religions which affirm that life is confined to but a single incarnation in the face of eternity proffer salvation only to their own believers and followers. Faith traditions which affirm a belief in reincarnation proffer a cyclic view of existence and an evolutionary model of the self. The Buddhist Wheel of Life or Wheel of Becoming, much like the Tree of Life encapsulates a theory of existence in a simple form that can be committed to memory. The cultural or spiritual view that we hold of death has a powerful effect on the way. The post-death state has also been the subject of theological speculation. Christianity has in earlier generations concentrated heavily on the reality of hell and purgatory as places of continuing existence where the soul atones.

The Tibetan writes:

> I speak about death as one who knows the matter from both the
> outer world and the inner-life expression: There is no death.
> There is, as you know, entrance into fuller life... For the
> unevolved, death is literally a sleep and a forgetting, for the mind
> is not sufficiently awakened to react to the storehouse of memory,

it is as yet practically empty. For the average good citizen, death
is a continuance of the living process in his consciousness and a
carrying forward of the interests and tendencies of the life ...
For the aspirant, death is an immediate entrance into a sphere
of service and of expression to which he is well accustomed and
which he recognizes as not new.[4]

The 24th Path is assigned to the Tarot Trump XIII, Death. This Trump
shows the familiar face of death. A skeleton clad in black armour sits astride
a white horse. Bodies lie beneath the hooves of his horses. The royal, the
young, the ordinary and the religious fall at his approach – there is no escape.
In the distance a pale river flows. Its far banks are in twilight. Here are
traditional images of death – the Grim Reaper and the River Styx. Yet here
is something else besides the certainty of death. Trump XIII also shows
images of spiritual transcendence. The figure of Death holds a banner, a
five-petalled rosette, and in the far distance the sun rises between two towers.
The banner displays the rose-cross which is a symbol of Tiphareth, the destination of this journey. The rising sun represents the continuous process of
recreation day by day, moment by moment. A dualist mindset separates birth
and death. It celebrates one and fears the other. A unified mindset views
both portals as aspects of one process of eternal becoming. Like the classic
yin and yang symbol, birth is in death, death is in birth, and both are united
by the process of becoming.

The fear of death, which is most often accompanied by the idea of
judgement, has long been used by orthodox institutions as an ideological
instrument to repress the human spirit. Medieval Europe was haunted by
the images and ideology of hell. The notion of the devil walks hand in hand
with historically frightening views on death and judgement. This triple
phantom has served to diminish, reduce and disempower humanity.

Tarot Trump XIII depicts one of humanity's greatest fears – the inevitability of death. Yet this very inevitability provides reason and justification
for engaging in a process of preparedness. Buddhism, in common with other
spiritual traditions, strenuously urges personal meditation on death. This
can take many forms. In some places such meditations are performed in
cremation grounds or in the vicinity of a corpse. Such immediacy both
shocks and awakens. Facing the inevitability of your own death brings a
sense of purpose and meaning to daily life. Quite simply, this realization
gives a perspective to all that you do.

Buddhism offers specific meditative practices which include first contemplating the disadvantages and advantages of engaging in this form of meditation. The inevitability of death and the uncertain extent of a lifespan are contemplated along with the understanding that at the point of death it is only the spiritual achievement garnered in life that has value. Neither possessions nor qualifications serve any purpose in the face of death. This form of meditation sets the context in which a more personal meditation can proceed. A second technique involves visualizing your own deathbed scene. Though death does not always take place peacefully in the presence of loved ones, such preparation is of great benefit for anyone with courage enough to undertake it. This form of meditation is further developed through a specialized spiritual practice which recapitulates the process of disintegration as the subtle and physical vehicles disengage. Many traditions suggest the simple practice of reviewing each day with a closing meditation or review. This not only brings a quality of mindfulness and continuity to life but also serves as a preparation for death. Not facing the reality of death is the worst preparation of all.

THE FINAL JOURNEY

Imagine yourself on your own deathbed as fully as you are able. See that your friends and family are gathered. Who will come to be with you at this important time? Who would not travel to be with you? Spend time in reviewing what you have done with the life now passing away. What do you discover?

This is a powerful meditation which has the potential to bring a real sense of renewal to daily life.

The Death of the Ego

> From now on, for the rest of our lives, we must make
> the effort to free ourselves from our ego.

Lama Sherab Gyaltsen Amipa, *The Opening of the Lotus*

Although this Trump is most often interpreted as physical death, and this is not an inappropriate meaning, it also and more importantly refers to the death of the ego with all its demands for self-satisfaction. This is a Path of deep transformation. This Trump is called the Child of the Great Transformers. The successful crossing of the gulf before Tiphareth represents a process of deep personal change. The expanded perspective of self and the universalizing nature of this shift brings a framework for choices, aspirations and intentions. The centre of consciousness is transferred from the Astral to the Ethical Triangle. While the forces of the Astral Triangle predominate, life choices remain haphazard, motives remain mixed, aspirations remain changeable. As the move beyond the Astral Triangle into the Ethical Triangle is established and stabilized, an abiding sense of life's purpose becomes known step by step. This inner direction finally becomes actualized as the personality becomes the servant, no longer the master.

Accomplishing the death of the ego is difficult. It does not happen without conscious effort and self-awareness. This goal is a major concern of Buddhism. Its teachings offer a clear path through the maze of self-delusion. 'The chief purpose of spiritual training is the transformation of the mind... This training should chiefly cause us to abandon our selfishness and initiate transformation of our mind.'[5] Beyond the miasma of egoistic consciousness, the seeds of the awakening enlightened mind emerge. This is the emergence of *Bodhicitta*. *Bodhi* refers to the awakening of Buddahood, *citta* refers to the mind. Bodhicitta is the awakening of the Buddha mind. This is the consciousness of Tiphareth. This Path is assigned to the letter Nun, signifying a fish. The symbolism of the fish cannot be separated from the symbolism of water. Water in any form represents the fluid nature of the unconscious; it represents the collective consciousness as ocean or individualized consciousness in the form of a droplet. Water represents the realm without boundaries. As one of the Simple Letters, Nun is assigned to the quality of movement. This too suggests the dynamic quality of life and progression. The element of water related to the Path signifies the universal waters of the womb which we have all inhabited. This is the place where rapid and purposeful transformation takes place. The 24th Path is assigned to Scorpio, which represents the process of spiritual transformation from one state to another. It signifies the unrelenting desire to penetrate deeply into life's most difficult or even forbidden areas, often through occult, metaphysical or spiritual practices. The two symbols representing Scorpio, the scorpion and the eagle, are very similar to the alchemical pair of eagle and toad. The one symbolizes the liberated spirit, the other represents spirit bound by earthly limitation. Scorpio is assigned to the Tree of Life more often than any other astrological sign. The Tree of Life is a graded pathway of multiple transformations.

The metaphysical paths of East and West reveal some remarkable similarities. Both systems offer a graded structure of holistic development. Both systems recognize that achieving the goal of transformed mind requires participation, involvement, commitment and assistance. The Eastern guru and the Western teacher or master serve the same purpose. The Lam Rim, the graded path to enlightenment, and the Thirty-two Paths of the Tree each represent the process of engagement. Psychosynthesis too has much in common with both the method and intent of Kabbalah and Buddhism. It also, 'definitely affirms the reality of spiritual experience', and recognizes that, 'there have always been a certain number of human beings who were not, and could not be satisfied with normal achievement'.[6] To these it offers a wider and higher type of psychosynthesis – namely, Spiritual Psychosynthesis:

> The basic premise or hypothesis is that there exists – in addition to those parts of the unconscious which we have called the lower and middle unconscious, including the collective unconscious – another vast realm of our inner being for the most part neglected by the science of psychology, although its nature and its human value are of a superior quality. This higher realm has been known throughout the ages and in the last decade some daring investigators have started to study it in a scientific way.[7]

This is an exciting and daring statement. Assagioli calls this the realm of the *superconscious*. It represents the level of mind which generates the superior manifestations of the human psyche: the creative imagination, intuition, aspiration and even genius itself. 'Viewed in terms of energy, we may consider the contents of the superconscious as energies having a higher frequency than some of the contents of the lower consciousness... The difference – and it is very real – consists in what is specific to the superconscious in terms of certain values.'[8] Just as Buddhism offers a specialized path towards the birth of the Bodhicitta mind, so at this stage Spiritual Psychosynthesis offers a particular and more specialized range of images and techniques. Both systems, however, still draw upon methods and approaches which are characterized by the active use of the imagination.

The key to so many meditative practices is visualization, which relies in the power of the imagination to create and engage with images in the mind. Buddhist visualizations too are often detailed and highly complex. Planting such images in the mind necessitates a developed imagination. The 24th Path is assigned to the Imaginative Intelligence. This Path connects Netzach, the Sephirah of the imaginative mind, with Tiphareth, which represents the birth of a new mode of thought. As the initiation of Tiphareth draws closer, the beginner's mind becomes eclipsed. The fragmented 'monkey mind', which jumps from thought to thought as a monkey leaps from branch to branch, has been transformed. The linear mind, self-limiting and incomplete, has been expanded. The stream of consciousness has been redirected. Jean Houston speaks of a 'holographic mode' of mind; Rudolf Steiner writes of 'continuous consciousness'. The Imaginative Intelligence is the vehicle on which this transformation rides. The Imaginative Intelligence is fully rounded, being both analytical and pictorial, intellectually grounded and emotionally authentic. The creative imagination carries with it the essence of transformation.

The Sepher Yetzirah states that the Imaginative Intelligence is so called, 'because it gives a likeness to all the similitudes which are created in like manner similar to its harmonious elegancies'. In other words, it is through the open and receptive nature of the imaginative mind that the personality forms a likeness similar to the harmonious elegancies projected by the higher self. Without imagination no change other than a naturally occurring, spontaneously generated process is possible. Imagination brings the emotional quality of rapport and empathy. The seed of compassion is planted through the imaginative facility, for without the simple ability to put yourself in another's shoes it is impossible to identify with the suffering of others. Should you doubt the power of the Imaginative Intelligence, imagine as fully as you can that you have just received news of the death of your closest and most dearly beloved friend!

It is through the Imaginative Intelligence that the transformation of being proceeds. The awakened imagination permits the internalization of transpersonal symbols, inner dialogue and imaginative evocation which constitute the curriculum of Spiritual Psychosynthesis. It is clear that this approach has much in common with the modus operandi of both Kabbalah and Buddhism. Assagioli suggests identification with abstract, geometrical and natural symbols and immersion in great mythic themes such as The Grail Quest and Dante's *Divine Comedy*. These themes have much in common with the renewing Mysteries of the past. Time may have elapsed but the potency of rebirth symbolism remains undimmed. It is through the Imaginative Intelligence that archetypal symbols become personal process. It is through the Imaginative Intelligence that the Victory of Netzach becomes the shining Beauty of Tiphareth. This is, as the birth of Bodhicitta, the realization of a mystical consciousness, the emergence of the holographic mind and the birth of continuous consciousness. Once the universality of life and mind has been revealed it becomes impossible to return to the localized perspective of the small self.

EVOCATION

Welcome to my kingdom. Come look upon my face without fear. I am your future and your past. My very name strikes a terror deep in your heart. For the world misunderstands my function. I am truly the great initiator. It is by me that you may measure yourself, not by that which you have gained. Consciousness alone cannot be destroyed. If you have become a being of light in your own right, by virtue of your own labours, then I shall merely be your ferryman. If you come to me as a corpse in the mind, I cannot create light where there has been none.

I am with you all the time. I am perpetually with you. Where is the child you used to be? If the child had not been transformed, you would be imprisoned within your own childish state. I am commonly known as Death by those who fear me, but by the wise I am called Child of the Great Transformers. Are you willing to be transformed? Your new self may only come to birth through the death of the infant personality. Thus are all initiates called the twice born. They are also those who face death-in-life. Do you seek the initiation into the greater life or are you content as you are? Will you journey or will you rest? Will you awaken or will you sleep? Do you seek me? I am the Great Transformation and I will transform you.

INTERNALIZATION – THE 24TH PATH: NETZACH–TIPHARETH

Construct the Temple of Netzach in the creative imagination. Find yourself standing beside the door of Death. The Archangel Haniel lifts the tapestry curtain so that you may pass.

You emerge upon a riverbank. The river is swathed in mist. It is early morning. Dawn is just breaking. Upon the far bank a sun rises between two towers. But this place has an eerie feel to it. The sky seems yellow in colour and a deep silence fills the air. You walk on and become accustomed to the scenery. Now you see that ahead of you two bodies lie entwined on the ground.

As you stand, you can hear the unmistakable sound of hooves but the early morning mist still obscures your vision. The sound of a horse neighing is somewhere close by. You hear the sound of metal on metal. The pale mist parts like a veil. A white horse now comes into view. Its rider is clad in black shining armour. He carries a banner emblazoned with a rosette.

It flutters in the early morning breeze. The horse is slowed as the rider sees you. The bridle of the horse jingles as horse and rider approach. Finally the horse is reined to a halt close to where you stand. You feel that the rider is scrutinizing you from behind the vizor. Nothing is said and a heavy silence hangs in the air. Questions are beginning to form in your mind. The rider slowly raises a gauntletted hand and lifts the vizor. From within, a whitened skull looks out at you from empty sockets. Now you know where you are and whom you are with. A cold fear grips you. You are transfixed to the spot. The rider of the pale horse dismounts and approaches you. The figure now stands directly in front of you. Words fill your mind though nothing is said. A question arises: 'Do you trust me?' This is a strange question, but you cannot escape from its challenge. You must answer from the heart. You may surrender to the unknown or flee and return to the familiar territory of waking consciousness. Make your choice and act accordingly now. You hear the sound of a sword being drawn from its scabbard. You have chosen the path of willing surrender. Death looks you right in the face. He gestures and bids you kneel before him. In token of your trust, you kneel before him in total surrender.

You recall the story of the Green Knight who came to Arthur's court and placed his head at the mercy of Gawain. Before you have time to dwell on the tale you hear the sound of steel upon air. Yet you are not afraid for you have done all that has been asked of you. You have given yourself willingly in total surrender.

The blade passes through you. Your head falls to the floor. Yet you have suffered no diminution of consciousness. Death himself has been trans-formed. The fearsome figure in dark armour has gone. You rise to see a beautiful woman with soft features and a gentle face, wearing a simple robe. She seems to radiate with a brilliant inner light. She smiles at your surprise and sweeps up the severed head with her hand. In an instant it is restored to you.

When you are ready, return the way you came into the temple. When you are ready, leave through the doorway. Finally, dissolve all images and return to ordinary consciousness.

EXERCITIA SPIRITUALIA

Take the Following as Subjects for Meditation:

- Child of the Great Transformers, Lord of the Gates of Death
- The letter Nun
- Movement
- Scorpio
- The Imaginative Intelligence

Make Notes on:

- Tarot Trump XIII, Death

Visualize the Following and Record your Experiences:

- The Temple of Netzach including the Archangel Haniel
- The Journey of the 24th Path

CHAPTER 15

Tiphareth – Beauty

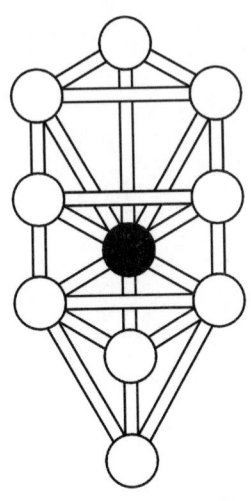

FIGURE 23 THE SEPHIRAH TIPHARETH

TABLE OF CORRESPONDENCES

God-Name: Jehovah Aloah va Daath – God made manifest in the sphere of the mind

Archangel: Raphael

Order of Angels: The Malachim, the Kings

Magical Image : A Child, A King, A Sacrificed God

Spiritual Experience: Vision of the Harmony of Things

Symbols: Lamen, Rose-Cross, Calvary Cross, Truncated Pyramid, Cube

Mundane Chakra: The Sun

Personal Chakra: The Anahata or Heart Chakra

Text: The Mediating Intelligence

Virtue: Devotion to the Great Work

Vice: Bigotry, Zealotry, Spiritual Pride

Titles: Zoar Anpin, The Lesser Countenance, Adam, Melekh, The King

Colour in Atzilut : Clear rose Pink

Colour in Briah: Yellow

Colour in Yetzirah: Rich salmon Pink

Colour in Assiah: Golden Amber.

Tarot Cards: The Four Sixes

Six of Wands: Victory

Six of Cups: Joy

Six of Swords: Earned success

Six of Pentacles: Material success

COMMENTARY

The Sixth Path is called the Mediating Intelligence because in it are multiplied the influxes of the Emanations; for it causes that influence to flow into all the reservoirs of the blessings with which they themselves are united.

The sixth Sephirah, Tiphareth, meaning Beauty, holds a special significance. It occupies the central position at the very heart of the Tree. It can be seen as the pivotal point on which the entire Tree is balanced. Placed on the Pillar of Equilibrium, Tiphareth is a place of balance and transformation where ascending and descending potencies meet. Tiphareth is called the Lesser Countenance, and is the place where Kether, the Great Countenance, is reflected. Tiphareth reflects the forces of The Supreme Mysteries into the lower reaches of the Tree while simultaneously representing the culmination of the forces represented by the Lesser Mysteries. Uniquely, Tiphareth is served by eight Paths. Three Paths connect Tiphareth with the Lesser Mysteries. Two Paths connect Tiphareth with the Greater Mysteries and three Paths make contact with the Supreme Mysteries. As the single Sephirah to stand in direct relationship to all three areas, Tiphareth is assigned to the Mediating Intelligence. Tiphareth is at the heart of the Microcosm formed by the surrounding Sephiroth – Hod, Netzach, Yesod, Chesed and Geburah.

Mystical Knowing

The Mystics show us this independent spiritual life, this fruition of the Absolute, enjoyed with a fullness to which others cannot attain. They are the heroic examples of the life of spirit – as the great artists, the great discoverers, and the heroic examples of the life of beauty and the life of truth.

Evelyn Underhill, *Mysticism*

Tiphareth represents a major shift in consciousness. It brings a mode of consciousness quite unlike the intellectual mind represented by Hod or the intuitive and imaginative mind represented by Netzach. The consciousness represented by Tiphareth includes the balanced powers of both Hod and Netzach, but it also brings a new level of mind which is best described as mystical. The word 'mystic' has its origin in the Greek Mysteries of Eleusis, through which people in huge numbers were initiated into revelation through ritualized drama. The initiates were referred to as *mystica*. The word 'mystery' (*mysterion*) comes from the Greek verb meaning to shut or close the lips or eyes. This source is therefore instructive; it indicates that the elements of mysticism were present in the Mysteries of Eleusis. Although sacred initiatory drama is a rarity today, its purpose is timeless: to precipitate personal revelation through the active and intense use of rebirth symbolism. The initiate or *mystica* was 'reborn into eternity'. This is a statement of gnosis, not of intellectual apprehension. Closing the lips is a gesture of silence and closing the eyes is a gesture of personal engagement. Silence has been much misunderstood in relation to the Mysteries. It should not be confused with secrecy. Silence relates to the ineffable quality of mystical knowing; what has been experienced cannot be conveyed. The revelation is personal, the experience is unique. The moment is transformative. This is the essence of the Mysteries as initiatory drama and of mystical experience itself.

The word 'mystical' did not become current until the late Middle Ages. Medieval theologians described this type of experience as 'experimental wisdom' or a 'stretching out of the soul into God through the urge of love'. Mystical experience is 'the raw material of all religion and is also the inspiration of philosophy, poetry, art and music, a consciousness of a *beyond*, of something which, though it is interwoven with it, is not of the external world of material phenomena, of an *unseen* over and above the seen'.[1] As this experience belongs to all spiritual traditions, it is not dependent on dogma or creed but is, rather, a fundamental aspect of the human condition. The mystical path has a universal nature. The description rendered by the Sufi mystic Farid-al-din in his allegory *The Conference of the Birds*, bears a striking similarity to the Kabbalistic model. He too begins with the allegory of a pilgrimage through seven valleys. The pilgrim travels through the seven valleys of The Quest – Love, Knowledge, Enlightenment, Detachment, Unity, Bewilderment and, finally, Annihilation.

Mystical experiences mainly divide into two types: the mysticism of love and union, and the mysticism of knowledge and understanding, though in reality the division is far from rigid. These two aspects reflect the nature of the 26th Path from Hod, the sphere of mind, and the 24th Path from Netzach, the sphere of the emotions. Tiphareth unites both knowing and feeling into gnosis personally revealed. Mystical states are characterized by three features: ineffability where the state of mind defies expression in terms that are fully intelligible to anyone who has not had an analogous experience; a noetic quality which brings insights into the depths of truths unplumbed by discursive intelligence; a consciousness of oneness, a timelessness. These qualities are reflected in the nature assigned to Tiphareth, meaning beauty. This title conveys the inclusive and revelatory nature of the integrated knowing of Tiphareth. It is simply beautiful. While watching the sun rise above the trees, the mystical poet Rabindranath Tagore experienced the following, which he later recorded:

> As I was watching it, suddenly in a moment, a veil seemed to be lifted from my eyes. I found the world wrapt in inexpressible glory with its waves of joy and beauty bursting and breaking on all sides. The thick cloud of sorrow that lay on my heart in many folds was pierced through and through by the light of the world, which was everywhere radiant. There was nothing and no one whom I did not love at that moment. I seemed to witness, in the wholeness of my vision, the movement of the body of all humanity, and to feel the beat of the music and the rhythm of a mystic dance.[2]

Though mystical experience is not an everyday event, it is a perfectly natural state of mind. 'This "mystical consciousness" is, of its nature, in some way a development and extension of rational consciousness, resulting in an enlargement and refining of perception, and consequently having a noetic quality, so that through it knowledge of the "real" is gained which could not be gained through rational consciousness.'[3] Dr R.M. Bucke, a pioneering figure in the study of mystical states, wrote the ground-breaking book *Cosmic Consciousness* in 1905. In it he described the impact of a mystical knowing:

> Like a flash there is presented to his consciousness a conception of the meaning and drift of the universe. He does not come to believe merely; but he sees and knows that the cosmos, which to his self-conscious mind seems made up of dead matter, is in fact far otherwise – is in truth a living presence. He sees that the life which is in man is eternal; that foundation principle of the world is what we call love. Especially does he obtain such a conception of *the whole* as makes the old attempts to mentally grasp the universe and its meaning petty and ridiculous.[4]

This definition still holds.

So often human awareness is polarized by apparent oppositions. Day and night are not opposed but opposing elements within a single cycle. Light and dark are not oppositions but part of a greater cycle. Spring in the northern hemisphere means autumn in the southern hemisphere. This division in our thinking and subsequent language runs deep. It lies at the heart of the internal map we construct of reality. 'In this realm of polar opposites man is imprisoned. He is conscious, therefore, of a division in his soul. His deepest spiritual instinct is to break through the polar opposition and find again the Primal Meaning so that he may once again be restored to the Undivided Unity which he has lost.'[5] A dualized consciousness perceives only yin and yang, but a unified consciousness perceives the whole and its parts simultaneously. Tiphareth brings the birth of a unifying consciousness. Unlike the lower Sephiroth which represent the consciousness of innate intellect and instinctual understanding, Tiphareth represents a level of consciousness that is not given but created from within like a skein of spider silk.

The birth of this new level of consciousness is represented by the symbolism assigned to Tiphareth. The spiritual experience of Tiphareth is the Vision of the Harmony of Things. This experience lies at the heart of mystical knowing. Unusually, Tiphareth has three magical images, each of which relates to this period of transition. The newly born child of Tiphareth represents the newly born consciousness. The majestic king represents the rulership of the real self and the sacrificed god symbolizes the willing surrender of the personality. Tiphareth is said to be Kether on a lower arc and Yesod on a higher arc. 'From the point of view of Kether it is a child, from the point of view of Malkuth it is a king, from the point of view of the transmutation of energy it is sacrificial god.'[6] Dion Fortune says, 'The importance of the Tiphareth stage in mystical experience lies in the fact that the incarnation of the child takes place here; in other words mystical experiences gradually build up a body of images and ideas that are lit up and made visible when illumination takes place.'[7] This is the consciousness of illumination. It is the consciousness of enlightenment.

Enlightenment and Illumination

All real artists, as well as pure mystics, are sharers to
some degree in the Illuminated Life.

Evelyn Underhill, *Mysticism*

In the Western experience the term Illumination is often used to describe this mystical revelation. It has much in common with the experience of enlightenment spoken of by the Eastern tradition. The enlightenment experience is a personal revelation, a direct seeing into the nature of things. It is the moment when the scales of illusion, projection and misidentification suddenly fall away to reveal naked reality. The experience is always transformative, often devastating and intensely private. Like the mystical experience it has an ineffable quality and conveys a sense of unity. Though there are similarities in mystical awakening and the experience of enlightenment, these experiences also reflect the special nature of the tradition in which they are rooted. The mystical awakening of the West is most often suffused with a sense of God's presence. However, the Eastern experience of enlightenment is marked not by a sense of personal relationship to a divine source but by an awareness of the ground of being. Otherwise, these experiences have too much in common to be quite different phenomena. The experience of enlightenment is a clearly stated goal within Buddhism, which seeks to precipitate this moment through the application of many practices, all designed to ripen the mind for the moment of awakening. Zen Buddhism seeks to precipitate the experience not by the gradual transformation of awareness but by breaking the small mind asunder at a single stroke with the cutting edge of its own special sword, the *koan*. The two main branches of Buddhism — Hinayana and Mahayana — offer different paths and goals. Mahayana Buddhism, that of the Greater Vehicle, seeks individual enlightenment for all sentient beings. Hinayana Buddhism, that of the Lesser Vehicle, seeks personal and individual enlightenment. In the Western tradition the experience of illumination is documented and known yet this has never become a broad goal. Curiously, both traditions take the image of light to convey the impact of this turning point. Accordingly Tiphareth is assigned to the sun and called *shemesh*, or the sphere of the sun. This symbol conveys both light and life. As sunlight illuminates a darkened room, so the experience of Tiphareth, mystical awakening or enlightenment, illuminates the mind.

The vocabulary may differ but both illumination and enlightenment effect a powerful and lasting revolution in understanding of meaning and purpose. The expansion of consciousness, release of latent powers and widening of vision do not fade but remain to form a new foundation for the forward journey. The truncated pyramid assigned to Tiphareth is a symbol of construction in progress. A plateau has been reached but the apex is still to be built.

In describing a personal experience, William James wrote, 'Directly afterwards there came upon me a sense of exultation, of immense joyousness, accompanied or immediately followed by an intellectual illumination quite impossible to describe.'[8] This mode of understanding is quite different from that represented at Yesod, which is predominantly psychic. Here impressions are picked up or conveyed via the intermediate image or symbol. But the illumined Tiphareth mind apprehends directly. This is gnosis. It is a mystical knowing, an illumined consciousness.

The Way of the Heart

My heart is with me and it shall not be taken away, for

I am a possessor of hearts who unites hearts. I live by

truth in which I exist.

Spell from *The Egyptian Book of the Dead*

The consciousness of Tiphareth is currently related to the Heart Chakra. This is a new correspondence which works well. The heart has most often been seen as the seat of life rather than the mind. The passions and the feelings are always related to the heart, not the head. Not surprisingly then, the symbolism of the Western Kabbalah and that of the Eastern *Sat-Cakra Nirupana* fit together. In both systems, the heart represents transpersonal love and universal compassion. As Tiphareth has a unique role among the Sephiroth, the Heart Chakra has a unique role too. Uniquely of all the centres, the Heart Chakra alone has a subsidiary centre. This is represented as an island of gems where a single tree grows. This is called the Kalpa Tree or the Wish Fulfilling Tree. It has the power to grant wishes made for the benefit of others. In other words, when all desires for the small self have passed away, the greater self is granted a power to fulfil the wishes of others. Motive is now everything. This is the awakened, compassionate and infinite heart of Tiphareth, which takes the needs of strangers for its own. The consciousness of Tiphareth is not easily reached. It appears on the horizon of consciousness only after the work of the Psychological Triangle has been effected. Tiphareth is approached only by crossing the gulf from the personal to the transpersonal, from the particular to the universal, to an unbounded and infinite perspective. Just as the universalizing qualities of heart cannot be awakened until the gulf separating the small self from the greater self has been crossed, in the metaphysics of Yoga the powers of the heart are also locked away until the key is forged from intent, motive and self-realization. The Anahata Chakra is locked by a psychic knot called the *Vishnu Granthi*. The heart is universally accorded a special significance. The *Sepher Yetzirah* calls the heart 'the king over the soul' and describes mystical experiences as a 'running of the heart'. Alice Bailey, mediator of the mind of the Tibetan, places great importance on the awakening of the heart:

> The first centre which the aspirant seeks consciously to energize and on which he concentrates during the early stages of his novitiate is the heart centre. He has to learn to be group conscious, to be sensitive to group ideals and to be inclusive in his plans and concepts. He has to learn to love collectively and purely and not be actuated by personality attraction and the motive of reward. Until there is this awakening in the heart he cannot be trusted to wield the creative powers of the throat centre for they would be subordinated to self-aggrandizement and ambition of various kinds.[9]

When group purpose is served with the same level of ambitious drive usually saved for self-interest, transformation can take place in the community and the world, not merely in the career.

The Virtue of Tiphareth is Devotion to the Great Work. This level of dedication is often seen as the gradual and cumulative result of many lives and many experiences. Such devotion is not often formed within a single lifetime. The Virtue of Tiphareth is uncomfortably close to its Vice. Devotion can easily spill out into its deviant form, a zealous spiritual obsession which cannot countenance any deviation from a prescribed practice and belief. Religious history is littered with examples of intolerant and bigoted behaviour; this is not the mystical awakening of the heart but its complete reverse.

The mystical awakening of Tiphareth changes everything. The illumined mind shines its light into the very heart of life at its ethical centre. Tiphareth represents the first point of contact between the Psychological and Ethical triangles. The move into the Ethical Triangle is a life-changing shift of perspective. Every choice and decision now reflects the gnosis of the Ethical Triangle. Entry into the Ethical Triangle and the Greater Mysteries brings hitherto unrecognized factors and forces into conscious awareness. The new perspective of being gives rise to the Buddhist Bodhisattva, a figure dedicated wholeheartedly to the service of others. In the Western mystical tradition, the Unreserved Dedication recognizes that service to the Great Work is the central cause for a lifetime's journey. Such vows made in full consciousness, backed by a focused will and pure intent, slowly bring about the changes required to fulfil this promise. As a symbol of the unfoldment and awakening taking place in the heart, the rose-cross is assigned to Tiphareth.

THE ROSE OF THE HEART

Place your awareness within the heart and there visualize a tiny rosebud. Call to mind feelings and memories of loving and of being loved. Continue to deepen your feelings of love. Allow the rose of the heart to begin to grow and unfold. Watch as the rose comes to its beautiful fullness. From deep within the centre of the rose see streams of radiant light emerging. Send these rays of light outwards in all directions. At the same time feel that loving kindness is flowing outwards without distinction.

Rebirth

Rebirth is not a process that we can in any way observe.

C.G. Jung, *The Archetypes and the Collective Unconscious*

Travelling the paths of the Tree brings a continuous process of transformation. It is a journey of self-discovery into the depths of the psyche. The route is marked by certain significant landmarks. Contacting the potencies of Tiphareth represents the first major landmark on the journey of ascent. It is the culmination of each of the preceding initiations of Malkuth, Yesod, Hod and Netzach. The initiation of Tiphareth brings the birth of a new level of consciousness which arises only with the passing of a dualized type of thinking. Here the small self of the personality is superseded by different needs. Contemporary psychology has travelled fairly comfortably so far but it begins to run out of conceptual language at Tiphareth, which commences where psychological understanding ceases. The regenerated, expanded and universalized centre of consciousness is without name in psychological terms. But in metaphysical vocabulary this accords with the Hindu 'atman' or the Christian 'spark', 'centre', 'apex of the soul' or 'ground of the spirit'. Terminology, both ancient and modern, may vary, but beyond the ephemeral phenomena of egoistic self there lies an immortal, constant and unchanging nature. This state of identification is sometimes referred to as the Individuality. This is the point at which psychological insight begins to fall away. The difficulty of precise language mirrors the fact that at Tiphareth we cast off into unfamiliar waters. Retaining and exploring the concept of the Individuality, as individuation expresses the process of becoming through a single incarnation, the concept of Individuality represents the principle of becoming through successive incarnations. The Higher Self might be thought of as an aspect of being which initially projects a blueprint into the incarnation process and later absorbs the quintessence of a life's experience. The meeting point for the ascending impulse from within the incarnate life together with a descending spiritual impulse is in Tiphareth. Tiphareth is called the Lesser Countenance. It is the place where Kether is reflected. Malkuth brings the Vision of the Holy Guardian Angel but Tiphareth brings the Knowledge and Conversation of the Holy Guardian Angel. This personified aspect of universal consciousness holds the keys to the greater blueprint and conveys a sense of destiny and life purpose.

All initiatory rites contain an element of rebirth, but for the initiation of Tiphareth the element of rebirth is especially strong. The personality cannot make this crossing. This brings a deep sense of death and rebirth. The initiation of Tiphareth is an important landmark in identity. As the limited perspective of the personality gives way to the greater perspective of the individuality, so the sense of identity is expanded by an awareness of the greater cycles of lives and deaths. In Tiphareth the heart opens, the mystical mind is founded and the personality becomes aligned with the greater purposes of the Higher Self.

EVOCATION

Welcome to my kingdom. You have travelled long and far to have found your way here. I have watched your struggles and disappointments, your false dawns and new delights. I am the faint voice calling from afar. I am the prompting from deep within. I am the homecoming and the safe harbour.

And now you are here by the dint of your own labour. See the rainbow – this is the path by which you have travelled. It is the path of your own being. Your colours are bright and clear. You alone have made this possible, for as the spider spins a web from within, so you have become both the path and the traveller. Here you are reborn as a child. Like a child, you will need to learn anew.

You are welcome to the realm of the Greater Mysteries. Here new ways of being will arise. A new perspective will take birth. A new code of private conduct will arise as the true significance of things great and small is grasped. Here your journey finds a new foundation.

This is the place of death and rebirth. Do not regret the passing of the partial or the waning of the temporary. Look forward instead to a fullness of being and richness of purpose. You have penetrated beyond the surface of life into its heart. You have lifted the veil which occludes the sight and released the knot which holds the heart in tight restraint. Look forward onto the endless path of infinite becoming and let your heart become your guide.

INTERNALIZATION – THE TEMPLE OF TIPHARETH

Construct the Temple of Tiphareth in the creative imagination. In the centre of the temple you see a six-sided stone altar. But as you approach you also see that it is set upon an island seemingly separated from the floor of the temple by a space. You stand as close to the edge of the floor as you dare and wonder how this altar is tended. The space is too far to be crossed with a step or even a leap. Yet new candles clearly are alight here. You pause in meditative thought, wondering how this is accomplished.

As you stand observing the space between yourself and the central altar, a ray of light pours through one of the many windows. It splits into many colours. A rainbow of light spreads across the floor. It stretches like a many-coloured path and even seems to cross the space between yourself and the altar. The light seems so real and brilliant that without thinking you put your foot upon it. The light seems as real as any path. Without hesitation you leave the safety of solid ground and find yourself stepping out with no visible means of support. Yet you are supported and you do not fall. You cross the space between yourself and the altar.

On the altar you see a triptych with images of a newly born infant, a sacrificed god and a king. Spend some time in contemplation of these images. When your meditation is complete, light a candle and make a wish for someone in need. When you turn to make your way across the space once more, you will find that the rainbow path has become a mosaic surface seemingly ever present.

When you are ready, leave through the doorway. Finally, dissolve all images and return to ordinary consciousness.

EXERCITIA SPIRITUALIA

Take the Following as Subjects for Meditation:

- Jehovah Aloah va Daath
- The Vision of the Harmony of Things
- A Child
- A King
- A Sacrificed God
- A lamen, the rose-cross, the calvary cross, the truncated pyramid, the cube
- The Mediating Intelligence
- Knowledge and Conversation of the Holy Guardian Angel
- The Sun

Contemplate the Following Questions and Record your Responses:

- How does the quality of Devotion operate in your life?
- How do the qualities of Bigotry, Spiritual Pride or Zealotry operate in your life?
- How does the nature of Tiphareth relate to the Heart Chakra?
- What other correspondences can you relate to Tiphareth?
- How do the four Tarot cards relate to Tiphareth?

Visualize the following and Record your Experiences:

- The Temple of Tiphareth including the Archangel Raphael
- The Journey to the Temple of Tiphareth

CHAPTER 16

The Twenty-Third Path: Hod–Geburah

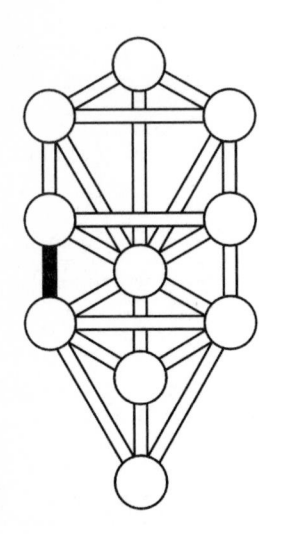

FIGURE 24 THE 23RD PATH:
HOD–GEBURAH

TAROT TRUMP XII,
THE HANGED MAN

TABLE OF CORRESPONDENCES

The Journey: Tarot Trump XII, The Spirit of the
Mighty Waters, The Hanged Man
Key: The Letter Mem, meaning water
Mother Letter: The Element of Water
Spiritual Significance: Elemental Water
Text: The Stable Intelligence
Colour in Atziluth: Deep Blue
Colour in Briah: Sea Green
Colour in Yetzirah: Deep olive Green
Colour in Assiah: White flecked Purple

COMMENTARY

The Twenty-third Path is named the Stable Intelligence, and is so called because it has the virtue of consistency among all numerations.

The 23rd Path connects the eighth Sephirah, Hod, with the fifth Sephirah, Geburah, which is directly above it on the Pillar of Severity. This Path is beyond the Initiation experience of Tiphareth and therefore builds upon the foundation of an already universalized consciousness. As part of the Ethical or Moral Triangle, the 23rd Path is intimately connected to the continuing refinement and development of a moral and ethical code.

Citta

The word citta denotes mind in its total collective sense
as being composed of three categories: *manas*, the
individual mind having the power and faculty of
attention, selection and rejection; *buddhi*, intelligence or
reason which determines the distinction between things;
and *ahamkara*, the I-maker, the state which ascertains
'I know'.

B.K.S. Iyengar, *The Concise Light on Yoga*

The 23rd Path is assigned to Tarot Trump XII, which is most often called the Hanged Man. However, this title is quite misleading. This is clearly not an image of execution. A more appropriate title might be 'The Hanging Man', the man suspended between heaven and earth. The figure hangs upside down suspended from a beam by a single foot. This vantage point brings a radical new perspective. It quite literally turns the world upside down. It reverses everything. Because the figure is hanging down in this way, his gaze is turned upwards into the higher reaches of the Tree.

This Path connects the Perfect Intelligence of Hod with the Radical Intelligence of Geburah. Hod is essentially a sphere of mind. Geburah is a sphere of radical transformation of karmic forces through evolution or revolution. The journey of the 23rd Path is one of revolutionary evolution;

it stands common sense on its head. The 23rd Path overturns biological models of evolution which place self at the centre. Neither the survival of the fittest nor the selfish gene holds sway here. This is the Path of No-self. This is a journey which reverses the ordinary conceptions of self. It stands the commonly held idea on its head. This is the Tarot Trump of the Hanging Man who sees the world quite differently to everyone else.

Western psychology is a young science which is still rooted in the empirical. Western metaphysics stems from a hidden tradition which is given little scientific credence. In the West, the arena of mind belongs more to empirical research than to philosophy and the nature of consciousness is still an open question. Eastern psychology is long-lived and blends seamlessly into a metaphysical dimension. The nature of consciousness carries none of the difficulties perceived by the Western analytical approach. Consciousness is described by the term *citta*. The verb *cit* means to perceive, to notice, to know, to understand, to long for, to desire and to remind. As a noun, cit means emotion, intellect, feeling, disposition, vision, heart, soul and Brahman. This is a powerful holistic definition which connects and embraces many aspects of being. This definition embraces the very fundamentals that Western culture has separated and fragmented: emotion and intellect, feeling and disposition. Also, according to this view, consciousness can be nurtured through cultivation, observation, progressive refinement and the development of detachment and renunciation; what we perceive, notice, know, understand, long for, desire and remind ourselves of can be altered under will. Finally, the same definition embraces the transcendent, through the possibility of vision, the awakening of heart, the language of soul and the immanence of Brahman. All are included in the concept of cit consciousness. Citta is the seat of intelligence and *mahat* is the universal consciousness. The relationship between individual consciousness and universal consciousness lies at the heart of the 23rd Path. It is an interface which the Western mindset does not acknowledge. In the temples of India, it is common to find two related sacred images, one of stone and one of bronze. The bronze image represents the personal or individual self and it is carried out in procession. The stone image is permanently fixed and represents the universality of soul. A complex metaphysical idea is thereby conveyed and preserved with utter simplicity. Buddhism too teaches that above and beyond the thinking process lies another level of mind. This is the True Mind. It is likened to the deep ocean, while the individual mind is but the wave briefly rippling across the surface. The practice of meditation awakens the lesser mind to the greater. It enables wave and ocean to blend in harmony and brings the personal and the universal into relationship. This teaching is the essence of the 23rd Path, which is the transformation of citta into bodhicitta. This level of mind has been likened to the Philosopher's Stone, the wish-fulfilling tree, the *jambu* tree laden with delicious fruit, a brave warrior destroying all sins, and the great fire at the end of the world destroying impurities. In other words, the Bodhicitta mind is the spiritual goal of transformation; it is abundant in the service of others, heroic and pure. The Bodhicitta mind develops only through conscious action designed to precipitate its gestation.

Consciousness is transformed through the application of wide-ranging holistic processes found under a single umbrella as meditation. A traditional Tibetan series of images, described as the Nine Stages of Mental Quiescence, describes the stages of the journey from inner chaos to calm, from mental confusion to clarity, from wild disorder to awareness. In the sequence, the nature of mind is symbolized by an elephant. At the outset the elephant is wild and untamed, and it is black, symbolizing the many initial hindrances to attaining mental control. But as the journey progresses, the elephant changes colour from black to white. It is accompanied by a monkey which dances wildly beside the path. This is the 'monkey mind', unfocused, scattered, fragmented and easily distracted. Both the monkey and the elephant require training if they are to be of any service. Five objects are depicted at the outset of the journey too. These represent the distractions provided by the world of the senses. The mirror symbolizes the distractions of form; the cymbals represent the distractions of sound; the bowl of fruit represents the distractions of taste; the conch shell holding perfume represents the distractions of smell; and the piece of cloth represents tactile sensation. Alongside the representations of the senses, flames are also depicted. These symbolize the energy and effort required at different stages of the journey. At the outset the flames are large but become smaller as the journey progresses. Finally the task becomes effortless and the flames disappear altogether. The path has six curves, representing Listening, Reflection, Recollection, Alertness, Joyful Effort and Familiarity. These are the challenges that must be mastered if the elephant and the monkey are to be tamed. Acquiring the state of Mental Quiescence is divided into nine stages. The first is called Initial Fixation. Here the man chases after the elephant, which is led by the monkey. Both the monkey and the elephant are coloured black. The man holds a goad, symbolizing alertness, but he is too far away to make contact with them. This represents the first attempts to control the mind. At this stage there is a lack of focus and external distractions are over-whelming. The next stage is called Increasing Fixation. The man now carries a rope in addition to the goad. The rope represents the power of recollect-edness. There has been some slight change in the representation of the elephant and the monkey. Small areas of white have replaced the previously all-black creatures. However, the man has not yet caught the elephant. The flames are still large and the elephant remains wild. Now effort has precip-itated the next phase, called Patchlike Fixation. The man has now succeeded in roping the elephant. The elephant's head is now turned towards the man. The head is now fully white and the elephant looks more peaceful. And now the elephant carries a rabbit on its back. A new distraction has appeared. Some degree of concentration has been attained but it is still liable to disappear at the first opportunity. At the fourth stage, called Close Fixation, alertness is now more important than recollection. Although the man holds the elephant by the rope, he is about to administer the goad. Now when concentration flags, awareness administers a corrective action. The elephant is becoming increasingly white, indicating that transformation is taking place. Considerable progress has been made since the start. At the fifth stage, Invigoration, excitement has no power to distract. For the first time, the monkey falls behind the elephant. Most of the elephant is now white. The next stage is called Pacification. Now, for the first time, the man walks in front of the elephant and the monkey. He exerts authority and leads the animals from the front. The elephant is now half-white and half-black. The flames surrounding the path are now much reduced. This stage is followed by Complete Pacification. The man now stands between the monkey and the elephant and both creatures seem obedient. Both rope and goad have been abandoned. Neither the monkey nor the elephant has much dark colouring left. The eighth stage is known as Singlepointedness. The monkey has dis-appeared and the elephant is totally white for the first time. Finally, in the ninth stage of Formal Fixation, the elephant and man lie down together in complete harmony. The man rides the elephant and in the last picture the elephant and man are returning the way they have come. The man carries a torch and there are flames in the background representing the newly estab-lished energy. On the last curve of the path, the man is depicted flying – an image of release and liberation.

Though this is an Eastern schema, it has universal application. Mental training commences at Malkuth. By the time the 23rd Path is reached much work has been accomplished in self-control, mastery and realization. It is upon this Path that personal consciousness gives way to universal con-sciousness. Citta is becoming transformed into Bodhicitta.

Bodhicitta

> By being inspired with Bodhicitta our whole nature
> changes, all actions and deeds undergo great change and
> we become a child of the Buddha.

Lama Sherab Gyaltsen Amipa, *The Opening of the Lotus*

Citta is the mind, the raw material of consciousness as yet unchanged by
the meditative processes which bring transformation. Bodhi refers to the
awakening of Buddhahood. Bodhicitta is the mind which wishes to attain
Buddhahood. Buddha means the enlightened one. Bodhicitta is the mind
seeking enlightenment. This is the model of transformation within Buddhism.
Siddhartha Gautama was a man like any other who sought and attained the
great awakening. He became Buddha.

Bodhicitta is the mind transformed by meditative processes and charged
by the desire to attain enlightenment. The level of mind gives birth to the
Bodhisattva, the living embodiment of the ideal. Sattva represents the highest
truth. The Bodhisattva life is one of total truth. These extraordinary aspirations can only begin to be formed within the Ethical and Moral Triangle
of the Greater Mysteries. This radically new ethical departure reverses any
value system centred on self. Lama Sherab Gyaltsen Amipa speaks about the
reversal of attitude needed to generate this selfless level of aspiration:

> If we wish to obtain enlightenment without delay we should
> reverse our attitude; in other words we should think of others in
> the way we used to think of ourselves. However, to obtain
> Buddhahood it is not enough to like others in the way we like
> ourselves; more than this we must prefer others to ourselves.[1]

Reversal is the central theme of the Tarot Trump assigned to the 23rd Path.

Buddhism's simple and everyday advice always centres on reversing selfishness. Instead of putting ourselves first, we are urged to treat others as our
best friends, and to do as little as possible for ourselves but as much as possible
for others. Self-love and egotism are said to be our worst enemies. Such
selfish qualities wait to be turned into spontaneous charity. 'By satisfying
the needs of others our needs will be met.'[2] 'The root of happiness is
altruism, the wish to be of service to others.'[3] In a Buddhist commentary, the
teacher Dharmakirti says:

When self exists, other is discriminated.

When self and other have formed, there is attachment and hatred.[4]

The Dalai Lama has said, 'Once there is a sense of solidly existent, palpable, reliable 'I', there is a discrimination of other – once there is 'I' there is also 'you', whereupon there is attachment to one's own side and anger towards the other side.'[5]

All of these views challenge and contradict the solidity, centrality and importance of the small self. Maslow's Hierarchy of Needs has been reversed. The greatest drive is now towards the universal application of selfless compassion, not the creation of a physical comfort zone. The Path of the Bodhisattva is one of reversal; the happiness of others comes before the happiness of self.

The desire of the Bodhicitta mind is to seek enlightenment for all others. It is awakened by compassion and universal love, represented by Tiphareth on the Tree of Life. The sixth Sephirah – Tiphareth, Beauty – represents the heart centre. It is the place where the heart unfolds to transpersonal love and where an even deeper commitment to all sentient life takes root. In the Western Mysteries, the Unreserved Dedication, a vow of universal service, can be offered when Tiphareth is entered.

In Buddhism, taking complete responsibility for all beings is called the Supreme Aspiration:

> May the jewel-adorned boat of the divine wisdom reach the remote shores of enlightenment by crossing the ocean of the two accumulations of energy, so that other beings may be helped.
>
> May the glory of the all-knowing Buddha spread the light of eternal joy.
>
> May all my wishes and those of other beings be granted.[6]

The Bodihisattva

Is the spirit of enlightenment, the Bodhimind, blended with your thoughts?

Master Ser-Ling-pa to his pupil Jowo Atisha

> ## TONG-LEN – GIVING AND TAKING
> Meditate on the desire to help others, starting with members of your immediate family. Visualize your mother standing in front of you. Visualize the difficulties and sorrows of her heart like a dark cloud emerging from it. Breathe this into your own heart.
> Visualize the gift of joy and happiness as a white cloud forming in your own heart. As you breathe out, see this white cloud replacing the darkness in your mother's heart. On the in-breath take in sadness and on the out-breath radiate joy.
> Extend this exercise to family, friends and anyone in need.

Buddhism places much value on the gradual and organic transformation of mind, from the raw material which is citta to the aspiration for enlightenment which is Bodhicitta, to the living and daily implementation of the enlightened mind through the way of the Bodhisattva. Although this is a Buddhist term, the state of consciousness represented has its equivalence across all spiritual traditions. This is the path of enlightened consciousness, universal love, boundless compassion, empathy and equanimity. All true spiritual teachers, saints, sages and shining exemplars have each found the great and abiding waters of truth.

The 23rd Path is assigned to the letter Mem. As one of the Mother Letters, Mem carries a special significance as the representative of elemental Water. Elemental water is unconfined and unbounded by any definition or limitation. Water represents consciousness. It is the reflecting astral mirror of Yesod and the dynamic process of the 25th Path. It is the higher consciousness of the water temple at Hod and the infinite seas behind the throne of the High Priestess. Now elemental water signifies the universal mind and the waters of the oceanic true mind. The term Dalai Lama, the office held by the spiritual leader of Tibet, means 'Great ocean'. This great ocean is the source of individual consciousness and the home to which personal consciousness can return. However, when this homecoming takes place the lesser can only give way to the greater. Aspirations, intentions and motivations become universalized. The small self naturally gives way in the certain awareness of the whole, and the figure of the Bodhisattva is born. The Tarot Trump assigned here is commonly called The Hanged Man, but it is also known as the Spirit of the Mighty Waters. Jung's words are as insightful as ever:

> The meeting with oneself is, at first, the meeting with one's own shadow. The shadow is a tight passage, a narrow door whose painful

constrictions no one is spared who goes down to the deep well.
But one must learn to know oneself in order to know who one is.
For what comes after the door is, surprisingly enough, a boundless
expanse of unprecedented uncertainty, with apparently no inside and
no outside, no above and no below, no here and no there, no mine,
no thine, no good and no bad. It is the world of water, where all life
floats in suspension; where the realm of the sympathetic system, the
soul of everything living, begins; where I am indivisibly this *and* that;
where I experience the other in myself and the other-than-myself
experiences me.

No, the collective unconscious is anything but an incapsulated
personal system; it is sheer objectivity, as wide as the world and open
to all the world. There I am the object of every subject, in complete
reversal of my ordinary consciousness, where I am always the subject
that has an object. There I am utterly one with the world, so much a
part of it that I forget too easily who I really am. 'Lost in oneself' is
a good way of describing this state. But this self is the world, and if
only a consciousness could see it. That is why we must know who
we are.[7]

This is the experience of the Hanging Man. Jung's own words accord well
with the symbolism of the Trump: 'it is the world of water'. This is the
journey of Mem and the Spirit of the Mighty Waters. When Jung speaks of
'a complete reversal of my ordinary consciousness', he reinforces the theme
of the Trump where the hanging figure sees the world from a reversed perspective. Finally, when he writes 'this self is the world', Jung affirms a mystical
view of reality. Only when everything that passes for reality is reversed is it
possible to gain the Spirit of the Mighty Waters. Reversal is the essence of
the 23rd Path.

The 23rd Path is assigned to the Stable Intelligence, a curious designa-
tion in the face of much watery and airy symbolism which cannot offer the
security of a foothold. But this is the rock-solid stability of *samadhi*, the state
of complete meditative absorption. This is the inner strength of the
Bodhisattva and the secure foundation of the Bodhicitta mind.

Tibetan Buddhism lays down a clear and graduated path for the
generation of Bodhicitta and the birth of the Bodhisattva through the Path
of the Six Perfections. When the Dalai Lama was asked, 'What is a path of
consciousness?' he replied, 'A path, or a vehicle, has the sense of a means of
progressing. When we speak of a path of consciousness, it is not like a super-

highway that might take one to Buddhahood. Buddhahood is achieved through mental development; therefore a path of consciousness refers to mental qualities.'[8]

The Path of Six Perfections defines the actions and practical assistance which gestate the birth of the Boddhisattva mind.

The Perfection of Giving is divided into four parts. These include the giving of *Dharma* in order to teach others; the giving of material aid, including property, clothing, shelter and food in order to assist others practically; the giving of refuge to all sentient beings in danger; and the giving of love which speaks for itself.

The Perfection of Ethics or Morality refers to a self-aware quality of mind which forestalls unwholesome physical actions; prevents speech being used to slander, gossip or lie; and averts negative mental traits such as covetousness, malevolence and holding wrong views. There are three kinds of ethics: restraint, cultivating wholesome qualities, and conduct designed to serve others at all times and in all situations.

The Perfection of Patience helps the mind to remain calm in the face of provocation or agitation: 'In previous times soldiers wore suits of armour to protect themselves from the weapons of their enemies. If in the same way we arm ourselves with patience, then no matter what attitudes or actions others have to us.'[9]

The Perfection of Patience also serves to accept suffering and mitigates against reacting to harm from others. Lastly, patience is needed to think deeply on all the points of Dharma teachings.

The Perfection of Diligence upholds commitment to Dharma and its practice. Diligence of mind protects against tiredness and generates the self-confidence to seek the highest spiritual aspiration.

The Perfection of Meditation or concentration brings the ability to remain mentally focused, both in the everyday experiences of life and in the practice of meditation.

The Perfection of Wisdom is based upon the realization of the true nature of reality, emptiness or Sunyata. It is the realisation of emptiness, the supreme wisdom, which takes the traveller towards the Supreme Mysteries of Being and Becoming. The transformation of being is almost complete. The emergence of a Bodhisattva figure, one dedicated in every word, deed and action to the well-being of others, represents the highest union of spiritual aspiration and physical incarnation. Although this is a rare choice, such figures inspire and empower by example; the Hanged Man is the man hanging upside down seeing everything from a unique and rare perspective.

EVOCATION

Welcome to this kingdom. Is this a realm you will choose, I wonder? If you could see what I see and know what I know then you too would be changed at the instant. For me all is reversed now. I remember when my passion was to work for myself, to make gain and achievement. I remember when ambition and desire drove me to succeed and conquer the world, but that was a long time ago. But from here, from this perspective, such games are hollow and empty. For I know the sham of separateness and the lie of independence. I see through the illusions of the world and the games that men play. From here I see the great waters, the ocean without end, the waters without separation, the experience without boundaries. I cannot be confined or limited, restricted or bounded. I have become like the ocean, I have become like the sky, I am of the infinite and the eternal. Knowing this I can accept nothing less. I am the hanging man suspended between heaven and earth. For me all is now reversed. I have turned my back upon the desires of the world. My one desire is that all sentient beings should be free from the cravings and desires of samsara. I seek nothing for the separated self which is but illusion. I have given my word.

INTERNALIZATION – THE 23RD PATH: HOD–GEBURAH

Construct the Temple of Hod in the creative imagination. Find yourself standing beside the doorway of the Hanged Man. The Archangel Michael draws back the tapestry curtain so that you may pass. You emerge into a low and dimly-lit corridor. From somewhere in the distant background, you hear the sound of men's voices chanting. A man dressed in the robes of a monk comes towards you. Smiling warmly, he places both palms together in a gesture of greeting. He turns and you instantly begin to follow. Now he stops before double doors. He opens the doors into a small dark room, lit only by flickering tapers. A group of monks sit in meditation. There is a space for you and you join them. In front of you is a long low altar set with statues and images which you do not recognize. But your attention is drawn to a painting which seems very familiar. A figure hangs suspended from a beam by only a single foot. He hangs down in space, looking at the world from an upside-down perspective. The image is compelling. You take this as your meditative focus. You notice that the painting hangs directly beneath another which is covered by a cloth. Entering meditation you recreate the image in your mind and find yourself hanging upside down, just as the image in the picture. From here the world looks very different. You recall the intended benefits of the headstand pose, which is supposed to invigorate the brain.

You emerge from your meditation to find yourself alone except for the monk who first accompanied you here. You have no sense of the time that has passed, so engrossed were you in the subject. Looking once again at the image of your contemplation, you see that someone has now removed the cloth concealing the second image directly above the first. It is an exact replica but painted upside down so that the figure now stands upright. In the upper world of the transformed Bodhicitta mind, the figure now stands poised. But in the lower world of raw citta and from the perspective of everyday reality the figure hangs upside down and sees reality in reverse. The great spiritual teachers of the world so often appear different as they shatter the accepted views with radical views and ideas that turn the world upside down.

When you are ready, leave the chamber and return to the temple. Finally, dissolve all images and return to ordinary consciousness.

Exercitia Spiritualia

Take the Following as Subjects for Meditation:

- The Spirit of the Mighty Waters
- The Letter Mem
- Elemental Water
- The Bodhisattva
- The Stable Intelligence

Make Notes on:

Tarot Trump XII, The Hanged Man

Visualize the Following and Record your Experience:

The Journey of the 23rd Path

CHAPTER 17

The Twenty-Second Path: Tiphareth–Geburah

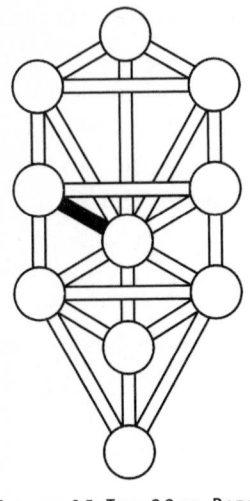

FIGURE 25 THE 22ND PATH:

TIPHARETH–GEBURAH

TAROT TRUMP XI,

JUSTICE

TABLE OF CORRESPONDENCES

The Journey: Tarot Trump XI, Daughter of the
Lords of Truth, Ruler of the Balance
Key: The Letter Lamed, meaning a goad
Simple Letter: Work
Spiritual Significance: Libra
Text: The Faithful Intelligence
Colour in Atziluth: Emerald
Colour in Briah: Blue
Colour in Yetzirah: Deep Blue Green
Colour in Assiah: Pale Green

COMMENTARY

The Twenty-second Path is the Faithful Intelligence and it is so called because by it spiritual virtues are increased and all dwellers on earth are nearly under its shadow.

The 22nd Path connects the sixth Sephirah, Tiphareth, with the fifth Sephirah, Geburah. It connects the Central Pillar of Equilibrium with the Pillar of Severity. As part of the Moral or Ethical Triangle, this Path deepens awareness and understanding of personal action and its karmic effects.

The Possibility of Rebirth

> We are brought up under an ideology that insists there is
> no truth in the idea of rebirth, but when we come into
> contact with Buddhist teaching we find that Buddhist
> tradition has always taken the truth of rebirth as a matter
> of course, and often lays great stress on it.

Martin Wilson, *Rebirth and the Western Buddhist*

The mystical awakening at Tiphareth forms the foundation upon which the 22nd and all other Paths emerging from Tiphareth are constructed. Tiphareth brings the certainty of a unifying vision which does not diminish or recede. From the new foundation of Tiphareth, looking upwards into the higher reaches of the Tree, the universalized self now seeks to understand the impact of consciousness as a far-reaching karmic factor. The experience of the 22nd Path follows upon the unifying and integrating initiation of Tiphareth. The 22nd Path brings the first challenge to the newly attained sense of wholeness and cohesion. The Path to the Sephirah Geburah brings a testing dynamic to bear.

The Sanskrit word for action is 'karma'. Every action leaves an imprint in the stream of consciousness. It is the fuel that drives the wheel of rebirth. The concept of karma seems entirely absent from the religious belief system of the West. Though individual actions and responsibilities carry moral implications, this is not the karma of word, deed, thought and action to be found in Buddhism. Western religion, being based on the notion of a single incarnation, has little need for a determining principle which makes no sense without the concept of many incarnations. Here is a fundamental divide between Western and Eastern belief or, more properly, between orthodox Western belief and Eastern philosophy, for the concept of re-incarnation has entered the Western spiritual arena in various ways. Both Plato and Pythagoras taught the concept of reincarnation. But it was never accepted into the doctrinal embrace of the Church. One of the earliest Church Fathers, Origen, affirmed reincarnation, but he was swimming against the tide and his beliefs were eventually declared to be pagan. Finally, it was the Emperor Justinian who sounded the death knell for the idea of reincarnation, at the Council of Constantinople: 'Whoever shall support the mythical doctrine of the pre-existence of the soul, let him be anathema.'

The Western understanding of reincarnation has always been closely related to the idea of a pre-existent soul as an entity in its own right, but this has never been the Eastern view. The Western interpretation is typically schismatic. To the soul is assigned all that is spiritual, to the body is assigned all that is material. This is not the Eastern view. The concept of soul as a returning entity is anathema to Eastern metaphysics, which affirms the dynamic relationship of becoming, not a fixed and static principle of being. It is no wonder that the West could not embrace its own view of reincar-nation. Instead Christianity, encumbered by a doctrinal plethora at the expense of a metaphysical philosophy, clung tenaciously to the hope of personal salvation through ideas of the second coming, bodily resurrection and personal judgement.

The idea of reincarnation is still relatively new in Western thinking, although recently it has become popularized through the general influx of Eastern metaphysics. However, an Eastern understanding of being and becoming has not travelled equally well. The Western mind still clings to the idea of a reincarnating soul moving from life to life, whereas Buddhism teaches the exact opposite. Consciousness moves from life to life as a flame lights a new flame. The Western mind is not comfortable with the level of ambiguity and paradox that sits easily in the Buddhist mind. The Western mind still seeks logical and rational answers where perhaps an openness of mind and heart might serve better.

Currently, rebirth is accepted within Buddhism, Hinduism and Sikhism. It is rejected by Christianity and Islam. Within Buddhism and Hinduism, rebirth is a mainstay of belief. Individual testaments are treated in a down-to-earth and matter-of-fact way. In the West, a number of independent researchers and groups are working to collect testament, story and evidence with a view to building up a body of material in order to investigate and explore the case for reincarnation. This methodology is typically Western in outlook. It is based on the assumption that the case for reincarnation can be proved by the accumulated weight of evidence. There is already a huge weight of evidence in favour of reincarnation. Tibetan Buddhism is itself a testament for reincarnation.

Acceptance of the idea of rebirth will never come from the weight of empirical evidence but must come from an internal recognition of its validity. Memories sometimes surface spontaneously; at other times far memory can surface under hypnosis. When the Dalai Lama was asked, 'Is it useful or advisable to be brought under hypnosis into one's former lives and inter-mediate states in order to understand better one's actual life?', he replied, 'I think it depends on the situation of the particular person. For some people, it could help in that they would remember virtuous activities in former lifetimes and thereby be drawn into more in this lifetime also; there would be cases of people who would remember an awful event in the past which might cause them great anxiety.'[1] Considerable testament from around the world has been collected in support of the theory of reincarnation. However, other than appearing as interesting reading material for an audience hungry for such news, what impact has this collective casebook made on the Western scientific or religious institutions?

The Path of Karma

If we desire real happiness in the future we must begin
to prepare the ground for it now.

Geshe Rabten, _The Treasury of Dharma_

The empirical tradition is impossible to escape; the casebook still has some value in turning the mind towards the idea. The lifelong work of Dr Hiroshi Motoyama provides a good starting point. He was born in 1925 to an unusually gifted and deeply religious mother. His spiritual life began early. When aged only five, mother and son together met the founder of the Tamamitsu sect of Shintoism, Reverend Kinue Motoyama. These two women instinctively felt that destiny had brought them together. The three settled in Tokyo where they later established a branch of the Tamamitsu shrine. Reverend Motoyama later adopted Hiroshi as her successor, and he took her name as his own. Throughout his life, he worked closely with his mother in the work of the shrine, as a spiritual counsellor.

In the 50 years since his counselling work began, Dr Motoyama has given more than 40,000 consultations. Many of these have revolved around karmic issues. His casebooks offer much food for thought. He was once approached by a shrine member with regard to her daughter, who at 21 had become severely depressed for no apparent reason. On entering a state of deep meditation Dr Motoyama saw the figure of a samurai and learned that he had been a chief retainer to Kiyomasa Kato, who had lived in the Suwa region located some 150 miles north-west of Tokyo. The warrior was named Hachirouemon Nakanose. Dr Motoyama saw that his young client had once been Nakanose's daughter who, because she had fallen in love with a young man but was not allowed to marry him, for social reasons, had committed suicide in her early twenties. Dr Motoyama also ascertained that in the past his client and her mother had been devout Buddhists, worshipping Amida Buddha at a temple in Suwa. In the present, he said her previous father Nakanose was now her maternal uncle, her lover was reborn as her brother, and her previous mother was again her current mother. He claimed that when she reached roughly the same age as Nakanose's daughter, intense emotions were triggered and resulted in depression. When these facts were made known to the family, they were surprised. The maternal uncle came from Suwa. Together the mother and daughter visited Suwa and visited the local temple. Here the aged priest remembered the tomb of Nakanose, which had been moved in living memory by his descendants. But there was still a small shrine to Kiyomasa Kato. Finally, in the historical archives of the province they found an entry for Hachirouemon Nakanose, listed 350 years ago.[2] Fact or fiction, fantasy or telepathy, invention or intuition, reality or illusion? What is your verdict?

Motoyama's long experience has led him to some very striking conclusions. In general, he has found that many present difficulties are rooted in a previous lifetime. In the case quoted, the family members of the present day were also those related to the tragedy of the past. He has concluded that, 'A family unit is not a chance entity but its members have normally known each other before, often many times.'[3] He also believes that the terror related to murders or other violent deaths lies at the root of schizophrenia. Though karmic factors might be anticipated in love and marriage, Dr Motoyama came to an unexpected conclusion. Far from being positive factors in recognizing one another, karmic forces often hid a darker truth. 'I have discovered that many troubled couples were not lovers in their former lives but enemies. In extreme cases, one partner may even have murdered the other. The person who was killed is motivated by revenge, and by marrying their killer they are in a position to do the most damage.'[4] He even found this to be the case with his own parents, who had a violent and unhappy marriage. Long after their divorce, his mother undertook an intensive 100-day period of prayer in the attempt to discover and dissolve the karma between herself and her ex-husband. In meditation his mother came to understand that during the reign of the Empress Jingu she had served the Empress as a Minister of State. The ambassadorial envoy from a Korean state had lived at court for many years. In this time, he had learned much about the inner working of government. Eventually the Minister of State felt that he had become a threat. Although the Empress wanted to spare his life, the Minister of State took it upon himself to murder the ambassador. The two major players in the scenario were to become Hiroshi's warring parents.

This single example raises many questions about the magnetic potency of karma to continually create relationships and circumstances. It is easy to understand how the symbolism of the wheel is related to the cycle of action. Hiroshi Motoyama takes the view that the purpose of life is to dissolve karma. In other words, liberation comes when karma is no longer an operative and unconscious force. As his own mother sought to be free from a future cycle of revenge and hatred in her long vigil of prayer and purification, so understanding the effect of karma brings self-awareness of thought and deed into the present moment. Suffering arises from karma, which in turn creates more karma. 'Karma is basically a result of the spiritual ignorance of the self that mistakenly believes it is an independent entity. As long as the self functions in this state of ignorance it is imprisoned in a continuous process of death and reincarnation within the dimensions of reality that are governed by the law of cause and effect.'[5]

To act without creating karma is to act without self-interest, desire or hidden motive. This is to act with the Intelligence of Transparency assigned to the 12th Path between Binah and Kether. Action without self-interest, deed without desire, such things do not come naturally or easily. 'Because people cherish self so much, surrendering it is a very frightening experience.'[6] Contemplating karma soon conveys a sense of the invisible ties that bind us all to the wheel of fate. Karma is clearly personal, but it is also national, racial and even global.

Moving towards a belief in successive lives poses many questions. If karmic factors can persist from life to life, how and by what mechanism does this happen? If a single life is not to be followed by either an eternal afterlife or the final cessation of consciousness, what is the nature of the intervening state? These are questions for which the West has few answers.

Buddhism however has a great deal to say about such questions. Not only does Buddhism offer teachings and practices which transform the mind in life, but the Bardo Teachings relate to death, dying and the intermediate state. These teachings are intimately related to the way that Tibetan lamas return time after time to carry on their chosen work.

The 13th Dalai Lama passed away aged 58 on the thirtieth day of the tenth month of the Water Bird, 1933. The official search for the new incarnation began in 1936. Signs and visions already indicted that the search should focus on north-eastern Tibet. Team leaders carried out searches listening carefully for local information. Kewtsang Rinpoche travelled in disguise as a servant while the Venerable Lobsang Tsewang dressed in the guise of the master. They were sent to investigate a boy in Chija Taktser. At the first meeting, the young boy pulled at a rosary of the 13th Dalai Lama being worn by Kewtsang Rinpoche, saying, 'Give me this.'

'Tell me who I am and I will give this to you,' replied Kewtsang Rinpoche.

'You are an Aka from Sera,' the boy replied.

'Who is the man in the inner room?'

'Tsedrung Lobsang,' came the answer.

When they left the next morning the boy begged to go with them. On their second visit, items once belonging to the 13th Dalai Lama were spread out, accompanied by other similar objects. The boy correctly chose the black and yellow rosaries, three quilts and, after much close scrutiny, a walking stick and a drum, which he immediately played. The team submitted a favourable report. After several months a coded telegram arrived back:

> Based on the evidence, such as his miraculous performances in all the tests, the striking similarity between the architecture and location of his house and the Regent's lake vision, reinforced by the prophecies of lamas and deities, the government hereby declare Lhamo Dondub, born at early sunrise on the sixth day of Gya month of the Wood Hog Year in the family of Chokyong Tsering and his wife Sonam Tsomo, to be the true reincarnation of the Thirteenth Dalai Lama.[7]

History has validated the choice and shown that, for Tibetan lamas at least, reincarnation is possible.

The Heart's Knowing

The three Mothers are Aleph, Mem, Shin

their foundation is

a pan of merit

a pan of liability

and the tongue of decree deciding between them.

The Sepher Yetzirah

The 22nd Path is assigned to Tarot Trump XI, commonly called Justice. This is a journey of self-conscious karmic awareness. It is a journey of the heart's knowing. Without rebirth, karma has no meaning and without karma rebirth makes no sense. The two concepts work hand in hand. Motoyama concludes that, 'Karma and reincarnation are the organizing principles of existence.'[8] Bringing a karmic dimension to an understanding of life can change the way we see identity and purpose. It has the power to alter the view of family relationships and radically change the perception of birth, death and ultimately of the nature of self. Turning to face personal karma may evoke memories or resonances of previous lives. It may bring the certain understanding that present circumstances, events or situations are rooted in the historical past. Self-awareness of the present avoids planting seeds which will rise up once more in the historical future. Contemplating the evolving role of consciousness in this way unites past, present and future in a single continuum.

The Initiation of Tiphareth has awakened the heart and opened it to remembrance and possibility. The surrender of the small self shifts the definition of identity from being to becoming. In recognition of the importance of the heart's knowing, many cultures have placed the seat of a directing intelligence in the heart, not the head. The stage is now set in which to contemplate karma and rebirth. The Tarot Trump depicts a crowned figure seated between two columns, much like the figure of the High Priestess. A veil is slung between the columns. The figure holds an upraised sword and a pair of scales. The everyday act of weighing one thing against another provides a powerful analogy for the weighing of actions and deeds. The scales universally signify the weighing of action, deed and outcome against intent and motive. The Talmud speaks of a pan of merit and a pan of liability. In the centre is the fulcrum and pointer represented by

Aleph as 'the tongue of decree'. The three Mother Letters – Aleph, Mem and Shin – together represent the two pans and the tongue of balance. This Trump is called Daughter of the Lords of Truth and Ruler of the Balance. In the ancient Egyptian system, the Judgement Hall belonged to Maat, the goddess of truth and order. Her symbol was the white feather against which the deeds of the heart were set. Thoth, the Lord of Wisdom, presided over the balance. The deceased stood in the presence of the 42 Assessors and spoke the words of the Negative Confession as the heart and its knowing was weighed in the balance.

This Trump is fittingly attributed to the astrological sign of Libra, the scales. Libra represents the qualities of Cardinal Air. Elemental Air represents the mind – like air, it is invisible. Yet it is these invisible thoughts, motives and aspirations that will be weighed. This is the knowing of the heart, for actions alone do not reveal the whole story. Libra is the seventh sign of the zodiac. Its glyph symbolizes the oxen yoke and the setting sun halfway below the horizon. Both these images represent perfect balance. Libra heralds the autumn equinox when daylight and darkness are equally balanced once more. Libra therefore epitomizes the balance point between opposites. At the point of perfect balance, equilibrium is maintained.

The Faithful Intelligence assigned to this Path implies the constant and enduring quality of the faithful friend or companion. This is the knowing of the heart. Through its workings, 'spiritual virtues are increased' and, 'all dwellers on earth are nearly under its shadow'. Karma has a purpose, which is to increase spiritual virtue. It is clear that all dwellers on earth are nearly under its shadow.

The Path is assigned to the letter Lamed, represented as the ox goad which prods and nudges the unwilling upon the journey. As a Simple Letter, Lamed is assigned to the quality of Work. This is reminiscent of the Great work of becoming which is the journey of transformation from life to life.

THE SCALES OF TRUTH

Imagine yourself standing before a pair of scales.

In one of the pans place, one at a time, all of the reasons why you are able to accept the idea of karma and reincarnation. In the other, place all of the reasons why you feel unable to accept the idea of karma and reincarnation.

When you have placed all your views in the balance, assess the current outcome.

The concept of karma has no meaning without its twin partner, rebirth. Rebirth is not conscious reincarnation but the result of the interplay of unconscious karmic forces. His Holiness the Dalai Lama speaks of the relationship between one life and the next.

> The quality of one's rebirth in the next life is determined by the quality of one's mental activity in this life. Generally speaking, we have no power to choose how we are born; it is dependent on karmic factors. However, the period near the time of death is very influential in terms of activating one from among the many karmas that a person has already accumulated and, therefore, if one makes a particular effort a virtuous attitude at that time there is an opportunity to strengthen and activate a virtuous karma. Moreover when one has developed a high realization and has gained control over how one will be reborn, it is possible to take what is called 'reincarnation' rather than mere rebirth.[9]

Unconscious rebirth and conscious reincarnation are differentiated by the work of self-realization. We are all bound to the wheel but, as Shinto priest, yoga practitioner and writer, Hiroshi Motoyama, reminds us, understanding the laws of being and becoming has a great value:

> I feel with increasing intensity that the most important thing for the future of humankind is not the ever increasing rewards of an affluent materialistic lifestyle, but it is rather the spiritual evolution of the race. It also appears that the fundamental necessity for accelerated spiritual evolution is a thorough understanding of the realities of our existence. And I don't believe this is possible without understanding the process of reincarnation and the details of karmic law. It is through this understanding that we can begin to learn to be free from the bondage of karma, to transcend the limits of the physical dimension, and to evolve into the Enlightened Being that we are all destined to become.[10]

EVOCATION

Welcome to my kingdom which is the place of absolute truth. I do not sit in judgement upon you but I call forth the record of your journey and it shall speak for itself. All is already recorded in the judgement hall. I hold the scales of truth and the sword of justice. Welcome to this path, traveller in eternity. You are here by virtue of your own effort and courage. You have arrived at the behest of your heart. You are here by no command, nor can any power on earth hold you. You stand here at your own request in accordance with your own choice and desire for truthful adjustment in the scales of truth. Your courage speaks of a long journey willingly undertaken. Your presence speaks volumes. You have the courage to dare, the willingness to know, the will to face the truth and the strength to absorb what you will discover in silence.

INTERNALIZATION – THE 22ND PATH: TIPHARETH–GEBURAH

Construct the Temple of Tiphareth in the creative imagination. Find yourself standing beside the doorway of Justice. The Archangel Raphael draws back the tapestry curtain so that you may pass.

You immediately find yourself at the bottom of a broad staircase. You begin to climb and reach a pair of closed doors. You have no option but to stand and wait, with a sense of nervousness and expectancy. The doors have an air of great age and antiquity. You wait patiently. Now the doors are being drawn back from within; slowly little by little they open to reveal a long low chamber with a vaulted roof. You know that you are awaited. You enter and the doors close behind you. On either side of the hall is a row of seats in single file. The low, vaulted ceiling creates a tunnel-like effect. A central aisle leads to the far end of the chamber. As you walk, you begin to recognize the faces of those seated on either side. There are family members and friends stretching back into childhood. As you pass you sense an unspoken recognition from each and every one. But soon the faces become unfamiliar; now you pass between people dressed in costume appropriate to another time and place. Yet though you cannot recall names, a flicker of recognition passes between you. As you walk on, the faces remain unfamiliar and the names unknown, yet a sense of connection remains; clothing and costumes change as people from distant times and places are represented here. At last you reach the far end of the chamber. You feel that all the eyes of the assembly are upon you. Seated on a throne on a raised dais a crowned figure is seated between two columns. Behind her, suspended between the columns, is a gauzy veil. In one hand she holds a sword which rests across her lap. In the other she holds a pair of scales. Now that you stand directly in front of her, your eyes meet directly in a deep but impersonal gaze.

Without speaking she lifts the sword. Its blade glints in the light. With the other hand she lifts up the scales; you see that a white feather has been placed in one of the pans – but what lies in the other? As far as you can see the second pan is quite empty, but as it begins to move you realize that it will hold the essence of your deeds, words, actions and thoughts, as expressed by the assembly of minds and hearts. From within the hall a palpable flood of feeling wells up. It is released into the hall in a single moment of remembrance. The pan quivers and shakes, rises and falls, falls and rises. You watch it reach its final place. Only you and the figure of Justice observe the final settling of the heart's knowing. This is a moment of private realization and personal communion. You may remain as long as you wish. When you turn to leave, the hall is found to be empty.

When you are ready, leave the chamber and return to the temple. Finally, dissolve all images and return to ordinary consciousness.

EXERCITIA SPIRITUALIA

Take the Following as Subjects for Meditation:

- Daughter of the Lords of Truth, Ruler of the Balance
- The Letter Lamed
- Work
- Libra
- Karma

Make Notes on:

- Tarot Trump XI, Justice

Visualize the Following and Record your Experience:

- The Journey of the 22nd Path

CHAPTER 18

Geburah – Severity

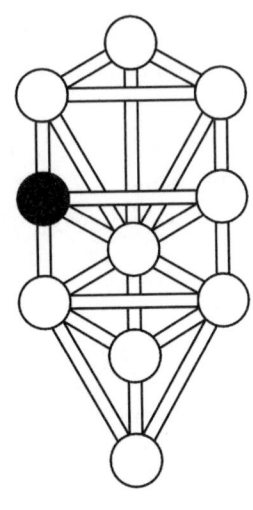

FIGURE 26 THE SEPHIRAH GEBURAH

TABLE OF CORRESPONDENCES

God-Name: Elohim Gebor – Almighty God
Archangel: Khamael
Order of Angels: Seraphim, fiery serpents
Spiritual Experience: The Vision of Power
Symbols: Pentagon, Five-Petalled Rose, Sword, Spear, Scourge, Chain
Magical Image: A Mighty Warrior in his Chariot
Mundane Chakra: Mars
Personal Chakra: The Anahata or Heart Chakra
Text: The Radical Intelligence

Virtue: Energy, Courage
Vice: Cruelty, Destruction
Titles: Pachad – Fear, Din – Justice
Colours in Atziluth: Orange
Colour in Briah: Scarlet Red
Colour in Yetzirah: Bright Scarlet
Colour in Assiah: Red flecked Black
Tarot Cards: The Four Fives
Five of Wands: Swiftness
Five of Cups: Abandoned Success
Five of Swords: Shortened Force
Five of Pentacles: Prudence

COMMENTARY

The Fifth Path is called the Radical Intelligence because
it resembles unity, uniting itself to Binah, Understanding,
which emanates from the primordial depths of
Chockmah wisdom.

The fifth Sephirah, Geburah, means Severity. With Chesed and Tiphareth, Geburah forms the Ethical or Moral Triangle of the Greater Mysteries. Geburah, the sphere of Severity, forms the polar opposite to Chesed, the sphere of Mercy. As Geburah gives its name to the Pillar of Severity, Chesed gives its name to the Pillar of Mercy. These two Sephiroth need to be viewed in a polarized relationship of opposites which find a balance point on the 19th Path assigned to the Trump named Strength. Geburah is reached from Binah on the 18th Path, from Hod by the 23rd Path and from Tiphareth by the 22nd Path. The 22nd Path represents the first conscious encounter with karmic factors; the 23rd Path represents the conscious steps which bring transcendence of karmic factors as Bodhisattva consciousness comes to birth; and the 18th Path represents the recurring drive to incarnate. This tight mesh of karmic influences is experienced through Geburah, which is also a sphere of karmic adjustment. It is therefore a powerful meeting place of karmic energies. It is perhaps no wonder that this is a sphere of severity represented by martial images.

Shared Karma

> Today, the harvest is ripe and mankind is reaping what it has sown, preparatory to a fresh ploughing in the springtime of the New Age, with a fresh sowing of the seed which will, let us pray and hope, produce a better harvest.

> **Alice Bailey, *Ponder on This***

Though the concept of karma carries no weight in international affairs, the concept of action certainly does. Karma means 'action', and it is not difficult to see how the actions of one nation impact on another. If the small self is motivated by personal considerations, then this is demonstrably true of the nation state which will fight and labour in its own interests. All actions, whether by individuals or states, have consequences and repercussions. Action is visible but karma is not. Karma represents seed sown long ago:

> Everything that is happening in the world today, and which is so potently affecting humanity – things of beauty and of horror, modes of living and civilization and culture, prejudices and likings, scientific attainment and artistic expression, and the many ways which humanity throughout the planet colours existence – are aspects of effects initiated somewhere, on some level, at some time, by human beings both individually and en mass.[1]

Unresolved hatreds, rivalries and deeply felt passions can suddenly ripen under new circumstances and erupt on the national or international scene with great force. Geburah is the sphere of shared karma; its manifestation is invariably dynamic as forces carrying a strong emotional charge seek expression. Conflict is most often about a clash of ideology, whether political, religious or economic. It will arise inevitably in a world composed of nation states. Apart from providing political cartoonists with an unlimited source of amusement, national characteristics are powerful forces. Hiroshi Motoyama is not alone in seeing a deeper spiritual dimension in nationhood. Taking the example of his native Japan, Motoyama writes, 'When we look at a country using the physical eye we can see only its physical characteristics, but when I look to Japan using non-physical perception I see a very different picture. I see a vast underlying spirit. This is the spiritual existence of the country which enabled the land itself to materialize on the physical plane.'[2] Motoyama continues, 'Each nation has its own spirit and that spirit has its own karma.' Like Motoyama, Blake envisaged Albion as the spirit within the land of Britain. Ideology separates as well as unites. Without a common meeting ground, when passionately held beliefs encounter equally passionate but different beliefs, conflict is inevitable. The battlefields of history are the graveyards of conflicting belief systems. The passage of history alone judges the rightfulness of causes. Spanish Catholicism felt justified in its conquest of South America and the annihilation of its native population. White Europeans felt justified in their great push across North America and the conquest of its native populations. Island Britain acquired an empire of continents and imposed the rule of a colonial master. The Age of Empires and of colonial rule is over. These ideas have lost their power. New ideas are on the rise. The communications revolution has breached the boundaries of nationalism. Globalism in many forms is on the march. The Spiritual

Experience of Geburah is the Vision of Power: this is the vision of an idea perfectly matched in time. The watchwords Liberty, Equality and Fraternity seized France with revolutionary zeal and brought about the downfall of *l'ancien régime*. Socialism was seeded as a counter to the excesses of capitalism and the effects of the Industrial Revolution. Marxism fired a revolution. The Vision of Power is the vision of a powerful idea – in fact, it is the vision of a vision. In the history of ideas and ideologies so many powerful themes begin with the vision of a single person. At the time the idea appears radical, shocking and utterly unattainable. But when the seed of vision is planted at the right time and in fertile soil, it takes root and has the power to overcome all obstacles. The USSR was transformed through the idea of *glasnost* – openness. Gandhi's vision of an independent India was made real and the mighty British empire was vanquished.

Translating vision into reality most often brings severity and requires the whole panoply of Geburah's armoury. Ideas whose time has passed do not disappear instantly like an extinguished candle flame but burn less brightly in the increasing vacuum of failing support. The clash of ideologies is fought out in the World of Action, Assiah, in the sphere of Malkuth. The feudalism of Russia was ended by the Russian Revolution. The slavery of America was ended by the Civil War, and America itself came to birth through its war against England. The defeat of Germany ended Nazi ideals of expansion and oppression.

In the terrible crucible of historical process it is possible to detect the slow accretion of humanitarian ideas and principles. The humanitarian principle, like the transcendent function, reconciles the oppositions presented by nationality and religious creed. Ironically, it often takes the horror of warfare to generate a humanitarian response. Professional nursing arose against the background of the human misery created by the Crimean War. The Victorian Florence Nightingale was initially alone in her vision of providing nursing care, but it was an idea whose time had come. The Red Cross organization and The League of Nations, which seeded The United Nations along with numerous other humanitarian bodies, were founded in response to the suffering caused by war. The Virtue of Geburah is Courage. Its Vice is Cruelty and Destruction. Yet courage is only seen in the face of cruelty and destruction. War and conflict bring both the Vice and Virtue of Geburah.

Human Rights

Contrary to popular belief, human rights are not about
abstract texts but about people, what they and their
neighbours are legally free to do and what obligations
fall on governments for guaranteeing those freedoms.

Sam Daws, *The United Nations*

Geburah and Chesed represent a dynamic polarity: the one is merciful, the
other severe. Chesed is the sphere of love, Geburah is the sphere of action.
Where Chesed represents a blueprint which is spiritually radical, Geburah
brings radical change in the world itself. Where Chesed represents a blueprint which brings Mercy to the individual, Geburah releases the stored
karma of individuals as part of the nation state. It brings severity and sows
the seeds of future karma. How many conflict situations draw upon the
memory of a distant battle, event or historical circumstance to stoke the fires
of present division? Where Chesed projects a blueprint for inner spiritual
dimensions, Geburah projects the desire to act directly in the outer world.
The polarity between these two powers comes together on the 19th Path
of Strength. Here the individual comes face to face with the karma stored
within the centres of the subtle bodies. It is this process of total transformation which cuts into the cycle of karma. However, the journey of the
19th Path is uncommonly undertaken. Karma rules. Whenever two parties
define themselves by difference, some degree of conflict will follow. The
greater the perceived differences, the greater the degree of conflict. A third
unifying factor alone has the power to break into this mindset. Only one
concept has the power to overreach all differences – that of Humanity itself.
Perhaps this is the Vision of Power today. Perhaps this is at last the idea whose
time has come. Buddhism urges that we treat all sentient beings *as if* they
had been good mothers to us in an unknown and forgotten existence. This
provides just the shift of identity needed to envision a fresh perspective and
break the mould of separation. This is the dawning of a New Age. It is said
to be characterized by a sense of brotherhood and the practical implementation of the ideals which will bring about a real sense of human family.
Perhaps this long task has already begun with the faltering steps towards a
reintegration of the spiritual and the physical as two dimensions in a single
interface. If the spiritual model of karma and rebirth is applied to human
existence, the abstract notion of the family of humanity at once becomes a
keen reality.

THE FAMILY TREE

Suspend disbelief for a moment. Imagine that you have lived a number of previous existences. Each life has provided the opportunity to create a family, who in turn may have done the same. Visualize the implications of lives in different cultures, different places and different times. Perhaps you have mothered and fathered many children, been the son or daughter to many a parent, both good and bad. This is the family of humanity extended through history. You have helped to create it in your own journey from life to life.

This is a new vision, as yet voiced by the few and ignored by the many. Yet this is where all visions begin, in the infinitesimally tiny flicker of new realization. It is a vision that changes the world. Where visions clash, Geburah is summoned. Only a holistic vision has the power to bring Mercy; until then, karma will be reaped with as much ferocity as it was sown. Each age stands for some two thousand years. This new vision of a united human family has a long gestation still to come. The family of humanity is more than a hopeful metaphor which appeals to a higher sense of vision and asks us to put differences aside. When His Holiness the Dalai Lama gave a talk to the members of the Theosophical Society in Illinois he began with a statement of common humanity:

> I will speak this evening on my usual topic – that is, about the
> importance of kindness and compassion. When I speak about this,
> I regard myself not as a Buddhist, not as the Dalai Lama, not as a
> Tibetan, but rather as one human being. And I hope that you in the
> audience will at this moment think of yourselves as human beings
> rather than as Americans or Westerners, or members of the
> Theosophical Society. These things are secondary. If from my side
> and from the listener's side we interact as human beings, we will
> reach the basic level. If I say 'I am as monk' or 'I am a Buddhist',
> these are, in comparison to my nature as a human being, temporary.
> To be human is basic. Once you are born as a human being that
> cannot change until death. Other things, education, rich or poor, are
> secondary.[3]

He continued with an overview of the many problems facing the world currently and with a plea for a shared responsibility:

> Each of us has responsibility for all humankind. It is time for us to

think of other people as true brothers and sisters and to be concerned with their welfare, with lessening their suffering. Even if you cannot sacrifice your own benefit entirely you should not forget the concerns of others. We should think more about the future benefit of all humanity.[4]

Such ideas have long been voiced. Throughout the bloody and divisive history of humanity, small voices have spoken up for peace and kindness. But perhaps now 'the family of humanity' is an idea whose time has truly come. The emerging Age of Aquarius offers the possibility of humanitarian goals and ideals in a way never before possible. Global communication shrinks the distances that once kept people apart. Environmental problems are shared issues not confined to one nation state. Boundaries of all kinds are shifting with great speed. Now at last, basic human rights are enshrined in law. The United Nations, the successor to the earlier League of Nations, was set up by the victors of the Second World War. It was a positive response to the horror of war. Rooted in the cruelty and destruction of war, the UN represents the energy and courage to make a radical change. Its founding Charter expresses a hope in a better future for all: 'The Charter is not perfect, but it is the only Charter we have. The challenge is not to devise a constitution for some future utopia but to make the best use of the Charter we have in this present, imperfect world.'[5]

Article 1: Purposes and Principles

1. To maintain international peace and security, and to that end to take effective collective measures for the prevention and removal of threats to the peace, and for the suppression of aggression or other breaches of the peace, and to bring about by peaceful means, and in conformity with the principles of justice and international law, adjustment or settlement of international disputes or situations which might lead to a breach of the peace.

2. To develop friendly relations among nations based on respect for the principle of equal rights and self-determination of peoples and to take other appropriate measures to strengthen universal peace.

3. To achieve international co-operation in solving problems of an economic, social, cultural, or humanitarian character and in promoting and encouraging respect for human rights and fundamental freedoms without distinction as to race, sex, language or religion.

4. To be a centre for harmonizing the actions of nations in the
attainment of these common ends. [6]

These word express sentiments rarely heard and enshrine ideals not often
lived up to. If such ideals seem unreachable or improbable, simply wander
down the byways of history to discover how values have changed.

Revolution and Evolution

We all want to change the world.

John Lennon

Geburah represents the reservoir of karma both great and small which
invisibly works its way to the surface through personal, national and racial
action. This is a Sephirah of dynamic action, represented by Mars the
Roman god of war. Martial energy permeates Geburah. Mars is also assigned
to the 27th Path of the Tower, which is also a Path of destruction and reconstruction. Mars represents physical power, active engagement and radical
change – these are the components of war. Humanity's ability and desire to
wage war seems to have no limit. From the earliest times to the most recent,
weaponry has been developed and warfare has never ceased. This unhappy
prognosis seems without remedy. War brings immense human misery, yet it
is at the same time the instrument of necessary change. The Magical Image
of Geburah is that of a Mighty Warrior in his Chariot. The symbolism is
unmistakably martial and potent. Geburah is represented by martial images
of the sword, spear, scourge and chain. These are double-edged symbols
representing defence in the hands of the oppressed and oppression in the
hands of the aggressors:

> Whenever there is anything that has outlived its usefulness, Geburah
> must wield the pruning knife; wherever there is selfishness, it must
> find itself impaled on the spearpoint of Geburah; wherever there is
> violence against the weak, or the merciless use of strength, it is the
> sword of Geburah, not the orb of Chesed, that is the most effectual
> counteractant; wherever there is sloth and dishonesty, Geburah's
> sacred scourge is needed; and where there is a removal of the
> landmarks set for our neighbour's protection, it is the chain of
> Geburah that must restrain.[7]

Geburah is a Sephirah of action. All action creates karma, like the ripples which follow a stone being dropped into water. The effects do not cease in the present moment but reverberate into the future. When Hiroshi Motoyama states that 'the earth, then, is composed not only of the physical plane but also of the astral and the causal worlds that belong to it', he draws a picture of reality which includes unseen but potent influences. The astral realm describes the accumulated feelings and emotions of individuals and groups; patriotic feelings for instance are powerful enough to have an influence on the course of events. Connected to Malkuth, the vast astral pool of Yesod provides an untapped reservoir of unresolved feelings, both positive and negative. The causal plane refers to the higher reaches of the Tree represented by both Geburah and Chesed, which together provide a reservoir of mental energy and ideas which is also acted upon in the world of effects, the Kingdom. Using physical power to implement a particular vision or to oppose a different vision must raise moral and ethical questions. Without facing the moral implications of action, applied force is no more than a restatement of the blunt idea that 'might is right'. Geburah is part of the Moral and Ethical Triangle. This Sephirah does not provide licence or justification for warring acts. As a channel for karma great and small, its greater purpose is aligned to that of Chesed, mercy. Where Chesed represents ideas and ideals which generate a merciful response and bring about peaceful goals, Geburah bears the weight of accumulated karma which by its nature seeks to be resolved through conflict. After the mystical and beatific experiences assigned to Tiphareth, the ascorbic nature of Geburah comes as something of a shock. As Dion Fortune has pointed out, 'Were it not that the Qabalistic doctrine explicitly lays it down that all the ten Sephiroth are holy, there are many who would be inclined to look upon Geburah as the evil aspect of the Tree of Life.'[8] Geburah is undoubtedly the most difficult of the Sephiroth to grasp. It shares certain qualities with both Binah and Chockmah, the Sephiroth of the Supernal Triangle. By, 'uniting itself to Binah', Understanding, Geburah partakes of the Binah nature. Its likeness to Binah gives a stabilizing potency. Perversely, its likeness to Chockmah gives a dynamic nature. These two influences permeate the nature of Geburah and provide an alternating rhythm of rise and fall, creation and disintegration. Geburah represents an ongoing dynamic process. 'If we watch life, we shall see that rhythm, not stability, is its vital principle.'[9] Geburah holds the seeds of change in stasis and the seeds of stasis in change. However, Geburah speaks not through the organic vocabulary of the natural world but through the voice of humanity at its most strident. Its images are martial, its message is one of dynamic action. Geburah is called the Radical Intelligence, from the Latin, *radix*, meaning root. This Radical Intelligence has the power to cut to the root of a society and a civilization; it is seen in the revolution and in the sweeping changes following war. Geburah wields the power of the pruning knife and the surgical blade. Its immediate effects are disruptive, often terrible, as the structures of a society fall. Geburah is also known as Pachad, meaning fear. But Geburah also has a third title, Din, meaning justice. The three titles convey the intertwined aspects of Geburah. Severe in mode and fearful in action, Geburah can also bring justice. The wheel of history turns relentlessly, fuelled by competing ideas of justice, freedom and power. The forces of Geburah are not specifically those of war, despite being characterized by so many war-like images. Geburah expresses the forces of destruction which are part of the rhythm of life. The nature of Geburah is implicit in the buds of spring and the leaf fall of autumn and in the rise and fall of civilizations. Everything has a life span, even stars are born and die. Great civilizations rise and fall: the marvels of Egypt, Rome and Greece are now ruins in the hot sun. Death and birth hold the balance of life. These twin poles reserve a balance in nature. Destruction, decay and dissolution are part of a natural cycle of rebirth and return. Nature provides her own limiting mechanisms which regulate growth and maintain a healthy balance. When undisturbed by external influences, nature holds the delicate balance required to maintain species and diversity. Unfortunately, environmental pressures now often add weight to the forces mitigating against balance and equilibrium. In the short term such imbalances become catastrophic crises, but in the very long term another level of equilibrium arises. Geburah offers symbols of reconstruction alongside its many symbols of destruction. The five-petalled rose, a symbol of Geburah, appears on the banner in Tarot Trump XIII, Death, as a symbol of renewal and rebirth. History shows cities and societies rise from the ashes, like the mythical phoenix. Every cataclysm and tragedy brings change. In its wake, society is never quite the same, but it moves forward.

EVOCATION

Welcome to my kingdom. I am the most feared encounter, yet you call me constantly from the depths of your collective vision. The seeds for my awakening are ever present in the ideals, values and beliefs that you live and die by. Look carefully to the beliefs that you hold to be good and true. All is not always as it seems. Where the seeds of division lie, the divided tree will grow and you will call me again. My lessons are terrible beyond measure, but you still call on me by my name Mars, the god of war. My path is truly double-edged. I bring justice and fear. I disclose the hero and the tyrant. I disclose courage and cruelty with the same breath. I bring the sword but also the rose. I am the warrior in defence of a belief. I am called fear but I am the reflection of your fear writ large in the theatre of the world. You are right to fear what can be done in the name of virtue and righteousness for my Vice is cruelty and destruction, and these will arise in equal measure to my Virtue of courage. I am the melting pot of civilization and the engine of change. I am your response to the seeds of the past.

INTERNALIZATION – THE TEMPLE OF GEBURAH

Construct the Temple of Geburah in the creative imagination. You are at once reminded of the amphitheatres of the past. Staggered seating in blocks leads down to an open circular area. In the centre of the space a broad open bowl of shining metal stands. A flame rises from within it. A figure wearing red stands beside it. This is Khamael, the organizer of today's event. The assembly sits in silent meditation. Khamael addresses you all:

'We are met to share the story of humanity. Each one of you carries a part of this story – not merely your living memory but through the DNA of your bodies and through the dust and forgotten memories of other places and times. The story of the world is not forgotten but indelibly printed upon a subtle level of reality sometimes called the akashic record. Each one of you here has a story to render.'

You enter more deeply into your meditation and unexpected images arise from the record of history. Events from the historical record of your nation's past come to mind. But now your consciousness is expanded and you are able to glimpse the effect of this idea on those people who seldom feature in the record of history. A palpable feeling begins to rise in the room. It contains sadness and sorrow, anger and grief, regret and remorse, dismay and disbelief. Limited by ideas of the time, every incarnation has its constraints and impelling drives. Now you have time to reflect on the ideas that drove your nation to act; now you have time to reflect on new ideas and vision.

Now Khamael calls each of you in turn to stand before him. As you watch the proceedings, you see that each person stands quietly before the flame. Then to your surprise Khamael reaches deep into the flames and draws out something which he hands over to each one. Now your turn arrives. You stand and walk to the arena. As you stand before the bowl with its flames, images from your meditation arise like fleeting phantoms. You feel that the fire calls them to itself and consumes them with a rising crest of flame. The flames drop back and Khamael reaches into the fiery furnace without harm. He draws out a small golden figure which he hands to you. It is a phoenix. You return to your seat and contemplate the meaning of these proceedings.

When you are ready, leave the way you came through the doorway. Finally dissolve all images and return to ordinary consciousness.

EXERCITIA SPIRITUALIA

Take the Following Subjects for Meditation:

- Elohim Gebor
- Khamael
- Seraphim, the fiery serpents
- The Vision of Power
- Pentagon, Five-Petalled Rose, Sword, Spear, Scourge, Chain
- A Mighty Warrior in his Chariot
- Mars
- Shared karma

Contemplate the Following Questions and Record your Responses:

- How do Energy and Courage operate in your life?
- How do Cruelty and Destruction operate in your life?
- How does the nature of Geburah relate to the Heart Chakra?
- What other correspondences can you relate to Geburah?
- How do the four Tarot cards relate to Geburah?

Visualize the Following and Record your Experiences:

- The Temple of Geburah including the Archangel Khamael
- The Journey to the Temple of Geburah

CHAPTER 19

The Twenty-First Path:
Netzach–Chesed

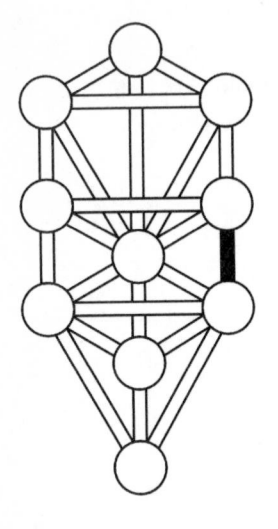

FIGURE 27 THE 21ST PATH:

NETZACH–CHESED

TAROT TRUMP X,

THE WHEEL OF FORTUNE

TABLE OF CORRESPONDENCES

The Journey: Tarot Trump X, Lord of the
Forces of Life, The Wheel of Fortune

Key: The Letter Kaph, meaning the palm of
the hand

Double Letter: Riches – Poverty

Spiritual Significance: Jupiter

Text: The Intelligence of Conciliation and
Reward

Colour in Atzilut : Violet – Blue

Colour in Briah: Rich Purple

Colour in Yetzirah: Bright Blue

Colour in Assiah: Rayed Yellow

COMMENTARY

The Twenty-first Path is the Intelligence of Conciliation and Reward and it is so called because it receives the divine influences which flow into it from its benediction upon all and each existence.

The 21st Path connects the seventh Sephirah, Netzach, with the fourth Sephirah, Chesed, which is directly above it on the Pillar of Mercy. The 21st Path bridges the Astral or Psychological Triangle of the Lesser Mysteries with the Ethical Triangle of the Greater Mysteries. In this capacity, the 21st Path forges links with the Individuality and creates a dynamic which moves beyond the limitations of the personality. This forward movement is represented by the symbolism of the turning wheel, also called the Lord of the Forces of Life. The 21st Path brings an expanded and broadened perspective on life through its entirely transpersonal symbolism. In connecting Chesed, the place of the Holy Powers, with Netzach, the 21st Path draws on the Occult, or hidden Intelligence, as a means of turning towards the nature of wisdom. Netzach is the realm of the instincts, both biological and cognitive. These powers, which are at the service of the self and its personal goals, are to be transformed into transpersonal goals and aspirations through the turning of the wheel.

The Circle of Life

When I began drawing the mandalas, however, I saw that everything, all the paths I had been following, all the steps I had taken, were leading back to a single point – namely, to the mid-point. It became increasingly plain to me that the mandala is the centre. It is the exponent of all paths. It is the path to the centre, to individuation.

C.G. Jung, *Memories, Dreams, Reflections*

The 21st Path is assigned to Tarot Trump X, the Wheel of Fortune. A wheel is suspended in the heavens. It has three sections, each inscribed with letters and signs. A sphinx bearing a sword sits at the top of the wheel and a strange

hybrid creature is attached to its outer rim. The four corners contain the
Holy Kerubs, each with a book. A serpent rides in the sky beside the wheel.
The wheel is a universal symbol of movement, change and dynamic life. It
is a circle turning upon its own axis to create a repetitive pattern. The wheel
found in every culture is a symbol of time and change. It is the sun disc,
the calendar, the zodiac, the wheel of destiny and the mandala. The Sanskrit
word *cakra*, meaning wheel, has passed into New Age vocabulary as chakra,
a wheel of living energy. The circle is an image of unity, the wheel is the
turning circle. The wheel of Tarot Trump X is composed of three separate
but interlocking rings. The outer ring is inscribed with the letters T, O, R
and A, which spell not only 'taro' but also 'rota', meaning wheel and law.
This piece of wordplay fuses the Tarot, the wheel and the law into a single
motif. The outer ring is also inscribed with the four letters of the
Tetragrammaton – Yod, Heh, Vau and Heh – which together render the
Holy Name of God. Each of the four letters also has an elemental attribution. Decoded elementally, the formula reads Fire, Water, Air and Earth. In
the spirit of Kabbalistic complexity, each letter also carries a number symbol
which in turn has meaning, and additionally each letter stands for one of
the four worlds – Atziluth, Briah, Yetzirah and Assiah. These represent the
Archetypal World, the Creative World, the World of Formation and the
World of Action. The outer ring therefore expresses the totality of creation,
from the spiritual to the material planes. It encompasses all that the Tree of
Life expresses, since the Sephiroth themselves are assigned to the four worlds.
It is a statement of totality and wholeness complemented by the additional
element of dynamic movement. The second inner ring is inscribed with
the symbols for the alchemical principles – Salt, Sulphur and Mercury. In
Eastern symbolism these are the three gunas – Tatmas, Rajas and Sattva.
Sattva is related to superconsciousness, which is symbolized by Mercury.
Rajas is related to activity, passion and desire, symbolized by Sulphur. Tamas
is related to inertia, subconsciousness and ignorance, symbolized by salt. The
fourth symbol is that of Aquarius, representing dissolution and also the
energies of the incoming age. This inner circle brings together the triplicity
of states of being and mind. The gunas are fundamental to Eastern metaphysics and form a foundation stone of the Ayurvedic tradition. A third
inner circle bears no inscription but is subdivided into eight segments. All
the circles radiate from and return to the central point within the innermost
circle. This place of unity is called the bindu point. It is the seed which
germinates the mandala. Tarot Trump X presents an image of wholeness
and unity. The forces of creation are represented here. But above all it is an

image of movement through time. As the wheel turns, so time moves on in cycles great and small from the daily cycle of 24 hours to the precessional cycle of 26,000 years. We most often understand the passage of time through the turning circle. The passage of time is an expression of earth's place in the cosmos and the interrelationships between the steadfast sun, the mobile moon and the wandering earth. The circular form is fundamental to a human understanding of life. It appears as the zodiac, the clock and the sacred circle of past peoples keen to unite heavenly patterns with life on earth. The Wheel of Fortune draws our attention to all the cycles of time which interweave to produce the framework in which human life is set. The image of the turning wheel is a universal one. Jung relates the details of a dream which bears an uncanny resemblance to the Wheel of Fortune. The Tarot Trump is the work of artistic construction, but the dream is the product of spontaneous psychic energy. The dreamer recalled the following:

> There is a vertical and a horizontal circle, having a common centre. This is the world clock. It is supported by a black bird. The vertical centre is a blue disc with a white border divided into 4 x 8 = 32 partitions. A pointer rotates upon it. The horizontal circle consists of four colours. On it stand four little men with pendulums, and round about it is laid the ring that was once dark and is now golden.
>
> The 'clock' has three rhythms or pulses:
>
> The small pulse: the pointer on the blue vertical disc advances by $1/32$. The middle pulse: one complete revolution of the pointer. At the same time the horizontal circle advances $1/32$.
> Finally, the great pulse: $1/32$ middle pulses are equal to one revolution of the golden ring.

Jung recorded that the dream was so potent as to bring the dreamer to a state of 'sublime harmony'. This is the potential power of a vision of wholeness. Jung described the dream as, 'the most complete union of opposites that is possible including that of the masculine trinity and the feminine quaternary in the analogy of the alchemical hermaphrodite'.[1] The dream carried such a numinous potency that it was given the name of The Great Vision.

A great vision has the power to uplift, inspire and even instruct. It conveys understanding beyond words and insight beyond explanation. The Trump expresses the same themes as those in the dream of the great vision. It brings dynamic opposites together in a pattern of unity. The wheel conveys the turning of cyclic time and suggests repeating patterns, both great and small, from the seasonal to the epic. The four elements as creative forces are expressed through the Tetragrammaton, the four zodiacal symbols, and through the sphinx, where the four are reconciled into one. This is the Path of the Conciliating Intelligence, which reconciles forces which are seemingly opposed and creates a synthesis from them. It conciliates the oppositions inherent in the four elements which are depicted upon the wheel and also in the background as the four fixed signs of the zodiac. The separated elements are reconciled by the sphinx, which represents a recreated synthesis of elemental forces. The sphinx symbolizes the work of recreation and regeneration at the heart of the Great Work in all ages and times. The sphinx is the newly-made being, reconstructed from the substance of the four elements. This is the Intelligence of Conciliation and Reward. The work of Conciliation brings its own Reward – namely, conscious choice. The sphinx bears a human head which symbolizes the achievement of consciousness and the victory of mind. The sphinx wields the sword which has been crafted from a sharpened awareness. The sphinx holds the power of liberation and may choose to be free of the wheel. In contrast, a hybrid creature is being carried upon the rim of the wheel. Consciousness is still undeveloped; it is carried unwittingly by the turning of the wheel.

THE CYCLE OF LIFE

How many cyclic rhythms affect your life?

Contemplate each of them in turn. What meaning do these have for you?

The Wheel of Existence

When he had seen all his own births and deaths he thought of other living things and he thought to himself: 'Again and again they must leave people they think of as their own and must go on elsewhere, and that without ever stopping. Surely this world is unprotected and helpless, and like a wheel it goes round and round.'

Buddhist Scripture

The idea of rebirth is fundamental to Buddhism. The wheel expresses the basis of the Buddhist philosophy of cyclic existence. Like the Tree of Life, the Wheel of Life expresses a metaphysical philosophy through symbols in the form of pictures. The Wheel of existence or Wheel of Being and Becoming is divided into four sections.

The centre of the wheel shows the three poisons. The pig represents ignorance, the cockerel represents greed and the snake represents hatred. These three contaminants give rise to the ten Non-Virtuous Deeds: killing stealing, sexual misconduct, untruthful speech, harsh speech, slander, frivolous talk, covetousness, malevolence, and attachment to misconceptions. Beyond the central circle is a second circle which is half-black and half-white. In the white half, people ascend; in the black half, people fall according to their karma.

The middle rim is divided into six realms, including the hungry ghosts and the hot and cold hells. The outer rim shows the twelve links of Interdependent Origination. The first of these is ignorance, represented by an old blind man. Next comes volition or karmic formation, represented by the potter making pots. Consciousness is next, represented by a monkey swinging from branch to branch as consciousness swings from one life to another. Name and form are represented by a person being carried across water in a boat, just as consciousness is carried by the body. The six senses are represented by an empty house with six windows. Next, two people come together to shake hands, representing the human contact that creates life. Sensation is represented by an arrow entering the eye. Craving is represented by the alcoholic searching to quell desire. Clinging is represented by fruit being plucked from a tree. Becoming is represented by a pregnant woman about to give birth. Finally, old age and death are represented by a corpse being carried away.

The entire wheel is in the grip of the red demon of Impermanence, who holds it in between her fangs. In the top-right-hand corner Buddha Shakyamuni stands on a cloud offering the *mudra* of protection. His right hand points towards the full moon in the top-left-hand corner. The full moon symbolizes purification, the third of the Four Noble Truths. The upright Buddha shows the way. The application *Dharma* is the way to control the ego and leave the suffering of *samsara* behind:

Cease to do evil.

Learn to practise virtue,

Purify the mind.

That is the teaching of all the Buddhas.

The Cycle of Life and Death

Through the power of ignorance, which is the first link
in the chain of the twelve dependent elements, we are
reborn in samsara.

Lama Sherab Gyaltsen Amipa, *The Opening of the Lotus*

Tarot Trump X, The Wheel of Fortune, is also called the Lord of the Forces
of Life. It is a mandala, an image of wholeness representing the forces of life
in balance, equilibrium and constant motion. This is a meditative image of
the interlocking relationships which propel life forwards. It too is an image
of cyclic existence. It shows the choice between the path of unconscious
rebirth represented by the animal-headed cynocephalus and the path of reincarnation represented by the sphinx. The one is being carried helplessly by
the turning of the wheel, the other sits just above the wheel, distanced from
its turning. The first has no choice but to be carried by the wheel, the
second can exercise the power of choice. Buddhism makes a clear distinction between rebirth, the involuntary result of karma, and reincarnation,
the conscious result of karma. Rebirth can only be transformed into reincarnation through the sustained development and evolution of consciousness.
'If rebirth was a given, and quite ordinary, reincarnation was not. Only those
who reached the highest levels of spiritual development, it was said, could
train their mind at the time of death to reincarnate consciously in the precise
place and circumstances they wanted.'[2]

Here is a prime symbol of transcendence with the power to relocate
the sense of self in eternal time. Integrating this symbol brings a profound
connection to the forces of life in the fullest sense. The symbolism of the
Wheel of Existence is deeply transformative, it has the power to put both
life and death in perspective. The wheel is a symbol of continuing change.
It is a reminder of the dynamic nature of life. This Path is assigned to
Jupiter, which represents the principle of expansion. Jupiter brings largesse
and abundance of heart, mind and being. It well represents the favourable
opportunities presented by the wheel, the auspicious face of fortune and
the expansive life processes which the wheel generates.

The letter Kaph is assigned to this path. It means the palm of the hand.
It reinforces the idea that each life expresses a personal destiny which can
be read in the lines of the hand. As one of the Double Letters it represents
the polarity of Riches–Poverty. Fortunes rise and fall, circumstances

change, situations shift and the wheel turns relentlessly.

Nowhere demonstrates the reality of the Wheel of Existence more clearly than the spiritual traditions of Tibet. Tibetan Buddhism is built upon the cycle of reincarnation. Its lamas return time and time again. Khamtrul Rinpoche, guru to Tenzin Palmo, was in his eighth incarnation as the head of the Khampagar in East Tibet. He had been recognized in a continuous line of succession since 1548. The current Dalai Lama is the fourteenth incarnation. It is common for lamas to provide some indications of future birth to assist those whose job it will be to locate the future incarnation. Buddhism is built upon the reality of reincarnation. Its lamas return by choice to pick up the same thread again. Every one has to pass the tests designed to show contiguity of consciousness. Examples of remembrance are legion. One of the most fascinating and recent stories of reincarnation is recounted in the book *Reincarnation* by Vicki Mackenzie. It tells of her friendship with Lama Yeshe, of his death and his rebirth as the Spanish child Osel Hita Torres. Lama Yeshe was among the first Tibetan lamas to teach in the West. His untimely death at 49 did not alter his intention. He was the first Tibetan lama to take a Western incarnation. He chose to incarnate in the West in order to continue his work. Not only did he indicate where he would be found in the time-honoured tradition, but he actively chose his future parents – a couple he knew in his adult life as the fully-fledged lama. This extraordinary and wonderful sequence of events is unprecedented outside Tibet, but this kind of experience lies at the very core of Tibetan spiritual life. In 1977, when he was teaching a two-week course, Lama Yeshe met Maria Torres, the woman who would give him future birth. The two became immediate friends even though Maria was not yet a Buddhist. 'I knew this was a man I could dedicate my life to,' she said. After Lama Yeshe died, it was the task of his close friend Lama Zopa to find the future incarnation. This too is regular practice within Tibet. Lama Zopa listened and watched for signs, exactly as he might have done in Tibet. Once, in a dream, Lama Yeshe had revealed he was about to take human form. Later dreams showed a small child crawling on the floor as a young Western boy. Maria Torres, as a close friend of the deceased lama, also had a dream. She stood in a cathedral where Lama Yeshe was giving a teaching. With everyone else she went up to receive blessings but when she was touched it was like blissful golden white water pouring through her. Lama Yeshe died on 3 March 1984, and Osel Hitta Torres was born on 12 February 1985, less than a year later. In all there were ten candidates who showed favourable signs, but the Dalai Lama was drawn especially to Osel's name in meditation.

At 14 months, Osel was brought to meet the Dalai Lama. After the meeting it was a long 15-hour drive to Dharamsala. Here Lama Zopa, following his own intuition, placed the toddler on Lama Yeshe's throne. In respect, he performed three prostrations and made a mandala offering to the young child. 'Here is your guru,' he said to the small group of Lama Yeshe's own students. It was a bold move which had startling results. 'With that, Osel, who until then had been exhausted and flopped back against the cushions, threw aside his bottle and was suddenly fired with energy. His whole demeanour changed. He sat bolt upright, wide awake, eyes shining, his face full of vitality. He picked up the dorje and bell in his small hands, the correct hands, and with tremendous gusto waved them in the air exactly as a Tibetan lama should. He put them down and repeated the action again and again, seven or eight times, all the time laughing, laughing. People began to cry. It was so like Lama Yeshe. He had come back to them.'[3]

This informal event was followed by the traditional Tibetan test in which the candidate is presented with a range of items belong to the previous incarnation and must successfully select them from a range including similar looking items. The 14-month-old Osel had to find Lama Yeshe's own *mala* and the correct bell from among eight pairs, which he did with great gusto and delight. It was at this point that he was formally recognized as the legitimate incarnation of Lama Yeshe. More informal signs were to follow.

In the grounds of the Tushita retreat centre is a house which once belonged to the Dalai Lama's own tutor. It contains his body, preserved in the Tibetan way, sitting peacefully in the lotus position in one of the rooms. On being taken there, Osel threw himself to the ground in three prostrations. Later that day at the stupa dedicated to his own root guru, Triang Rinpoche, he circled it clockwise in the proper fashion and stopped to perform prostrations. Perhaps even more remarkable however was the day when the newly incarnate Osel Ling met the recognized incarnation of Triang Rinpoche, whose stupa he had recently reverenced. The two children, one aged 14 months, the other aged four, exchanged gifts with excited and mutual delight.

In the middle of March 1987 Osel Ling, aged two, was enthroned. He wore the ceremonial lama's robes and on his head the high-crested yellow pandit hat, the badge of office. Osel behaved impeccably. For the next three hours Osel sat on his throne watching the proceedings with a stillness, composure and majesty that went far beyond his years:

The high point of the ceremony was when the lamas, led by Lama Zopa Rinpoche, lined up before him, did prostrations in homage and then humbly offered the child their gifts. Without prompting, Osel took each gift, placed the holy object next to the crown on his head, in the lama's way of showing reverence, and then handed it to his attendant. That done, he placed a chubby hand on the head bowed before him in blessing. He did it again and again through the entire ranks of the Tibetan hierarchy and then the rows of Westerners.[4]

After the enthronement Osel played in the garden like any other child of two.

Maria Torres has had the extraordinary and unique experience of knowing the man and mothering the child. Her words provide a fitting conclusion to this continuity of consciousness turned by the wheel of becoming. 'For me the purpose of Lama Osel's life is to finish the job started by Lama Yeshe. Lama Yeshe could not help Westerners as much as he wanted because he was limited by his Tibetanness. He chose to be reborn in a way where he could work more effectively with the background of Tibetan Wisdom and Western science. I believe he will truly be able to reach people.'[5]

This is the Intelligence of Conciliation and Reward. Through the turning of the wheel, a disparate consciousness is gradually transformed into a sense of continuity. Conciliation, the harmonious union of once unrelated aspects of being, proceeds with every revolution. Conscious participation is reward itself. Lama Yeshe, through his own spiritual attainment, returned once more to his chosen work and close friends through a new incarnation, Osel. Through the turning of the wheel, the transformation of rebirth brought both a reconciliation and a reward. The reward of this Path is the gift of expanded awareness, subtle understanding and depth of relationship that comes from a total re-identification of self. This is indeed the Wheel of Being and Becoming and Lord of the Forces of Life.

EVOCATION

Welcome to my kingdom. Come to me through the simple analogy of the wheel. Take this simple image of turning and rotation, of revolution and change, and internalize its nature into your being. Plant the seeds of a cyclic understanding within yourself and you will enter into a deeper understanding of life. I am the Lord of the Forces of Life and this is my domain, from the cycle of the seasons, to the cycle of the ages, all turn upon the wheel.

Consciousness too has the opportunity to evolve as the wheel revolves again. Incarnate life is a precious opportunity to gather momentum. Why let the turning of the wheel carry you as a helpless passenger when you can become master of your own fate?

Come to my kingdom when you are ready to seek the greater life and the fullest expression of your being. I am the sphinx, guardian of the wheel, Lord of the Forces of Life. I hold the mysteries of being and becoming. I preside at the portal of life and death which is the single door to the wheel of existence. Time moves, everything changes, nothing stands still. Everything is in motion. The wheel turn ceaselessly.

INTERNALIZATION – THE 21ST PATH: NETZACH–CHESED

Construct the Temple of Netzach in the creative imagination. Find yourself standing beside the doorway of the Wheel of Fortune. The Archangel Haniel lifts the tapestry curtain so that you may pass.

Find yourself climbing up a green hill. The land rises quite steeply. With every step you gain a wider view of the land beneath and the sky above. It is a brilliant day of clear light and fast-moving clouds. As you walk, the sky provides a constantly changing panorama of light and shade, shape and form. At last you reach the top, a broad area of green with a wonderful view over the surrounding land.

The day is warm, the scenery enchanting. You lie down on the earth and look up into the sky, falling more deeply into an interior state of reflective awareness. The clouds are in constant motion against the setting of the sky. In your mind patterns and familiar images form and reform. As you watch, it seems to you that the clouds take on the shape of a great wheel suspended in the sky. It seizes your attention and fills your mind, and you find yourself moving into a deeper meditative awareness. Briefly it seems that fleeting clouds assume other shapes – a sphinx sits atop the wheel bearing a sword and a strange composite beast is dragged along as the wheel turns.

Your sharpened attention brings even more passing shapes into sharp relief. Clouds gather and seemingly take up positions at four points on the wheel, assuming the likeness of bull, man, eagle and lion. No sooner have you imprinted these images in your mind than movement brings change. Clouds move, shapes dissolve, images fade. But through some whimsy of nature you have seen the wheel and have planted its form deep in your mind. Soon the clouds have passed on their way. Nothing remains except your memories.

When you are ready, leave and return to the temple. When you are ready, leave through the door. Finally, dissolve all images and return to ordinary consciousness.

EXERCITIA SPIRITUALIA

Take the Following as Subjects for Meditation:

- Lord of the Forces of Life
- The Letter Kaph
- Riches – Poverty
- Jupiter
- The Intelligence of Conciliation and Reward

Make Notes on:

- Tarot Trump X, The Wheel of Fortune

Visualize the Following and Record your Experiences:

- The Temple of Netzach including the Archangel Haniel
- The Journey of the 21st Path

CHAPTER 20

The Twentieth Path:
Tiphareth–Chesed

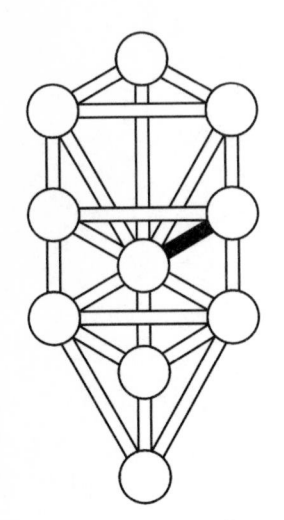

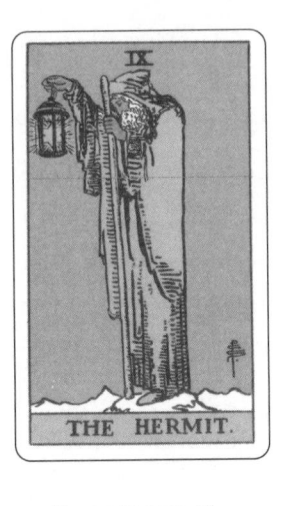

FIGURE 28 THE 20TH PATH:

TIPHARETH–CHESED

TAROT TRUMP IX,

THE HERMIT

TABLE OF CORRESPONDENCES

The Journey: Tarot Trump IX, Prophet of the
  Eternal, Magus of the Voice of Power
Key: The Letter Yod, meaning a hand, also a
  sperm
Spiritual Significance: Virgo
Colour in Atzilut : Yellowish Green
Colour in Briah: Slate Grey
Colour in Yetzirah: Green Grey
Colour in Assiah: Plum
Text: The Intelligence of Will

COMMENTARY

The Twentieth Path is the Intelligence of Will and it is so called because it is the means of preparation of all and each created being and by this intelligence the existence of the primordial wisdom becomes known.

The 20th Path connects the sixth Sephirah, Tiphareth, with the fourth Sephirah, Chesed. It leads between the central Pillar of Consciousness and the Pillar of Mercy. Emerging from Tiphareth it carries a redefined new consciousness towards its next level of expression. Tiphareth brings the Vision of the Harmony of Things. It conveys a mystical or holistic knowing which brings certainty of the unified ground of being. This revelation of enlightenment is so radical that all further journeys upon the Tree are rooted in this realization. The initiation conferred at Tiphareth provides a foundation for succeeding journeys into the infrastructure of the Ethical Triangle. These journeys increasingly represent the rarer qualities of the human condition – altruism, selfless behaviour and universal goals. The upper and lower reaches of the Tree are divided by the symbolism of the veil, the gulf and the knot. The veil can be parted, the gulf can be crossed, the knot can be released. Beneath Tiphareth ego rules, beyond Tiphareth the ego is no longer in charge.

The 20th Path, the Intelligence of Will, represents the journey between the Mediating Intelligence assigned to Tiphareth and the Cohesive or Receptive Intelligence assigned to Chesed. It connects the Spiritual Experience of Tiphareth, the Vision of the Harmony of Things, with the vision of Chesed which is the Vision of Love. This is the journey of The Hermit.

The Path of The Hermit

The purpose of life is to realize our spiritual nature and to do that one has to go away and practise, to reap the fruits of the path, otherwise you have nothing to give anyone else.

Tenzin Palmo, *Cave in the Snow*

The 20th Path is assigned to Tarot Trump IX, The Hermit. This figure is based in historical and religious tradition. The renunciation of worldly things found in every religious tradition gives rise to the hermit existence. Retreating into inaccessible places such as caves, lonely huts or the depths of a forest, single-minded followers of every creed have in the past chosen the life of the hermit. Preferring solitude and a life of religious practice above worldly comfort, the hermit existence has always included privation and intense hardships. For the hermit, ancient or modern, Eastern or Western, life is sustained by belief and daily practice; all else has been stripped away.

Tarot Trump IX depicts a traditional hermit figure. Wrapped in a grey cloak, the hermit stands alone in a snowy and frozen landscape undistinguished by any features. He stands and lifts the lamp to light the way. The lamp is a universal symbol of light in the darkness. It represents the beliefs which bring light to life and signifies the light of wisdom and truth. It is the flame of enlightenment which shines out in the darkness. For support the hermit leans upon a staff. This represents spiritual practices which bring belief to life and thereby provide support in daily life. The life of the hermit is a solitary one. Though he walks alone, he walks purposefully and with direction. This is neither an escape from life nor an inability to be among people, but a willed act of spiritual seclusion. Without the sustaining power of the interior life through contemplation and meditation, solitary months in conditions of hardship resemble imprisonment. Yet this is no prison but the path to liberation of being. Spiritual practice has the power to turn common sense upside down. Buddhism still actively employs the retreat. Some are quite brief, others commonly cover a number of years. This is the path of the hermit today.

In 1976, the Buddhist nun Tenzin Palmo began living in a cave in the Himalayas. She did not leave until 1988. She spent 12 years living as a contemporary hermit. Her story is told in the book *Cave in the Snow* by the journalist Vicki Mackenzie. There can be no doubt that most people would find the conditions under which she lived quite unendurable. Difficult physical circumstances and the challenges produced by mental and emotional isolation created a testing environment that few would choose. These are in fact the conditions used to punish and imprison, but when interviewed Tenzin Palmo spoke with affection of her hermit life. 'I was very happy there and I had everything I wanted.' Without comfort, companionship, diversion or distraction, her life was stripped to its very core. In fact she had no intention of leaving, even after 12 years. Her cave life was unexpectedly interrupted by a local superintendent of police bearing a Quit India notice. Had it not been for this unwelcome beaurocratic finale she might still be 13,000 feet up in the Himalayas.

Born Diane Perry, daughter to a Bethnal Green fishmonger, the future Buddhist hermit felt misplaced in life even as a child. She always had a deep sense that her destiny lay outside London's East End, 'I knew there was something else I had to with my life.'[1] Even as a child she wanted to be a nun but she knew there was no calling to Christianity. At 18 a book on Buddhism opened the door to the life where she belonged. This was the path that eventually led to the mountain retreat. The total change of identification from Cockney Diane to Buddhist nun is an object lesson in the curious and deep voice of karma which speaks even to the young child. 'The last thing I wanted to be was a Tibetan Buddhist,' Diane Perry thought with conscious reasoning and rational mind. Yet a deeper, more insistent, non-rational voice was also present. An innate sense of knowing and of recognition became her guide. It took her away from a life in England towards a most unexpected new identity in India. It is impossible to read the story of her life without observing the play of karmic forces. She left England, aged 20, for India and went to Dalhousie, the first home for the Tibetan community in India. On her twenty-first birthday she met the Lama Khamtrul Rinpoche who had come to visit the school where she lived. He was a Tibetan lama in exile, she was a young Western woman. But in the moment of their meeting, mutual recognition spoke with the voice of certainty. Within hours of the meeting she stated that she wanted to be a nun and asked if he would ordain her. Three weeks later Diane Perry was no more and Drubgyu Tenzin Palmo was born. The transformation was complete. The journey from her first encounter with Buddhism at 18 to her ordination at 21 had taken only three years. She had undoubtedly come home. The journey towards the cave was still to come.

In 1976 Tenzin Palmo was feeling the need for somewhere quiet. Her time since 1964 had been busy and fruitful. Hearing about a mountain cave, she set out with a group of friends on an exploratory trip. They found no more than an overhang on a natural ledge, open on three sides to the elements with a sheer drop into the valley. The roof was low and in total the space measured no more than 10 feet by 6. But she decided it was the perfect spot. Some home improvements followed – a partition to create a storage area, scooping out the floor to give standing room, the installation of a wall, window and a door, a covering of mud and cow dung on the floor and walls, the levelling of the ledge and the erection of a stone perimeter wall.

This was the future home of the Glorious Lady who Upholds the Doctrine of the Practice Succession. With a little furniture and a few possessions, Tenzin Palmo, aged 33, moved in. She did not leave the cave until she was 45. Between November and May the area was subject to snowdrifts. One year the site was quite engulfed by an avalanche in which 35 local people were killed. In complete freezing darkness, she had to dig her way out from entombment. She imposed a routine which included four three-hour meditation sessions each day. Sitting in the traditional meditation box, less than 3 feet square and raised off the ground to keep out the damp, it was the space she inhabited most often. In the traditional lama way she learned not to sleep. This is a glimpse of the life of a modern-day hermit. Her outer life was difficult, monotonous and demanding, her interior life was much the same. Tenzin Palmo says of being in retreat:

> ...there's a pattern that emerges. At first it is very interesting. Then you hit a period when it's excruciatingly boring. And then you get a second wind after which it becomes more and more fascinating until at the end it's much more fascinating and interesting than it was in the beginning. That's how it is even if you're doing the same thing four times a day for three years. It's because the material begins to open up its real meaning and you discover level after level of inner significance. So, at the end you are much more involved in it and totally identified with it than you were at the beginning.[2]

In solitude and simplicity there is no escape from the mind, only the deepening experience of it. When asked if the journey had been worth all the effort she replied:

> It's not what you gain but what you lose. It's like unpeeling the layers of an onion, that's what you have to do. My quest was to understand what perfection meant. Now, I realize that on one level we have never moved away from it. It is only our deluded perception which prevents our seeing what we already have. The more you realise, the more you realise there is nothing to realise. The idea that there's somewhere we have to get to, and something we have to attain is our basic delusion. Who is there to attain it anyway?[3]

THE CAVE

Imagine yourself in a cave high up in an isolated region. It has been prepared for you. Supplies have been laid in and the basics of life are present. You are faced with a choice. If you wish the cave can become your home and your retreat. How would you organize your day? How would you spend your time? What mental problems would you expect to encounter? How long will you be able to stay here unsupported by friends and the trappings of the 21st century? What qualities of being would you need to sustain this life? Would you want the life of the hermit even for a single day?

The solitary Hermit on Tarot Trump IX is also called Magus of the Voice of Power. Tenzin Palmo speaks with a voice of authority and experience. This is the voice of power because it is the voice of truth. There is much power in the voice of the hermit, made wise by inner knowing. Prince Siddhartha Gautama, who became the Buddha, abandoned his wealth and set out into the world seeking the truth of all existence. Like the traditional hermit, he renounced the comforts of the world. He first devoted himself to yoga and next passed six years in extreme asceticism. Finally, after many years he sat beneath the Bo Tree and there at last saw into the true nature of existence. On the first night he saw his previous lives pass before him. On the second night he saw the cycle of birth and death and the karma which governs it. On the third night he came to understand the Four Noble Truths: the knowledge of suffering, the source of suffering, the removal of suffering, and the ways to remove suffering. He had become enlightened. Prince Siddhartha had become the Buddha. He preached his first sermon at Benares, and his five former companions became his first followers. Buddha himself travelled around India for 44 years. His voice rang with the unmistakable sound of truth which has the power to change the way people see the world. Jesus too undertook solitary periods of spiritual withdrawal. For 40 days he retreated to the wilderness, where he was tempted to renounce his own beliefs.

The Hermit is the Magus of the Voice of Power and also the Prophet of the Eternal. The first words of truth spoken directly with the force of insight and revelation become the seed of a new path. The Sermon on the Mount and the sermon at Benares set new forces spinning in motion. In time, the spoken word becomes the written word so that future generations might benefit. The Hermit becomes the Magus of the Voice of Power who becomes the Prophet of the Eternal. The hermit Siddhartha Gautama became the Buddha who founded Buddhism. Jesus Nazarene became the Christ who founded Christianity.

The letter Yod is attributed to this path. It signifies the first dynamic principle of creation. It is the tiny seed, rich in the potential of becoming. The letter Yod is the first quarter of the Tetragrammaton, the Holy Name of God. It represents elemental fire and it also signifies a hand. Placed here in relation to the journey of the Hermit, the letter Yod speaks for the dynamic power embodied in the voice of truth and its ongoing impact. It is the seed of wisdom which changes the world. The 20th Path leads from Tiphareth to Chesed, which is the sphere assigned to Wisdom and to all those teachings which bring wisdom to birth. It is therefore through the intelligence of the 20th Path 'that the existence of the primordial wisdom becomes known'. The Sephirah Chesed is the reservoir from where the Primordial Wisdom flows into the world through the shared voice of those who take on the role of prophet of the eternal. The 20th Path is the Intelligence of Will. Intent, choice and autonomy are registered through application of will. Tenzin Palmo's long retreat was an act of will which survived all obstacles: cold, hunger and even an avalanche. The spiritual quest begins with an affirmation of will. In the Western tradition, this is enshrined in the fourfold axiom, 'To Dare, To Know, To Will and To Be Silent'. Daring implies courage, risk-taking and adventure. It suggests leaving the safe haven of familiar views and acceptable beliefs. It speaks of a pioneering spirit and a willingness to move into the unknown. Diane Perry did just this. She naturally observed the first virtue of the spiritual path, Discrimination, which is the Virtue of Malkuth. She made choices and acted upon them. This is the Intelligence of Will. The Vice of Malkuth is inertia, a demonstrable lack of will.

Emptiness

> Emptiness is the ultimate nature of all phenomena.
>
> **Geshe Rabten, *Treasury of Dharma***

Both religion and science seek to answer fundamental questions about the ultimate nature of reality and existence. Buddhism expressly teaches that the ultimate nature of all phenomena is emptiness. Moving from Tiphareth towards Chesed deepens the personal quest into the ultimate nature of reality. The Initiation of Tiphareth brings a mystical awareness and a universalized consciousness. It also redefines the understanding of both self and reality. The journey of the 20th Path deepens this understanding. The quest for the Primordial Wisdom now becomes all-encompassing as the influence of Chesed draws closer. The Primordial Wisdom, as its name suggests, encompasses the primordial, which is the root nature of reality. The Intelligence of Will assigned to the 20th Path is a means of preparation; 'by this intelligence the existence of the Primordial Wisdom becomes known'. It is therefore also the means of preparation necessary to receive the teaching of emptiness. This is considered to be a difficult and even dangerous advanced teaching. It can be understood only after a firm foundation for mind and body has been established. It is said that this doctrine raises great dangers if approached too soon or without the necessary mental skills. Seeking emptiness without wisdom is likened to walking along a narrow path at the edge of a cliff or to catching a poisonous snake. Misconception and misunderstanding lie ahead for the unwary. This is not the concept of Nihilism or of non-existence, but of an awareness of the difference between how we believe things exist and how things actually exist. Geshe Rabten states very clearly that 'to negate the real existence of everything and say that nothing exists is a great error'.[4] All objects do exist but not as they appear to us as independent and self-sufficient entities. They exist in a state which is completely dependent upon, related to and connected with the consciousness that perceives them. It takes on qualities and characteristics projected by the mind. Geshe Rabten tells us that, 'Whatever we perceive appears in a manner deformed by this ignorance. Hence, the actual object appears to us mingled with a fiction projected by the ignorance in our mind.'[5] In other words, sensory perception produces false mental images which we take to be real. 'We must realize that they do not exist in reality as they appear to our minds, and yet they do exist conventionally in a way that we are at present unable to understand. Our usual attitude is that phenomena exist precisely as they appear to us and that we cling to the appearance, exaggerating it unrealistically so that the delusions of attachment, hatred and so on arise. By managing to understand that things do not exist as they appear, we will gradually be able to stop these gross delusions.'[6] 'The doctrine of emptiness is undoubtedly beyond the grasp of the rational mind. But its direct realization is considered to be the means of attaining liberation from cyclic existence.' This is what Tenzin Palmo struggled with in her cave, and in one form or another this is what the hermits of the ages have left the society of men to find. The realization of the doctrine of emptiness only follows upon the stabilization of mental quiessence, a high degree of concentration and a firmly founded ethical conduct. The realizations on this path are a development of the unifying glimpse seen through the Initiation of Tiphareth.

Now comes a more sustained and complete seeing into the nature of reality. The phenomenal world of appearance and separation belongs to the realm below Tiphareth.

New Birth

> Birth is a journey. Second birth is as great a journey.
>
> **Jean Houston, *A Passion for the Possible***

This Path is assigned to Virgo. The virgin birth represents the second birth into selfhood, self-generated and self-created. As a mutable earth sign, characterized by service, Virgo brings a practicality and an adaptability to the work of the world. This Path is assigned to The Hermit, the solitary spiritual traveller supported only by the lamp and the staff. But where and when does the spiritual quest begin in earnest? How does knowledge of spiritual truth awaken? For many, the time for awakening is limited – when the spiritual journey is conceived to be demarcated by the boundaries of birth and death. But a single lifetime provides very little opportunity for the fullness of the journey. For others the spiritual path is not deemed to be bounded by the demarcation points of birth and death and is therefore not limited to one lifetime but remains open-ended and continuous. The 20th Path, that of The Hermit, is 'the Intelligence of Will and it is so called because it is the means of preparation of all and each created being and by this intelligence the existence of the Primordial Wisdom becomes known'. It is through the development of will that choice is first exercised, and through the applied will that the Primordial Wisdom becomes known. The Primordial Wisdom is represented within Chesed as the patterns and blueprints for the Holy Powers. Is it conceivable that the wisdom and understanding of Chesed might even be gained within a single lifetime? The biographical details of significant spiritual teachers indicate very strongly that awakening comes early and quite spontaneously. Such individuals do not take the route of the many towards a spiritual path but stand strong in the light of spiritual awareness, even as young children. At the age of 12, Jesus was speaking of his father's work. Mother Meera, who is considered to be a contemporary incarnation of the Divine Mother, was an unusual child too. She states that she was born with full knowledge of her divine status and that divine forces were involved in her growing up and education. By the age of three she spoke openly of entering into various lights. The visionary abbess, Hildegard of Bingen, was another extraordinary child.

When she had scarcely learned to speak she sought to convey something of her unique and remarkable vision to others. Later she wrote that this visionary gift had been imprinted on her while still in her mother's womb. At eight she was offered to the nearby Benedictine monastery. At 15 she became a nun. Like the 18th-century mystical poet William Blake and the 20th-century founder of anthroposophy, Rudolph Steiner, she saw what others did not. This early awakening to another dimension of life is not uncommon. Indeed it is part of the bedrock foundation which supports the mystical life.

The Path of The Hermit is a journey of single-minded dedication to spiritual truth, but emerging as it does from Tiphareth, it is already rooted in a universalized consciousness and mystical sense of unity. The 20th Path paradoxically may appear to be a solitary one, but it is taken on behalf of the many. Tibetan Buddhism, the path of the Greater Vehicle, seeks the enlightenment of all sentient beings as its goal.

The 20th Path is partnered by the 22nd Path, which is also intimately connected to the concept of karma. Leading from Tiphareth to Geburah, the 22nd Path is one of karmic adjustment in the Hall of Maat. The 20th Path leading to Chesed via the journey of The Hermit is also a deeply karmic path. In the initiatory system created within the Hermetic Order of the Golden Dawn, Chesed is assigned to the grade of *Adeptus Exemptus*, indicating that karma has been transcended. This is affirmed again by the symbolism of the 21st Path, which rises into Chesed from Netzach carrying the symbolism of the wheel and cyclic existence. On the 20th Path the Intelligence of Will is the means by which the existence of the Primordial Wisdom becomes known. Living by the Primordial Wisdom, by whatever name it is known, brings the possibility of incarnation as a conscious choice, not an unconscious impulsion. Transcending karma is derived only from self-rulership of Chesed, the long evolutionary journey of The Hermit, and many existences attached to the wheel. Such a journey makes a master of wisdom.

EVOCATION

Welcome to my kingdom. I dwelled in the world among men and after many lives the absurd ploys by which lives were directed and ruled became transparent and meaningless to me. I sought to look beyond the everyday world into the world of causes. I spent many lives in study and contemplation. Yet I have also been part of the world again, for the eternal wisdom has much to say about life in the world. Many have come to sit at my feet and hear of the ways of the spirit and the eternal path which is always to be found in any circumstances. I have imparted my knowledge freely, knowing that the seeds of wisdom take time to mature and come to fruition. I have known and seen every human experience. I have lived them all. Now wherever I walk I am attuned to the voice of inspiration which resounds in the secret places. It tells of things to come and patterns still to be unfolded. I speak of such things only when asked. I seek like minds who will also become as lamps in the darkness for others to follow. I will plant the seed of wisdom through the word which is holy. I have no need for name or identity, I know who I am. I am the Prophet of the Eternal and the Magus of the Voice of Power.

INTERNALIZATION – THE 20TH PATH: TIPHARETH–CHESED

Construct the Temple of Tiphareth in the creative imagination. Find yourself standing beside the door of The Hermit. The Archangel Raphael lifts the tapestry curtain so that you may pass.

You find yourself in a bleak and barren landscape. It is cold and the terrain is difficult. You feel utterly alone. Which way will you go? Where are you? Although you set out, it is without any sense of direction or purpose.

Suddenly from the gloom ahead you see a single moving light. You run to find out what this light is. Now you see that the light is carried by an aged man. You catch up and fall in step with him. His pace does not slow. He turns and looks at you under the light of his lantern. You walk together side by side. He walks on with steady tread and with eye fixed on the distant horizon. The light from his lamp gives out a steady beam. He walks with a determination which you cannot match. Your mind is filled by thoughts of home and family, of friends and familiar places. This journey seems to be taking you further away into a desolate and unknown land. At last you are prompted to ask where he is going. He replies simply, 'home'. Now he stops and looks at you. 'This journey is not for you today but I will travel on your behalf. On my arrival, a white dove will be released.' With these words he turns and continues on his way. Soon he is gone. You make your way back but this time the path is much easier, you simply follow the footprints.

When you are ready, return he way you came to the temple. When you are ready, leave though the doorway. Finally, dissolve all images and return to ordinary consciousness.

EXERCITIA SPIRITUALIA

Take the Following as Subjects for Meditation:

- The Prophet of the Eternal, Magus of the Voice of Power
- The Letter Yod
- Virgo

Make Notes on:

- Tarot Trump IX, The Hermit

Visualize the Following and Record your Experiences:

- The Temple of Tiphareth including the Archangel Raphael
- The Journey of the 20th Path

CHAPTER 21

Chesed – Mercy

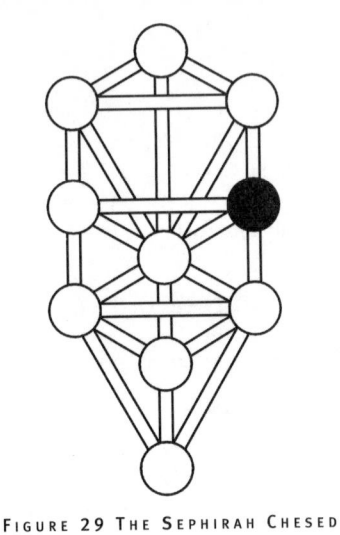

FIGURE 29 THE SEPHIRAH CHESED

TABLE OF CORRESPONDENCES

God-Name: El – Lord
Archangel: Tzadkiel
Order of Angels: Chasmalim, meaning
  The Brilliant Ones
Magical Image: A Mighty Crowned and
  Throned King
Virtue: Obedience
Vice: Bigotry, Hypocrisy, Gluttony, Tyranny
Titles: Gedulah, Love, Majesty,
  Magnificence
Spiritual Experience: Vision of Love
Mundane Chakra: Jupiter
Personal Chakra: The Anahata or Heart
  Chakra

Text: The Cohesive or Receptive
  Intelligence
Symbols: The Solid Figure, Tetradhedron,
  Orb, Wand, Pyramid, Sceptre, Crook
Colour in Atziluth: Deep Violet
Colour in Briah: Blue.
Colour in Yetzirah: Deep Purple
Colour in Assiah: Deep Azure, flecked
  Yellow
Tarot Cards: The Four Fours
Four of Wands: Perfected Work
Four of Cups: Pleasure
Four of Swords: Rest from Strife
Four of Pentacles: Earthly Power

COMMENTARY

The Fourth Path is called the Cohesive or Receptive Intelligence because it contains all the Holy Powers and from it emanate all the spiritual virtues with the most exalted essences. They emanate one from another by virtue of the Primordial Emanation, the Highest Crown, Kether.

The fourth Sephirah, Chesed, gives its name to the Pillar of Mercy, just as the fifth Sephirah, Geburah, gives its name to the Pillar of Severity. Together Geburah and Chesed form a polar opposition which is reconciled and harmonized through the journey of the 19th Path, Strength. Where Geburah holds images of war and strife, Chesed conveys images of peace, stability and wisdom. As the fourth Sephirah on the Path of Descent, Chesed is the first emanation beyond the division rendered by the Abyss. It is the first Sephirah beyond the Supernal Triangle formed by Kether, Binah and Chockmah. These three Sephiroth together form the Greater Countenance, or Macroprosopos. Chesed is the first sphere of the Microprosopos, the Lesser Countenance. It therefore reflects what is beyond the Abyss onto a lower plane. These powers assigned to Chesed arise first in Kether, from where they are differentiated into Chockmah and Binah and then refracted through the prism of Daath into Chesed. Chesed receives powers from the Supernal Triangle. It is a place of archetypal ideas. These are precipitated and made real through the process of descent into manifestation.

Archetypal Patterns

Chesed, then, is the sphere of the formulation of the archetypal idea; the apprehension by consciousness of an abstract concept which is subsequently brought down the planes and concreted in the light of the concretion of analogous ideas.

Dion Fortune, *The Mystical Qabalah*

Chesed is the Sephirah where particular archetypal patterns are held. The higher reaches of the Tree are concerned with the transpersonal guiding

principles, causative impulses and archetypal patterns which are embedded
in manifested life. Just as science seeks to recognize and understand the most
basic laws of the universe, so spiritual science seeks to find and apply basic
universal laws. The laws of physics are few, but matter takes an infinite variety of forms and expressions. Esoteric philosophy also seeks to understand
the basic principles, but in contrast to a scientific perspective assigns a quality of mind to the very framework and structure of nature. 'Esoteric science
teaches that the divine mind formulates archetypal ideas in order that substance might take form.'[1] In other words, this is the realm of the plan, the
abstract idea and the blueprint. Chesed represents the formulation of the archetypal idea. This principle operates at the most practical of levels – construction
always follows vision, implementation follows idea. Chesed is the realm of
the archetypal pattern or primal idea which is replicated and reflected in the
physical world. This is not a new concept. It has much in common with Plato's
philosophy. He put forward the notion of the Ideal Form as the primordial
and transcendent image stored up in a supra-celestial place of eternal forms.
This is the realm where the primordial idea has much in common with the
nature assigned to Chesed. This concept well describes the function of
Chesed. Chesed is called the 'Cohesive or Receptive Intelligence'. To cohere
is to gather, hold and cement together disparate parts and render them whole.
More than just a temporary assembly, the cohesive unit engenders a sense of
unity and completeness. Chesed is assigned to the Cohesive Intelligence. As
the Receptive Intelligence, Chesed receives influences from the Supernal Triangle
which are transformed through its form-building nature to provide a new
level of cohesive patterning.

As the first Sephirah beyond the Abyss on the Path of Descent, Chesed
holds patterns which can be reached through exalted states of consciousness. Chesed, 'contains all the Holy Powers and from it emanate all the
spiritual virtues'. In other words, the archetypal patterns held within Chesed
are those holy powers or powers of wholeness which give rise directly to
'spiritual virtues with the most exalted essences'. Chesed holds not archetypal
physical laws but archetypal spiritual laws.

Chesed is connected to Tiphareth and Geburah within the Greater
Mysteries, to Chockmah within the Supreme Mysteries, and to Netzach
within the Lesser Mysteries. The nature of the several connecting paths
throws light on the nature of Chesed. Chesed is reached diagonally from
the 20th Path, which connects it with Tiphareth. This is the Path of The
Hermit, the solitary spiritual traveller in search of wisdom. This is a route
of preparation; 'by this intelligence the existence of the Primordial Wisdom

becomes known.' Chesed is reached vertically from the 21st Path, which connects it from Netzach. This is the Path of the Wheel of Fortune, Lord of the Forces of Life. This Path describes how the turning of the wheel brings the Intelligence of Conciliation and Reward. Chesed is reached from the 19th Path, which connects it horizontally with Geburah. This is the Path of Strength. As a lateral journey, this Path is required to bind the opposed forces of Chesed with Geburah. It is the Path of 'the Intelligence of all the secret activities of the spiritual being'. Finally, Chesed is reached from the 16th Path, which connects it from above with Chockmah. This is the Path of the Triumphal or Eternal Intelligence, represented by the Hierophant or Revealer of Secret Things. Taken together these four paths speak directly of a direct contact with the Primordial Wisdom. The Hermit approaches in a solitary quest seeking wisdom. The Wheel is the vehicle which provides unlimited opportunities to find the first seeds of wisdom. Strength is in dynamic partnership with the nature of wisdom. The Hierophant holds the power of initiation into the Perennial Philosophy.

The Wisdom of Chesed arises originally, 'by virtue of the Primordial Emanation, the Highest Crown, Kether'. But this primordial pattern only becomes accessible through Chesed, which is to be found on the near side of the abyss. Even then, the archetypal wisdom of Chesed is only directly accessible to a spiritualized and evolved consciousness which rises to meet it. But through its reflection down into more immediate realms, the path towards wisdom is to be found through the Lesser Mysteries and connects directly with Netzach and indirectly with Hod.

Chesed is represented by images of wise rulership. The Mighty, Crowned and Throned King of Chesed exemplifies the law giver and wise ruler. The rules that are held here are the archetypal patterns of wisdom. Chesed is assigned to Jupiter, the traditional king of the gods in the Roman pantheon. Astrologically, Jupiter represents the principle of expansion and bounty. Jupiterian qualities are abundance, largesse and bounty. The Vices of Chesed are the unbounded vices of Jupiter. Bigotry is the excessive valuing of a single belief; hypocrisy is excessive outward behaviour unsupported by congruent thinking; gluttony is just sheer excess; tyranny is reliance on a single authority. The Virtue of Chesed is Obedience. But this is not the blind obedience given to an external authority; this is the natural and spontaneous following of the holy powers established in the inner kingdom of self-rulership.

The Spiritual Experience of Virtue of Chesed is the Vision of Love. This is not the personal love that cements family, friends and close relationships, which belongs to the Lesser Mysteries, but the unlimited and unconditional love as a factor in creation itself. This is the root expression of love itself. Though it is difficult to comprehend, mystics often affirm the overwhelming experience of cosmic or divine love.

Kingship

> The abhiseka of form is a process of bringing the
> student up, raising him or her from the level of an infant
> to a king or queen.
>
> **Chogyam Trungpa, *Journey without Goal***

This kingdom is characterized by Love, Majesty and Magnificence. Majesty is the term traditionally applied to the ruler and to holders of the office of rulership. In the context of Chesed, the term speaks of rulership from within, but also to the majestic stature which accompanies a realized individual. Beyond the personal level, Majesty refers to Chesed itself as the source of abundance and largesse in the kingdom. Just as the laws of physics determine and shape the world, so spiritual laws apply too. These are the Holy Powers assigned to Chesed which, 'emanate all the spiritual virtues with the most exalted essences'. Realizing the nature of spiritual law brings self-authority, liberation and autonomy. This is the real kingship of being. The Mighty Crowned and Throned King is none other than the universal self. The quality of magnificence speaks once more of the rare and awesome qualities of being which the realization of spiritual virtues brings. This is not an assumed air of authority or a given authority that comes with an office, but the natural authority which spontaneously flows from inner wisdom. It may be rare but it is a quality with the power to change the world. It is paradoxically the magnificence of being only expressed by the self who has consciously become no-self. This is the magnificence of the universal, the triumphal and the eternal.

This sphere of kingship is the sphere of full self-realization. The wise and merciful ruler of Chesed presents the traditional symbols of royal authority – the orb, wand, sceptre and crook. The orb caries all the symbolism of the circle but translates it into a third dimension – of the globe or sphere, representing totality. The wand is an image of authority and directive power; it has no practical use. Like the conductor's baton, it serves to direct and orchestrate as a means of authority and decision. The sceptre combines both wand and orb into a single symbol of dominion and authority. This is not the outer kingdom, however, but the inner kingdom of the psyche.

The crook is derived from the distant agricultural past. It speaks of the role of the shepherd and the flock. The Egyptian god Osiris, and all pharaohs in imitation of him, carried a crook as part of the royal insignia. It defines the king as the shepherd of the people. This image has long moved from the purely secular realm. The bishop's crosier is derived from the shepherd's crook and lineage of the good shepherd.

Curiously, the symbolism of royal insignia also plays a large part in the *abhiseka* transmission of Vajrayana Buddhism. The abhiseka is an initiatory ceremony in which the student is cleansed with water, crowned with a jewelled crown, and given a sceptre, a bell and a new name. This empowerment takes its form directly from the first presentation of Tantra when the Buddha donned royal attire to teach the first tantra to King Indrabhuti. The symbolism is purposeful. 'In the abhiseka form we actually bathe ego, coronate ego and give ego a sceptre. Finally, when ego finds itself with everything it wants, it begins to flop, it begins to be so embarrassed that it becomes non-existent. Then we can build a new kingdom of egolessness. This is the Tantric Way.'[2]

THE THRONE OF WISDOM

Imagine that a very special day has come at last. Preparations have been under way for a considerable time. Today you will sit upon the throne of wisdom. You wait in a small antechamber. You wear a simple robe of white. Two attendants appear bearing a shallow bowl holding water scented with rose petals. You wash your hands and dry them with a soft towel handed to you. Now you are escorted to the door where you wait.

You hear a trumpet sound from somewhere close by. The door is opened. You see a long aisle and a raised dais at the far end. You begin the long walk towards the front of the hall. Your attendants walk behind. Soon you see that the hall holds friends, family and those to whom you are linked by mutual care.

Finally you reach the raised dais, where you stand and wait. The symbols of royalty are now carried in. The attendants place a cloak of the realm on your shoulders. A jewelled crown is placed on your head. The orb and sceptre are given to you. A new name is whispered into your ear. All present cheer you.

You stand and give a speech of acceptance in which you explain the meaning and significance of each aspect of the royal insignia.

Chesed is assigned to the symbol of the pyramid, an image of the journey itself. Its base is set four square on the earth, but its apex stands in the heavens. The pyramid of Chesed is complete, whereas the pyramid assigned to Tiphareth is truncated, indicating that the journey is still unfinished. Chesed is the last of the Sephiroth before the Abyss which cannot be crossed. The solid figure assigned to Chesed indicates the relationship between the idea and the actual, the abstract and the result, the plan and the realization. Chesed is the sphere of the abstract principles and archetypal pattern. It contains the holy powers which emanate the spiritual virtues. The spiritual experience of Chesed is Love, its name means Mercy.

The Masters of Wisdom

The sphere of the masters is said to be in Chesed.

Gareth Knight, *A Practical Guide to Kabalistic Symbolism*

This is the domain of the Primordial Wisdom glimpsed by the way-shower travelling on the 20th Path. Chesed is traditionally assigned to the Masters of Wisdom. In its broadest sense this concept describes those who have through the ages sought and found wisdom, risen to the heights of human consciousness and returned with a new vision which changed the course of history. When the individual is directly in contact with spiritual law, an intervening authority has no power. Chesed brings self-rulership. The pure vision of Christ, the Anointed, seeded Christianity, which has in turn changed the history of men and nations. The idea that love could be an active power for good was revolutionary. It was a new vision. The enlightenment of Siddartha Gautama, the Awakened, became the core of Buddhism, which in its turn changed the history of men and nations. The idea that enlightenment could be an active power for good was revolutionary. It was a new vision. This is the presence of Chesed in the world. Religion is based on a set of ideas. Chesed is the Sephirah of archetypal ideas. The abstract inspires the actual. This takes place through the conduits of the 21st Path into Netzach and the 20th Path into Tiphareth. The 21st Path connects Netzach with Chesed. This links the creative imagination to the higher emotions of the personality. When the creative imagination is gripped by the power of an ideal, the resulting fusion releases a dynamic impetus of hope, intent and aspiration which seeks actualization. Lofty ideals such as 'liberty', 'equality' and 'fraternity', or 'democracy' and 'freedom', have affected the course of history. When fired by a powerful ideal, the imagination has the power to become the springboard for forward momentum and projected action as the ideal seeks realization in the world of effect. Curiously, the Vices of Chesed – bigotry, tyranny, gluttony and hypocrisy – may grip the individual with obsessive compulsion. The power of the idea can never be underestimated as a guiding force in the physical world. The Virtues of Chesed bring empowerment through freedom and autonomy, through authorizing the individual as ruler. The Vices of Chesed disempower the many as the few steal authority and freedom. The 22nd Path also connects the Wheel of Fortune to Chesed. Rising from Netzach, meaning Victory, the wheel brings the concept of a long and slowly evolving journey of time and change. Ideas only succeed in gripping mass vision at the curious confluence of right time and place. History is littered with the examples of ideas misplaced in time – failed rebellions, quashed hopes, smashed aspirations and destroyed ideals.

The 20th Path connects Chesed with Tiphareth. This Path is assigned to the Intelligence of Will. It is the Path walked by the lone traveller, of the solitary hermit in search of truth and wisdom. This is the Path of the masters of wisdom, both known and unknown, who have shaped the religious and spiritual development of the world by the clarity of their vision, the strength of personal inspiration and power of realization. This is indeed the Intelligence of Will. Such walkers have made the Primordial Wisdom visible and accessible for those not able to walk so far unaided.

According to Dion Fortune, the place of contact between the Masters of Wisdom assigned Chesed and their disciples in the world is through the sphere of Hod. Engagement with the Sephirah Hod awakens the lower mind into a reflective but conscious stillness which is a presage to vision and inspiration that cannot take place without spaciousness of mind. As the first engagement with Hermetic Wisdom, Hod is a necessary preparation for its full flowering as the Primordial Wisdom of Chesed. As a water temple, Hod provides a reflecting mirror where the archetypal forms projected from Chesed can be briefly glimpsed in the mind. As part of the Astral or Psychological Triangle and the Lesser Mysteries, Hod has a proximity to the consciousness of Malkuth which makes working through the mind relatively accessible. Working directly with the potency of Chesed, on the other hand, is beyond the remit of the many. As the Sephirah of ceremonial forms, Hod provides a many-faceted vehicle with which to touch upon the timeless wisdom reached at Chesed.

The 19th Path connects Chesed with Geburah, but the 19th Path is one of a Secret Intelligence. This is a Path of silent, personal, inner, spiritual transmutation which works directly upon the karmic grid that is Geburah. From the place of karmic freedom that is Chesed, this work goes unrecorded. In the Western Mystery Tradition, the esoteric grade assigned to the grade of Chesed is that of *Adeptus Exemptus*. It carries the notion that the bearer has reached a place of exemption from the pull of karma and can enter incarnation as a conscious choice. Buddhism too recognizes that beyond a level of spiritual mastery, incarnation is a choice. The seeds that impel incarnation have been extinguished. When liberated from the impulsion of personal karmic action, energy can be used to dissolve seeds of shared karma. The desire to serve humanity as a whole has become so spontaneous and natural that it is not extinguished even by death.

Chesed is the Cohesive Intelligence but also the Receptive Intelligence. It receives influences from Chockmah directly from the 16th Path. This route connects the Supreme Mysteries with the Greater Mysteries. The 16th Path is assigned to the Triumphal or Eternal Intelligence. This journey is symbolized by the Magus of the Eternal, outwardly called the Hierophant or The Revealer of Secret Things.

All Paths may be undertaken in two ways, either on the Path of Ascent or Descent. On the Path of Ascent the individual emerging from Chesed journeying towards Chockmah might be thought of as a Magus of the Eternal, pure being, rooted in eternal truth. On the Path of Descent, the Hierophant, as the archetypal initiator into the Mysteries of Being and Becoming, takes on a role as a mediator between humanity and the archetype of Primordial Wisdom. In this way, images, ideas and symbols of the Eternal Triumphal Intelligence that is the Primordial Wisdom are reflected into the accessible Sephirah Hod through the Perfect Intelligence, as a reflection of the Absolute.

EVOCATION

Welcome to my kingdom. Come when you are able. Until you seek this journey unaided, look to those who have travelled here ahead of you and returned laden with the treasure which is wisdom. The seekers of wisdom have been many. Philosophers and sages, saints and seers, visionaries and hermits – these have sought me out and discovered my true nature. For I do not hide but await discovery with delight.

Mine is the realm of spiritual truth which is also love and mercy. For the truth is merciful to all. I hold the laws of being and becoming. I hold the Primordial Wisdom which does not belong to one time or place. This wisdom belongs to all times, all places and all peoples. I give this truth endlessly for it bestows the blessing of freedom and liberation. But though my wisdom is everywhere and abundant, it is invisible until needed and called for.

I hold the pattern of being and becoming. My truths are subtle and delicate. When you have understood these truths and hold them as dearly and closely as breath itself, you will have earned the right to be crowned and enthroned in the Hall of Wisdom.

INTERNALIZATION – THE TEMPLE
OF CHESED

Construct the Temple of Chesed in the creative imagination. Find yourself standing with a guide by a single door. It opens with the unexpected speed of an automated process. Your guide takes you by the hands. You take a single step forward. You step out, seemingly into space. At first you see nothing but pinpricks of light against darkness. Your guide urges you to take another step and in doing so you realize that you stand in the infinite realm of the heavens. Here all orientation fails – there is neither direction nor compass point. You stand in space, neither falling nor floating but standing, for this is the place of mind and the habits of your mind permit you to find a footing here in this place without footing. Wherever you look the darkness is irradiated by pinpoints of light. All about is wonderful and extraordinarily glorious; there is the munificence of an unknown place You remain in contemplation for as long as you wish. When you are ready to continue, tell your guide, who will understand every thought in your mind with total clarity. At your request the journey shall continue.

From your vantage point, a pinprick of light seems to be in motion. Your attention becomes fixated upon it – it is certainly moving towards you. You watch closely and the light begins to take on the shape of a small and narrow boat. It has a single sail decorated with the emblem of a blazing sun. This is the Ship of Solomon, as recounted in the fable of the Chymical Wedding. The boat draws alongside you now and you step in with your guide.

The boat holds a richly decorated bed, and at its head lies a crown, the crown of Solomon. At the foot of the bed lies a sword, the sword of David. The bed has three spindles, one snow white, one blood red and the other emerald green. These are taken from a tree grown from a cutting taken by Eve from the Tree of Knowledge of Good and Evil. The boat moves with

ease against the starry backdrop. All around stars shine. You have no idea of
the intended destination. You have no sense of either the passing of time or
of movement. You pass into a deeper state of meditation. The boundaries
between inner and outer space have dissolved. You are deep in the inner
space of timeless reality.

Now something new enters your awareness. In the darkness a bright
light shines out. Your vessel glides towards it with the certainty of a homing
bird. Appearing, seemingly from nowhere, you see a fountain of white light
gushing like a geyser from a hot spring. But unlike any earthly geyser it
towers so far above you that it is lost to sight. Your vessel stops beneath its
cascading waterfall. As if in response to your presence the white light is now
shimmering and pulsating with rainbow colours. You are caught in a shower
of radiance that is both light and energy; each colour has its own vibration
and note. The colours play over you and seemingly even through you, for
your boundaries seem fluid and open. You are immersed in radiant colour
and shimmering light. You are played upon by sound and living energy.

Your guide reaches out and extends a chalice. You accept it and, holding
it out, it is at once filled with radiance. You raise it in the face of eternity,
giving thanks for all that you have come to know. Now you take communion from the fountain of the seven lights.

You return the cup to the guide, who throws it high up into the air. It
begins its descent, falling slowly and gracefully like a feather caught on a
breeze. You watch it moving away, still shining with an inner light; you
know it will continue to fall to earth for others to sup from too, in the form
of a Grail. Now rest. The guide covers you. The boat will return you to
the temple.

When you are ready, leave through the door. Finally, dissolve all images
and return to ordinary consciousness.

EXERCITIA SPIRITUALIA

Take the Following as Subjects for Meditation:

- El
- Tzadkiel
- Chasmalim – The Brilliant Ones
- A Mighty Crowned and Throned King
- Love, Majesty, Magnificence
- Jupiter
- The Vision of Love
- The solid figure, the tetradhedron, the orb, the wand, the pyramid, the sceptre

Contemplate the Following Questions and Record your Responses:

- How does Obedience operate in your life?
- How do Bigotry, Hypocrisy, Gluttony and Tyranny operate in your life?
- How does the nature of Chesed relate to the Heart Chakra?
- What other correspondences can you relate to Chesed?
- How do the four Tarot cards relate to this Sephirah?

Visualize the Following and Record your Experiences:

- The Temple of Chesed including the Archangel Tzadkiel
- The Journey to the Temple of Chesed

CHAPTER 22

The Nineteenth Path: Chesed–Geburah

FIGURE 30 THE 19TH PATH:

CHESED–GEBURAH

TAROT TRUMP VIII

STRENGTH

TABLE OF CORRESPONDENCES

The Journey: Tarot Trump VIII, Daughter of the Flaming Sword, Leader of the Lion, Strength

Key: The Letter Teth, meaning a serpent

Simple Letter: Taste

Spiritual Significance: Leo

Text: The Intelligence of the secret of all the activities of the spiritual beings

Colour in Atziluth: Greenish Yellow

Colour in Briah: Deep Purple

Colour in Yetzirah: Grey

Colour in Assiah: Reddish Yellow

COMMENTARY

The Nineteenth Path is the Intelligence of the secret of all the activities of the spiritual beings and it is so called because of the influences diffused by it from the most high and exalted sublime glory.

The 19th Path connects the fourth Sephirah, Chesed, with the fifth Sephirah, Geburah. It therefore bridges the two Pillars of Manifestation. This is a placement of considerable power, for it reconciles the forces of Mercy and Severity upon the twin pillars of the Tree. If the opposing forces represented by the polarity of Chesed and Geburah are to become balanced, a third transcendent principle must arise. Like the lateral 27th Path below it, the 19th Path is one of dynamic change and transmutation. The 27th Path, represented by the journey of the Tower, uses mental and emotional energy as it its raw material, fuelling transformation within the personality. The 19th Path, as part of the Ethical or Moral Triangle within the higher reaches of the Tree, uses latent karmic and potential spiritual energy to create a new fusion of being.

The Royal Path

> A Lyon Greene did in her Lapp reside
> (The which an Eagle fed), and from his side
> The Blood gush'd out: The Virgin drunck it upp,
> While Mercuries Hand did the Office of a Cupp.
> The wondrous Milk she hasten'd from her Breast,
> Bestow'd it frankly on the Hungry Beast
> And with a Sponge his Furry face she dry'd
> Which her own Milk she had often Madefy'd
> Upon her Head a Diadem she did weare,
> With fiery Feet she'Advanced into the Aire;
> And glittering Bravely in her Golden Robes
> She took her Place amidst the Starry Globes.

The Cantilena, verses 32–4

Alchemy is known as the royal art. Its goal is transformation. It takes its vocabulary and modus operandi from the stages and processes of transformation played out upon metals and various substances which were seen to be analogues to the parallel process of personal transformation. Alchemy presents an arcane and symbolic language rich in fabulous beasts and mythical figures, which also signify stages and processes of the psyche. The lion is a central image which takes three different forms. The green lion is the raw energy of nature before it is subject to the applied will. The red lion represents the inner natural forces under perfect control. Finally, the old lion represents the purified consciousness which is achieved as a result of the Great Work. Tarot Trump VIII shows the red lion and a woman. She is called the Daughter of the Flaming Sword and Leader of the Lion. She does not hunt or kill but subdues, tames, and unites with the forces of the red lion. She wears a garland of flowers and fearlessly opens its jaws. She has clearly succeeded in subduing the fearsome powers of the lion. Her robe is white, signifying simplicity, innocence and the power of spiritual gnosis. She is very like the figure of the Magician in Tarot Trump I who also wears the white robe and is likewise dignified by the lemniscate symbol of infinity. Kundalini is always considered to be a feminine power. She is Para Shakti. In alchemy the white phase refers to a period when a new feminine principle appears in consciousness, bringing more fantasy, vivid dreams and a receptive sensitivity. The white phase is one of the pre-forms of the final stone and a presage of the elixir of health.

The red lion as the transformed green lion represents the many changes that have already taken place through the stations of the Tree. The quality of greenness – fresh, raw and new – refers to the state of natural energy which accompanies the beginning of the journey at Malkuth. From Malkuth to Tiphareth via the intervening Sephiroth and Paths, the green quality of the lion has matured to red as a result of intensive patterning projected from consciousness. The application of mind through holistic meditative practice brings mastery and self-awareness. The powers of the red lion are now at the disposal of consciousness in a harmonious partnership. This is not a depiction of passions and instincts under conscious will – which belongs more to the realm of Netzach – but a representation of the natural energies imbedded in the mind-body-spirit unity. This Path is assigned to, 'the Intelligence of the secret of all the activities of the spiritual beings'. This is a depiction of the serpent power which is the secret but natural energy implicit within everyone.

This is the phenomenon of serpent power, known in the East as *kundalini*, which simply means 'coiled'. It is the personal aspect of the universal life force. The figure of Strength represents a feminine consciousness; the red lion represents the reservoir of the secret spiritual and natural energy imbedded at the heart of being. To bring this energy into conscious awareness is to become conscious of the universal life force. The awakening of the serpent energy is a universal phenomenon that has been recorded by the worldwide community of spiritual travellers. This experience belongs not in the territory of the green lion, the training ground for the energies of being, but in the matured and stabilized realm of the red lion.

The 19th Path is assigned to Tarot Trump VIII, called Strength. This Path is assigned to the letter Teth, meaning a serpent. This is the Path of the serpent power. The regal lion and coiled serpent are one and the same. The symbolism of the serpent remains misunderstood in the Western mind, where it is identified almost solely with the serpent of the Garden of Eden. Elsewhere, without the weight of biblical reference, the serpent holds positive associations. It signifies rebirth, since the snake grows by shedding its skin. The concept of rebirth or continuous dynamic change is central to the development and process of the psyche; the conjunction of opposing qualities precipitates a new state of being which is a new state of understanding, a new birth within consciousness. The Tarot Trump shows a woman holding a lion by its open jaws. Animal symbolism represents that part of the human psyche which needs to be trained and mastered. Eastern iconography often uses the symbol of the elephant to represent the raw untrained mind. The elephant has great power and when mastered becomes an invaluable servant and helper. Western iconography represents the same process through the symbolism of the lion. As the king of the beasts, the lion represents the danger and power of untamed force.

The Intelligence of the Secret

The object is to awaken Kundalini through ritual practices and to enable her to ascend up the *sushumna nadi* through the cakra system. When it reaches the topmost cakra the blissful union of Shiva and Shakti occurs. This leads to a far-reaching transformation of the personality.

Georg Feuerstein, *Yoga, The Technology of Ecstasy*

The goal of Yoga is the unification of being. Yoga means to yoke. Kundalini Yoga is a specialized branch of Yoga which seeks to unite, to bring the potentiality of the deepest and most hidden energies into consciousness. It is therefore an arcane and esoteric branch of Yoga which, like alchemy, is rich in symbols and transformative practices. This knowledge has always been preserved and transmitted as a carefully guarded secret:

> Great Goddess! This science of Shiva is a great science,
>
> it had always been kept a secret. Therefore, this science
>
> revealed by me, the wise should keep secret.

Siva Samhita, verse 206

When Sir John Woodroffe went to India in search of this knowledge he was rebuffed time and again. It took a decade of dedicated searching to finally find and translate *Sat-Cakjra-Nirupana* and *Paduka-Pancakra*, which eventually appeared in English as *The Serpent Power* by Arthur Avalon. Woodroffe can take the credit for bringing this body of knowledge to the West long before the West was actually ready to receive such arcane teaching. However, his pioneering sense has been vindicated. Perhaps now, his prophetic words carry a real ring of truth: 'All the world (I speak of course of those interested in such subjects) is beginning to speak of Kundalini Shakti.' In the early years of the 20th century the materially grounded Western mindset was not ready to hear even a basic Tantric premise; namely, that the universe is a creation of pure consciousness. Now in the early years of the 21st century, Western culture is more receptive to such metaphysical ideas. Kundalini, the serpent power, is a conceptualization of a subtle spiritual energy. Until a general concept of life force or living energy has become acceptable, the concept of kundalini can have no reference point. Now the West has gained, even if mainly through adoption, a conceptual framework which can incorporate a more specialized refinement. The Western mindset is now ready to receive Kundalini Shakti.

Yoga has become accepted and, though its higher spiritual aspects are less often stressed at the expense of its physical dynamics, a broad range of literature is widely available. As a complete philosophy of being, slowly and organically Yoga re-patterns the life energies through a combination of *asanas* (postures), *pranayama* (conscious breathing), meditation, mental development and spiritual awakening. Now the broad acceptance of many energy-based therapies, such as acupuncture and shiatsu, has established a general holistic understanding of a unified mind-body-spirit interface, along with a general appreciation of vital energy as an expression of this trinity. Knowledge of the chakras, *Sat-Cakra-Nirupana*, has now permeated and penetrated the Western mindset. The current Western thirst for spiritual knowledge has brought a wide dissemination of a once-secret knowledge. The tools for spiritual awakening are now in the hands of the many. Books about the chakras, the wheels of subtle living energy, are now easily available. The classical texts, *The Serpent Power* and *The Secrets of the Golden Flower* are easily obtainable. The stage is now set for deepening encounter with Kundalini Shakti.

The Serpent Power

> The science of Kundalini is one of the most advanced
> and difficult branches of Yoga.

Swami Rama, *The Awakening of Kundalini*

The phenomenon of kundalini remains unidentified by modern science, which has little interest in either the subjective or the spiritual. Despite being outside current scientific explanation, kundalini, by whatever name it is known, is a universal phenomenon well known to spiritual practitioners. This is the energy of life itself. In the Japanese tradition it is known as *ki*. In the Chinese tradition it is known as *chi*. In the Yogic system it is known as *prana*. Although knowledge of the chakras is now commonplace in the West, contemporary easy access to such information should not reduce the importance of the subject. This branch of Yoga was once kept secret outside the dedicated relationship between teacher and pupil. The chakras provide the blueprint for spiritual awakening. By changing patterns of thinking, the energy of a chakra is changed. Kundalini cannot rise fully into the head centres until the obstacles which exist in mind, body and energy field have been dissolved. Creating this clear channel of light is the work of building the *Antakarana*, the rainbow vehicle, the refined sheath of consciousness. Spiritual awakening cannot take place without refinement and purification of the subtle vehicles of consciousness. Yoga works directly upon the subtle energies through body-work, breath control and techniques of mind. Buddhism affects the subtle energies indirectly by working on the qualities of being expressed by each of the chakras as keys to levels of consciousness. There is a reciprocal relationship between the chakra as a vortex of living energy and the thoughts, feelings and desires of consciousness which constitute the energy of the centres. Energy follows thought, thought follows energy.

The serpent power can only be understood in relation to the full energetic network which interpenetrates the physical body. This subtle energy system is the, 'secret of all the activities of the spiritual beings'. The blueprint for subtle energies provides the route map for the journey into self-realization. Kundalini, as the coiled and latent current, is at rest within the centre of subtle energy at the base of the spine. When awakened through the trigger of a spiritual practice, this dormant energy will begin to move through the routes already present in the subtle anatomy. As the two Pillars of Severity and Mercy act as opposing dynamics on the model of the Tree, so the rising serpent power will flow alternately through two channels called *Ida* and *Pingala*, which are respectively hot and cold currents. Like a serpent which sways slightly from side to side as it rises, the serpent power zigzags between two opposing dynamics when it rises up through the subtle channels of the spine to the top of the head. One pathway brings a hot fiery solar current, the other brings a cooling lunar current. The combined effect of the two energies is to draw up the awakening life force from the base of the spine towards the crown of the head. The effects and impact of this awakening is impossible to convey through the limited medium of the word. Spiritual energies are not metaphorical but literal powers which hold the key to a radical, dynamic and once secret transformation. The awakening of kundalini brings new levels of consciousness to birth as it rises up through the centres of chakras. When kundalini reaches the centres of the head, like a flower the thousand-petalled lotus of the Crown chakra opens and brings the infinite consciousness of spiritual awakening. A new level of consciousness is born, blending the universal and the individual in a seamless marriage of expansive energy. This is the quantum leap on the journey of becoming.

Jung's deep understanding of symbols led him naturally into the area of Tantra and Eastern mysticism as a pioneering force. His unfailing ability to recognize symbols of psychic transformation, even when such symbols had been lost, ignored, forgotten and devalued, led him to explore Indian Tantra, European alchemy, Taoism and Kundalini Yoga. Jung's special interest in kundalini began with a patient whose dream symbols indicated some degree of kundalini awakening. As early as 1912 Jung wrote psychological interpretations of passages from the Upanishads and the Rig Veda. Another contemporary pioneer was Count Hermann Keyserling who, deeply impressed with Indian metaphysics, established the school of wisdom at

Darmstadt. In his book *The Travel Diary of a Philosopher*, Keyserling, contended that the new psychology emerging in the West was a rediscovery of what was already known in the East: 'Indian wisdom is the profoundest which exists ... the further we get, the more closely do we approach the views of the Indians. Psychological research confirms, step by step, the assertions contained ... within the old Indian science of the soul.'[1] Keyserling was unequivocal in his admiration: 'The Indians have done more than anyone else to perfect the method of training which leads to an enlargement and deepening of consciousness.'[2] It was at Darmstadt that Jung met Richard Willhelm, and in 1928 Jung wrote a psychological commentary to *The Secret of the Golden Flower*. This early foray by a small group of like-minded individuals open to a new spiritual infusion was well ahead of its time. Yet where this pioneering group cut a narrow trail others have now followed, creating a broad and open pathway.

Karma and Kundalini

> How and where is karma stored? What conditions induce
> karma to manifest and lead a person to incarnate?

Hiroshi Motoyama, *Karma and Reincarnation*

The subtle energies or sheaths of consciousness hold imprints of all life experience as energy. All chakra work, whether directly through the discipline of Yoga or indirectly through the application of a philosophy of living, will slowly change the nature of the subtle energies and the flow of life force. However, the chakras also hold karmic seeds. Working upon the self in whatever way will release these potencies. Karma is stored in the matter of the subtle vehicles of consciousness. Since the 19th Path brings together the forces of Geburah and Chesed, this journey is well named Strength, Geburah. Severity holds the seeds of karma already sown. Chesed, Mercy, holds the patterns and imprints of the Primordial Wisdom which release karma. The 19th Path brings these two karmic powers together through the experience of the serpent power which releases karma and dissolves seeds stored in the subtle bodies. This baptism of fire simultaneously burns up karma stored in the akashic record of Geburah and purifies and aligns the *antakarana* in the image of Chesed. Kundalini has been a secret wisdom; it is a difficult and even perilous journey. The process is one of transformation and rebirth. However, this is also a path of immense challenge. The process is not gentle and mild but fierce and unpredictable. The serpent rises with the fire of the lion. Often roaring as it rises, it transforms as it moves through the wholeness of being which is the mind-body-spirit interface. The process is not controllable but dynamic and self-propelling. The serpent will rise and fall again many times until the channel ahead is fully prepared without obstacle – physical, emotional, mental or spiritual. All this will take place, as Gopi Krishna testified, in the crucible of the body. When the serpent rises fully from the base of the spine and unites with its destination at the top of the head, the thousand-petalled lotus of the fully realized human being opens like a crown of fire. This is the Path of Teth, which is the serpent but also the lion.

Kundalini Yoga provides an effective model upon which the process of personal transformation can take place:

> It sees the aim of human development as bringing about an approach
> to and connection between the specific nature of the non-ego and
> the conscious ego. Tantra yoga gives a representation of the condition
> and the developmental phases of this impersonality, as it itself in its
> own way produces the light of a higher suprapersonal consciousness.[3]

It is possibly only a New Age conception that spiritual awakening comes with ease. Misplaced metaphors of light detract from the labour of self-reconstruction. This is the Great Work, nothing less. Plumbing the depths and scaling the heights places every act, deed, word and thought in the spotlight of consciousness. Transformation requires total honesty, integrity and fearlessness.

The testimony of Gopi Krishna provides probably the fullest account of this process. He documented his own trials and many tribulations with the detached eye of an observer and captures both the wonder and the terror of being a lonely traveller in foreign and unexplored terrain. For him, as for most, the sudden awakening was unexpected. Despite having studied both meditation and Yoga, Gopi Krishna was quite unprepared for his own awakening. His journey into kundalini began in 1937:

> I sat breathing slowly and rhythmically, contemplating an imaginary
> lotus in full bloom, radiating light … I suddenly felt a strange
> sensation below the base of the spine. The sensation was so
> extraordinary and so pleasing that my attention was forcibly drawn
> towards it. The moment my attention was thus unexpectedly
> withdrawn from the point on which it was focused, the sensation

ceased ... suddenly, with a roar like that of a waterfall, I felt a
stream of liquid light enter my brain through the spinal cord ...
The illumination grew brighter and brighter, the roaring louder,
I experienced a rocking sensation and felt myself slipping out of my
body entirely enveloped in a halo of light. It is impossible to describe
the experience accurately.[4]

His story is a compelling one. His relationship with this living energy was
to continue for the rest of his life. At times he was no more than a curious
bystander observing the drama taking place in his body and mind. He was
completely transformed by the process, which never ceased:

The process is still at work in me, but after twenty-five years I am
still lost in amazement at the wizardry of this mysterious energy
responsible for the marvels which I witnessed day after day in my
own mortal frame. I regard the manifestation with the same feelings
of awe, adoration and wonder with which I regarded it on the first
occasion; the feelings having increased in intensity and not
diminshed.[5]

Living with kundalini led him to see an evolutionary purpose:

From my own experience, extending more than a quarter of a
century, I am irresistibly led to the conclusion that that the human
organism is evolving in the direction indicated by mystics and
prophets and by men of genius, by the action of this wonderful
mechanism located at the base of the spine.[6]

He knew its difficulties and dangers but concluded that 'The awakening of
Kundalini is the greatest enterprise and the most wonderful achievement in
front of man'.[7] His words may yet hold a prophetic note.

The West now has its first generation of chakra apprentices. Where
chakra work has commenced, kundalini in one degree or another will surely
follow. Gopi Krishna saw kundalini as a powerful healing force, a unifying
power with the capacity to bridge the schism between religion and science
and the herald of a new understanding into human nature:

This is the immortal light, held aloft by nature from time
immemorial to guide the faltering footsteps of erring humanity
across turns and twists, ups and downs of the winding path of
evolution; the light which shone in the prophets and sages of
antiquity, which continues to shine in the men of genius and seers

of today, and will continue to shine for all eternity, illuminating the vast amphitheatre of the universe for the marvellous, unending play of the eternal, almighty, queen of creation, life.[8]

His extraordinary testament has become a classic text in its own right. Gopi Krishna travelled on the 19th Path for most of his life.

THE RAINBOW

Sit in meditation and using the creative imagination build the seven chakras. Flood each centre with coloured light, assigning the colour red to the Base Chakra, orange to the Sacral Chakra and yellow to the Solar Plexus Chakra. Fill the Heart Chakra with a green light and the Throat Chakra with blue. Flood the Brow Chakra with indigo and the Crown Chakra with violet. Holding all of the colours in place, on an in-breath draw a current of light upwards from the base of the spine and release it on an out-breath in a cascade through the top of the head. Repeat this three times. Finally, dissolve all images and return to ordinary consciousness.

EVOCATION

Welcome to my kingdom where a secret knowing awaits. I am one part of a secret wisdom. I am the fire that sleeps within and watches in unknown silence. I am the sleeping serpent who waits in anticipation for the time of awakening. I am known in many places and by many names to the walkers in wisdom. Yet our time will come, for I am the evolutionary impulse to awaken. But feel no impulsion to call me until the compulsion first calls upon you.

I walk in the guise of the lion or the serpent for I am the carrier of a powerful presence. So I test both courage and faith. Yet my gifts are great and my trials are small in comparison to the bounty that I offer. I bring the secret of gifts of being which cannot be described. Yet such gifts bless the history of humanity through those who came in search of me. I bring the Intelligence of the secret of all the activities of the spiritual beings. I am the maker of true visionaries. Mine are those who serve humanity the most and in return ask for the least. I am the maker of the wise servant. This is the essence of my secret which I offer openly and freely to all.

INTERNALIZATION – THE 19TH
PATH: GEBURAH–CHESED

Construct the Temple of either Geburah or Chesed in the creative imagination. Find yourself by the door of Strength. The Archangel lifts the tapestry curtain so that you may pass.

Find yourself on a path set in a wood. Almost immediately, you hear the roaring of a lion. The sound sends a tremor of fear through you but you walk on. The roaring grows louder. The trees part and you come upon the most unusual and unexpected sight. A woman dressed in white, garlanded with flowers, strokes the head of the lion with all the gentleness and tenderness of a close friend. She looks up momentarily and sees you, but straightaway returns her attention to the animal by her side. She is quite without fear as she strokes the lion's head. Her confidence and ease inspire you to draw a little closer. Now you see the redness of the lion's coat, which shines with a brilliant copper lustre, and you feel somehow that this is not a beast of the world but an emblem of an unseen power. This realization gives you further confidence and you step forwards again. The woman reaches out and with a smile takes your hand and places it on the lion's head. You are unafraid, her demeanour is so calm and reassuring. At once, and to your surprise, the lion's head gives off a fiery heat quite unlike that of any living creature. Now the lion begins to roar. The sound is like a deep vibration moving through everything in the vicinity. It is a sound that seems to penetrate to the core of your body. With every roar, you feel that a resonant wave is moving somewhere deep inside your being. You look into the eyes of the woman at your side; she remains calm and reassuring. She closes her eyes and you do the same. Now the red lion and the woman in white fade from view and from awareness. You still hear the rhythmic roaring of the lion but now the sound seems to have moved within your body entirely. With the rise and fall of every roar you feel that a rhythmic wave is flowing in an undulating response somewhere deep in your being. You sense the heat from the closeness of the lion, but now you feel that the heat has also moved from outside to inside. You find yourself slipping more deeply into a state of heightened awareness as the roaring rhythm and the fiery heat fill your mind.

Holding your consciousness in place, you watch all that is unfolding with the detached eye of an observer. Be attentive to all that is happening – physically, emotionally, mentally and in the realm of your highest feelings. Be aware of any sensations of light moving through the body. Be fully aware of all that is happening. Even while immersed in the fullness of the moment, a part of your mind knows that all intensity will fade. When you open your eyes, you will find yourself alone.

When you are ready, return the way you came to the temple. When you are ready, leave through the doorway. Finally, dissolve all images and return to ordinary consciousness.

EXERCITIA SPIRITUALIA

Take the Following as Subjects for Meditation:

- Daughter of the Flaming Sword, Leader of the Lion
- The Letter Teth
- The symbolism of the serpent
- Leo
- Strength

Make Notes on:

- Tarot Trump VIII, Strength

Visualize the Following and Record your Experience:

- The Journey of 19th Path

CHAPTER 23

The Eighteenth Path: Geburah–Binah

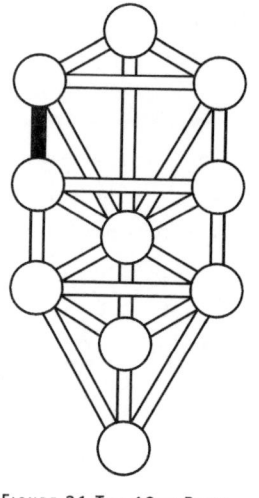

FIGURE 31 THE 18TH PATH:

GEBURAH–BINAH

TAROT TRUMP VII,

THE CHARIOT

TABLE OF CORRESPONDENCES

The Journey: Tarot Trump VII, Victory, Child of the Powers of the Waters, Lord of the Triumph of Light

Key: Cheth, meaning a fence

Simple Letter: Speech

Spiritual Significance: Cancer

Text: The Intelligence of the House of Influences

Colour in Atziluth: Amber

Colour in Yetzirah: Maroon

Colour in Briah: Rich bright Russet

Colour in Assiah: Dark greenish Mauve

COMMENTARY

The Eighteenth Path is called the Intelligence of the House of Influences, by the greatness of whose abundance the influx of good things upon created beings is increased, and from its midst the arcana and hidden senses are drawn forth, which dwell in its shadow and which cling to it from the Cause of all Causes.

The 18th Path connects the fifth Sephirah, Geburah, with the third Sephirah, Binah, on the Pillar of Severity. This journey thereby links the Ethical Triangle to the Supernal Triangle on the journey of ascent and reflects the influence of Binah into the Ethical Triangle on the journey of descent. This Path forms one of the three Paths of the Supreme Mysteries. The Greater Mysteries have been accomplished through the 20th, 21st, 22nd and 23rd Paths. By connecting Binah with Geburah, the 18th Path relates the form-building power inherent in Binah to the karmic storehouse represented by Geburah. As the reservoir of all that has been, and still awaits the journey of descent, Geburah provides the force to match the form of Binah. Where karmic desire stored in the akashic record arises and meets archetypal form, incarnation arises. The charioteer inhabits the chariot.

The Mysteries of Incarnation

The entire subject of rebirth is but little understood at present. Its modern interpretation, and the emphasis which has been laid so strongly on small and unimportant details, have distorted and diverted the wide sweep of the subject and ignored the true import of the process; the broad general lines of the incarnation process have been largely overlooked.

Alice Bailey, *Ponder on This*

The 18th Path is assigned to the Tarot Trump VII, commonly called The Chariot. An impressive figure stands in a chariot drawn by two sphinxes, one black and one white. The figure is crowned with a wreath of laurel surmounted by a star and wears a breastplate and body armour. He holds a wand tipped with a golden cone but carries no reins. The chariot is topped with a starry canopy and bears a winged disc and a heraldic device. In the background is a walled city and a river flows just behind the chariot.

Although this Trump is commonly known as the Chariot, both Chariot and Charioteer need to be considered together, for the driver and the vehicle, consciousness and form, are inseparable. The Charioteer is called Child of the Powers of the Waters and Lord of the Triumph of Light. Elemental water signifies the depth powers of the unconscious, the unlimited realm of the collective unconscious and the infinite expanse of the life-giving waters. The Charioteer knows all these waters. Binah's influence is close by. Hers is the realm of the great sea, Marah. As a feminine sphere of archetypal form, Binah brings the possibility of infinite life through successive rebirth from the timeless waters. This Tarot Trump is assigned to Cancer, which brings another water influence. As the sign for mutable water, Cancer represents the quality of movement, symbolic of the incarnating drive projecting into time and space. The astrological sign of Cancer represents the fourth house of the zodiac, which symbolizes childhood and all the formative influences of this period. Cancer also represents the mother, the family and the ancestors. It therefore points directly to birth and to the wider familial group. As a water sign Cancer bestows a natural sensitivity and emotional depth which have the power to turn life experience into self-awareness. The sign of Cancer is ruled by the moon, the ruler of ebb and flux which also signifies the incarnating currents. The Charioteer wears lunar epaulettes showing that the influence of the moon is understood and honoured. The chariot represents the vehicle of manifestation. In other words, it is the incarnating vehicle of the physical form. It is shaped by the subtle influences carried from life to life as karmic seeds. The chariot is pulled by the twin sphinxes – one black, the other white. The sphinxes represent the balanced power of the four elements, harmonized and united in effort. The sphinxes bring an effortless power to the chariot. These have now become the motive power for the incarnating life force. The Charioteer applies neither reins nor goad of any kind. He is master in his own house. Power now resides in consciousness alone. The chariot is cubic in design. It is the vehicle of incarnation. Its six faces represent the four directions and the Great Above and the Great Below. Its fours pillars are reminders of the four directions and the four elements in endless and infinite combination. The chariot represents all the possibilities and experiences that incarnate life can offer. Its four-square structure represents stability and balance. Four is also the number of a carbon-based life form. The Charioteer wears a shining square upon his breast. The chariot is emblazoned by the emblem of Shiva set in a heraldic shield. This fusion of Eastern and Western metaphysics once again represents a unifying principle. This level of awareness transcends all cultural labels. The winged disc is a symbol beloved of the ancient Egyptians, representing freedom, liberation and spiritual transcendence. The chariot represents the incarnating form and the physical life to be set under the stars. The cycle of incarnation requires a physical form. As the solid and enclosing armour protects and defends the charioteer, as a house provides a dwelling place for its inhabitants, as a city contains the life of a people, as the shell houses the hermit crab, so the incarnating form provides the means of experience in the physical world. The Charioteer wears a zodiac belt. Which astrological combination will best serve the future incarnation?

These are the mysteries of incarnation. The Charioteer, the Child of the Waters and the Lord of the Triumph of Light, stands with confidence in the chariot. He rules from within. As an initiate of the Supreme Mysteries of birth and death, he wears a starry crown set on a laurel wreath and carries a sceptre of authority tipped with a cone shaped as the pineal gland. This Trump is also known as Victory. This is the victory of supreme self-realization over the gates of life and death, even over nirvana and samsara. All oppositions have been reconciled. The Charioteer is rightly called the Lord of the Triumph of Light, consciousness has been transformed, the Bardo realms of light have been mastered. He exemplifies the awakening that the Path of Wisdom brings.

The Body of Light

The time has come however when the fact that there is an energy body underlying the nervous system must be recognized by the world at large, and when the nature of the seven centres, their structure and location should be grasped technically, and when the laws of their unfoldment should be widely known.

Alice Bailey, *A Treatise on White Magic*

The Charioteer is the Lord of the Triumph of Light. This is the victory of awakened self-consciousness, visibly demonstrated in the self-created, coherent and unified body of light. The vehicle of consciousness, the chariot, is the *antakarana*, the refined vehicle constructed from living energy through a directed and purified consciousness. This is the Great Work. It is the task of not one lifetime but many.

Although the subtle vehicle is always open to and changed by mental and emotional energy, the work of refining the *antakarana* begins with intent on the 28th Path, which is that of the Natural Intelligence, where the chakras are represented as seven stars. This is the natural inheritance yet it is also the secret wisdom. This blueprint is a part of the Occult Intelligence of Netzach, to be activated and actualized by the willed imagination. It is on the 27th Path of the Exciting Intelligence that the dynamic potency of the living energies begins to become apparent. The gradual refining of the subtle energies magnetizes higher levels of energy, which are drawn gradually towards the threshold of consciousness. The 27th Path represented by Mars and Scorpio is a journey of radical transformation and polarity, both vertical and horizontal, as revealed through the imagery of The Tower. As the 27th Path consolidates the work of the Lesser Mysteries and the Psychological Triangle, so the 19th Path consolidates the work of the Greater Mysteries and the Ethical Triangle. The processes of the Greater Mysteries are intimately related to karma and the storehouse from the past and for the future. This is the Path of Strength represented by the letter Teth, the serpent. This is the arisen kundalini, The journey of the 18th Path represents the realization of the Natural Intelligence first depicted on the 28th Path.

The 18th Path rests upon the foundation constructed through the expansion of consciousness and the refinement of the antakarana through these paths. This is the Intelligence of the House of Influences. It is an understanding of the influences expressed through the centres of consciousness as powerful factors in the development and unfolding of a life. The subtle energies represented by the chakras form the intermediary between body and mind, consciousness and form, chariot and the charioteer. The centres can confer 'abundance' and 'the influx of good things'. The sevenfold blueprint offers a model of being and becoming. Following its secret wisdom, 'the arcana and hidden senses are drawn forth'. This is a Path of self-realization. Now, the blueprint for becoming has become actualized and through it the victorious figure of the Charioteer as Child of the Power of the Waters and Lord of the Triumph of Light has arisen. The secret wisdom has been applied and become a gnosis of the heart.

THE CHARIOTEER

Imagine yourself standing beside a chariot. It towers over you and sits upon heavy wheels. Two beasts stand between the shafts. Run your hand over the framework, feeling its weight and power. Soon you will be expected to take charge of this vehicle and to gain control over it.

This appears a formidable task. You step up and put on the armour hanging from one of its four pillars. Strapping on the breastplate brings a warmth to your heart and a sense of purpose. The epaulettes at your shoulders convey an ability to bear responsibility with sensitivity. The zodiac belt gives you a sense of unlimited connection. The crown brings mental acuity and self-confidence. Finally, the wand brings authority and autonomy. The charioteer is ready. The chariot awaits. The two beasts now sit quietly awaiting your word.

Are you ready to assume control?

The Secret Wisdom

Then, beyond this secret wheel – the wheel of birth –

he finally gains access to the realm of Braham, where

subject and object being in harmony, are emitted within

the Self and by the Self.

Stanzas of Abhinavagupta, verse 140

The House of Influences is the full mind-body continuum. The Intelligence of the House of Influences is the conscious and actualized knowing of the mind-body continuum. Such knowing has always been a secret wisdom, though few seek it; transcendence remains the highest yet rarest human aspiration. Few seek the self-mastery exemplified by the Charioteer. He has become the Lord of the Triumph of Light. He has created the body of light as a reflection of a transformed consciousness. But this is no easy task: 'it is most difficult to bring about the rearrangement of the forces flowing through these vortices, and to learn to function consciously through the higher centres, subordinating the lower ones'.[1] Alice Bailey draws a clear distinction between the lower and higher centres. The three centres below the diaphragm – the base of the spine, the sexual centre and solar plexus – provide the necessary energy for survival, reproduction and the exercise of personal will. 'These are, at present, the most potent in average humanity and the most "alive",' says Alice Bailey.

Knowledge of the chakras has seeped into the Western mindset ever since the theosophist Charles Ledbeater brought such ideas to a late Victorian audience. He was followed very slowly by others who also saw value in these Eastern ideas. But outside esoteric circles there was little general interest until much more recently, when the trickle of books, classes, teachers and exponents has become a veritable torrent. The subject of the chakras has risen in popularity over the last decade. Drawing upon an original Eastern infusion, the West has now evolved its own style and approach to the subject. Yet even now, the fullness and significance of the subject does not seem to have been conveyed. Though some outstanding exponents have emerged, the Western approach has often tended towards presenting a technology of chakra-awakening in place of presenting a spiritual framework in which chakra-awakening will naturally take place. Though this energy is now being used in new therapeutic and healing ways, it is important to also set this sevenfold blueprint in its fullest context. In it lies the means through which the body of light is created. The Charioteer reminds us of this as he rides from life to life: 'The subject is of vital importance to the modern aspirant, for the mechanism of the heart, the throat and the eye – constituting part of the inner structure which he must learn to use – has to be mastered and consciously employed before any true creative work is possible.'[2] The transfer of energy and focus between the higher and lower centres is crucial, according to Alice Bailey. These three centres represent the overwhelming drives for the vast majority. The lower centres encapsulate the abiding concerns of Western culture – to own, to create a family and to be materially successful. These first three chakras express a self-centredness which may be considered socially desirable, but spiritual awakening does not stir until the opening of the heart centre. Alice Bailey states that these centres, which are currently the most active, require to be re-organized and re-orientated. By contrast the four centres above the diaphragm are the least developed and awakened within the community as a whole. The root centre provides a strong sense of physical power. It carries a strong sense of personal survival and territorial identity. Without the softening impact of other centres, this energy brings greed, avarice and a fear of losing control or possession. This primitive and self-serving energy is very much alive in the world today. Territorial disputes, conflicts over boundaries and possession – all express aspects of the base and basic centre. The sexual centre is also necessary and important in evolutionary terms, yet it is also clear that without an inter-nalized controlling mechanism, indiscriminate sexuality is damaging. Sexual abuse of many kinds is still rife and its effects are devastating. Even though

this centre brings a receptivity and sensitivity to others which seeks expression through many forms of relating, its main drive is towards sexual expression. The Solar Plexus Chakra expresses the will to be and to do. It is the place of the personal will and the seat of those much valued attributes – ambition, drive, focused energy and self-determination – which are so necessary in career building. This too is another self-serving force which puts self-interest above anything else. It is easy to live through the first three chakras – in fact, it is impossible not to draw on these energies, which are instinctive. Crossing the gulf, leaping forwards towards the embrace of the heart is difficult. Yet these centres bring the much-needed qualities of universal compassion and pure altruism. It is through the higher centres that a love for humanity and life itself will flower. There is no financial, material, social, emotional, sexual or other gain to be had. If such a transfer of energy and values were to take place on a large enough scale it would precipitate both a personal and a cultural revolution. Perhaps this silent revolution is already taking place.

These are the influences in the House of Influences, 'by the greatness of whose abundance the influx of good things upon created beings is increased'. These are the influences which bring an 'influx of good things' by the grace of an abundant source. But where are such things to be found? They are to be found 'from the midst', where 'the arcana and hidden senses are drawn forth'. In other words, the knowledge of these subtle forces is to be found not in surface appearances but 'in the midst', deep beneath the surface. To reach the middle point demands a journey into the depths of being. It is through the journey to the centre that the secret influences are discovered, recognized and drawn forth or brought to the surface. The journey of the 18th Path is one of mastering key hidden influences. It is on this path that the arcana, the secret things, are drawn forth. The Intelligence of the House of Influence brings an inner knowing and mastery of the forces of influence. It signifies the opportunities and circumstances whereby the individual awakens to the nature and reality of hidden and subtle influences immanent within incarnate life. Such subtle energies and forces are not accessible to anything other than consciousness itself. As the journey touches the higher reaches of the Tree, so many of the touchstones by which we now operate are called into question by a deeper and timeless wisdom. The cult of personality, the stock in trade of the media and all media-related industries, is revealed in the mirror of Yesod as no more than a glamorous and superficial illusion. Beyond the personality which is the mask for a single incarnation lies the realm of the Individuality and its greater cycle of successive lives and varied personalities. Approaching such concepts tests all logical mental processes to the limit. Here is a concept without proof, an idea without substantiation, a rationale beyond the rational. Nevertheless, a wide view of history and a broad view of human nature will reveal individuals who have in fullness and consciousness lived out this pattern. Such individuals are the exception not the rule; such lives display the rare, not the usual. Such people provide uncommon models in a world dominated by commonly held models of spiritual impoverishment.

The Charioteer exemplifies the Triumph of Light. He has by virtue of a long spiritual journey acquired an Intelligence of the House of Influences. He has followed the secret wisdom enshrined in the *Sat-Cakra-Nirupana*, the knowledge of the chakras. He has constructed the body of light which is sometimes called the rainbow body. The Charioteer knows that the seeds of future karma rest within the body of light. The theory is that every action we create, be it positive, negative or neutral, leaves an impression on the mind that will later act as a subconscious predisposition or instinct. A person who creates evil will cause his mind to become laden with a heavy subconscious predisposition towards cruelty. Conversely, a person who creates goodness through acts of love, wisdom and kindness will increase a predisposition towards these qualities. This karma or action affects our mind and personality in this life and consequently also influences the patterns our life will take. But, more importantly, at the time of our death the karmic seeds we carry within the mind strongly affect our future evolution. Karmic seeds are stored within the chakras.

The seeds of sexual attachment are stored within the Muladhara Chakra.

The seeds of attachment to emotions and imagination are stored within the Manipura Chakra.

The seeds of attachment to love and compassion are stored in the Anahata Chakra.

The seeds of attachment to the processes of purification are stored in the Vishuddi Chakra.

The seeds of attachment to knowledge and wisdom are stored in the Ajna Chakra.

Motoyama concludes that, 'Once karma has been stored in the seed state, it lies latent until conditions arise that cause it to manifest.'[3]

In the book *A Treatise on White Magic*, Alice Bailey provides a new insight into the Hermetic axiom, which she relates directly to the awakening of the chakras:

To Dare:
These words give the clue to the subordination of the personality, and have a close connection with the solar plexus, the great clearing house of desire and of astral forces, and also the main centre of the transmutative work.

To Know:
These words concern the Ajna centre, the centre between the eyebrows. A hint lies in the words 'Let the Mother know the Father.' It has relation to the marriage in the heavens.

To Will:
These words relate to the ultimate achievement, when, by an act of combined will of the soul and of the lower man, unification and realization are brought about. It concerns the centre at the base of the spine.

To Be Silent:
This phrase relates to the transmutation of the lower creative energy into the higher creative life. The sacral centre has relapsed into silence.[4]

In other words, on this Path those influences which work upon an incarnation are recognized and mastered. This is the nature of the work of the Supreme Mysteries. Mahayana Buddhism offers teachings which relate directly to this process. Its history is a living testament to reincarnation as a conscious and willed act of rebirth. This is the Path of the Charioteer who chooses to ride out into incarnation. It is the victory of the human spirit and the Triumph of the Lord of Light.

EVOCATION

Welcome to my kingdom which is your rightful inheritance too. The question 'Who are you?' has been posed many times. Are you now in a position to speak with the authority of self-knowledge and awareness? How many times have you ridden out onto the field of incarnation to return empty-handed, dazed by forgetfulness and bedazzled by what you have seen? How many more times will you ride out into new birth and new circumstance before awakening can take root? Who is master in your house, which is the House of Influence? Have you attained control over the elemental powers in your nature or are you pulled and driven by desires and impulses with a life of their own? Are you yet crowned by the awakened mind? Have you gained the staff of authority? Do you understand the influences which carry you from life to life in vehicles suited to different tasks and experiences? When you are at one with such influences, you will no longer be driven but will call yourself master in your own home. Know that you will always stand beneath the starry heavens. Know that you will always be a child of the zodiac. Know that you will always find elemental powers at your disposal. These are the influences that you must acknowledge and master through self-awareness. Then the unlimited powers of infinite possibility will flow into whatever form you inhabit. And you shall understand what it means to be a Child of the Powers of the Waters and Lord of the Triumph of Light.

INTERNALIZATION – THE 18TH PATH: GEBURAH–BINAH

Construct the Temple of Geburah in the creative imagination. Find yourself standing beside the doorway of the Chariot. The Archangel Khamael lifts the tapestry curtain so that you may pass.

You find yourself in a corridor. Somewhere close by you hear the sounds of a workshop. Hammers ring out in a repeating pattern. You walk on briskly and the corridor opens into busy workshop. In the centre is a furnace. Workmen busily go about their tasks. The smell of molten metal fills the air. There is a great sense of frenetic activity; even though you walk freely among the people no one pays you any attention and you wonder if you have become invisible. Yet as you walk among them you hear your name mentioned and you realize that this workshop is operating on your behalf.

Now in one corner of the room you see the focus of their great work. A magnificent chariot stands ready. You see hanging from one of its columns a breast plate, epaulettes and crown, waiting for the charioteer. It seems to you that the work is near completion. Everything looks to be almost ready for the charioteer to ride out. But overhearing the workmen it is clear that seven jewels are to be placed on the inside of the chariot, hidden from view, and the Overseer in the House of Influences is waiting on inspiration and guidance in this matter.

You see him on the far side of the room sitting quietly, deep in reflective thought at a table on which you see a small pile of gemstones. It is clear that he is pondering on the final selection because he picks up the stones and allows them to run through his hands. You too become totally caught up in his contemplation. As the stones play through his hands, thoughts run through your mind. With a sudden intuitive flash, you perceive the true arrangement and understand its significance for the charioteer who will ride out in the chariot. You see him set aside seven stones, counting them out with care. He lays them out in a vertical array and covers them with a soft cloth. With a contented air, he rises from his seat and leaves the workshop.

Now you are alone. You go over to the chariot knowing that you are its rightful owner. You put on the crown and the breastplate and stand four square in the chariot. There, hidden on the inside are seven small depressions waiting to receive the seven stones. Then the chariot will be ready and you will ride out again.

When you are ready, leave and return to the temple. When you are ready, leave through the doorway. Finally, dissolve all images and return to ordinary consciousness.

EXERCITIA SPIRITUALIA

Take the Following as Subjects for Meditation:

- Victory, Child of the Powers of the Waters, Lord of the Triumph of Light
- The letter Cheth
- Speech
- Cancer
- The Intelligence of the House of Influences

Make Notes on:

- Tarot Trump VII, The Chariot

Visualize the Following and Record your Experiences:

- The Temple of Geburah including the Archangel Khamael
- The Journey of the 18th Path

CHAPTER 24

The Seventeenth Path: Tiphareth–Binah

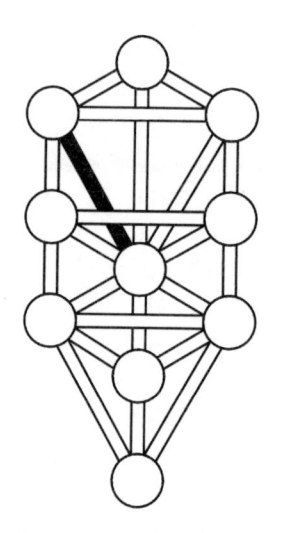

FIGURE 32 THE 17TH PATH:

TIPHARETH–BINAH

TAROT TRUMP VI,

THE LOVERS

TABLE OF CORRESPONDENCES

The Journey: Tarot Trump VI, The Lovers, Children of the Voice, Oracle of the Mighty Gods

Key: Zain, meaning a sword

Simple Letter: Smell

Spiritual Significance: Gemini

Text: The Disposing Intelligence

Colour in Atziluth: Orange

Colour in Briah: Pale Mauve

Colour in Yetzirah: New Yellow leather

Colour in Assiah: Reddish Grey inclined to Mauve

COMMENTARY

The Seventeenth Path is the Disposing Intelligence which provides faith to the righteous, and they are clothed with the Holy Spirit by it, and it is the Foundation of Excellence in the state of higher things.

The 17th Path connects the sixth Sephirah, Tiphareth, with the third Sephirah, Binah. Binah is part of the Supernal Triangle which represents the impersonal powers and creative laws within creation. Tiphareth is part of the Moral or Ethical Triangle which forges connections to a greater and extended perspective of life. The 17th, 13th and 15th Paths each connect the Greater Mysteries with the Supreme Mysteries. The 13th Path is the Uniting Intelligence, 'the essence of glory' and 'the consummation of the truth of individual spiritual things'. The 17th Path is the Disposing Intelligence, called 'the Foundation of Excellence in the state of higher things'. The 15th Path is the Constituting Intelligence; 'it constitutes the substance of creation in pure darkness'. These three Paths serve as two-way connections between the centre of the Tree at Tiphareth and the highest triad of forces represented by Binah, Chockmah and Kether. Together these three Paths bring an increased awareness of the ultimate nature of reality. These three Paths bring initiations into the most sublime aspects of being, the substance of creation, the state of higher things and the truth of individual spiritual things. The 13th Path shows the feminine face of wisdom as initiator. The 15th Path shows the face of wisdom as divine law. The 17th Path shows the face of wisdom through the balanced polarities of male and female forces.

Fire from Heaven

> I will pour out my spirit upon all flesh;
>
> your sons and daughter shall prophesy,
>
> your young men shall see visions.
>
> Even upon the menservants and the maid servants,
>
> I will pour out my spirit.

The Book of Joel, 28–9

On this Path, travellers become, 'clothed with the Holy Spirit'. It is the, 'Foundation of Excellence in the state of higher things'. The Holy Spirit is a Christian doctrine rooted in the biblical account of Pentecost. 'When the day of Pentecost had come, they were all together in one place. And suddenly from heaven there came a sound like the rush of a violent wind, and it filled the entire house where they were sitting. Divided tongues of fire appeared among them and a tongue rested on each of them. All of them were filled with the Holy Spirit and began to speak other languages as the spirit gave them ability.' This is an extraordinary account. What does it mean?

After Pentecost the Holy Spirit became available to the Christian community. It was taken as a sign of God's continuing presence in the world after the death of Jesus. The inception of the Holy Spirit also conferred spiritual gifts such as healing and prophecy, through which God's work might continue through the Christian congregation. In many ways the Holy Spirit is a purely Christian conception. However, although the term 'Holy Spirit' may belong to the Christian tradition, the nature of the experience, or one which may be described in very similar terms, may indeed belong to the universal community of spiritual pilgrims.

This central Christian experience has much in common with accounts of the risen kundalini. Emerging from a quite different world view and model of self, the relevant accounts bear similarities which are worthy of comparison. Although the rising of kundalini and the descent of the Holy Spirit may seem at first to have nothing in common, the commonality remains worth pursuing. The Holy Spirit is always depicted as entering through descent, whereas kundalini is always depicted as entering through ascent. However, when kundalini has risen through the six centres and finally rises into the Crown Chakra, its effect is to cause the many petals of the lotus to invert and descend onto the head like a close-fitting cap. This metaphorical language implies that kundalini first rises from within but then, at its crowning, descends. Kundalini is represented by the serpent, which in the Western mind has become the most maligned of all creatures since its part in the first fall from a state of grace in the idyllic Garden of Eden. The Holy Spirit is invariably symbolized by a white dove. This gentle image conveys a softness of contact which is not always matched in mystical literature. The experience of Western mystics reveals the same kind of turbulence as that documented by Eastern mystics. The Christian mystic, St Teresa of Avila, wrote that 'The noises in my head are so loud that I am beginning to wonder what is going on. My head sounds just as if it were full of brimming rivers and a host of little birds seems to be whistling not in the ears but in the upper part of the head where the highest part of the soul is said to be.' Mystical accounts from East and West document these highly personal and intensely spiritual events; boundaries dissolve, emotions are intensified, the divine presence seems palpable.

A metaphorical model holds great power, it demands obedience and loyalty to is own internal symbols. It is doubtless as difficult for the practitioner of Kundalini Yoga to appreciate parallels with the descending dove of the Holy Spirit as it might be for a devoted Christian to appreciate parallels with the risen serpent. The one is an Eastern blueprint, the other is a Western blueprint. Jung anticipated the difficulties in attempting to cross-match the two symbolic representations: 'Kundalini Yoga is a symbolic formulation of the impersonal experience in the Eastern way. It would cause us a great deal of trouble to understand in our Western way what the East tries to convey through its symbolism.'[1] However, a few have crossed the cultural barrier, though not without difficulty. In 'Christian Mysticism and Kundalini', Mineda J. McCleave writes of his own spiritual struggle 'to understand the meaning of God, Christ, the Holy Spirit, love, good, evil, heaven and hell'. He pursued his personal quest with much devotion and intensity:

> On April 6, 1976 I was in very deep prayer expressing a strong need for God's intervention in the affairs of my life. Unexpectedly, I was jarred out of my prayer by what felt like a current of energy that seemed to enter my body through my left foot. Subjectively it felt like an electrical charge of nervous energy moving with extreme rapidity up the inside of my left leg, passing thorough my genitals and then dispersing through my upper back. The current was constant for four days and nights, and with it there was a continuous feeling of great body heat. I felt as though I was burning up from the inside out. Relatives could feel heat emanating from the front and back of my head while their hands were an inch away from me. It was a frightening experience. I had somehow triggered a current through intense prayer, but I had no knowledge of how to stop it.[2]

Though the original episode subsided in intensity it continued to operate at a less intense threshold:

> I felt as if my basal metabolism had skyrocketed, my mind was hyperactive as I tried to understand what was taking place. Physically I went through a variety of symptoms including anorexia, headaches, trembling, fever with concurrent chills, nausea and dizziness.

Emotionally I went up and down the keyboard of euphoria, joy, bewilderment, anxiety, depression and the familiar despair. I was at times deluded and often disorientated.

Unusually, McCleave, whose Christian orientation never failed, had been drawn to a wide spiritual literature. Though typically warned against the dangers of occult literature, he place his trust in God and continued to read widely. By happenstance he found the works of Gopi Krishna, where he immediately found supportive parallels with his own story. When McCleave first read Gopi Krishna's book, it was without understanding. Later he turned to it again in a new light. McCleave recognized in himself the physical, mental and emotional characteristics of kundalini, aroused but not fully risen. As a devout Christian, McCleave needed to find a bridge between the two models. Finally, 'by the grace of God I was led to an open minded, tolerant, compassionate, caring Christian psychiatrist. He was not afraid of Kundalini.' McCleave was able to bridge the two different models of mystical transformation and concluded that 'The Christian mystics, unaware of the Hindu term, described the same phenomena, but named the animating, motivating spiritual force at work within them as the Holy Spirit'.[3]

Traditional accounts of kundalini and the iconography of Christianity are filled with the imagery of fire which simultaneously purges, destroys and yet renews. Although mystical Christianity is typically filled with images of fire as a metaphor for divine love, this imagery and symbolism also belong to the many mystical traditions of the world. The experience of fire is described as an uncontrolled body heat, sometimes as a vision of fire, or as a flame or light which though present does not consume. The poem written by St John of the Cross speaks through the metaphor of fire:

> Oh flame of love so living,
> How tenderly you force
> To my soul's inmost core your fiery probe.
>
> Oh lamps of fiery blaze
> To whose refulgent fuel
> The deepest caverns of my soul grow bright,
> Late bloom with gloom and haze,
> But in this strange renewal
> Giving to the belov'd both heat and light.

St John of the Cross, 'Song of the Soul in Intimate Communication and Union with the Love of God'

The Tarot Trump depicts a tree alight with 12 flames, each triple, reminiscent of the letter Shin as representative of spiritual fire. The naked Adam, or the Shiva principle, stands before the flaming tree. Both Gopi Krishna and Mineda McCleave, like other unknown and unnamed spiritual pilgrims, learned that the fiery metaphor was more literal than literary.

Shiva and Shakti

> In Kundalini Yoga, Shiva is associated with the chakra at
> the crown of the head and Kundalini Shakti with the
> chakra at the base of the spine.

Mary Scott, *Kundalini in the Physical World*

The Tree of Life continually demonstrates the law of polarity. Unity gives rise to duality which eventually permits multiplicity and complexity. Opposites attract and result in the creation of a third new factor. If homogeneity prevailed, nothing new could come into existence. This is the law of polarity which takes many forms – as yin and yang or the archetypal male and female powers. In Tantric philosophy these same forces are embodied as Shiva and Shakti. Neither can exist without the other. Shiva's power is a static quality and remains identified with unmanifest consciousness. The power of Shakti is dynamic and creative. She is referred to as the mother of the universe, the creator of the universe, of life and mind.

The Tarot Trump of The Lovers shows two naked figures, one male and the other female. The naked female stands in front of a tree entwined with a serpent. The naked man stands before a tree alight with 12 flames. Behind them an angelic being fills the upper sky. The scene is reminiscent of the biblical Garden of Eden. All the components are present – Adam and Eve, the tree, the serpent and the apple, the angel and even the sword, since this Trump is assigned to the letter Zain, meaning a sword. But this is not an image replicating the expulsion from Eden; rather, it is an image of the sacred marriage between the twin powers imbedded within creation. The sword divides wholeness into parts which then take on the appearance of being separated. The sword is one of the quaternity of elemental symbols: the rod, the cup, the sword and the pantacle. It represents the function of the intellectual mind which divides, analyses and separates. The sword of the mind slices Shiva from Shakti, yet the lovers ever seek reconciliation and unity. This Trump is assigned to Gemini, which as another Air sign also signifies the function of mind. As representative of the twins, Gemini symbolizes both unity and duality. As twins emerge from the same womb and often share an inexplicable mutual understanding, so the natures of Shiva and Shakti can be likened to that of cosmic twins. This is the essence of the divine marriage.

This principle of polarity operates in many ways, both in the macrocosm and the microcosm. As a woman represents Shakti, so a man represents Shiva. There is of course an abiding attraction across the sexes which brings male and female together as lovers. But this polarity is also operative at much more subtle levels of being. Shiva is assigned to a place within the Crown Chakra at the top of the head. Shakti is assigned to a place within the Root Chakra at the base of the spine. The two remain separated until a spiritual awakening takes a particular form, when Kundalini Shakti rises through each of the chakras to the Sahasrara Chakra, the abode of Shiva, to there consummate the sacred marriage. The child of this union is cosmic consciousness, the flowering of the thousand-petalled lotus, the Sahasrara Chakra. When Shiva and Shakti meet in the Crown Chakra, the coming together of these two forces brings intense stimulation and hyperactivity to the neural configuration in the head, including the 12 cranial nerves. This physical explanation should not detract from the affective quality of the experience, which brings feelings of bliss, universal love and intense joy. In the Eastern tradition this moment of cosmic awakening is described through the symbolism of the opening lotus. In the West this same experience is depicted by a halo of shining light or flames. Might these not be one and the same experience, described in different language through the particular lens of cultural and spiritual expectation?

DOVES AND SERPENTS

Take both these images as focal points for your contemplation. Use this iconography to meditate on the meaning of these two quite different symbols.

The State of Higher Things

The higher realm has been known throughout the ages.

Roberto Assagioli, *Psychosynthesis*

This Path is, 'the Foundation of Excellence in the state of higher things'. Christianity speaks of the Holy Spirit and Yoga speaks of kundalini. Excellence in the state of higher things cannot appear until total nakedness of being exists. Stripped of ego, emptied of the needs of personality, the empty vessel waits to be filled. As the Path of the Disposing Intelligence, the 17th Path clothes with the Holy Spirit. The naked pair, Adam and Eve or Shiva and Shakti, await the coming of such clothing. Both the descent of the Holy Spirit and the rising of kundalini bring what might be termed the gifts of the spirit. Both the experience of the Holy Spirit and the experience of the risen kundalini are related to the experience of the 17th Path, which provides the 'Foundation of Excellence in the state of higher things'. Whether the Disposing Intelligence, 'the Foundation of Excellence in the state of higher things', is to be dressed in the form of the dove or the serpent is possibly a cultural perspective. Whether these two kinds of experience are identical or just broadly similar or quite different remains an open question. Their commonality, however, is compelling. This mystical trans-formation, by whatever name it is known and through whatever metaphor it is described, brings the active and practical manifestation of 'higher things'. Such manifestations are unusual but not without precedent and belong to the universal tradition of spiritual powers. These spiritual gifts are quite unlike the psychic flowering which begins at Yesod and takes shape as clair-voyance, clairaudience or telepathy. Such abilities still retain a highly personal element. But the prophecy, oracular ability, direct knowing, healing and visionary powers which accompany this level of awakening always have an impersonal and numinous quality. These gifts seem to flow spontaneously, often unbidden, usually unstoppable, like water in a conduit. The individual in whom such gifts are evident invariably ascribes ownership and control to a divine or other source, for the working of such gifts always *feels* utterly and completely non-personal. The higher realm, the state of higher things, originates not from the personality but from another and quite different reality. It is a transpersonal source of inspiration and connection which is represented by Metatron, the Archangel of Kether. Tarot Trump VI, The Lovers, is also known as the Children of the Voice and the Oracle of the Mighty Gods. These titles express this transpersonal yet intimate relationship. The child is the offspring of the voice, the oracle is in the service of the mighty gods. The source of wisdom lies with the voice and the mighty gods, but the manifest form lies with the oracle. During Pentecost, 'they were filled with the Holy Spirit and began to speak other languages as the spirit gave them ability'. Gopi Krishna also developed some remarkable linguistic gifts and powers which could not be explained by formal learning.

The higher state of things is the realm of the mystic. It belongs to the spiritual walker far along the path. The rarity of the territory makes it difficult to assess, understand and evaluate. The descriptions of these unique encounters are also close to testaments given by the obviously insane, the clearly deluded and the mentally sick. The defining difference is that the mystic is demonstrably sane in every other aspect of life. The true spiritual gifts convey an authenticity, prophetic words ring with truth, healing brings ease, insight is potent. Self-delusion masquerading as spiritual power is palpably paper-thin.

The 17th Path connects the Greater Mysteries of the Ethical Triangle with the Supreme Mysteries of the Supernal Triangle. The Supernal Triangle is not fully accessible to the human mind other than indirectly through analogy or reflection. Although it is separated from the remainder of the Tree by the Abyss, the Supernal Triangle is of course inseparable from the Tree. However, just as the individual is subject to the law of gravity for instance, so the individual is also subject to the supernal realm through its impersonal functions. These three Paths connect the mystical and unified consciousness of Tiphareth to a level of reality beyond full self-realization; each brings a deepening of the gifts of the spirit.

Is the Disposing Intelligence of the 17th Path, which provides 'faith to the righteous and clothes with the Holy Spirit', to be relegated to the pages of history? If it is the Foundation of Excellence in the state of higher things, may not the higher states remain open to all peoples and at all times?

Adopting the kundalini model as one worthy of research, Lee Sannella, a contemporary investigator into the kundalini phenomenon, has observed an increase in recorded cases. Furthermore, he anticipates a continuing increase. He notes, 'Today kundalini awakenings occur more frequently, with and without training ... people experience kundalini phenomena more frequently because they are actually more involved in lifestyles conducive to psychospiritual transformation.'[4] Sannella sees that a broadly based cultural and spiritual infusion is in progress. 'Many are engaged in Yoga, Vedanta and the different schools of Buddhism – Zen, Vajrayana, Mahayana, Theravada. An even larger number of people pursue psychic arts like dowsing, "chan-nelling", magic, witchcraft and psychic healing, and many more have a passive interest, if not a fascination for, such matters.'[5] This grass-roots spiritual upsurge is not without its transformative impact, both individually and collectively. In the West, knowledge of the chakras, *Sat-Cakra-Nirupana*, has been at work for a generation or more now. Like seeds broadcast in fertile soil, this too will yield a future crop. It may result in a more broadly based Foundation of Excellence in the state of higher things.

This Path takes us deeper into the realm of mystery and reframes the injunction 'Know Thyself'. It represents the mysterious and wonderful transformative possibility of the human condition which all observers of higher states know to be true. Jung recognized the transformative effect of kundalini: 'When you succeed in awakening the kundalini so that it starts to move out of its mere potentiality you necessarily start a world which is totally different from our world.'[6] From a Christian perspective the Holy Spirit brings renewal: 'With God's Spirit human beings are given a wonderful power and force. It is not at their disposal, yet it can clearly be perceived. It questions them and yet builds them up. The Holy Spirit is a liberating, perfecting power … The Spirit takes God's creatures into a new life.'[7] McCleave, whose encounter with spiritual fire served to reaffirm his Christianity, finally concluded that 'there is a Living God – a vibrant, active, creative Being who is the silent mover of all things'.[8]

Gopi Krishna came to see an evolutionary purpose to the energies working in his body. He described it as, 'energy not yet known to science, which is carrying all mankind towards the heights of superconsciousness'.[9] He saw this palpable but unknown and undefined energy as the driving force behind the next major evolutionary impulse. Perhaps this may prove to be the case.

EVOCATION

Welcome to my kingdom if you truly wish to know the reality of high things, for I am the foundation of excellence in such matters. When you discover the way into my realm, nothing will appear to be the same, so think wisely and well before you seek me.

I bring you the contact with a new reality. I bring you a new foundation. My nature has been described in many different ways, so dispose of labels and merely know that some have found my kingdom and write of it with words of allegory and simile. For it is not possible to write directly of this but only through reflection. Here unity is restored but briefly and even in this union you will be transformed.

My nature is that of mystery. For I cannot explain myself in words that you will grasp. But in our meeting there will come knowing. And from this knowing will come a new beginning. And from this beginning, you will arise reborn with the gifts of the spirit resting upon your shoulders.

INTERNALIZATION – THE 17TH PATH: TIPHARETH–BINAH

Construct the Temple of Tiphareth in the creative imagination. Find yourself standing beside the doorway of The Lovers. The Archangel Raphael lifts the tapestry curtain so that you may pass.

You find yourself walking upon a path in an open plain. Ahead of you in the far distance you see the shape of a mountain peak rising up from the plain. Time passes. As you watch the mountain top, clouds begin to gather above it. As you continue to walk, you watch the clouds which form and hover over the summit. Now your journey has a clear destination. The mountain and the clouds above it magnetize your mind as you continue on your way. Ahead of you in the distance something else attracts your attention. As you approach, you can see more clearly that two trees rise up from an otherwise perfectly flat plain.

The tree on the left bears four fruits. The tree on the right appears to be aflame with fruits of living fire. This enigmatic and mysterious sight galvanizes your whole being. You step forwards once more. A serpent uncoils itself from the foliage of the fruit tree and begins to wind itself around the slender trunk. The second tree bears fruits in the form of 12 living flames burning with a brilliant light. You want to move closer to touch these fantastic trees, but the trees are two and you are one. You will have to choose which of the two trees to stand beside.

Now you enter your own deep meditation, while you contemplate which tree has the deepest call upon your soul. When you come to a decision, move closer into the embrace of the tree of your choice. As you turn to stand with your back to the tree, at that instant all your outer clothing disappears, stripped away from you as if by some superior but gentle force. Now you stand naked in front of the tree you have chosen. A soft rustling sound from the other tree attracts your attention. A naked figure of the opposite sex steps out as if from nowhere to stand beside you. You both stand naked and stripped of all pretence. You turn towards each other and without speaking extend a hand. This gesture coincides with the sound of thunder. You turn your gaze to the horizon in the distant background. Clouds begin to swirl and move as if life stirs within them. As you watch the clouds open, sunlight pours from the heavens and it seems that a most beautiful figure takes shape in the clouds. You are mesmerized as an angelic being takes form and raises both hands in a sign of benediction and blessing. Light pours forth in streams of brilliance, bringing a new wave of intensity to your being. The shimmering light coalesces and takes on the shape of a white bird. It hovers and you feel the beating of its wings in the air. You reach out to the other figure, your hands touch and meet. Now you embrace.

When your embrace has run its course, you prepare to leave. When you are ready, return the way you came to the temple. When you are ready, leave through the doorway. Finally, dissolve all images and return to ordinary consciousness.

EXERCITIA SPIRITUALIA

Take the Following as Subjects for Meditation:

- Children of the Voice, Oracle of the Mighty Gods
- Zain, meaning a sword
- Smell
- Gemini
- The Holy Spirit
- Kundalini

Make Notes on the following:

- Tarot Trump VI, The Lovers

Visualize the Following and Record your Experiences:

- The Temple of Tiphareth including the Archangel Raphael
- The Journey of the 17th Path

CHAPTER 25

Binah – Understanding

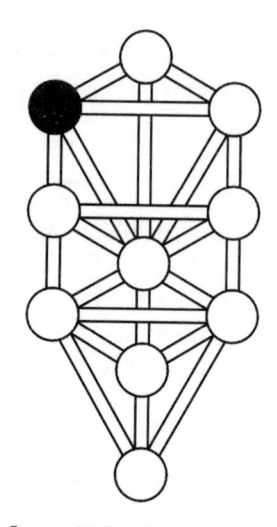

FIGURE 33 THE SEPHIRAH BINAH

TABLE OF CORRESPONDENCES

God-Name: Jehovah Elohim – God and Goddess

Archangel: Tzaphkiel.

Order of Angels: Aralim, meaning thrones

Magical Image: A mature woman

Mundane Chakra: Saturn

Virtue: Silence

Vice: Avarice

Titles: Ama, the Dark Sterile Mother; Aima, the Bright Fertile Mother; Khorsia, the Throne; Marah, the Great Sea

Spiritual Experience: The Vision of Sorrow

Personal Chakra: The Ajna Chakra.

Text: The Sanctifying Intelligence

Colour in Atziluth: Crimson

Colour in Briah: Black

Colour in Yetzirah: Dark Brown

Colour in Assiah: Grey flecked Pink

Symbols: The Yoni, The Vesica Piscis, The Cup, The Chalice, The Outer Robe of Concealment

Tarot Cards: The Four Threes

Three of Wands: Established Strength

Three of Cups: Abundance

Three of Swords: Sorrow

Three of Pentacles: Material Works

COMMENTARY

The Third Path is called the Sanctifying Intelligence, the Foundation of Primordial Wisdom, it is also called the Creator of Faith, and its roots are in Amen. It is the parent of faith, whence faith emanates.

Binah or Understanding is the third Sephirah. It emanates directly from Chockmah, Wisdom, the second Sephirah. Where Chockmah is the first Sephirah of Force, Binah is the first Sephirah of Form. Chockmah and Binah therefore set up the primal polarity of opposites which are replicated throughout the Tree on succeeding planes. Chockmah represents the powers of archetypal maleness, the force of the Great Father. Binah represents powers of archetypal femaleness, the form of the Great Mother. At these levels these attributions are not related to gender in any way but to a primal polarity. Binah is found at the head of the Pillar of Severity. Chockmah is found at the head of the Pillar of Mercy. Kether represents a state of singular unity which divides itself into a primal polarity. The dynamics of the Supernal Triangle are reflected downwards into the Tree. On the Path of Descent unity gives rise to duality, but on the Path of Ascent oppositions are resolved by the third transcendent function. In this way dynamic movement and change are continuous in both directions and on all planes simultaneously.

The Perennial Wisdom

> With Wisdom, God established the earth, and with
> Understanding, He established the heavens, and with
> His Knowledge, the depths were broken up.
>
> **Proverbs 3:19–20**

Chockmah is the Sephirah called Wisdom, but Binah consolidates this potency and is called the Foundation of Primordial Wisdom. This is not the worldly wisdom accrued through human life experience since the qualities of Binah are beyond self-realization. It is instead the constellation of primordial patterns which are involved in the organization of creation and are implicit wherever form arises. Binah is derived from the root *Beyn*, meaning 'between'. Chockmah represents a unified state, but with Binah comes a separation which permits division and differentiation. This will become nature's own pattern, the secret wisdom of myriad forms. The Primordial Wisdom provides a blueprint. It is eternal and changeless within the paradigm of creation, but also capable of infinite variety and complexity. Binah is assigned to the God-Name Jehovah Elohim. Elohim is a feminine noun with a masculine plural ending, which makes translation difficult. Dion Fortune suggests 'God and Goddess', William Gray suggests 'God the Mother', while Gareth Knight emphasizes the bipolar marriage of the divine feminine and masculine.

Nature's wisdom is multi-faceted and veiled. An ancient Egyptian inscription from the statue of Neith at Sais reads, 'I am all that has been, that is and will be. No mortal man has yet been able to lift the veil which covers me.' The Veil of Nature is the Goddess herself.

In the spiritual allegory, *The Chymical Wedding*, the character of Christian Rosencreutz steps forward to lift the coverlet of the naked Lady Venus. This act carries all the implication of naked revelation. It symbolizes the desire to uncover nature's secret. It was a bold allegory to present when the prevailing mindset was unable and unwilling to contemplate scientific enquiry. To lift the veil of nature is to seek her secrets and to know her most intimate ways. Decoding nature's blueprints brings responsibility and presents unique and difficult challenges as society is again discovering through rapid break-throughs into genetic territory. Knowledge may bring power but it does not always bring wisdom.

Binah is called the Foundation of the Primordial Wisdom. This Ageless Wisdom has many guises and forms, but its essence is unchanging because it is derived not from a single human revelation but from nature's own blueprints and patterns. To come to know these patterns is to become wise in nature's ways. To be initiated into nature's patterns is to understand the processes and relationships which govern the world around us. Such under-standing becomes the foundation of all fields of knowledge. Here is the gulf which divides revealed religion from natural religion. Natural religion grows from observation, understanding and intuitive realization. Nature is the both the teacher and the model. Change and diversity are implicit. Revealed religion claims to be once and for all time, a fixed and immutable series of laws usually encapsulated as the Word of God. The friction between these two models is ongoing, even at the dawn of a new millennium.

The newly discovered *Hermetica* assigned an authority to the realm of nature that proved instrumental in breaking the prevailing taboos which did not permit exploration of investigation into nature:

God smiled and bade Nature be; and there came forth from his voice a being in a woman's form, right lovely, at the sight of whom the Gods were smitten with amazement; and God the Forefather bestowed on her the name of Nature and he conferred on Nature the government in the world below and bade her be productive of all manner of seeds.[1]

Binah is assigned to the Sanctifying Intelligence. To sanctify is to make holy. Every society sanctifies ideas and values, which are marked out through emblems, epiphanies and events. Such cultural and spiritual values carry a special weight and gravitas. A society without a sense of the sanctified sacrifices the transcendent dimension for the preferred goal of utilitarian gains. The resulting sense of shared soul loss is always apparent, if unspoken, and such societies are most often short lived. Demarcating the sacred, naming what is sanctified, represents a clear statement of values for any cultural group. Shared values bring organization and structure, qualities attributed to Binah. Choosing where importance lies is a cultural and social process. Most often the sanctified experience accords a dignity and honour to human existence and sets the individual in both a personal and cosmological context at the turning points of life and death. The sacred enclosure, the *temenos*, is the place where sanctification is recognized and validated. Gareth Knight says that the archangel Tzaphkiel assigned to Binah is, 'the archangel of the archetypal temple'.[2]

This Path is called, 'the Creator of Faith'. It is 'the parent of faith, whence faith emanates'. Faith implies a religious belief or creed, but this Path does not call upon creed, invoke doctrine or lay down dogma. It is instead the source of faith. It is the place of a natural revelation. This lies at the heart of the Sanctifying Intelligence. When brought face to face with the magnitude, enormity and infinite variety of life, wonder and awe arise spontaneously in response to creation's own creativity. These are the sentiments and feelings revealed religion seeks to elicit through its formalized channels. When the complexity, multiplicity and interdependence of diverse creation is understood, the Sanctifying Intelligence, the desire to commemorate and celebrate, arises as a natural response. This understanding is the creator of faith, not in creed, doctrine or dogma but in creation itself. To have faith implies a deep trust or conviction in a sustaining reality. Holding faith with Binah is to place trust in nature herself. She is the parent of faith.

The Doorway of Life

There are few figures which carry so much meaning as
the simple Vesica.

Robert Lawlor, *Sacred Geometry*

The number of Binah is three. This is the realm of the Supernal Mother as
the giver of form. As a form-giving Sephirah, Binah provides a new
dimension for the impulse received from Chockmah. The wealth of female
images assigned to Binah supports the idea of this Sephirah as cosmic womb
and place of generation, where potentiality is seeded and takes secure hold.
Among its symbols is the Vesica Piscis, the archetypal womb. It is formed by
the interface where two circles overlap. It perfectly symbolizes a state of
unity in the process of becoming dual. The central overlapping area forms
a fish-shaped matrix. The geometry of the shape, which contains $\sqrt{3}$, gives
rise to the hexagon, the $\sqrt{3}$ rectangle and all regular polygons. Robert
Lawlor describes the Vesica as, 'a form generator in that all regular polygons
can be said to arise from the succession of vesica constructions'.[3] Though the
roots of 2 and 5 can also be derived from the Vesica, it mainly emphasizes
the $\sqrt{3}$ which is intimately linked to the formative process. It is the $\sqrt{3}$ which
divides the volume form of the cube. Binah is assigned to Saturn, which
represents limitation, boundary and form. This relationship is clear in
Malkuth, where Saturn brings limitation through physical form. Saturn
signifies the coalescing function of Binah, which brings boundaries to freely
flowing force. In her capacity to contain and bind the free-flowing impetus
of Chockmah, Binah is called the Dark Mother, but she is also called the
Bright Mother Aima in her capacity to bring forth created life from this
same containment. Binah brings containment and organization to the fluid
and dynamic activity of Chockmah. The Spiritual Experience assigned to
Binah is that of Sorrow. The very containment that brings organization and
structure also brings cycles of life and death. From the perspective of Binah,
all is subject to the cyclic laws of life and death. All the offspring of the
Great Mother will be subject to this without exception. The Vice assigned
to Binah is Avarice, representing an imbalance between dynamic force and
constraining form. The Elohim related to Binah represents the first
Constriction created by the Infinite Being, Ain Soph. The principle of containment is implicit to Binah. When form becomes too constraining and
binding, organization has exceeded its purpose. There is an unwillingness to

cede to forward momentum or dynamic movement. There is instead the desire to capture and hold onto structure and form. Such an avarice would be contrary to the impetus for evolution which is also implicit here.

THE DOORWAY OF LIFE

Draw a circle of any radius about any centre A. At any chosen point on the circumference of the circle, B, swing another circle of equal radius. As the initial circle, unity projects itself outwards into a perfect reflection of itself, there is an area of overlap defined by the two centre points A and B and the intersection of the two circumferences. The area and shape is known as the Vesica Piscis.

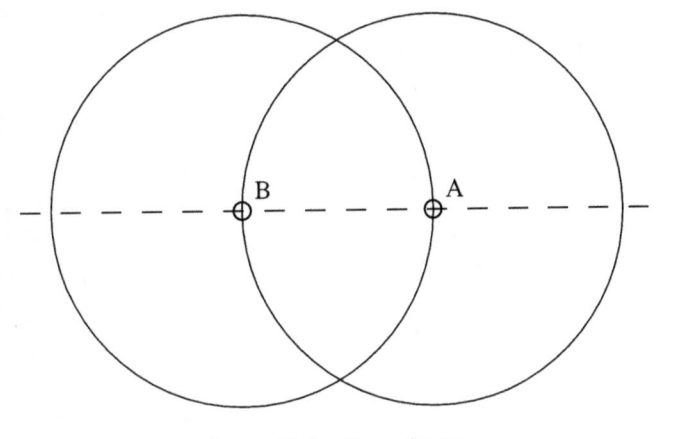

FIGURE 34 THE VESICA PISCIS

The line AB naturally unfolds into the equilateral triangle. As the equilateral triangle unfolds outwards it successively defines the sides of the square, the pentagon, the hexagon, the octagon the decagon and the dodecagon.'

Robert Lawlor, *Sacred Geometry*

The Black Goddess

The Black Virgin stands for the healing power of nature.

Ean Begg, *The Cult of the Black Virgin*

Binah's colour is black, which is also the colour assigned to Saturn. Black is also the colour attributed to the *prima materia*, the virgin substance in the language of alchemy. Binah is also called Marah, the great sea. She is the supernal mother. The image of a Black Virgin is still found and worshipped today in a completely Christian setting. Images of the Black Virgin are to be found in France, Spain, Mexico, Austria, Belgium, Brazil, the Czech Republic, England, Germany, Malta, Poland, Switzerland and Turkey. This is not just the Christian Virgin Mary but a rich amalgam of earlier exotic and mysterious elements absorbed in the progress from the formal inception of her cult in AD 431, when Mary was proclaimed Mother of God at the Council of Ephasus. The cult of the Black Madonna as the Virgin Mary links Christianity with pre-Christian worship and continues to unconsciously represent the qualities of the Sephirah Binah. The Virgin Mary is called Stellar Maris, the star of the sea. The cult of the Black Madonna is one of the forgotten and dismissed traditions of the Divine Feminine. Its longevity and cultural depth have been rediscovered by 20th-century commentators such as Ean Begg who have reinstated its true significance and established the ways in which the more ancient traditions of Goddess worship became absorbed into a Christian cult of the Divine Feminine. In yet another curious interweaving, Binah is assigned the title *Khorsia*, meaning the throne, and the order of angels assigned here is the *Aralim*, meaning thrones. This image conveys a sense of stability and order, but additionally it recalls the much earlier pre-Christian Mother of God, She of the Throne. She was Isis, mother of Horus. She is often depicted as suckling her infant son or holding him upon her lap in a familiar image. Matthew Fox takes a radical view of the meaning of the throne and sees it as the seat not of clerical power but of the divine feminine: 'The word cathedral was invented in the twelfth century. What cathedral meant in the twelfth century was the throne where the mother goddess sits ruling the universe with wisdom and compassion and justice for the poor and oppressed.'[4]

The divine feminine is still a source of inspiration and wisdom. The writer and poet Robert Graves openly describes how the White Goddess as Muse entered his life and mind as poetic inspiration; powerful coincidences followed in her wake: 'Poetry, it may be said, passes through three distinct stages: first, the poet's introduction, by Vesta, to love in old-fashioned forms of affection and companionship; next his experience of death and the recreation at the White Goddess's hand; and lastly a certitude in love, given him by the Black Goddess, his more-than-Muse.'[5] In recognizing her initiatory role at a personal level, Graves also sees a wider significance, most especially in the relationship between the sexes:

> The Black Goddess is so far hardly more than a hope whispered
> among the few who have served their apprenticeship to the White
> Goddess. She promises a new pacific bond between men and
> women, corresponding to a final reality of love, in which the
> patriarchal marriage bond will fall away. Unlike Vesta, the Black
> Goddess has experienced good and evil, love and hate, truth and
> falsehood in the person of her sisters; but chooses what is good,
> rejecting serpent-love and corpse flesh. Faithful as Vesta, gay and
> adventurous as the White Goddess, she will lead men back to that
> sure instinct of love which he long ago forfeited by intellectual
> pride.[6]

In these words, Graves restates the inherent power of the Goddess as the
healing agent of nature recognized by Ean Begg too. This is a power which
can heal men and women by stripping away the false values of stereotype and
social imprint accrued through the centuries. This is a power which can
undo the patriarchal marriage bond by simply revealing the outworn nature
of manipulation and ownership. This is a power which always brings
wisdom. It is not for the faint-hearted. Graves writes as a poet, in praise of
the Goddess. Poetry in the hands of the Muse-Poet is close to the Sanctifying
Intelligence of Binah. Such words bring utterly truthful revelation. The
Goddess speaks not just to poets and women in need of comfort but to all
those in search of truth. Her salvation is deep and nourishing. Lifting the veil
of the Goddess, seeing into nature, brings its own rewards as well as risks.
Knowledge, the precursor of Wisdom, comes from the curious drive of the
awakened mind. Though it may seem hardly credible, its opposing force,
the ignorance and fear of nature, has enjoyed considerable power and prestige
in the long history of humanity. The unwillingness to observe and understand nature has been a powerful force for preserving prejudice. These two
forces may seen warring in the long struggle between the orthodox Church
and the unorthodox Perennial Wisdom, between natural religion and
revealed religion. Much territory once claimed by the Hermetic Wisdom
as a secret philosophy has now passed easily into various branches of
knowledge. Engagement with nature brings knowledge derived from inves-
tigating, observing and interacting with nature as a whole system. Ean Begg
rightly considers that 'The Black Virgins are often associated with esoteric
teaching and school of initiation.'[7] This is certainly true of perhaps the most
famous of all the Black Madonnas, at Chartres. Contemporary visitors may

enjoy the spectacular stained-glass windows and architectural splendour but probably fail to understand the unorthodox and radical stream of Christianity which inspired them. Chartres Cathedral stands as a testament to the practical significance conveyed by the cult of the Black Virgin as initiator into a holistic and universal philosophy. Chartres represents an almost forgotten 12th-century spiritual renaissance which arose from the powerful mingling of Christian Scholasticism and Neo-Platonism. This same initiating presence is much needed today. This is the power which reinstates real love by dissolving the projections of the intellect which masquerade as love. This is the power which awakens the soul at the centre of human life. This is the divine feminine. 'The feminine principle is not a theory but real and has a will of its own which we ignore at our peril.'[8] Difference is the motive force of creation; its mainspring depends upon the tension between the opposites. As a blueprint, Kabbalah offers a system of polarized tensions which spring from a unified state. Once separated these polarities generate constellations which have an independence from the original source. As independent powers, the dual forces have a unique identity but still retain a relationship to each other and the wider whole. This is the classical yin-yang polarity. The two forces with separated qualities have the potential to generate an entirely new quality from their interaction. As oriental philosophy speaks of yin and yang, so the Perennial Wisdom personifies these forces as also being male and female. These powers are clearly not personal but impersonal, transpersonal and supra-personal. Belonging to the realm of nature, these powers must assume larger than life proportions and easily take on the role of gods. The divide between monotheistic and pantheistic religions is wide and seemingly unbreachable. Pantheism carries a taint of idolatry and even theological confusion as deities proliferate with time and circumstance. But pantheism most often recognizes both the one and the many, while monotheism recognizes the one but denies the many. It is most noticeable that monotheistic religions find no place for the divine feminine while pan-theistic religions include the feminine dimensions. For Kabbalah, the feminine dimension begins with Binah and is reflected downwards through the Tree into Netzach, and is eventually actualized as the Virgin, the Queen and the Bride at Malkuth. The repression or distortion of the feminine principle has brought implications not just for women but for all. Kabbalah offers a remedy of balance. Binah, the Supernal Mother, is both equal and opposite to Chockmah, the Supernal Father. Here is the opportunity to begin to heal a schism which has plagued Western culture for too long. 'Recognition of a female god image should expand our awareness of the majesty and mystery of god. Our prior dependence on a relatively narrow image of the divine as male, particularly as male parent, may have stifled our faith and limited our experience of god.'[9]

EVOCATION

Welcome to my kingdom. I am the Supernal Mother. I am mother to all the Great Mothers and their many daughters. I am reflected in the goddess whose names and faces are many. I am seen in the nature of the divine feminine where paradox and cycle, ambiguity and change are honoured, not despised. From unity comes duality, from duality comes plurality, from plurality comes multiplicity. I can be seen in nature for I am the Foundation of the Primordial Wisdom. I am nature's own truth. I am the goddess matrix. I am mother to Wisdom even though my name is Understanding. I am the understanding of the laws hidden deep in creation. I know them all and make them holy so that you shall not pass them by without recognition. I bring the Sanctifying Intelligence to preserve the Primordial Wisdom in perpetuity. I am the feminine face of the creative power. I am the builder of form and the organizing principle which contains the life force. But I am also the sorrowful mother, for all that is born through me will also die. I am the divine feminine. In my most exalted and sublime state, I am beyond the reach of human consciousness. I am the builder of worlds and the giver of form. I am the generator of a million forms, of endless variation and infinite possibilities. But do not be confused by appearance. My laws are few but my manifestations are without number. Take delight in variety, rejoice in multiplicity. Pay homage to what you see. When you forget my nature you lose yourselves in deceits and phantasms of the mind.

INTERNALIZATION – THE TEMPLE
OF BINAH

Construct the Temple of Binah in the creative imagination. You approach the doorway and stoop slightly to enter. You cross the threshold and find yourself in a dark interior, which now appears to be much larger than you had expected. Slits high up in the walls admit fingers of light which fall onto the ground. You hear women's voices in the background, chuckling and laughing. The sound is reassuring and lively. Your eyes begin now to adjust to the levels of light.

You had in some way expected to find an altar set up in a visible place, but looking around you see no statuary of any kind. The floor beneath your feet is made of stone. A shaft of brilliant sunlight breaks through and hovers like a finger over a single stone. Its illumination reveals that a different stone has been inset into the expanse of the floor. You walk over to where the light shines. Standing on the stone, you realize that a pathway has been laid out. You step forwards and begin to pick out the pathway against the broad expanse of the dark floor. You need to pay attention. Each step becomes a moving meditation in awareness as your foot is slowly and carefully placed. The path curves gently outwards, taking you on a journey which fills the four corners of the space. Then it curves inwards and you soon realize you are walking in a spiral towards the centre. Your mind and body become totally absorbed in the journey. Time has no relevance. Drawing nearer to the centre at last, you see that it is marked by a dark circle. Soon you will stand at the centre of the spiral. As you finally draw close, you realize that the dark circle is in fact an opening. Standing directly at the open mouth you look down. Now you have a choice – to return the way you came or continue.

As you reflect on your decision, a candle flickers in a far corner. As you watch, a chain of light begins to form around the square. As you have walked, unknown women have silently taken up positions along each side of the square and watched you. Now that you have reached the centre, candles are lit to sanctify your journey.

Looking down you see a spiral staircase. You make a decision and step forwards into the opening and the darkness below. Momentarily you find your way down by touch alone, but as the staircase turns you have a sense of increasing light. There is soft light somewhere below and you continue with confidence. The staircase opens onto a chamber lit by a flickering candle. You stand in an underground natural cave. The air is cool. You hear the sound of water close by. You can just make out a natural pool formed from the rock. It is decked with tiny candles set in niches and perched on stones. You move closer and kneel beside the cupped pool. Its far side is set into the rock wall. Now that your eyes have become used to the light you suddenly see shapes emerging from the cave wall. Is it a natural feature or has something been created here? Surely, emerging from the back wall, lapped by the waters of the pool, is the form of a great throne. And on the throne the figure of a woman emerges in rough stone; she bears the shape of a child who sits directly on her lap facing forwards, looking at you. This is not a statue carved with precision but more a trick of nature and light in unique combination. You sit back in wonder and take time to reflect. Finding an unlit candle, you light it and give thanks to whatever unknown circumstances or peoples have created this shrine of natural rock and water. You reach out and dip your fingers in the pool. Tasting the water you find it to be bitter with the minerals and salts of the earth. When you are ready, leave and return to the upper hall, which will be empty except for the square of candles laid out in recognition of your journey.

When you are ready, leave through the doorway. Finally, dissolve all images and return to ordinary consciousness.

EXERCITIA SPIRITUALIA

Take the Following as Subjects for Meditation:

- Jehovah Elohim
- Tzaphkiel
- Aralim
- A mature woman
- Saturn
- Ama, the Dark Sterile Mother; Aima the Bright Fertile Mother
- The Primordial Wisdom

Contemplate the Following Questions and Record your Responses:

- How does Silence operate in your life?
- How does Avarice operate in your life?
- How does the nature of Binah relate to the Brow Chakra?
- What other correspondences can you relate to Binah?
- How do the four Tarot cards relate to Binah?

Visualize the Following and Record your Experiences:

- The Temple of Binah including the Archangel Tzaphkiel
- The Journey to the Temple of Binah

CHAPTER 26

The Sixteenth Path: Chesed–Chockmah

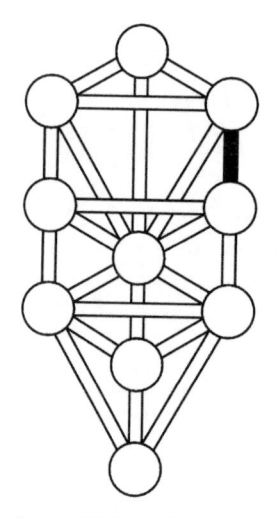

FIGURE 35 THE 16TH PATH:

CHESED–CHOCKMAH

TAROT TRUMP V,

THE HIEROPHANT

TABLE OF CORRESPONDENCES

The Journey: Tarot Trump V, the Hierophant,
the Magus of the Eternal
Key: Vau, meaning a nail
Simple Letter: Hearing
Spiritual Significance: Taurus
Text: The Triumphal or Eternal Intelligence
Colour in Atziluth: Red Orange.
Colour in Briah: Deep Indigo
Colour in Yetzirah: Deep warm Olive
Colour in Assiah: Rich Brown

COMMENTARY

The Sixteenth Path is the Triumphal or Eternal Intelligence, so called because it is the pleasure of the glory, beyond which is no other glory like it, and it is so called also the paradise prepared for the righteous.

The 16th Path is to be found on the Pillar of Mercy between Chesed and Chockmah. It forms the polar opposite to the 18th Path which is to be found on the Pillar of Severity between Geburah and Binah. Both these Paths connect the Sephiroth of the Ethical Triangle with the Sephiroth of the Supernal Triangle and thereby connect the Greater Mysteries of Becoming to the Supreme Mysteries of Eternal Being.

Eternal Life

> Lift your heads, throw down your hands and weep no
> more. The eye of creation looks upon you. Look back
> you are crystal reflecting fire. In your own becoming
> there is light – enough to lead you home.

> **Normandi Ellis, *Awakening Osiris***

The 16th Path is described as the Triumphal or Eternal Intelligence. Currently the term 'eternal' has become glibly attached to the concept of love expressed by two people. The phrase 'eternal love' is used to encapsulate the highest ideal and to express the idea of undying and unconditional love. Outside this usage the term is little applied since concepts of infinity belong more to the realm of contemporary physics, while concepts of eternal being come from the mouths of mystics, poets and visionaries. The realm of the eternal is not the most commonplace. Yet this is the Path of the Eternal Intelligence which is at the same time Triumphal. Eternal life is the salve offered to the community of believers by particular religious traditions. But what does this mean? Most often it is used to describe entry into a permanent, unchanging, heavenly, post-death state which is 'with God' in some way. The idea of this idyll is indeed comforting. Physical life is often nasty, brutish and short. Entry to eternal life is ensured by admittance into the body of the faithful through acceptance of its doctrines and sacraments. Here is the perfect covenant. Traditional religions have most often interpreted the doctrine of salvation which is the promise of eternal life in this way. But what of those never admitted into the body of the faithful? What eternal place awaits them? In a linear mindset which characterizes the schismatic thinking of the past, solutions are always framed in an either/or context. Either a physical life merits eternal life or it does not. Either the individual has joined the body of the faithful or has not. Either an eternal life 'with God' or an eternity without God! These stark and uncompromising choices are produced by the same mindset that divides body from spirit, humanity from nature. The polarized mind always divides, separates and categorizes, offering only an either/or solution. Mental projections make fearful demons. Buddhism speaks often of transforming the mind as the path to liberation.

The distinctions which appear so solid and immovable to the dualized mind simply dissolve in the light of a unified consciousness. When the either/or dichotomy has been transcended a new paradigm arises which is not divisive but inclusive, not fragmentary but unifying. The journey of self-realization through the Tree of Life is a journey of transformation. The progress from the Lesser Mysteries of the Astral or Psychological Triangle to the work of the Greater Mysteries represented by the Moral or Ethical Triangle precipitates a new way of thinking, not metaphorically but literally. This Path, in common with other Paths in the higher reaches of the Tree, takes that new level of mind for granted. The substance of the Ethical Triangle and the nature of the Supernal Triangle may only become connected in consciousness through the transformed mind. Jean Houston describes this new type of mentation as 'hieroglyphic' in recognition of the holistic mindset evidenced in Egyptian thought. 'In hieroglyphic thought many disciplines and knowings converge in a synergistic way.'[1] As a stone dropped into a pond creates a series of concentric ripples which emanate from the centre, so a single seed thought dropped into the seed bed of the transformed hieroglyphic mind will set off a series of interconnected associations and resonances. This is quite different to the linear mind in which only a limited one-dimensional response may arise. The hieroglyphic mind is the holistic mind, which is also the holographic mind. This is the transformed mind and the quantum mind in which there are no boundaries. Jean Houston places much value on the emergence of this form of consciousness, not just personally and individually but collectively and culturally as an agent for change in the world. This mode of consciousness carries the seeds of change and dynamic movement because of its holistic, unifying, healing and connective nature. 'By thinking hieroglyphically, analogically and symbolically in charged multi-patterns with webs of meaning, we can begin to create changes in our forms – in our bodies and our minds.'[2] Jean Houston states with some optimism, 'I suspect that we are again on the verge of hieroglyphic thinking.' This massed breakthrough constitutes the Aquarian Initiation. It might prove to be the seed of the next evolutionary step for humanity. The holographic mind, in direct contrast to the linear mind, sees not limited options but endless possibilities, not a single chance at conforming to a pre-packaged model being but an infinite variety of means on the path of becoming. Where some religions balance the context of a single life against an eternity of being, others embrace the cyclic nature of life and death as the means of eternal becoming. This Path is assigned to the Triumphal or Eternal Intelligence. In other words, the intelligence which is able to place life within the context of eternity is itself triumphal. This gnosis is the central revelation of all Mystery teachings. The Hierophant is the Revealer of Secret Things.

The Hierophant is an archaic and unfamiliar term. It is taken from the office of the key celebrant to the ancient Mysteries of Eleusis, which provided the major initiatory process of the pagan classical world. Though precise details have never been revealed, the nature of the Mysteries is well understood. 'In the mysteries the individual undergoes an indirect transformation through his participation in the fate of the god.'[3] As the Eleusinian Mysteries centred on the mythology of Demeter, the fate of the participant was bound with hers as she set out in search of her abducted daughter Persephone, who had has been snatched away to the underworld by Pluto. The Eleusinian Mysteries, much like the earlier Mysteries of Isis and Osiris, focused on the loss and subsequent reunion with the beloved. These mythic elements provided the vehicle for deep contemplation. The participants share in the grief and loss of Demeter. When Demeter, and Isis too, triumph at the moment of reunion, so the participants share in the triumphal moment. This is the Triumphal Intelligence which is simultaneously the Eternal Intelligence. It is the Eternal and Triumphal Intelligence which comes to understand both the portals of life and death.

The nearest contemporary equivalent to these ancient Mysteries might be the Christian passion play of Oberammergau, which uses drama as a sacred vehicle. However, this event does not match the degree of involvement and engagement of the ancient mystery dramas in which all were participants, not observers. There was no audience at Eleusis, all were *mystai*.

The process of re-identification had two stages, beginning in the month of February when the Lesser Mysteries were celebrated at Agrai. These ceremonies were presided over by key personnel from Eleusis and provided a stage of preparation for the later turning point of self-realization. Like the Lesser Mysteries assigned to the Tree of Life, these Lesser Mysteries served as the foundation which begins the work of redirecting attention from outer daily life to matters of eternity and the soul. The Greater Mysteries followed in the month of September and lasted for ten days. This phase included an opening procession, a purifying plunge into the sea, new clothing and sacrifice. The huge procession created a new sense of shared identity and a common human goal; the plunge in the sea provided the opportunity for personal purification; and the new clothing represented both the new identity and the possibility of a new beginning. It served to divest partici- pants of a mundane identity and prepare them to face the contemplation of eternity. In this way the identity was refocused, re-orientated and redirected. Finally, on the 19th of the month the assembly, possibly numbering up to 3,000 people, moved in solemn procession to the *telesterion*, the Hall of Initiation. It was here that the Mysteries proper took place. The preparations had made the participants receptive to the numinous power of Demeter, mother of the corn, and her daughter. All was primed to release the moment of revelation when the central epiphany was displayed. By a process of re- orientation, begun gradually but finally locked tight in a climactic experience, the participant reached a moment of utter transcendence and personal gnosis. Historians may like to quibble over the exact nature of the epiphany at Eleusis. The specialization of history teaches nothing about the means of sacred psychology and its methods. It is no surprise that historians remain confused about the modus operandi of these events. Whether ear of corn or daughter of the corn, the symbolic message is the same. The ear of grain reveals the wholeness of the human cycle, the community of souls, the life of the individual, the rendering of body from essence and the infinite cycle of seed and harvest which is eternal life. The returning Persephone reveals the balance of death-in-life and life-in-death, the cycle of mother and daughter which is the path of becoming, the renewing cycle of the year, and the re-emergence of new life from death. This immersion in the mythos through dramatic engagement provides a holistic, hieroglyphic, holographic framework which permits multi-dimensional realizations to arise. Drama is a holistic medium. Sacred drama channels this holistic medium for a specific purpose.

The drama of Eleusis initiated its participants into a triumphal secret, the

Triumphal or Eternal Intelligence of the 16th Path, 'so called because it is the pleasure of the glory, beyond which is no other glory like it, and it is so called also the paradise prepared for the righteous'. This was a mass initiation into the cycle of life and death. The Homeric Hymn says, 'Blessed is he who among the earthbound men has been privileged to see these mysteries. But he who has not been initiated into the sacred rituals and does not participate in them has no like destiny, once he is dead, among the watery darkness.' Understanding the meaning of death liberates life. This Path connects the transient and phenomenal realm of human life to the greater eternal realm of the Supernal Triangle. This Path is one of gnosis where things were enacted (*dromena*), things were shown (*deiknymena*) and things were spoken (*legomena*). This is not the place for doctrine or dogma, teaching or texts; it is the place of personal experience, involvement and participation. It is the place of revelation, the way of precipitated insight. The Hierophant is the eternal initiator into the mysteries of being and becoming. He is rightly called the Magus of the Eternal.

The Way of the Mysteries

> Come let the whole people build me a great temple and
> an altar beneath it, at the foot of the Akropolis and its
> high walls. I myself will found my mysteries, that you
> may piously perform them and render my heart
> propitious.

The words of Demeter, *The Homeric Hymn*

The historical record shows the significance of the Mysteries in both Egypt and Greece and later of the smaller mystery cults which also belonged to the ancient world. All of this has ostensibly vanished. The Mysteries of Eleusis were finally destroyed. The historian Eunapios, himself initiated at Eleusis, recorded the prophecy given by the last Hierophant who foretold of its imminent destruction. He prophesied that his own role would be usurped by a foreigner, the sanctuary would be destroyed, the worship of the two goddesses would come to an end, and the site would be overrun by barbarians and men in dark garments. All this came to pass when Alaric, King of the Goths, invaded Greece in AD 396, followed by monks.

Are the Mysteries and their initiatory functions to be consigned to the pages of history? Was the value of the Mysteries only possible within a mindset that has long vanished in the ancient world or did the Mysteries enshrine a universal and eternal truth which is always available to anyone at any time? Arthur Versluis asks, 'How does initiation, how do the Mysteries relate to modern life, to the present?'[4] Having posed the question, he attributes enormous value in the message of the Mysteries. 'Although modernity consists in the forgetting of the nature of the Mysteries, none the less it is in them that the *centrum* of life is ever to be found, in them that our meaning consists; initiation is a universal, ever the path to true knowledge.'[5] Its message is timeless, triumphant and eternal. It is a message that the modern world may have forgotten in the distracting light of technological wizardry. Nevertheless, it is still a message that people need to hear if the values of the heart are to be sustained. 'If the modern world is to recover from the delerium of scientism and technologism, from the accelerating confusion of her own inventions, it is necessary first of all that one returns to the universal wisdom which lies at the heart of all traditions.'[6] The outer form of the Mysteries may have perished but the symbols remain as alive and potent as ever. It is therefore through symbolism, eternal and triumphal, that we may, even in the present time, re-connect with and draw upon the deep waters of the eternal wisdom, the *Sophia Perennis*.

Though the outer form of the Mysteries has clearly vanished, a lasting imprint remains as an indelible thread in the Western philosophical tradition. 'The Egyptian Mystery tradition has continued to influence Western culture profoundly, albeit in an underground manner, not least through the Qabalah and the Hermetic teachings, both of which directly reflect Egyptian cosmology.'[7] The Egyptian culture may be distanced in time but its holistic spiritual tradition was in some small way inherited by the Greeks, who in turn contributed to a particular philosophical development. Platonism is evident in medieval Christendom, and the Mystery tradition persisted through the works of Dionysius the Areopagite and others. The Primordial Wisdom has always been present throughout the growth of western civilization. The way of the Mysteries is the Path towards Wisdom.

The 16th Path is attributed to the Simple Letter *Vau*, which signifies a nail. A nail joins or holds two surfaces together, interpenetrating both of them. The 16th Path joins the Greater Mysteries with the Supreme Mysteries, the Ethical Triangle with the Supernal Triangle. As the third component of the Tetragrammaton, the letter Vau signifies elemental Air and the quality of mind which is like wisdom, invisible but vital to life.

The 16th Path joins the Illuminating Intelligence of Chockmah with the Cohesive or Receptive Intelligence of Chesed. Chockmah is the

Sephirah which holds nature's most basic and primal laws. Chesed contains
'all the holy powers from which emanate all the spiritual virtues'. Receptivity
to the holy powers of Chesed initiates into its spiritual virtues. Chockmah
is the Sephirah wisdom; Chesed is the Sephirah mercy. The possibility of
admission into the Primordial Wisdom is a merciful blessing which places
the keys to life and death with the individual. The 16th Path connects
Chesed and Chockmah. It is the Path of a secret revelation made known
through the office of the Hierophant.

The Hierophant sits between two columns, much like the twin pillars
of manifestation. The decorative motifs on the capitals are designed to be
reminiscent of the reproductive system and symbolize both emergence from
and return to the womb as the source of life. Life descends down through
one pillar, taking on incarnation; life ascends through the other pillar, leaving
incarnation. Together the two pillars represent the cycle of life so central to
the Triumphal or Eternal Intelligence.

The Hierophant, the Revealer of Secret Things, wears the two colours
of body and spirit, much like the figure of the Magician. The two tonsured
acolytes wear robes of roses and lilies reminiscent of the two flowers also
seen on the Trump of the Magus of Power. Together the red rose and the
white lily represent the powers of the red and the white, the Macroscosm
and the Microcosm. The Hierophant wears a lamen marked by three crosses
representing the three states assigned to the Lesser, Greater and Supreme
Mysteries. Likewise, the Hierophant holds a triple-barred sceptre and wears
a triple-layered crown. The crossed keys on the dais are the keys which the
blessing of the Hierophant gives as the Revealer of Secret Things. These are
the key to the Eternal Intelligence and the key to the Triumphal Intelligence.

The Eternal Wisdom

> Entry into the primordial wisdom cannot be
> accomplished through mere visualisation, mere fantasy,
> for it is not psychological.

Arthur Versluis, *The Egyptian Mysteries*

The ageless or eternal wisdom is not defined by dogma or doctrine. If the
Primordial Wisdom is in the Egyptian Mysteries of the distant past, in the
philosophy of Greece as well as in the Eastern religions and the architecture of medieval Christendom, then it is clear that it not housed in or

confined to one place. Its message is eternal and it is held waiting in countless symbols and manifold metaphors. It will find expression in every age and time. When repressed and threatened by an opposing and powerful doctrine, the Ageless Wisdom will become the province of the few who will enshrine the same truths in new guise. The eternal wisdom can never be confined to a doctrine or dogma or be enclosed between the covers of a single book. This is the journey of the initiate, not the intellect. This is a truth which, like water, can fill many containers and take many shapes, yet its essence does not alter. It is the eternal wisdom. Different names and new symbols change nothing for those taught how to apply the key which unlocks the buried code. In the far future the eternal wisdom may become enshrined in the vocabulary of cyberspace and the symbolism of the space age. In the past the eternal wisdom has been expressed through the language of alchemy, the cycle of nature, the vocabulary of architecture and countless other mythological and symbolic containers which each have the power to render archetypal forms into expressible ideas. The Ageless Wisdom is not an intellectual understanding but a gnosis of the heart which encompasses the mysteries of being and becoming.

EVOCATION

Welcome to my kingdom which is that of the triumphal and eternal. I am always present, for the abiding questions of human life remain the same. How is it possible to reconcile the momentary passing of a human life, sometimes no more than the duration of a breath, with the face of eternity? What is the meaning in this paradox, that of the temporal and eternal set side by side sharing the same moment? And what of death, the implacable enemy of joy and delight? What role is assigned to this player on life's stage? Recall that in your life you have posed this same question many times to good people of different faiths. Each time you have received a different answer. Each time you have left empty-handed. But you do not seek second-hand answers or opinions, only where truth can be found.

And so you have submitted yourself to this new quest, half in hope, half out of curiosity, but you are not alone for many pilgrims walk this way with the same thought. Though you come with expectation of an answer, I can tell you nothing. All is to be experienced. Words belong to the realm of illusion, separation and projection. Mine is the realm of wisdom, not of empty words. I can tell you nothing. But I have the power to reveal what you seek. For I am the Hierophant, the Revealer of Secret Things.

INTERNALIZATION – THE 16TH
PATH: CHESED–CHOCKMAH

Construct the Temple of Chesed in the creative imagination. Find yourself standing beside the doorway of the Hierophant. The Archangel Tzaphkiel lifts the tapestry curtain so that you may pass.

Find yourself at once in the company of pilgrims, upon a broad and dusty road lined with green trees giving some shade. You wear the new white linen of one seeking initiation. You have already undergone rites of purification and preparation. You have dipped yourself in the sea seven times, each one accompanied by words of private confession. You have divested yourself of worldly concerns and worries. Now your thoughts rest elsewhere. You have come to contemplate the meaning of human life in the face of eternity. Like an empty container, you have come to be filled.

Now the swell of pilgrims draws near to the sacred precinct and the Hall of Initiation. The crowd waits patiently in the early morning sun to be admitted. In response to a signal, you all begin to move towards the entrance. Now you reach the large open door and enter into the coolness of the stone building. The dark hall is lit by many candles set in niches cut into the walls. In the centre at the far end of the hall an empty throne flanked by two columns stands on a raised dais, decorated with the insignia of two keys. Though the crowds are many, fate blesses you with the opportunity to gain a place just in front of the throne, behind two shaven-headed figures in robes decorated with roses and lilies. The crowd fills the hall and everyone sits on the stone floor in an orderly manner. There is an air of optimistic expectancy but also the spirit of naked openness as you all wait together.

A hushed and expectant stillness fills the air at the stately entrance of the Hierophant. He wears three robes: an outer robe of red, an inner garment of white, and an undergarment of blue. The lamen set about his shoulders is decorated with three crosses, his crown is set with three tiers. He holds a sceptre topped by a triple cross. You reflect that his title means the Revealer of Secret Things, and you wonder what he might reveal to you. The hall begins to darken as attendants move silently, extinguishing the candle flames. Now lights are lit upon the dais, gradually highlighting the figure of the Hierophant. Light is thrown upwards too, picking out the carvings on each of the pillars. You see these shapes very clearly and they too seem to have a message for you.

Now a sound enters the great hall. It has the devastating familiarity of mourners grieving at the loss of a loved one. From unseen doors beyond the enthroned Hierophant, two lines of women enter into the hall, one from either side. The sound of their weeping and lament is unmistakable. They sweep the entire length of the hall carrying the funeral lament on high. Hearing the dirge of loss awakens the feeling of mourning in the crowd and an atmosphere of palpable sorrow descends on the hall. You remember those who have passed and in the privacy of your own mind contemplate your own passing. Will you too be mourned?

Now the hall is totally silent. The Hierophant stands and slowly turns to face the pillars. He raises the triple cross in a gesture of authority and in a deep and resonant voice sounds a phrase quite unknown to you. He calls out with the same imperative three times. Now he turns back to face the hall. A young girl, neither child nor maiden, turns with him, called from the far reaches of the darkness. She wears a circlet of spring flowers on her head and is dressed in a loose and flowing robe of white. In her hands she holds a woven casket which she offers to the assembly. At the sight of her, the mourning women give out a new cry, which is of life itself. The ululation of women fills the air and the sound is taken up by the women in the assembly. Now the cry of life fills the great hall. The atmosphere changes from mourning to rejoicing. Now the young girl begins a solitary procession around the hall. She bears the casket, carrying it gently and with great reverence, as if it were a newborn child to be shown to its loving family. All eyes are upon her as she walks. At last her circuit is complete. She returns and stands once more in front of the dais between the two priestly figures. The Hierophant is gone, his throne is empty. The young girl mounts the dais, followed by the two acolytes. She passes instantly from view, moving behind the throne set between the pillars. The two attendants turn and stand one on either side of the throne. Each figure bangs three times upon the floor in unison with a heavy wooden staff. The proceedings in the hall are closed.

You sit quietly as the assembly disperses in solemn silence. Leave the Hall of Initiation and return to the temple. When you are ready, leave through the doorway. Finally, dissolve all images and return to ordinary consciousness.

EXERCITIA SPIRITUALIA

Take the Following as Subjects for Meditation:
- The Magus of the Eternal
- The letter Vau
- Hearing
- Taurus
- The Eternal or Triumphal Intelligence

Make Notes on:
- Tarot Trump V, the Hierophant

Undertake the Following and Record your Experiences:
- The Temple of Chesed including the Archangel Tzaphkiel
- The Journey of the 16th Path

CHAPTER 27

The Fifteenth Path:
Tiphareth–Chockmah

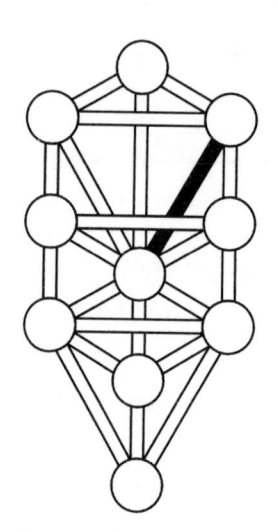

FIGURE 36 THE 15TH PATH:

TIPHARETH–CHOCKMAH

TAROT TRUMP IV,

THE EMPEROR

TABLE OF CORRESPONDENCES

The Journey: Tarot Trump IV, The Emperor,
Son of the Morning, Chief among the
Mighty
Key: The letter Heh, meaning a window
Simple Letter: Sight
Spiritual Significance: Aries
Text: The Constituting Intelligence
Colour in Atziluth: Scarlet Red
Colour in Briah: Red
Colour in Yetzirah: Brilliant Flame
Colour in Assia : Glowing Red

COMMENTARY

*The Fifteenth Path is the Constituting Intelligence and it
is so called because it constitutes the substance of creation in
pure darkness, and men have spoken of the contemplation;
it is that darkness spoken of in scripture,
'and thick darkness a swaddling band for it.'*

The 15th Path connects the sixth Sephirah, Tiphareth, which lies at the
heart of the Tree, with the second Sephirah, Chockmah. Tiphareth is part
of the Ethical Triangle but Chockmah is part of the Supernal Triangle. This
Path therefore bridges two levels, that between the Supreme and the Greater
Mysteries. It connects the Sephirah which is Beauty with the Sephirah
which is Wisdom.

The Lawgiver

> The main challenge of our times is to link the inner
> world of the self with the outer world of society, and to
> see both within the larger context of the natural world.
> To do this effectively, I believe, we must come to
> appreciate that self, society and nature all derive from a
> common source, that each is a necessary partner in some
> larger creative dialogue.

Danah Zohar and Ian Marshall, *The Quantum Society*

The 15th Path connects Tiphareth with Chockmah. The 15th Path shows
a king seated on a throne. This is an image that for many has the unwelcome
overtones of patriarchal lawgiver and ruler. The effects of the masculine
rulership are self-evident. History tells its own story, but the Son of the
Morning is not the enforcer of a social law but the steward of a deeper law
which belongs to nature, not to men. As the Son of the Morning, the
Emperor expresses his secret allegiance to Venus, the morning star, the
Empress and the kingdom of Natura.

Chock means 'rule' or 'decree'. This is the Path of the lawgiver. Rooted within the Supernal Triangle, however, this is not the law of *jurisprudence*, which is culturally determined and always relative, but a deeper and universal commonality. This Path represents not the land but creation itself. This is a representation not of a patriarchal ruler but of natural rule. This is not a gender-based issue but an issue of natural law. This king rules not over society but within nature. Here is a crowned and bearded king. The image is reminiscent of that assigned to Kether. Kether's Magical Image is of a bearded king seen in profile. Where Kether's image is designed to elude, here the king is seen full face. This image is not hidden but revealed. In other words, what is hidden and immanent within Kether has here been made manifest. The laws within Kether, imprinted indelibly on the fabric of creation at the moment of the Big Bang and unfolded through Chockmah, are now made accessible and visible via the 15th Path which connects Chockmah to Tiphareth. Tiphareth represents a personal revelation of the wholeness and unity of the implicate order. This is the realization of Beauty. The realization of the mystic is essentially no different to that of the contemporary physicist. The one grasps the wholeness of creation emotionally and from within the heart as a personal and private realization; the other grasps the wholeness of creation intellectually and as part of a shared field of knowledge which thereby preserves an emotional distance. Sometimes the two worlds may overlap:

> I was sitting by the ocean one late summer afternoon watching the waves roll in and feeling the rhythm of my breathing, when I suddenly became aware of my whole environment as being engaged in a gigantic cosmic dance. Being a physicist, I knew that the sand, rocks, water and air around me were made of vibrating molecules and atoms and that these consisted of particles which interacted with one another by creating and destroying other particles. All this was familiar to me from my research in high-energy physics, but until that moment I had only experienced it through graphs, diagrams and mathematical theories. As I sat on the beach my former experiences came to life; I 'saw' cascades of energy coming down from outer space, in which particles were created and destroyed in rhythmic pulse; I 'saw' the atoms of the elements and those of my body participating in this cosmic dance of energy; I felt its rhythm and I 'heard' its sound, and at that moment I *knew* this was the Dance of Shiva, the Lord of Dancers.[1]

In that brief moment the physicist Fritjof Capra crossed over into the territory of the mystic. It was such a powerful turning point that the now famous book *The Tao of Physics* was seeded in that vision. For Capra it was another moment on a new trail. For so long the science of the West and the mysticism of the East had seemed to be implacably opposed world views, but Capra suddenly glimpsed the common ground, the nature of reality itself. He gradually came to realize that, 'a consistent view of the world is beginning to emerge from modern physics which is harmonious with the ancient Eastern wisdom'.[2] This is the realm of both the Emperor and the Empress.

This is the Path of the Constituting Intelligence; it is 'the substance of creation'. In connecting Chockmah with Tiphareth, the 15th Path connects the Mediating Intelligence of Tiphareth with the Illuminating Intelligence of Chockmah and joins the Vision of God face to face with the Vision of the Harmony of Things. This Path brings a personal experience of the ultimate nature of being. For a theistic mindset this is the Vision of God Face to Face, for a non-theistic mindset this is the personal experience of Emptiness. For the physicist this is a glimpse into the ground of being. This experience can be deeply moving, intensely emotional and totally transforming. The highly trained Fritjof Capra freely admits bursting into tears as his understanding was instantly turned from an intellectual appreciation to a personal knowing. He moved from analysis into gnosis in that brief and unique glimpse as the window onto creation was suddenly opened to him.

The 15th Path is assigned to the letter *Heh*, which is symbolized by a window. As a Simple Letter it is attributed to the quality of Sight. As the second letter of the Tetragrammaton, the letter represents a fundamental aspect of creation itself. This Path brings a direct viewing, a personal seeing into the ground of being. It is the experience of Beauty at the sight of Wisdom. On the Path of Ascent from Tiphareth, forces within creation become apparent to the mind ascending from Tiphareth. On the Path of Descent the forces of creation become increasingly discernible to those seeking the ultimate nature of being.

As the representative of the implicit order, the Emperor holds a sceptre and a globe. The sceptre, constructed by a circle above the two arms of a cross, resembles both the Egyptian ankh, the key of life, and the symbol for Venus. Both symbols blend non-linear with linear elements. Venus is assigned to the Trump of the Empress who partners the Emperor as twin representatives of the forces immanent within creation. Although this Trump appears to express solely the male current, it simultaneously encompasses the feminine creative force through the Simple Letter Heh, which also stands for the feminine creative power. In the same way, although the Trump of the

Empress appears to express solely the female current, her pregnancy encompasses the masculine creative forces.

The globe is an image of totality. These images of rulership are closely related to the images of Chesed which also share the insignia of kingship. At Chesed, the sceptre and orb express dominion over the inner realm and the magical image of king throned and crowned is the self fully realized. These images of kingship should not be mistaken for signs of worldly authority and power, nor for a masculine interpretation of leadership. The king is but another symbol. Jung elaborated on the importance of king as a symbol in alchemy: 'The king represents a superior personality exalted above the ordinary. The outward paraphernalia of kingdom show this very clearly. The crown symbolized his relation to the sun, his bejewelled mantle is the starry firmament, the orb is the replica of the world.'[3] Despite these worldly images, this remains an inner journey towards the inner kingdom.

The Law

> And $E=mc^2$ is quite literally the law of all creation.
>
> **Nigel Calder, *Einstein's Universe***

Einstein may indeed have discovered and expressed the law of all creation, but hymns of praise are unlikely to be addressed to this formula. Though proven accurate, the formula of creation does not provide values to live by – but perhaps a revolutionary breakthrough in the future will provide further refinement. Yet Einstein's discovery cannot be ignored; he too peered through the open window into creation and saw its fundamental constitution. Einstein has provided the Illuminating Intelligence; the key to creation has been unlocked, its immanent beauty is, if anything, made even more visible. Current scientific understanding is unprecedented. Cosmology and particle physics are providing a more precise language and explanation for a territory that mystical systems have long recognized. The cross-fertilization between Western science and Eastern mysticism might indeed give rise to a new value system rooted in the ground of being yet open to the journey of becoming.

There can be little doubt about the rapidity of change currently underway in the West. Changing times breed uncertainty and unease as old values become powerless and diminish in authority. New values which lack the strength of tradition and the comfort of familiarity may appear flimsy, but reaction to clearly changing values is also the result of already imbedded values. For those of a conservative disposition and fixed view, the emergence of a multi-faceted, non-hierarchical spirituality, rooted in eclectic and wide-ranging sources, is as the appearance of dragons' teeth in the land. The many-headed hydra of religious inclusiveness is feared as a sign of dilution and diminution, not welcomed as a sign of understanding. For those fed on a strict diet of religious doctrine and dogma, the broadening impact of spiritual values has been a welcome expansion of possibilities. Organized religion in the West faces a crisis of confidence. Whether welcomed or feared, there can be no doubt that patterns of social and political relationships are changing rapidly. Changing inner values will result in new outer forms. Azliluth precedes Assiah. In the descent of power expressed on the Tree, Malkuth is the final emanation. It is the result of energy both emotional and mental. Changes begin first at the level of mind.

Change is now evident throughout society in new patterns of family, community, business, and even nation. The time for externally imposed rules and categorical doctrine is passing. Emperors once held sway, both literally and metaphorically, as lawgivers, final arbiters and images of authority for individuals and nations. But as an early troubadour of the New Age once sang, 'The times, they are a-changing.' Different times call out for different solutions. In *The Quantum Society*, Danah Zohar and Ian Marshall anticipate the possibilities offered by the opportunities of changing values:

> If then we want to change society, we must begin by changing the way that we think. Ephemeral changes to our daily thoughts about what kind of society we would like are inadequate for any social transformation. Thinking on this level leads more often to 'trendy' solutions for half-understood problems. Real social transformation requires that we change our basic *categories* of thought, and that we alter the whole intellectual framework within which we couch

UTOPIA

If social reality could mirror the 'laws of nature', what basic laws would you cite in your chosen constitution?

If a masculine-orientated society were to shift more towards a society based on natural law, what changes and effects would you anticipate?

What social changes do you support?

What social changes do you hope for?

What features would you include in your own utopian ideal?

experiences and perceptions. We must in effect change our whole
mindset and learn a new attitude and learn a whole new language.[4]

The authors suggest a new model of society based on a new model of reality,
a quantum society, 'stemming from a conviction that a whole new paradigm
is emerging from our description of a quantum reality and that this paradigm
can be extended to change radically our perceptions of ourselves and the
social world we want to live in ... Rooted in the nature of physical reality
itself – a society drawing its laws and principles, its self-images and its
metaphors from the same laws and principles underlying all else in the
universe.[5] This bold idea fully encapsulates the Hermetic axiom 'As Above,
so Below'. The authors suggest that the following features, derived from a
quantum model of reality, have the potential to provide an important basis
for a new model of social reality. Many of the trends cited are already
emergent.

Holistic in Setting
The interdependence of nations has never been clearer. Global commerce,
travel and the revolution in communications is currently effecting widespread
social and political change. The worldwide web is here to stay, both as
practical reality and as a new metaphor. Isolationism is no longer a possibility.
A powerful trigger, whether political or economic, now reverberates through
the entire global system.

Personally Meaningful in Operation
Social organizations must provide a sense of individual value, purpose and
meaning in order to balance the age-old dichotomy between the individual
and society. Societies based on the extremes of social organization have
proved hollow. The time is ripe for a new model of self, community and
society.

Plural in Expression
The ongoing revolution in communication makes a pluralistic vision both
possible and inescapable. Diversity can become a source of strength and
creativity. Confidence in a single truth, rigorously upheld and widely shared,
is giving way to the desire for a broader, multi-faceted, inclusive and
embracing value system.

Responsive in Practice

The mechanistic model and its metaphors have proved too rigid to channel the full range of human potential. Organic metaphors include paradigms for adaptability, growth and evolution. A new model must be more flexible and less hierarchical.

Emergent by Nature

The top-down social and political structures imposed by tradition, hereditary revelation or outside authority no longer suit the mood and needs of the time. Responsibility at grass-roots level needs to be encouraged and validated.

Green through Choice

Environmental issues such as pollution, global warming and dwindling resources transcend national and political boundaries. The old paradigm which treats nature only as a infinite storehouse is visibly seen to have created many of the current problems. There is a hunger for an integrated philosophy which places value on the natural world.

Spiritual by Consensus

The decline of orthodox and structured religion is being matched by a rising interest in informal and unstructured spirituality. The need for personal meaning and human values must be acknowledged if a new model is to provide a sense of meaning.

Scientific in Strength

Science and religion have long been considered to be antagonistic to one another. But the radically new scientific understanding now emerging harmonizes with a spiritual perspective. As a reflection of the quantum scientific model, the quantum social model represents a healing of the old antagonism.

Natural Law

> It is my conviction that in quantum physics we now
> have the foundation of a physics upon which we can
> base both our science and our psychology, and that
> through a wedding of physics and psychology, we too
> can live in a reconciled universe, a universe which we
> and culture are fully and meaningfully part of the whole.

> **Danah Zohar,** *The Quantum Self*

The social model put forward by Zohar and Marshall has much in common with the essential features of the Aquarian Initiation. It too is characterized by a holistic, environmental, inclusive, empowering, and pluralistic spirituality rooted in the very constitution of reality. Although the entire Thirty-two Paths of Wisdom may be seen as the vehicle for bringing this initiation to birth, both the 15th and the 28th Paths share a special relevance. Under the aegis of the Star as a form of the Goddess, the journey towards the Natural Intelligence begins. It is completed here on the 15th Path with the realization of nature's own law, the quantum field, emptiness and the ultimate ground of reality. The intrinsic link between these two journeys is extraordinarily potent. In a vision Aleister Crowley was led to swap the attributions of these two Paths, a practice that others have also chosen to follow. This is the Path of the Constituting Intelligence, the 'substance of creation in pure darkness'. The 28th Path is that of the Natural Intelligence. Seeking natural law must inevitably lead to the very heart of reality at the deepest and most profound levels open to us.

The 15th Path is assigned to the astrological sign of Aries. As a Cardinal Fire sign, Aries represents a dynamic and initatiting force. It is ruled by Mars and shares many of the Martian qualities of courage, action and radical movement. This is the sign of change *par excellence*; this is not the gradual transforming process symbolized so often as the Scorpion process but the much more sudden and impulsive need to be rid of the old, the dated and the outworn. As the first sign of the zodiac, Aries heralds the spring, symbolized by the ram, this is the energy of beginnings. It is an appropriate sign for the dawn of a New Age, for new values and new hopes. The lawgiver sits upon the ram-headed throne robed in red, the colour of both Mars and Aries.

The connection between the beliefs that we hold and the society that we create is demonstrated most readily through the historical perspective. It is easy to look back upon the cherished beliefs of the previous generations with all the superiority that hindsight brings. Earlier scientific views of the world may appear to be nothing more than superstition – but how will future generations look back on the scientific models in which we too have put so much faith? The Copernican revolution has given way to the Newtonian revolution, which in turn is giving way to the Quantum revolution. Each leap in understanding brings new values and ideas in its wake. When Danah Zohar writes, 'Today's physics requires that we learn to see the physical world in different terms', she is already anticipating the new values that might arise in its wake. 'I believe that a wider appreciation of the revolutionary nature of quantum reality, and of the possible links between the quantum processes and our own brain processes, can give us the conceptual foundation we need to bring about a "positive revolution" in society.'[6]

The quantum universe that is now arising with Western science has much in common with the Buddhist concept of emptiness. Grasping the teaching of emptiness, the essential nature of reality is considered to be the highest wisdom. Chockmah is the Sephira which is Wisdom. The 15th Path leads to Chockmah. Is it possible to see any reflections of a belief system based on the quantum model in the belief system of Buddhism which leads to an understanding of emptiness? Buddhism is especially tolerant of paradox, finding harmony in the reconciliation of opposites. Where paradox presents an either/or choice to the linear mind, the holographic mind embraces both, seeing not opposition but duality awaiting transcendence. The linear model predominates the Western mindset. 'Quantum physics has called this whole either/or way of thinking into question. When dealing with quantum reality, we have to learn a new both/and kind of thinking. We have to learn to get beyond apparent contradiction. For people schooled for centuries in the either/or mould this can be difficult.'[7] This is the full scope of the paradigm shift – to embrace a revolution that begins in the mind. 'What will the future bring?' asks Jung in *The Undiscovered Self*. It is the opening question. Writing in 1956 in a different political world, he would have been unprepared for the changes that have followed. Deploring the heavy hand of the state as the devourer of the instinctive need for religious expression, he could not have anticipated the breakdown of power from within. Nor did he foresee the technological revolution just waiting in the wings. Perhaps he might have applauded the shift of values in the making. He saw that history and the psyche are inextricably intertwined: 'Our psyche which is primarily responsible for all the historical changes wrought by man on the face of this planet remains an insoluble puzzle, an object of abiding perplexity – a feature it shares with all Nature's secrets.'[8] Perhaps in the quantum model, nature's secrets and the insoluble puzzle of the psyche might at last come together to create a constitution to live by.

EVOCATION

Welcome to my kingdom if you desire to see the ultimate face of reality. If you have sought its knowing with every waking breath and heartbeat, then follow your quest to its utter limit. Many are happy to settle for less. The appearance of reality like a multi-coloured garment is familiar and comforting, but how many choose to strip away the garment to see what is beneath? Yet what lies beneath the world of appearance is astonishing and extraordinary. Though many have claimed to have seen my face and heard my word, I am not to be found in words.

I am the law, but perhaps all is not as you think in the inner kingdom. I am the Constituting Intelligence. I am the inner constitution of the world of form. My world is inseparable from you, as the flame is from the coal. I am the lawgiver. I show you the face of the law that cannot be changed. I show you the face of ultimate reality. I show you what is real. I show you the world within the world.

Do you still seek me out? Do you dare to know? What is your true will? Shall you be at peace, keeping the silence of the ages? These are my questions to you before you come seeking me out. Once you have seen my face, you will never forget what you have come to know. I am the Emperor ruler of the inner kingdom.

INTERNALIZATION – THE 15TH PATH: TIPHARETH–CHESED

Construct the temple of Tiphareth in the creative imagination. Find yourself standing beside the doorway of the Emperor. The Archangel Raphael lifts the tapestry curtain so that you may pass.

Find yourself walking in a strange landscape. It is like nothing you have ever seen on earth. The sky is red and distant shapes, though familiar as mountain outcrops, seem to be red as well. You stand on a narrow and rocky path climbing towards steep mountainous terrain. As you walk everything here seems to be in a primal state. In the distance you hear the rumbling of sounds deep in the earth and feel the vibration tremors far below. This seems to be a land in the making, wild and primal.

You continue on your way upwards, picking out a pathway of grey rock. The path crosses fields of rock still spewing lava and cuts its way between high boulders. Everywhere you look the processes of creation are active; showers of sparks suddenly fill the air and the smell of sulphur and gas travels on the wind. Just as you begin to wonder if you are alone in this strange and alien landscape you hear the low, vibrating sound of a horn.

You follow the sound to its source. To your surprise, here in this wild landscape sits a crowned king on a stone throne, constructed from the very substance of the land he rules. It is adorned with four carved rams' heads. The ruler wears a robe of red like the kingdom around him. In one hand he caries an orb and in the other he carries a sceptre. He seems quite unperturbed by the work of creation taking place so visibly and noisily around him. You approach his throne and instinctively kneel before him. He reaches forward and places the orb in your hands. You hold it gently. It feels warm to the touch. Holding the sphere, reminiscent of the globe of the earth, you begin to enter a meditative state. The sphere seems to be vibrating with a life that you do not understand. You open out your two hands to cup it more gently. It begins to shine and shimmer with an inner light. Its hard exterior surface is changing to a fast-moving vortex of light. Now it has given up all sense of weight and instead is resting lightly on your hand like a ball of spinning energy. You feel the Emperor leaning forwards. Extending the sceptre, he touches you gently at the nape of your neck. A white light flashes through you in an instant. When you look up, you are quite alone. As you stand to depart, you suddenly realize that the landscape has changed. No longer wild and primeval, the mountains are clothed with green trees; a river flows in the distance and birds fly in the sky.

When you are ready, return the way you came to the temple. When you are ready, leave through the doorway. Finally, dissolve all images and return to ordinary consciousness.

EXERCITIA SPIRITUALIA

Take the Following as Subjects for Meditation:

- Son of the Morning, Chief among the Mighty
- Heh
- Sight
- Aries
- The Constituting Intelligence

Make Notes on:

- Tarot Trump IV, The Emperor

Visualize the Following and Record your Experiences:

- The Temple of Tiphareth including the Archangel Raphael
- The Journey of 15th Path

CHAPTER 28

The Fourteenth Path: Binah–Chockmah

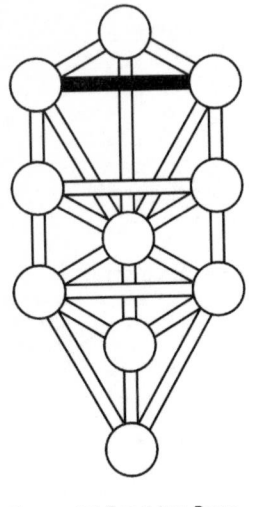

FIGURE 37 THE 14TH PATH:

BINAH–CHOCKMAH

TAROT TRUMP III,

THE EMPRESS

TABLE OF CORRESPONDENCES

The Journey: Tarot Trump III, The Empress,
Daughter of the Mighty Ones
Key: Daleth, meaning a door
Double Letter: Wisdom – Folly
Spiritual Significance: Venus
Text: The Illuminating Intelligence
Colour in Atziluth: Emerald Green
Colour in Briah: Sky Blue
Colour in Yetzirah: Early spring Green
Colour in Assiah: Bright Rose or Cerise rayed
pale Green

COMMENTARY

The Fourteenth Path is the Illuminating Intelligence and it is so called because it is that Chasmal which is the founder of the concealed and fundamental ideas of holiness and of their stages of preparation.

The 14th Path connects the second Sephirah, Chockmah, Wisdom, with the third Sephirah, Binah, Understanding. As one of the three lateral journeys of the Tree, this is a Path of adjustment and blending where opposite powers are brought into harmony. The 27th Path reconciles the duality of Hod and Netzach, balancing intellectual mind with instinctive emotion, thereby providing the integrating experience for the Astral or Psychological Triangle of the Lesser Mysteries. The 19th Path reconciles Geburah with Chesed and thereby serves to provide the integrating experience for the Ethical or Moral Triangle of the Greater Mysteries. The 14th Path reconciles the potencies of Chockmah and Binah where dynamic and free-flowing force meet organization and structure as the integrating experience for the Supernal Triangle of the Supreme Mysteries. Each of the three lateral Paths also connects the two Pillars of Severity and Mercy which represent the powers of force and form.

Blueprints for Being

> Each of us, faced with the mystery of our existence and experience, has to try and find some way of making sense of it. We have a choice of philosophers: the mechanistic theory of nature and of human life, with God as an optional extra; or the theory of nature as alive, but without God, or the theory of a living God together with living nature.
>
> **Rupert Sheldrake, *The Rebirth of Nature***

Blueprints for being, whether scientific or religious, exert a powerful influence. Models of creation and explanations of evolution provide a perimeter holding the beliefs and values which arise like reflections within its embrace. Once models of creation were entirely religious, and being dressed in the language of definitive revelation assumed an infallible authority. Models of reality derived from a scientific perspective at last have a place too. Perhaps now at the dawn of the 21st century a new blueprint for being will emerge to reconcile the old antagonisms. A culture lives by its own model of reality and imitates its favoured blueprint through values and beliefs which echo the prime model. A model of reality must illuminate if it is to serve as a blueprint for being and behaving. The 14th Path is assigned to the Illuminating Intelligence. The idea that the world was flat was not an effective model to live by. This was a fearful belief but people lived as if it were true. The idea that the earth and not the sun lay at the centre of the solar system was a projection, not a fact. But cultures lived in accordance with this belief. Eventually the door was opened to an Illuminating Intelligence, one based in the truth and actuality of nature. A new blueprint for being was born. It permitted a monumental cultural, religious and scientific shift.

A model of reality should illuminate our understanding. By throwing light on the nature of the physical world, blueprints offer models which can be applied to bring about an intended outcome. Based in an intelligence which illuminates, advances in medicine, technology, and science become possible. We live at a time when models of reality which have served well for centuries are now proving to be inadequate and partial representations. The revisioning force is coming principally from science, through both physics and the biological sciences. Just as Newtonian physics has proven inadequate to describe micro events, so Euclidean geometry is proving inadequate at a micro level.

Quantum physics and fractal geometry are establishing new models of reality. These developments are exciting and revolutionary. The quantum model is quite unlike any previous blueprint. Where once a single ill-fitting theistic description proscribed possibilities, now a plurality of descriptive blueprints reveals the complexity and wonder of creation. Choosing a model of reality to live by may appear to be an intellectual choice but, as Sheldrake has pointed out, the choice of a guiding light is much more a matter of intuition and the values that we already hold to be dear at heart. He examines the most common types of explanatory models and finds three main categories:

According to the first theory, all creativity emerges from the mother principle: It is inherent in nature, and emerges from blind, unconscious processes such as the workings of chance. It wells up from material activities. New patterns of organisation, new morphic fields, just spring into being spontaneously. The second theory proposes that all creativity comes from the father principle. It descends into the physical world of space and time from a higher, transcendent level which is mind-like. In the Platonic tradition this eternal intelligence is the source and abode of the ideas reflected in the world of nature...

Thirdly, there is the theory that all creativity comes from an interplay between the mother and the father principles, or, more abstractly, from below and above. It depends on chance, conflict and necessity, the mother of invention. It arises in particular environments, at particular times; it is rooted in the ongoing processes of nature. But at the same time it occurs within the framework of a higher system of order. Creativity occurs not just upwards from the bottom, with new forms arising from complex systems by spontaneous jumps; it also proceeds downwards from the top, through the creative activity of higher-level fields.[1]

The Quantum model of reality may prove to be the most mysterious, magical and spiritual of all paradigms yet put forward. It contains elements that might be ascribed to both the mother and father principles, as opposing yet interconnected forces.

The 14th Path is represented by Tarot Trump III, The Empress as the embodiment of Mother Nature. But she is also called the Daughter of the Mighty Ones. These Mighty Ones are Chockmah and Binah, the Supernal Mother and the Supernal Father. This Path brings the powers of these Sephiroth into a relationship with each other. Though Binah and Chockmah separately express different aspects of creation, their potencies meet upon the 14th Path in a deeper and more complex evolutionary development. These complementary and opposite effects together interact to generate the ongoing momentum for life.

On the 14th Path, the forces and powers imprinted at the Big Bang and implicitly held in the creative matrix, meet in a new relationship. The 14th Path lies within the realm of the Supernal Triangle of archetype and cosmic blueprint in its highest form. As the lateral girders of the Supernal Triangle, the 14th Path is not one of physical manifestation which belongs to Malkuth. Despite the attribution of The Empress, this is not an encounter with nature manifested as physical form but a statement of relationships and interplay of forces implicit within nature. This Path is one of causation, not effect. It is a path of foundation. It represents an evolutionary stage which draws to itself all the forces and principles, laws and operations through which the material world and its many life forms will arise. As the potential for physical life was already present in the moment of the Big Bang, so the potentiality for and inevitability of conscious life are seeded on this the 14th Path.

This Path is assigned to the letter *Daleth*, meaning a door. It is the doorway through which manifest life will eventually arise. This Path belongs to, 'that Chasmal (Brilliant One) which is the founder of the concealed and fundamental ideas of holiness and of their stages of preparation'. This is a Path where the concealed and fundamental ideas are founded. Nature's laws are indeed concealed. We see the result of the law, not the law itself. We see and interact with the phenomena of the natural world, not with the concealed and fundamental which lie in the world of atoms and molecules and beyond that, with particles and waves of energy. This is a Path of foundation and preparation.

Might nature's implicit and concealed laws be described as 'the ideas of holiness'? The idea of holism is being boosted by the newly emergent Quantum model. Might this extraordinary holism also be thought holy? This is a place of preparation for the evolutionary journey to be unfolded. This is the Path of 'the founder of the concealed and fundamental ideas of holiness and of their stages of preparation'. It is the Illuminating Intelligence. This is a model of being which illuminates.

The 14th Path forms the underpinning substrate which is the inner world of dynamic energies under hidden and implicit law. The Sanctified Intelligence assigned to Binah renders the hidden laws holy and is the Foundation of the Primordial Wisdom. As Binah is called the Superior Mother, so Malkuth is called the Inferior Mother. What is envisaged as archetype in its pure and ideal form will come to pass in less pure form – varied, diluted and modified, refracted into a thousand new images. What is founded through the Supernal Triangle will find physical expression in the World of Action. The archetype of Natura, Mother Nature, the Empress of the 14th Path, reinforced by the Magical Image of the mature woman assigned to Binah, will find a reflection in the Magical Image of Malkuth, a young woman crowned and enthroned.

The *Chasmal*, the Brilliant One, of the 14th Path comes into being through the polarized relationship between Chockmah and Binah. The word Chasmal comes from two words: *Chash*, meaning silence, and *mal*, meaning speech. This paradoxical 'speaking silence' points out the

> ## WHAT'S IN A NAME?
>
> Take the familiar creation story from Genesis. Read it aloud, substituting the female Goddess for the male God.
>
> 'In the beginning when Goddess created the heavens and the earth, the earth was a formless void and darkness covered the face of the deep, while a wind from the Goddess swept over the face of the waters. Then Goddess said "Let there be light", and there was light. And Goddess saw that the light was good. And Goddess separated the light from the darkness. Goddess called the light Day and darkness she called Night, and there was evening and there was morning, the first day.'
>
> Record how reading these words makes you feel.

harmonized conjunction of the two modes of consciousness assigned to Binah and Chockmah. Silence belongs to the unified Wisdom of Chockmah and speaking belongs to the separating Understanding of Binah. It is possible that the word Chasmal was used as a mantra. Formed from two sounds – *Sh* from the letter Shin and *M* from the letter Mem – Chasmal may set up an oscillation between the left and right hemispheres of the brain representing Binah and Chockmah consciousness. 'In our present terminology Chasmal would be the interface between Binah consciousness and Chockmah consciousness.'[2] This concept is entirely in keeping with the placement of this Path as the girder between Binah and Chockmah. Might it even be possible that the 'Brilliant One' refers to a unified state of heightened consciousness which emerges as a speaking silence from the harmonious balance of left and right brains?

The Great Goddess

And then it struck me that we are all children of our earth. It does not matter what country you look at. We are all earth's children, and we should treat her as our mother.

Aleksander Alexsandrov, cosmonaut

The Tarot Trump of The Empress shows a mature woman seated outdoors upon a throne. She carries a sceptre and beside her is a shield emblazoned with the astrological sign for Venus. She is crowned with a diadem of stars and wears a necklace set with spheres. Her robe is decorated with pomegranates and her rounded figure suggests pregnancy; wheat springs at her feet and in the background there is a waterfall. She is Mother Nature, fertile and abundant, set in her own realm of the great outdoors. Growing crops and running water are symbols of abundance. Her pregnancy speaks of the renewing and gestating potency of nature. In her speaking silence, she poses the same question asked by philosophers, empirical researchers and enquiring minds: what is the nature of nature? What is the nature of the laws governing nature? Were eternal laws imposed on nature from the outset by a creator God or have the laws of nature evolved through time, circumstance and opportunity? What is the balance between dynamic forward-moving evolution and the equilibrium within creation?

Nature has long been described through a feminine metaphor. The mother principle once lay at the heart of a blueprint for being. In an age nursed on images, motifs and praise to the creator as God the father, it is timely to remember that this is a relatively new blueprint for being. Ancient cosmologies most often assigned the realm of earth to the mother and the realm of sky to the father. This polarity expresses a relationship between the earth and the heavens, the eternal and the finite, the temporal and the spiritual. Over time the balance of power between these two realms has shifted. The realm assigned to God the Father has subsumed the realm of the Great Mother. In the shift from the mother to the father, cerebral values came to replace direct interaction with the world. In the new model of being, nature worship acquired a taint, but this was not always the case.

Under an earlier and different representation of reality, nature was personalized and personified as the universal mother, the source of life. She was revered as the Great Goddess, mother of all. Deity was worshipped in feminine guise for millennia. The figure of the Empress embodies all the great mothering goddesses. She is the archetypal mother behind all the life-giving goddesses in human history. This is the Path of the Goddess matrix. This is the Path of the Empress; she is the embodiment of the powers of reproduction, regeneration and renewal.

This is the Path of the mother of all Great Mothers. The letter assigned to this Path is Daleth, signifying a door. This is the doorway into life; it is the womb of the Great Mother which is also the *vesica piscis* of Binah. The Empress sits enthroned, wearing a robe decorated with pomegranates, the many-seeded fruit sacred to the grain goddess Demeter. Without the renewing powers of nature implicit in seed, flower and fruit, the world would have ceased its seasonal round of growth long ago. These simple wonders sustain human life and call forth a human response. The spirits of the rice are thanked with festival and dance in Bali. The corn mother is thanked by the Hopi people, who see themselves as children of the mother. The women of ancient Greece descended into caverns to leave offerings in an annual cycle of engagement with the fertilizing power of the earth. This spirit of thankfulness preserves a relationship between the world of people and the natural world. Harvest was once a time of shared thankfulness, but in the West, at least, the agrarian cycle and its customs have faded into folk memory.

The realm of the Great Goddess is not limited merely to the agrarian cycle. Her realm is the infinite universe. The Empress sits with wheat at her feet but she also wears a crown of stars. Nature provides all. Her many epiphanies, anathema to those of monotheistic sentiment, express the fullness, richness and sanctity of life itself. The Goddess is centred at the heart of a constellation of values, experiences and ideas which affirm inter-connectedness, relationship and human experience. Elinor W. Gadon summarizes the nature of goddess worship in *The Once and Future Goddess*:

> The Goddess religion was earth-centred, not heaven-centred; of this world, not otherworldly; body affirming, not body-denying; holistic, not dualistic. The Goddess was immanent, within every human being, not transcendent; and humanity was viewed as part of nature, death as part of life. Her worship was sensual, celebrating the erotic, embracing all that was alive. The religious quest was above all for renewal, for the regeneration of life, and the Goddess was the life-force.[3]

How might our contemporary attitude to nature be summarised? Matthew Fox places our attitude to nature at the heart of a new creation of spirituality: 'The issue of grace lies at the heart of an ecological consciousness, for it presents us with the issue of how we envision our relationship to nature.'[4]

The Gaia Hypothesis

So in what sense is Gaia alive? And what difference does it make if we think of her as a living organism, as opposed to an inanimate physical system?

Rupert Sheldrake, *The Rebirth of Nature*

This Path is assigned to the Tarot Trump of The Empress. She represents all and any of the earth mothers from the distant past, when a different mindset prevailed. She is one among many earth goddesses. The scientist James Lovelock has brought her name to current attention through his Gaia Hypothesis. When working on a project in which he compared the atmosphere of earth with that of Mars and Venus, he noted that earth's atmosphere was constant over long periods despite being composed of a mixture of unstable gases. This realization led Lovelock to search for the earth's self-regulating mechanisms, and from this idea of self-regulation the Gaia Hypothesis was born. His ideas were not well received by the scientific community of the late 1960s and early 1970s. Likening the earth to the ancient Greek goddess Gaia irritated the scientific mindset of the day. It was a metaphor too far. 'Metaphor they seem to see as pejorative, something inexact and therefore unscientific.

In truth, real science is riddled with metaphor. Science grows from imaginary models in the mind and is sharpened by measurements that check the fit of the models with reality.'[5] Now, almost 30 years later, in the light of environmental disasters and the rise of ecology, the holistic view of earth provides a new model at a time in need of new models. Lovelock has attempted to breach the barriers around the life sciences with his vision of a new holistic discipline to combine the study of rocks with the evolution of life:

> I have called the science of Gaia, geophysiology. Just as physiology takes a holistic, systems view of ordinary living organisms such as plants, animals, and microbes, so geophysiolgy is holistic science of large living systems, such as the earth, in which the organisms are dispersed. Geophysiology is a hard and rigorous science whose study is the properties of these large systems.[6]

It is perhaps significant that the Gaia Hypothesis has made an appearance at a time when the women's movement has done much to reinstate the significance of the Great Goddess as a model for women. But the domain of the Great Goddess is not just an arena for personal empowerment. It is both a cosmological and individual pattern for reclaiming what has been devalued, forgotten and discarded. This is not a gender battle for equal opportunities or women's rights, but a far deeper issue. Why should it now matter that the Great Goddess has been dethroned? What value might there be in describing nature through a feminine metaphor? What insights might such a blueprint bring?

The 14th Path is one of balance and harmony between the masculine and feminine polarities. But this balance has been weighted in favour of the masculine dimension for so long that it is difficult to disentangle the tightly woven mesh of social, economic and political factors set in place to confine the feminine and her constellation of values. This imprisonment has carried a loss in its wake. We do not live by bread alone but by our values, and the Age of Reason has led us into a cul-de-sac. Technological domination has brought a false sense of security and power. The technological skills of the modern world are wonders indeed, but nature cannot be tamed. Unusual weather patterns, unexpected floods and searing heat waves are as threatening as any foe. As new frontiers of knowledge are breached, space exploration becomes thrilling and important, but suffering and poverty still dominate millions of lives each day. Material goals do not assuage, only a holistic philosophy nourishes the whole person. Only a holistic philosophy can feed the whole person.

When the qualities of Chockmah and Binah are harmonized and no longer separated, the seeds of a different philosophy will find fruitful soil. When the Illuminating Intelligence of Chockmah is seen to give rise to the Sanctifying Intelligence of Binah as the Foundation of Primordial Wisdom, then an Illuminating Intelligence will arise. This revisioning of nature will generate new possibilities. New blueprints for being will arise in an intellectual climate of genuine curiosity and openness; new models of reality will permit and encourage new ways of thinking about the world. Without the invigorating possibilities derived from new models, culture becomes frozen and atrophies through a false sense of loyalty which demands adherence to a single pattern.

Lovelock's intended geophysiology is a statement of hope; it is a different way of looking at the world. Ecology is a new science that takes a holistic perspective. 'Ecology is the prototype of a new holistic vision of science which will recognise these involuntary metaphors and acknowledge, in the way that myth does, the symbolic as well as the symbiotic nature of our earth-household.'[7] The 14th Path asks that we examine the views that we hold about the laws within nature. At the dawn of the 21st century, we at last have the opportunity to harmonize the scientific with the holy and to celebrate the divine marriage of the father and the mother, Chockmah and Binah.

EVOCATION

Welcome to my kingdom. Some call me the Great Mother, for I am the mother of all forms and all worlds. Some call me the Great Goddess, for I am the mother of many divine daughters. Some call me the Empress, for my empire is without boundary and without end. From my throne I look out and see the kingdom of the Emperor who also has dominion in the inner worlds without form. Behold the sacred marriage in the interior realms of creation.

I am the source and the doorway to life. I endlessly recreate myself. I give birth to myself in a multitude of forms. I am infinite potential and unlimited possibility. My sign is Venus, for I am love without end, pouring myself into creation lovingly conceived. I am the power that gives rise to nature. I am the world of the world within the world. I am the mother of all that shall be. I am ever pregnant, endlessly bringing creation into being. I am the doorway and the womb of life. This is my gift – endless creation and infinite variety. Nature's own realm covers me in a veil of appearance and delight. I am the Illuminating Intelligence which shines at the heart of creation. I am the Empress; creation is my kingdom.

INTERNALIZATION – THE 14TH
PATH: BINAH–CHOCKMAH

Construct the Temple of either Binah or Chockmah in the creative imagination. Find yourself standing beside the doorway of the Empress. The Archangel lifts the tapestry curtain so that you may pass.

Find yourself walking through a wood. It is late summer, the trees are in full green. As you walk, open your senses to the life of the wood. Beneath your feet the leaf litter is soft. And there is the deep, dark aroma of mingled wood and earth. Above you sunlight filters through the greenery with a diamond brilliance.

Now a sound reaches you. You hear a woman's voice. She cannot be far away. The voice is deep and rich like the woodland itself. Curiosity aroused, you quicken your step. The trees begin to thin out and ahead you see a clearing. In the centre, on a throne softened with velvet and cushions, sits a woman. She sings to herself, enwrapped in a lullaby. As you step forward, she sees you and stops her song. But she is neither afraid nor perturbed by your presence. Instead she gives a knowing smile as if she had been expecting you all along. You step closer. Now you can see her more clearly. She wears a gown of white silk decorated with fruits, which you recognize as pomegranates. As she turns slightly upon her seat, you realize that she is pregnant. She wears a crown of 12 stars which rise from a wreath of laurel, and a necklace of spheres above a jewelled collar. Resting by her side is a heraldic shield in the shape of a heart emblazoned with the astrological sign for Venus. In the foreground, around her seat, wheat is ripe. In the background, water cascades from a wooded outcrop and collects into a pool. She beckons you to come closer. You step through the golden corn so that you stand right in front of her. She looks deeply into your eyes, never losing contact for even a second. From within the folds of her gown she draws out a sceptre and raises it over you as if in token of blessing. At the same time she moves forward and takes your hand and places it firmly on her belly, enfolding it with her own hand. At the instant, everything around you suddenly and without warning changes, shifting from the everyday and the familiar to the unknown and extraordinary. You feel you are being propelled into a new dimension. You have no control; you look towards your body but there is no body to be seen, yet your mind is fully aware and registering every nuance of the experience. Though you see no body you can still sense a comforting hand holding yours in some unknown way. Your consciousness registers a region of scintillating darkness without orientation. Tiny brilliant lights flash momentarily and then are gone. You have no sense of scale or direction. You are reminded of the vastness of space, but you know this is not outer space. From somewhere in your awareness, you hear a voice singing again. 'I am the prima materia, and this is my kingdom.' The voice is comforting – its human quality reassures you that all is well. This new focus of awareness has an instant impact. The whirling, dancing, dizzy darkness ceases; you are back in the glade but quite alone.

By the foot of the draped throne there is a single pomegranate. You pick it up, knowing that inside are many jewelled seeds. Its feminine redness will remind you of this visit to the Empress, the Daughter of the Mighty Ones.

When you are ready, leave and return to the temple. When you are ready, leave through the doorway. Finally, dissolve all images and return to ordinary consciousness.

EXERCITIA SPIRITUALIA

Take the Following as Subjects for Meditation:
- Daughter of the Mighty Ones
- Daleth
- Wisdom – Folly
- Venus
- The Illuminating Intelligence

Make Notes on:
- Tarot Trump III, The Empress

Visualize the Following and Record your Experiences:
- The Temple of either Binah or Chockmah including the Archangel
- The Journey of the 14th Path

CHAPTER 29

The Thirteenth Path: Tiphareth–Kether

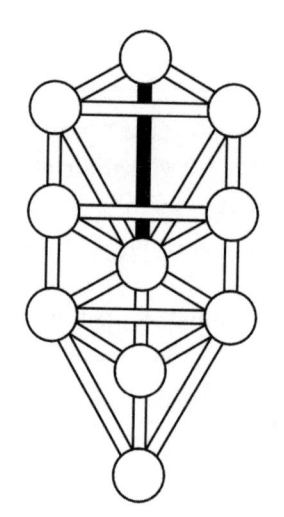

FIGURE 38 THE 13TH PATH:

TIPHARETH–KETHER

TAROT TRUMP II,

THE HIGH PRIESTESS,

PRIESTESS OF THE SILVER STAR

TABLE OF CORRESPONDENCES

The Journey: Tarot Trump II, The High
    Priestess, Priestess of the Silver Star
Key: The Letter Gimel, meaning a camel
Double Letter: Peace – War
Spiritual Significance: Sirius, The Moon
Text: The Uniting Intelligence
Colour in Atziluth: Blue
Colour in Briah: Silver
Colour in Yetzirah: Cold pale Blue
Colour in Assiah: Silver rayed sky Blue

COMMENTARY

The Thirteenth Path is named the Uniting Intelligence,
and it is so called because it is itself the essence of glory.
It is called the consummation of truth of individual
spiritual things.

The 13th Path joins the 25th Path and the 32nd Path. Together these three Paths form the backbone of the Tree. This Central Pillar formed by the three Paths joins Kether, the Crown, with Malkuth, the Kingdom, in a direct line. This Path passes through the Lesser Mysteries of psychological adjustment, the Greater Mysteries of ethical development and the Supreme Mysteries of spiritual realization. The Central Pillar of Consciousness connects the Crown, the source, with the Kingdom, the manifest world. The 13th Path is one of unification and homecoming. Arising from the non-dual mindset of Tiphareth, the 13th Path crosses the Abyss and leads directly into Kether. The 11th and 12th Paths also connect directly to Kether but these Paths remain confined to the Supernal Triangle, whereas the 13th Path rises or descends into the Ethical Triangle and the sphere of Beauty which is accessible to human consciousness. This is the Uniting Intelligence.

The Divine Feminine

> We stand on the threshold of a Goddess religion, which
> by virtue of its membership and its aims, is non-
> hierarchical, decentralised, locally-manifest, in its many
> and various ways. Goddess spirituality addresses directly
> the problems of our own world now.

Caitlin Matthews, *Sophia, Goddess of Wisdom*

The 13th Path is assigned to Tarot Trump II, The High Priestess. The office of High Priestess has been obliterated by the forces of a patriarchal society which is unwilling to invest the feminine with any spiritual authority. It is ironic, then, that the 13th Path, which holds such a key position upon the Tree, is assigned wholly to the powers of the Divine Feminine. The rediscovery of the divine feminine might be seen as one of the challenges of our time:

A discussion of the nature of the feminine principle and the laws which govern it is of vital importance to both men and women today, for, as we have seen in our Western, twentieth-century culture, this principle has been neglected and its requirements have been met only by stereotyped and mechanised observances of conventional customs, while the care and tendance of the life-giving springs, which lie in the depths of nature, have been disregarded. For these sources of spiritual or psychological energy can only be reached, or so the myths and ancient religions say, through a right approach to the feminine essence of nature, whether this functions in inanimate form or in women themselves. It is therefore of the greatest importance that we seek to establish once more a better relation to the feminine principle.[1]

Kabbalah offers a system of polarized opposites and balanced forces. Both the masculine and feminine powers are accorded a rightful place in the overall schema. Taoism offers the complements yin and yang; Hinduism offers its pantheon of gods and goddesses. The ancient Greeks envisaged both gods and goddesses, as did the Romans, the Egyptians and the Sumerians. Monotheistic cultures are, historically speaking, of recent origin. Christianity offers a grudging place to the feminine powers through the Virgin Mary, but even now society is still weighted in favour of masculine archetypes. The idea of the divine in a feminine form is still found to be shocking and totally unacceptable by the majority. Change, however, is slowly dawning, appearing organically as the Aquarian current takes root and brings in more humanizing and balanced solutions. At the beginning of the 21st century we are in need of a new holistic philosophy which encompasses all levels of human experiences, from the physical to the spiritual, while simultaneously embracing both modes of human expression, the masculine and the feminine. Because power has been so strongly vested in the masculine dimension for so long and in so many ways, any shift of emphasis towards balance may appear radical. Yet some rebalancing is vital. With remarkable anticipation, the Jungian therapist and writer Esther Harding foresaw the need for this in the early 1950s:

In order to gain a new vantage from which a fresh world philosophy may perhaps be built up, a renewed contract with the deeper levels of humanity is needed so that a really vital relation may be established with the laws and principles which activate humanity. Perhaps the most important of these inner laws which need fresh exploration today are the masculine and feminine principles.[2]

In reality it is the relation with the feminine principle which cries out to be re-addressed, after millennia of neglect and denigration. The quest towards the feminine is not merely personal but potentially transformative for society as a whole. 'A new relation to this woman principle is urgently needed today to counteract the one-sidedness of the prevailing masculine mode of Western civilisation.'[3] Some 50 years on, the Goddess and her retinue are making a tentative reappearance once again. Reclaimed by feminists, political activists, spiritual pioneers and women in need of nourishment, the names of the Goddess are sounded again. However, the realm of the Goddess does not belong to women alone but to all. In the initial stages of reclaiming the Goddess as an image of empowerment, role model, archetypal pattern, blueprint for wholeness, image of womanhood and symbol of liberation, women have chosen to reclaim and honour this homecoming alone. Enraged by an enforced estrangement from the divine feminine, many women are adamantly against sharing this bounty with those seen as her captors and tormentors. Reclaiming the Goddess and redefining the reciprocal relationship for a new time has rightly been the task of those few who felt themselves called into her service, whether as scholars, academics, devotees or priestesses. Now that the spearhead has been established and made secure, it is perhaps time to open the door of the house of wisdom for men too. A separate development institutes another imbalance. Masculine powers are best dissolved by bringing men into the service of the Divine Feminine. Historically, men served the goddess Isis as both devotees and priests. Women's Mysteries belong to women, Men's Mysteries belong to men, but Transcendent Mysteries belong to humanity. Excluding men from a relationship with the feminine serves no value. In fact, it denies the very salve needed to heal the wound of the ages. 'Men also need a relation to the feminine principle, not only that they may better understand women, but also because their contact with the inner or spiritual world is governed not by masculine but by feminine laws.'[4]

THE BLESSINGS OF THE FEMININE

In what ways might Western society benefit from a rediscovery of the feminine? Where are these values needed? Where does resistance to feminine values stem from?

This Path is assigned to Tarot Trump II, The High Priestess. A woman robed in soft blue sits between two pillars. A crescent moon rests at her feet, nestled in the folds of her robes, and she wears an equal-armed cross on her breast. A veil decorated with pomegranates hangs suspended between two pillars. Behind the veil it is possible to catch a glimpse of the waters behind her. The priestess wears a crown and sits with the scroll of the law on her lap. This Trump recapitulates many familiar images; a female presence dignifies both moon and water, these are the images which relate to the depths of the unconscious, to Eros and to feminine poles of both values and divinity. Yet this place is far removed from the realm of Yesod and the unconscious has no place with the Supreme Mysteries. This is the realm of the supraconscious and the initiation of Daath. It is said that Yesod is Daath upon a lower arc. Now we have arrived at Daath, the invisible most enigmatic of all the Sephiroth. Initation into the realm of the moon begins at Yesod and forms the foundation for another initation at Daath, the higher octave of Yesod.

The Mysteries of Isis

> All men at one time or another have fallen in love with
> the veiled Isis whom they call truth.

Evelyn Underhill, Mysticism

Tarot Trump II is also called the Priestess of the Silver Star, which is Sirius, the most brilliant star in the sky. Called Sept or Sodpet, Sirius is the star beloved by the Egyptians. Its heliacal rising announced the rising of the Nile, and the two events together inaugurated the new year. This is the star of Isis and this is her priestess. Isis remains a potent figure in the tradition of the Mysteries. Like the figure of Demeter who was likened to her, Isis presided over the Mysteries of being and becoming in the sacred dramas of Egypt. Like Demeter, Isis too travelled in disguise, searching out the body of her beloved. She also attempted to bestow the gift of immortality on an infant with disastrous consequences. Yet the initiation into immortality is the gift of this Path. This is the truth concealed in the scroll of the law, which is *tora*, but also *taro* and *rota*, the wheel and the tarot. This is the essence of the law and it is feminine in nature. It is the transforming, dynamic, ever-turning, energy of life, which is elusive, powerful, magnetic, enigmatic and mystifying. This is the nature of feminine energy. This is Shakti as prime initiator, teacher and guardian of the Supreme Mysteries of being and becoming. It is impossible to comprehend the femine principle through an intellectual or academic approach. Anyone who seeks to understand the Supreme Mysteries through intellectual study or rational analysis and empirical research will be sorely disappointed. These mysteries of being and becoming are revealed only through the development of higher consciousness. This is the place of the Throat Chakra, called Vishuddi, which means to purify. The High Priestess wears a robe of blue, symbolizing elemental water once again. The symbolism of water has accompanied the journey upon the central pillar. At Malkuth, Scorpio, as one of the fixed signs of the zodiac, represents elemental Water. At Yesod water represents the pool of the collective unconscious. It is the mirror in which a self-image may be seen and the astral mirror of the collective whole. The 25th Path commences with the pool of Yesod and stretches upwards towards the realms of Tiphareth. It is a Path of desert trial where the life-giving waters of spiritual rebirth are much needed. The 13th Path is another journey of trial which culminates in the experience of the High Priestess. She sits before a veil. Behind it are the infinite waters of continuous creation. This is her realm. The Central Pillar is that of consciousness. It is the way of mystical ascent. Every step on this Path of Ascent has posed challenges and tests. Each one – facing the personal unconscious, opening towards the collective unconscious and awakening to higher consciousness and finally merging with supraconsciousness – has been precipitated by interaction with the central pillar. Each phase has been accompanied by the realization of new aspects of being. The realm of Yesod brings the awakening of psychic gifts. A deeper, integrated and illuminating consciousness appears through the mystical awakening of Tiphareth. At Daath psychic, spiritual, intellectual, imaginative, emotional and instinctive powers are harmonized. The personality has given way. The Individuality sits on the throne of wisdom. Travel upon the 13th Path provides the consummate experience which unifies and unites all that has gone before into a single unbroken stream of consciousness. Curiously, Tantric texts speak of the evolution of consciousness passing from the watery realm by means of the crescent to the fiery region of the sun and from there to the place of air and to the full moon. In these same texts it is said that whoever reaches the full moon sees the three periods and is long lived. This is the gateway of the great liberation. This Path is assigned to the letter Gimel, which signifies a camel. This ship of the desert is capable of travelling long distances without water as it draws upon its own internal reserves. In the same way the traveller upon the 13th Path needs to be utterly self-sufficient and self-sustaining. Like the 25th Path from which this rises, this Path represents the next phase of testing. By virtue of the in–depth interior journey, wisdom has accrued like nectar. Now it becomes possible to ride upon the waters with safety in the moon boat of the goddess. This is the boat of immortality.

Boats and Temples

> In the first stage of the initiation the human being entered the boat of the goddess and journeyed with her over the floods to the region of the sun … In the temple of the goddess, the human being, whether man or woman, is face to face with himself, his own instincts, his own emotion. He must experience himself to the uttermost.

> **Esther Harding, *Woman's Mysteries***

Tarot Trump II offers an open invitation to the temple of the Goddess. The initiate can embark in her boat and become one of her company. The boat is not a familiar contemporary symbol but in a historical culture where boats were commonplace, the symbolism was natural. Like the chariot, the boat represents a vehicle, but unlike the chariot, which is designed to move over land, the boat moves over water. The chariot is the vehicle of physical incarnation, the boat is the vehicle of spiritual immortality. In a culture nourished by a single river, the Egyptians naturally understood the symbolism of the boat as safe passage from shore to shore and the means of journeying upon water. This meaning was especially vivid in a culture where life was placed on the east bank of the Nile and where the dead were housed on the western side in the company of the setting sun. The boat was often used to portray the passage of time, especially when conjoined with the symbolism of the sun. Model boats were often included with funerary possessions. The soul joined the company of the gods in the Boat of Millions of Years. This boat sails through time carrying mortals and gods together. The boat therefore ferries the living and the dead from place to place, from realm to realm. It is the means of safety in the flood, the means of escape in danger, the means of transport in life. It is the means of sailing upon the river of life. This is quite different from swimming in the same waters, which implies effort, the necessary skill and even the possibility of drowning. Sailing on the waters implies safety, ease and a mastery of the water that comes from closeness and long familiarity. Riding in the boat of the Goddess can take place only after the Lesser Mysteries of the Moon have been assimilated and integrated. In other words, the journey as a passenger or guest can take place only after a long apprenticeship to elemental water and the light of the moon has been fully served. Personal drives must give way to the transpersonal or the boat of immortality will have no meaning:

> To enter the boat of the Goddess implies accepting the uprush of instincts in a religious spirit as a manifestation of the creative life force itself. When such an attitude is attained, instincts can no longer be regarded as an asset to be exploited for the advantage of the personal life; it must be recognised that the personal I, the ego, must submit to the demands of the life force as a divine being.[5]

The boat of time is the solar boat, but the boat of the goddess is the moon ark, which also appears in Hinduism, another spiritual culture nourished by a great river. It is the moon boat which carries the soul to a new incarnation. The word 'ark' is derived from the Hindi *argha*, which means crescent. In the presence of a great river the new crescent moon would appear from the darkness of invisibility riding as a reflected image upon the waters. Ishtar, another moon goddess, was known as the ship of life. Isis also had a boat festival, *Navigium Isidis*, to celebrate the first sailing of the year. After having come to understand the waters by virtue of a long personal journey, the initiate is ready to embark on the boat of the goddess and receive the gift of immortality. This arises as a self-revelation, a certain knowing, a mystical perception. However, 'The immortality promised by the moon is not an unending life in a golden city, ever renewed life like the moon's own, in which diminishing and dying are as essential as becoming.'[6] This is the initiation into the fullness of the moon. With the full light of the moon comes wisdom, often personified as a dove – a representative of Sophia the Holy Wisdom of the Gnostics. 'In psychological terms, he who attained the realm of the full, or complete, moon has gained knowledge of the unconscious, as past source, origin; he has power in this present world; and has insight into the realm of the future. He has become in a certain sense timeless, he has transcended the limitations of time. He has gained immortality.'[7] Tantric texts also speak of longevity, a knowledge of past, present and future and spiritual liberation as the gifts of the full moon. But this is the moonlight not of Yesod but of Daath, which corresponds to the Throat, not the Sacral Chakra. The Throat Chakra, or the Vishuddi, is named from the word *shuddhi*, meaning to purify. The process referred to is quite specific and unusual. Tantric teachings of both Hinduism and Taoism reveal that there is a small spot near the top of the brain, towards the back of the head, which holds a small amount of liquid secretion. This spot is called the *bindu visargha*. 'It is symbolised by the full moon and the crescent moon together; the full moon represents the point for which individualisation begins. The crescent moon expresses the fact that only a portion of the infinite sahasrara is manifest and perceptible.'[8] Nectar is secreted from the awakened Sahasrara Chakra and collects in the bindu visargha, from where it drops and is stored in a minor psychic point in the upper part of the epiglottis. If the powers of the Throat Chakra have been sufficiently awakened, the nectar has the power to rejuvenate the body, bringing longevity and purifying poisons. Purified by the harmonious interaction of the bindu visargha and Vishuddi Chakra, the nectar descends and penetrates the entire body. Yogis are well known for feats of physical endurance and self-mastery. There are documented cases of yogis being buried underground for 40 days. Tantric texts claim that this nectar reduces the body's need for nourishment. Motoyama found that an awakened Vishuddi Chakra, in conjunction with the *bindu* and *lalana* centres, brings conscious control of metabolism, respiration, food intake and digestion. The awakening of the Vishuddi Chakra is said to bring high-level telepathy, indestructibility, a full knowledge of the sacred texts which expound the law of the universe, the ability to endure without food or drink, and the ability to know past, present and future.

The final initiatory sequence of the moon is completed with the gift of soma, a drink brewed from the moon tree. Its gift is the power of immortality, wisdom and creative inspiration. Who would refuse such blessings? The Rig Veda says:

We've quaffed the Soma bright,
And have immortal grown;
We've entered into light,
And all the Gods have known.

EVOCATION

Welcome to my kingdom. I welcome all who find the bridge of return. I am the Uniting Intelligence. I affirm balance in all things. See that I sit between the opposing pillars of the temple Boaz and Jachin in the house of Solomon the wise. But these also signify the presence of the powers of the

Great Mother and the Great Father, Binah and Chockmah. I am at peace with both the divine parents.

I watch the rise and fall of civilizations both great and small, for my throne is always occupied by one who watches. I see the movement between these two poles as cultures and societies take their stand. I have seen each extreme exercise of power and know that peace comes through harmony and balance. War follows upon the misuse of archetypal power. I am called the Uniting Intelligence. I join what others cannot. I am the peacemaker and the healer, for where there is unity strife cannot prevail. From my withdrawn place, I simply watch and record the unfolding of the totality.

If you would seek the Feminine Mysteries, begin with the moon, my most ancient of signs. Attune yourself to the mysteries of moon and water, ebb and flow. Let these currents and tides bring you into my inner kingdom. Come ride in the boat of millions of years and drink the nectar of the gods. I show you infinity, unbounded possibility and immortality. Drink deep and quench your thirst for the knowing of the heart. I am the Uniting Intelligence. Let body, mind, heart, spirit and soul become as one in the path of being and becoming. My sign is the ship of the desert. I will carry you home.

INTERNALIZATION – THE 13TH PATH: TIPHARETH–KETHER

Construct the Temple of Tiphareth in the creative imagination. Find yourself beside the door of the High Priestess. The Archangel Raphael draws back the tapestry curtain so that you may pass.

You find yourself walking along a narrow path rising between sharp and steep cliffs. The path takes you inescapably to a ravine crossed only by a narrow bridge slung from side to side. If you are determined to make the crossing you must place all your courage and faith in the possibility of a safe passage. There is no other way to proceed. Put your foot upon the bridge and begin. Although it sways from side to side with every step, you will make the crossing.

Once on the other side, the landscape is open and easy. On the skyline at the top of a gentle slope, you see a building. You arrive to find that it is a small temple of white marble with a classical portico. You enter. This temple is not large and your eyes soon adjust to the gentle light. Directly ahead of you, not very far away, a woman is seated on a raised dais. She does not speak but you feel she is fully aware of your presence. She is robed in a gown of soft blue. It falls in folds that gather at her feet like water. Her robe is embroidered with an equal-armed cross upon her breast, and a scroll rests in her lap. She wears a lunar crown displaying the full and partial moons. Blue drapery descends from it, covering her shoulders and arms. Behind her hangs a veil suspended between two columns of black and grey stone. A gentle breeze lifts the veil slightly. You wonder what lies beyond.

Her eyes meet yours and hold your gaze. Though she does not speak, you somehow know that this is the Temple of the Goddess and here is her eternal servant. She beckons you to draw closer to her. You step forwards and once again she meets your gaze. You feel that she is looking deep into your soul, learning everything there is to know about you. Finally she releases her gaze. She rises from her seat and moves towards the veil. With a sweep of her arm, she draws it back to reveal the waters of a vast sea. You step forward. There is nothing but water. But moored directly in front of you is a small boat. There is room for only one person. The boat has a single mast and a sail decorated with the insignia of the full moon.

While waiting on your decision, the High Priestess draws out a chalice from within the folds of her robe and offers it to you. You take the chalice in both hands and drink from it. In your heart you know that this is soma. You drink deeply, recalling its fabled blessings.

Now you are ready to journey in the moon ark. You step into the boat and lie down to rest. This boat will ride under your direction. You easily fall into a deeply contemplative state. In your mind you review your own past, contemplate the present moment and seem to have a sharpened awareness of your future path. Time seems to stand still as you float upon these cosmic waters. When you feel that your journey is complete, just think of going home and the moon ark will make its way back to safety. As your boat nudges the shoreline once more, you notice that night has fallen and a single white star shines more brightly than the others. You disembark. The temple is nowhere to be seen but you know you have travelled far under the aegis of the goddess and her watchful priestess.

When you are ready, make your way back and return to the temple of Tiphareth where you may spend some time in contemplation. Finally, dissolve all images and return to ordinary consciousness.

EXERCITIA SPIRITUALIA

Take the Following as Subjects for Meditation:

- The High Priestess
- Priestess of the Silver Star
- Gimel
- Peace – War
- Sirius
- The Moon.
- Soma
- The Uniting Intelligence

Make Notes on:

- Tarot Trump II, The High Priestess

Visualize the Following and Record your Experiences:

- The Temple of Tiphareth including the Archangel Raphael
- The Journey of the 13th Path

CHAPTER 30

Daath – The Invisible Sephirah

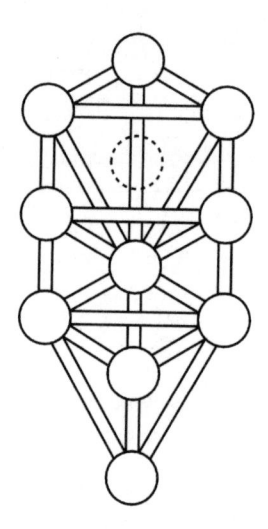

FIGURE 39 THE SEPHIRAH DAATH

TABLE OF CORRESPONDENCES

God-Name: A conjunction of Jehovah and Jehovah Elohim

Archangel: The Archangels of the Cardinal Points

Order of Angels: Silver serpents

Magical Image: A head with two faces looking both ways

Virtue: Detachment, Perfection of Justice and the application of the virtues untainted by personality considerations, Confidence in the Future

Vice: Doubts about the Future, Apathy, Inertia, Cowardice, Pride

Titles: The Invisible Sephirah, the Hidden or Unrevealed Cosmic Mind, the Mystical Sephirah, The Upper Room

Spiritual Experience : Vision across the Abyss

Mundane Chakra: Sothis or Sirius

Personal Chakra: The Vishuddi or Throat Chakra.

Text: None

Colour in Atziluth: Lavender

Colour in Briah: Silver Grey

Colour in Yetzirah: Pure Purple

Colour in Assiah: Grey, flecked Yellow

Symbols: The Condemned Cell, The Prism, The Empty Room, The Sacred Mountain, A Grain of Corn, The Absence of any Symbol

Tarot Cards: None

COMMENTARY

Daath, or Knowledge, is unique among the Sephiroth – historically, it was not considered a full Sephirah. It first arose as the conjunction between Wisdom and Understanding, Binah and Chockmah. Accordingly, the God-Name assigned to Daath is a conjunction of Jehovah and Jehovah Elohim, representing a conjunction between the God-Names assigned to Binah and Chockmah as the meeting point of the archetypal male and female forces. The title Knowledge also carries the connotation of knowing through intimacy rather than a mere abstract body of knowledge. The Sepher Yetzirah emphatically states, 'Ten is the number of the ineffable Sephiroth, ten not nine, and not eleven.' Daath remains as an invisible Sephirah. It is not always represented on the Tree and in contrast with the other Sephiroth it is represented by a broken line which implies a liminal nature. Daath's status among the Sephiroth is therefore unique.

The Invisible Sephirah

Modern research has led to sufficient evidence to justify its [Daath] being regarded as a Sephirah in its own right, but in rather an especial way. It is thus termed the invisible Sephirah.

Gareth Knight, *A Practical Guide to Qabalistic Symbolism*

Daath takes its station astride the Abyss which separates the Supernal Triangle from the rest of the Tree. This placement adds to its unique nature. Like the once unknown black holes of space and time, Daath represents a place of transition and transmutation. The Magical Image assigned to Daath is that of a head looking both ways. Like Janus, the god of January, the twin faces see the past and the present. But unlike the Roman god Janus, Daath presides not at the threshold of a simple year but at the threshold of Being and Becoming. The two faces of Daath look both upwards towards the Supernal levels and downwards into manifestation simultaneously. The spiritual vision of Daath is the Vision across the Abyss. This too implies looking both ways, seeing ahead into forbidden territory while holding on to the safety of a known shore.

The extended journey through the Tree of Life is punctuated by two gulfs in continuity. The first of these precedes Tiphareth. This gulf is called the Veil of Paroketh. It represents the great leap required in order to awaken the qualities and powers of the heart before the mystical and universalized consciousness of Tiphareth is attainable. The second Abyss separates the Supernal Triangle of the Tree from the Ethical and Moral Triangle or the Supreme Mysteries from the Greater Mysteries. This is not a gulf that should be negotiated. The Spiritual Experience of Daath is the Vision across the Abyss. This is not the journey into the Abyss. Entering the Abyss is regarded as a one-way journey which dismantles even the Individuality. Like the black hole, Daath is a dangerous place. Not even light can escape the black hole. The event horizon is a fatal zone. The black hole offers no escape, transformation is lethal. Daath perhaps represents a quantum leap from which there can be no return. The Supernal Triangle represented by Kether, Chockmah and Binah is a transpersonal domain of cosmic creation. The Abyss symbolizes the gulf between the hidden forces of creation and the fabric of creation.

Daath is called the Unrevealed Cosmic Mind. This is a place of cosmic dimension and infinite horizon. Daath is not a Sephirah where the human mind can feel comforted or comfortable. Gareth Knight suggests that genuine contact with the forces of Daath is dangerous. 'Explosive would be the contact with the universal subconscious containing the whole past history and inner stresses of the Logos.'[1] It is simply not possible for the human mind to know the full history of the cosmos in which we have a part. Daath is called Knowledge. This is an infinite and unbounded realm of discovery. Our knowledge of the cosmos has grown by geometric progression in the last century. Yet by comparison we know only a little of the cosmic story. But our desire to know, to reach out and to understand is a remarkable and constant human quality.

Despite not being considered a full Sephirah in the past, the unworldly and cosmic qualities represented by Daath have appeared in our time. Daath is the Sephirah of Knowledge and it is the quest for knowledge that has taken humanity into space. Daath's cosmic qualities now make sense in an age familiar with space travel and the whole genre of science fiction and science fact that has accompanied this forward march into the unknown. In an age without this metaphor, the terrain ascribed to Daath would remain beyond grasp. But metaphors from deep space provide useful analogies. Even before the space age had taken hold, Aleister Crowley suggested that Daath might best be considered as not of the same dimension as the other Sephiroth. Such ideas now have current reference points in the realms of space exploration, whether as fact or fiction. Other dimensions and the possibility of other life forms have become commonplace and popular ideas. With recent advances in cosmology and the technologies available to view the physical reality of space, the wonder of the intergalactic universe becomes steadily more apparent. One of the most surprising and astonishing recent discoveries is that of 'dark matter'. Although it is now estimated that as at least 90 per cent of the universe consists of dark matter, it remains an unknown and enigmatic mystery. This vast force, like the hidden bulk of an iceberg, has powerful gravitational effects and may possibly become a future force in cosmic contraction. Daath is the Sephirah Knowledge, which is infinite and unbounded as dark matter itself. Cosmological data has a unique value in establishing mind-reeling statistics which place earthly life in a vast panorama of cosmic creation. Cosmic metaphors and analogies open the mind to the possibility of totally new phenomena. Danah Zohar, author of *The Quantum Society* (with Ian Marshall) and *The Quantum Self,* finds in the language of contemporary physics excellent vocabulary for new models of social and cultural vision: 'Physics is a universal language. The knowledge that it gives us and the images and metaphors associated with this knowledge are the common currency of every people on earth.'[2] The extraordinary phenomena of creation are to be found not just in the micro world of particle physics but in the macro world of cosmology. The strange and undiscovered realm of intergalactic space provides a paradigm in which to set the enigmatic and invisible Sephirah Daath which is Knowledge. Factual knowledge changes the models that we hold of reality and of ourselves. We are at the moment in the throes of a scientific and biological revolution which will continue the process of revision and redefinition.

DARK MATTER

Take the idea of dark matter as a theme for meditation.

'Recent estimates of the amount of dark matter in the universe vary from around 90 to 99 per cent. In other words, the familiar kinds of matter we know about make up only 1 to 10 per cent of this total. The magnitude of this mystery is staggering. It is as if physics has discovered the unconscious. Just as the conscious mind floats, as it were, on the surface of the sea of unconscious mental processes, so the physical world floats on a cosmic ocean of dark matter. This dark matter has the archetypal power of the dark, destructive Mother; it is like Kali, whose very name means "black". If there is more than a critical amount of dark matter, then the cosmic expansion will gradually come to an end, and the universe will begin to contract again, pulled in by gravitation until everything is ultimately devoured in a terminal implosion, the opposite of the Big Bang – the Big Crunch.'

Rupert Sheldrake, *The Rebirth of Nature*

The Quantum Leap

We live in a quantum universe; everything – the stars,
the planets, the carbon atoms, life and, if part of the
physical world, consciousness itself – obeys the laws of
quantum mechanics.

Danah Zohar and Ian Marshall, *The Quantum Society*

Daath is a unique Sephirah. Unlike other Sephiroth which correspond to
recognizable aspects of the human psyche, Daath offers no refuge on a
human scale. It is too close to the Abyss and too closely related to the
Supernal Triangle to be of human dimension. Daath has little relevance for
mortal life. Its scope is simply beyond human imagination. Although it is
possible to touch upon this region and to understand its purpose in
meditative contemplation, this is not a place for mortal minds. Gareth Knight
describes Daath as the sphere where 'the Supernal Planning of the whole
Universe and the shining goals of the future is held'.[3] Daath is said to be
Yesod upon a higher arc. Like Yesod, which may be likened to the astral
mirror on which images from the akashic records may be glimpsed, Daath
too is imprinted with the knowledge of the past and future. The third Virtue
of Daath is Confidence in the Future. This is the infinite future stretching
into aeons and great ages still to come, not the conceivable tomorrow or
just another year or even the inconceivable possibility of another century. Yet
the Virtue of Daath is the certain knowing that all is working out as it
should. From the limited and engaged perspective of daily life, this Virtue
often proves elusive, most especially as the timescale represented at Daath is
not one of human dimension but of the unfolded future aeons still to come.
Like intergalactic space, Daath is not a realm where mortal minds can feel
comfortable. Its cosmic scale and totally impersonal nature does not offer
warmth to the human spirit.

The utterly impersonal nature of Daath is emphasized by its three Virtues.
Its first Virtue is Detachment, its second is the Perfection of Justice and its
third is Confidence in the Future. Its opposing Vice is Doubt about the
Future. The human mind cannot conceive such timescales or such dimensions. Daath is not a place where accommodation can be made for the
mortal mind. Taken together these three qualities represent complete
detachment from the karmic wheel. It is attachment which creates karma
and sows the seed of future incarnation. True detachment, free from karma,

creates detachment from the Wheel of Rebirth itself. The second virtue, The Perfection of Justice, suggests that despite every indication to the contrary, all of manifest creation below the abyss is an externalization of karma on a vast scale. Moreover, the final Virtue, Confidence in the Future, suggests that the hidden forces of karma will continue to drive creation from within. At a time of international tension, confidence in the future is always difficult to muster.

The symbols assigned to Daath speak of a separation and isolation which might also be understood in terms of the loneliness of space. The grain of corn, the condemned cell, the empty room and the sacred mountain – each symbol indicates the sense of separation which Daath brings.

Grain has a long history as a symbol of renewal and rebirth. The ear of wheat conveyed the understanding of immortal life to the initiates of Eleusis. The corn sheaf left standing in the field at harvest time represents the spirit of the corn; future life is preserved and honoured. Sprouting corn forms the epiphany at the heart of the Osirian Mysteries. As the green-faced god of vegetation and renewal, Osiris is also the god of the underworld and lord of the land of the dead. But the single grain of corn assigned to Daath holds no renewing promise. Its solitary state is mournful. When it is ground, which is the necessary fate of grain, no seed corn will remain. Nothing will remain – flour and husk will be separate. The grain of corn is but a single nub.

The condemned cell is a frightening and disturbing image representing the fate of the Individuality which is dissolved by the crossing of the Abyss. Once absorbed beyond the Abyss, the process of becoming through the experience of incarnation is needless. There will be no further journeying into possibility and circumstance. The Individuality as the reflected blueprint for the Greater Countenance has no further purpose.

The symbolism of the empty room is perhaps less frightening, but it is nevertheless a place of extreme isolation and separation from others. Daath brings a detachment which can be inhuman since it is concerned not with day-to-day events or everyday human experiences but with the ebb and flow of cosmic tides.

The sacred mountain is perhaps the most comforting of all Daath's symbols for it has an earthy familiarity. The sacred mountain is a place of quest and endeavour. It represents the upward journey and signifies the process of vigil and retreat. Gaining the summit brings a unique moment of clarity and vision. After the experience of summit, descent is the only possibility. Moses received the Ten Commandments on Mount Sinai. It is also perhaps possible that he received the essence of Kabbalah there too. The image of the sacred mountain makes it clear that this is the point beyond which the mortal mind cannot travel except through ultimate dissolution.

Each of Daath's symbols expresses its solitary and isolating impact. But this unremitting collection of sorrowful images is redeemed at least by the symbolism of the prism. When refracted through a prism, white light splits into its seven component colours and forms a rainbow. This image appears in the lower reaches of the Tree as the *antakarana*, the rainbow bridge which symbolizes the seven levels of consciousness represented by the chakras and also by the seven great rays. Perhaps this sevenfold blueprint represents a fundamental theme of creation which Daath receives and holds in its capacity as the Unrevealed Cosmic Mind.

Having made clear the strange and disturbing qualities associated with Daath, there will always be intrepid travellers who seek absolute reality with complete determination and unswerving determination. Aleister Crowley did not seem deterred by the possibility of the abyss. He even called himself 'The Babe of the Abyss', indicating that he felt, mistakenly or not, that he had ventured into these realms. Gareth Knight suggests that 'The safest way to work with Daath is through the Isis mythology for this relates to the bright positive side of Daath.'⁴ In other words, Isis provides a mediating figure who walks safely in both the human and the cosmic world. She is a wife and mother but also carries the title of Queen of Heaven. Like the face which looks both ways, she is both a cosmic and human figure. As Queen of Heaven she reigns in the upper world. As mortal wife and mother she walks in the lower world. As a winged goddess Isis represents the power of spiritual flight and liberation. Gareth Knight says of her wings, 'their influence and meaning could be "felt" and still can be'.⁵ She therefore represents the possibility of safe passage. Isis is intimately related to the star Sirius. Many words have been written about Sirius, the dog star and the brightest star in the sky. The Tarot Trump of The High Priestess is assigned to the 13th Path which crosses the Abyss. This is the safest route. It does not move through the Abyss but passes over it. Yet it is not possible to tread the 13th Path without touching upon cosmic reverberations and eternal realities. But under the guidance of the Priestess of the Silver Star it is possible to still keep a firm foothold:

> The form of Isis can be built up in the Daath colours or alternatively in blue, for the force has much to do with the 'Blue Ray' of the higher mind. For general purposes the best way is to visualise a huge pillar of Egyptian sculpture and within it the clear-cut lines of the

goddess seated upon her throne, with vast wings that would encircle the Universe; on her head the Solar disk of Sirius. The column should tower up to the uttermost limits of the Universe and equally penetrate to the uttermost depths.[6]

This image unifies the above and the below; it connects the heights with the depths. Her encircling wings both protect and encompass. She is a wisdom goddess seated upon the throne of wisdom in the kingdom of creation. This is the inner nature of the human quest to understand the cosmos and our place in it. Knowledge has a most valuable place, but only wisdom may cross the abyss.

EVOCATION

Welcome to my kingdom which is hidden and veiled from mortal knowing. I hold the knowing of that which has passed since time itself first began. I preside over what has been and what will be. My realm is not for you. Though you may seek to unravel my mysteries and fathom my nature in your rightful quest to know the origins and roots of all, your knowledge is but an abstraction of what has passed. I preside over time unimaginable and unknowable. I preside over possibilities beyond your conception. I stand at the doorway of the eternal being and endless becoming. I look both ways and see into both realms. But to you I offer neither substance nor solidity, safety nor security. My realm is not for the incarnate. I can give you few familiar analogies to ease your questing mind, nor can I offer you anything that you need. This realm is not for mortal minds. Mine is an invisible realm of many possible futures and multiple intended outcomes. I am unity undisturbed by differentiation. I am knowledge undivided by separation. My realm is that of the eternal present. This kingdom is not for you. Remain on your side of the Abyss and contemplate the infinite from the safety of the mortal mind. Contemplate the Vision across the Abyss but let your journey cease. This realm is not for you. Here the seeds which shall become, arise like sparks. The shape of tomorrow is already here. Karma arises. The Perfection of Justice prevails. The cosmic mind shall keep its secrets. You have no power in this realm. This realm is not for you. Return then to places where you are powerful and well received.

INTERNALIZATION – THE TEMPLE
OF DAATH

Construct the Temple of Daath in the creative imagination. You awaken from a deep and long sleep to find yourself in a perfectly empty room. It has neither table nor chairs, no bedding or adornment. High up in one of the walls is a narrow window. Worst of all it has no door of any kind. Panic sets in immediately as you search for an escape route. Soon you realize that there is no way out and begin to calm yourself. You wonder how you have come to be here and what purpose this place might have. You begin to retrace the steps of your own spiritual journey from wondering to waking, from awareness to amazement, from the specific towards the infinite. Such thoughts and memories bring a strong sense of calm; you realize that whatever happens in this place is also part of that same journey. You put your worries aside to the best of your ability and affirm your confidence in the unfolding of all events in this place.

Time passes and you find yourself missing the sound of human voices, the warmth of laughter, the touch of another person. Allow your mind to dwell on the simple pleasures and joys of being human, remember friends and family, fellow travellers and teachers. If you had the power to choose between staying in this place of separation, waiting upon some unknown event and transformation, and being transported to the earthly realm of experience with all its conflicts and difficulties, which would you choose? Reflect on this question deeply and come to a true decision of the heart. Be patient and calm, for you have no power here to affect the outcome. Perhaps another mind much greater than your own watches and knows when action shall be precipitated. Meanwhile, use this timeless place to meditate on time, even while you have no sense of the passing of time. The isolation of this place challenges everything that you are and have become. It challenges your sense of self and purpose, your faith and even your adherence to the path of truth. Doubts and fears arise to tease and torment your equanimity. But face each fear with certainty and quell each worry with confidence. As you conquer your own fears one by one, you become even more confident that there is some unrevealed purpose in your presence here. Now you are ready to both accept and receive the meaning of this place.

The room unexpectedly seems to be growing lighter, as if the sun were rising just outside. Light begins to stream into the room through the narrow window. Suddenly the rising light strikes a prism invisibly imbedded in the glass of the window. Immediately a rainbow light is cast into the room.

It spreads out across the floor. You sit in its path and the colours play upon your body. This is a moment of sheer delight and wonder. You want this moment to last indefinitely, even as you know that it must pass. Yet while it lasts you feel bathed in celestial light and have a sense of great blessing. All too soon the white light passes the prismatic window and the colours are withdrawn. Once again you are alone, but you have been changed by your own meditation and blessed by the seven great lights. You lie down to rest and you know with absolute certainty that when you awaken you will be restored to the parameters of your earthly life, for you have affirmed total confidence in the workings of the future.

When you are ready to leave, dissolve all images and return to ordinary consciousness.

EXERCITIA SPIRITUALIA

Take the Following as Subjects for Meditation:
- Jehovah – Jehovah Elohim
- Archangels of the Cardinal points: Uriel, Gabriel, Michael, Raphael
- Serpents
- A head with two faces looking both ways
- Sirius
- The Abyss
- The Vision across the Abyss
- The Invisible Sephirah, the Hidden or Unrevealed Cosmic Mind, the Mystical Sephirah, The Upper Room
- The Condemned Cell, The Prism, The Empty Room, The Sacred Mountain, A Grain of Corn

Contemplate the Following Questions and Record your Responses:
- How do the qualities of Detachment, Perfection of Justice and Confidence in the Future operate in your life?
- How do the qualities of Doubt about the Future, Apathy, Inertia, Cowardice and Pride operate in your life?
- How does the nature of Daath relate to the Throat Chakra?
- What other correspondences can you relate to Daath?

Visualize the Following and Record your Experience:
- The Journey to the Temple of Daath

CHAPTER 31

The Twelfth Path: Binah–Kether

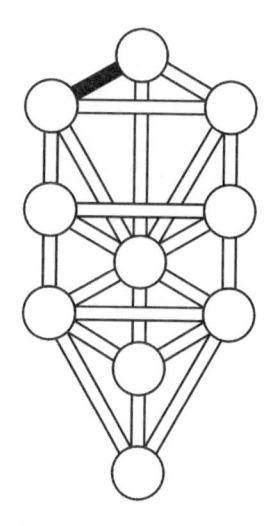

FIGURE 40 THE 12TH PATH:

BINAH–KETHER

TAROT TRUMP I,

THE MAGICIAN

TABLE OF CORRESPONDENCES

The Journey: Tarot Trump I, The Magician,
    The Magus of Power
Key: The letter Beth, meaning a house
Double Letter: Life – Death
Spiritual Significance: Mercury
Colour in Atziluth: Yellow
Colour in Briah: Purple
Colour in Yetzirah: Grey
Colour in Assiah: Indigo flecked Violet
Text: The Intelligence of Transparency

COMMENTARY

The Twelfth Path is The Intelligence of Transparency because it is that species of magnificence called Chazchazit, which is named the place whence issues the visions of those seeing in apparitions.

The 12th Path connects the first Sephirah, Kether, with the third Sephirah, Binah. It parallels the 11th Path between Kether and Chockmah. As Chockmah is found at the head of the Pillar of Force, so the 12th Path is found at the head of the Pillar of Form. This Path connects Kether, the source of the Pillar of Consciousness, with Binah, the head of the Pillar of Severity. It links Kether, the source of creation, with the organizing principles of Binah. As part of the Supernal Triangle, this is a Path of cosmic dimension and transpersonal principle.

The Path to Wisdom

We need to develop not only the wisdom that understands conventional reality, especially the causes of happiness and suffering, but also the wisdom that understands ultimate reality, because it is only then that we can eliminate the ignorance that is the root of all suffering, and its causes, and achieve liberation.

Lama Zopa, *The Ultimate Healing*

The 12th Path between Kether and Binah parallels the 11th Path between Kether and Chockmah. The 12th Path leads to the Supernal Mother. The 11th Path leads to the Supernal Father. The 11th Path leads from Kether to Chokmah, which is Wisdom. The 12th Path leads from Kether to Binah, which is Understanding. The Sephirah Binah is designated as 'the Foundation of the Primordial wisdom'. The 11th and 12th Paths from Kether jointly bring wisdom into existence. The 12th Path is assigned to the Intelligence of Transparency. It makes visible what is veiled. It brings the consciousness of transparency to bear. Vision is clear, clarity is achieved. The Intelligence of Transparency is described as 'that species of magnificence called Chazchazit', meaning seership. This is the 'place whence issue the visions of those seeing in apparitions'. On this Path it becomes possible to see clearly. Seership, the ability to see with the eyes of inner vision, is described as 'that species of magnificence'. In other words, this level of seership is rare and magnificent. This is not the personalized clairvoyance of Yesod, not even the universalized vision of Tiphareth, but the highest of all visionary possibilities which permits a direct seeing into the nature of ultimate reality.

The 11th Path of the Scintillating Intelligence is described as the curtain before the Face of the Cause of Causes. The image of the curtain and the idea of a window suggested by the quality of transparency are closely related. The curtain and the window can be opened or closed. The open curtain and the open window permit light and vision. The closed curtains conceal light, the closed window seals space. The 11th and 12th Paths open directly onto Kether on the Path of Ascent or directly onto creation from the Path of Descent. Together, the Intelligence of Transparency and the Scintillating Intelligence bring the *Lux Occulta* into appearance. Kether is called the Hidden Intelligence, it is the primal Lux Occulta, the hidden light. The Primordial Point of manifestation cannot be perceived directly except by the reflecting mirrors of the created universe. The 12th Path reveals or makes clear what is unrevealed and hidden within Kether. The 12th Path connects the Hidden Intelligence assigned to Kether with the Sanctifying Intelligence assigned to Binah. The notion of the Hidden but Admirable potency of Kether inspires a sense of both reverence and wonder. Yet, though 'hidden' and 'occult' should convey the same meaning, it is clear that the two words have come to assume quite different meanings. The term 'occult' has become loaded with negative associations. It is ironic that the term has become one which arouses fear and misunderstanding when it is assigned to Kether, the crown of all creation. This journey renders the occult, and occluded or hidden laws transparent. Binah renders them sacred or sanctified. This is the essence of the Hermetic quest. This Path is assigned to Tarot Trump I, The Magician, The Magus of Power.

Every society has produced its own tradition of magical practitioners, either covertly or overtly depending on the value given to the magical arts in their many guises. This in turn derives from a view of the world. The magical world view has often found itself at odds with the religious world view. Placing ultimate authority with the figure of God takes authority away from individuals not sanctioned by the power structure created in God's name. Both religion and magic seek to tread the same territory, which is that of ultimate reality, but each takes a differing view of where acceptable boundaries lie. Where the boundary is placed is a matter of cultural choice. The boundary between religion and magic has often become blurred. Walking in the shared overlapping space can be dangerous. Organized religion requires group conformity, shared and agreed doctrines, common and widespread observances. As a hierarchical organization, the structure represents the needs of the many, not the few. But solitary and non-conforming minds – the few – also arise and seek reality through individual and independent ideas. These are the two faces of religion: the exoteric and the esoteric. The exoteric aspect of religion is the outer, public, structured face which provides the organizational body, the doctrinal beliefs and the prescribed forms of worship. The esoteric aspect of religion is the inner, private, interior, experiential aspect of religious practice which draws its vitality from personal spiritual practice. There is often some overlap between these two divisions in a single faith tradition. Ultimately, the Path to Wisdom can only be born through engagement with deep personal practice.

The 12th Path connects Kether, the Crown and source, with Binah, Understanding. The 12th Path connects Kether, the Lux Occulta, with Binah, the Foundation of the Primordial Wisdom. It is through Understanding that the Hidden Intelligence within Kether becomes articulated and known. This is the way of the Western Mystery Tradition, which includes the Hermetic Path. The quest to understand and sanctify what is hidden and admirable has produced a tradition of mystical philosophers and philosophies – including Plato, Pythagoras, Kabbalah, Hermetic Magic and the Rosicrucian current. In searching to understand nature's law, as the foundation of wisdom, the West has produced a Perennial, Timeless and Ageless Wisdom.

As the laws of physics are few in number, so too are the basic principles of the wisdom tradition. The Magical Injunctions to Dare, to Know, to Will and to Be Silent encapsulate the Hermetic ethos and still provide entry into the tradition. Placing these injunctions in a historical context gives real meaning to their application. When certain areas of intellectual enquiry were restricted or unacceptable, the first injunction – to dare – was required to break through the prevailing taboo. To stand against the cultural norms called for intellectual bravery, non-conformity and independence of thought. In an age of sanction and religious authority, this quest may even have entailed some personal risk. The desire to know, which expresses a thirst for knowledge and learning, might also be a liability in a time when ideas are controlled and patrolled. Owning particular books, expressing certain views or upholding divergent interests might indeed court danger, punishment, excommunication or, ultimately, even death. The exercise of personal will implies choice and discrimination, which is the Virtue of Malkuth and the entry point into the spiritual path. This betokens a willingness to follow an inner calling regardless of the prevailing opinion and speaks of the power to engage and motivate the individual will without the support or validation of others. The fourth injunction needs no explanation. In an age when charges of heresy could be levied, silence was the policy of the wise. In today's open and liberal intellectual climate these injunctions no longer carry the implicit threat that once made magic a dangerous and lonely pursuit. The Western Path of Wisdom throughout history has engaged pioneering thinkers, intellectual rebels and brilliant scholars. But history also reveals the boundaries of the mainstream mindset, for some especially bold travellers became casualties of the prevailing prejudice.

The House of Wisdom

> Happy is the man that findeth wisdom, and the man
> that getteth understanding.

Proverbs 3: 13

The 12th Path is assigned to the letter Beth, meaning a house. As a Double Letter it carries the additional meaning of Life–Death. As the Path which leads to the Foundation of the Primordial Wisdom, the imagery of house building seems entirely appropriate. Binah is the Sephirah of form and organization. It sanctifies the Primordial Wisdom made transparent through the 12th Path. In other words, Binah enshrines the laws which render the hidden visible, in a form that can be more plainly recognized and understood. Just as the house builder constructs a house from the imagined concept of a house, so Binah provides principles and structures which permit organization.

Curiously, architectural symbolism has deeply entered the metaphorical language of the Western Mystery Tradition. As a holistic enterprise which engages mind, body and soul through planning, construction and vision, architecture has long been connected with Natural Wisdom. As a symbol, the house has a great deal to yield. In contrast to symbolism related to the natural world, the house represents the conscious action of human abilities. As a symbol for the self, the house provides a wealth of allegories and images.

The edifice speaks of appearances and the public face of the persona. Its foundations signify preparation and the ability to endure and survive crisis. The basement suggests secrets and the private world of the unconscious. An attic conveys undiscovered territory and long-forgotten memories. Shared rooms convey relationships. The state of repair and level of maintained care represent self-esteem and feelings of personal worth. Even architectural features such as doors, windows and stairs offer a symbolic vocabulary. The window, coincidentally symbolized by the letter Heh, symbolizes the quality of transparency, two-way vision and the admission of light. A doorway symbolizes crossing a threshold and a change of status. An open door signifies a state of welcome and openness; when closed it signifies patience or challenge. A staircase signifies progression and movement. The developmental phases and physical processes of construction also offer a rich symbolic language. Planning demands forethought, imagination and the precise skills of measurement. It is most often a shared venture of teamwork and diverse skills. The architectural metaphor works so well perhaps because architecture combines both practical and precise skill and imaginative and creative ideas. Its processes and methods, scope and results provide a rich symbolic vocabulary to express the work of consciously constructing the self modelled on a chosen blueprint. This is a symbolic language which perfectly fits all processes which seek to impose order on chaos, organization on disorder and structure on fluidity. Even the tools of construction can take on symbolic connotations. Metaphors of preparation and labour naturally lend themselves to the task of reconstruction.

The metaphor of planned construction is nowhere more evident in a spiritual system than in Freemasonry, which created an entire initiatory system based on the metaphors, images and symbolism of building and construction. The mundane tools of construction – compass, trowel and tracing board – were transformed into spiritual tools for reconstructing the self. The workaday system of apprentice and master took on a new level of meaning under the watchful eye of the divine architect.

Though probably a fading force as a movement for psycho-spiritual growth at the dawn of the 21st century, Freemasonry has played a significant historical and cultural role as an initiating process for individuals with a keen sense of self-realization. Freemasonry spread quickly throughout Europe and the American colonies at a time of mainstream religious stagnation. Freemasonry incorporated many Kabbalistic elements in a threefold degree system comparable to the three triangles represented on the Tree of Life. Its rituals and paraphernalia may seem somewhat theatrical to current sensibilities but Freemasonry modelled itself in part upon the initiatory vehicle of the ancient world, sacred drama. During its most vigorous phase Freemasonry played a part in shaping history, most notably in the founding of the United States. Both Benjamin Franklin and George Washington were Freemasons. The one-dollar bill bears all the hallmarks of masonic symbolism. The pyramid and the eye of the Great Seal of the United States are undoubtedly symbols derived from the Western Mystery Tradition, which owed some allegiance to the Mysteries of Egypt, whether real or imagined. The eagle is a symbol of spiritual liberation and freedom. The paired opposites, the laurel of peace and arrows of war, express a Kabbalistic sense of balance and specifically belong to the Double Letter Gimel which is assigned to the 13th Path. The American constitution with its separation of powers designed to create a structure of mutual checks and balances may even be rooted in the Tree of Life. 'It is not unreasonable to think that the framers of the constitution, serious thinkers of their time, designed it to reflect their understanding of natural law; nor is it unreasonable to think that they might design a government which, like the cathedrals of an earlier age, provided instruction to the individual citizen about his own nature.'[1]

It remains curious that the historical influence of the Primordial Wisdom has been so easily forgotten. Hermetic principles have been instrumental in the cultural, political and spiritual shaping of Western civilization, but this is mostly unknown or ignored. The Renaissance was inspired by a redis-covery of the ancient past and its perceived wisdom. This is a value system which is philosophical and mystical but also practical, as the flowering of Renaissance culture proved. At times its most practical concepts were even being poured into a Christian mould, almost seamlessly. The Age of Scholasticism drew relatively painlessly on a Platonic and Neo-Platonic world view which resulted in an early and forgotten renaissance of the 12th and 13th centuries. This early movement for spiritual renewal culminated in the building of Chartres Cathedral, which stands as a testament to the practical elements of a mystical philosophy. Sacred architecture by its nature provides the perfect vehicle for the expression of metaphysical ideas and mathematical constants. In the universal tradition of sacred architecture, the Cathedral at Chartres expresses a Perennial Wisdom in cannon and measure. Building God's house on earth has long been a passion for humanity. From the temples and pyramids of Egypt to the cathedrals of Europe, the desire is unchanged – to represent the sacred in stone. This relationship between physical construction and mystical philosophy gives rise to a particular view of geometry and mathematics which itself becomes a secret teaching.

It remains entirely plausible that such a mystical tradition of measure was handed down through the medieval masons' guilds, generation after generation, from master to apprentice. Currently, architecture and mystical philosophy are the estranged partners in a long-forgotten marriage. However, some contemporary architects – Keith Critchlow, for example – are restoring architecture to the Perennial Wisdom where it has always belonged.

The house represented by the letter Beth expresses the organizing nature of the Sephirah Binah. The reconstructed and personalized house of self is the goal of the Mysteries, the goal of psychosynthesis and the proper goal of all religious or spiritual systems. This is the nature of the 12th Path as the conduit for the 'will to be' which serves to translate pure being into the processes of becoming. As a Double Letter, Beth symbolizes the polarity of life and death. When the house of self has been designed and built by others, it becomes a prison cell, a place of living death. It cannot become a home. Only when the house of self represents the authentic and true nature can it become a home for the spirit and the house of life.

THE HOUSE OF SELF

Imagine that you are out walking in a wood on a pleasant day. Your path leads you to a clearing and there you see a house. First approach and take in as many details as possible. Does it have a discernible style or belong to a definite historical period? Assess how well it is cared for. If you wish, knock and then open the front door. Describe everything that you see in as much detail as possible. How many rooms can you find? Perhaps someone will show you around.

To finish your exploration, leave the house and return the way you came. When you are ready, dissolve all images and return to waking consciousness. Does the image of the house that spontaneously arises tell you anything about yourself?

The Way of the Magician

You have asked me to train you in High Magic's Way.
Why do you wish to be trained? What is your real
motive? Do not make the mistake of thinking that this
can be answered without a good deal of careful thought.

W.E. Butler, *Apprenticed to Magic*

The 12th Path is assigned to Tarot Trump I, The Magician. This figure represents the universal tradition of magic makers – whether shamans, sorcerers, shape-shifters, wise men, wizards or magi – who populate both fact and fiction as characters with the power to make things happen. Both kings and commoners have sought the assistance of magical practitioners in matters of importance. The trials and tribulations of life have often called out for the gifts of prophecy, far-seeing, vision, or even friendly intervention. This is the Path of the Magician, who in the highest guise consciously assists the forces of evolution by working in harmony with the laws of the universe rendered transparent through this path. The figure of the Magician, like the Fool, wears two robes – one of white and one of red. These are alchemical colours signifying the process of transformation implicit to this path. The white robe of spirit is covered by the red robe of the body. The two are bound by a jewelled serpent girdle holding its tail in its mouth. The serpent is a familiar image in the Western Mystical Tradition. Symbolizing the depth of understanding of the underworld and the constant process of growth through the shedding of its skin, the serpent represents both wisdom and initiatory journey. Moreover, the serpent of wisdom holds its tail in its mouth as a symbol of silence, the fourth magical injunction. The Magician stands with one hand uplifted towards heaven while the other points downwards to the earth. This gesture clearly states the Hermetic maxim 'As Above, So Below'. Like a lightning conductor, the person of the Magician conducts the supramundane forces into the world with conscious intent. The lily and rose together symbolize the Macrocosm and the Microcosm. This is a magician in the Hermetic tradition seeking to unite the Great Above with the Great Below. The Magician is also called the Magus of Power. This is a figure of authority and knowledge, best exemplified perhaps by John Dee, mathematician, astrologer, collector of manuscripts and books, historian of science, consultant to mariners, speaker with spirits and adviser to Queen Elizabeth I.

This Path is assigned to Mercury, who is also assigned to the Sephirah Hod which acts as the first introduction to the Hermetic Path. Under the aegis of Mercury, this is a journey into the mind through learning and knowledge. Hermetic magic is not the sympathetic magic of instinct but the conscious intent to seek out nature's own rule book as a basis for magical intervention.

The figure of the Magician stands behind the table where the symbols of becoming are laid. These are the four elemental weapons of rod, cup, sword and pentacle, signifying the four elements Fire, Water, Air and Earth.

These are also assigned to Malkuth, the Kingdom, where the elemental qualities take physical form. The four elemental weapons represent the fourfold symbolism which runs through Kabbalah linking the Great Above to the Great Below. The cup, rod, sword and pentacle also represent the four fixed signs of the zodiac, which are elsewhere depicted as the lion, eagle, bull and man. These are the four worlds of creation: Atziluth, Briah, Yetzirah and Assiah. These are the personal qualities of being: spirit, mind, feelings and body. On the path of self-realization these qualities of being provide the alchemical laboratory where the work of reconstructing the self is founded. This Trump is an image of the Great Work. It commences here on the 12th Path in descent and is completed on the 12th Path in ascent.

EVOCATION

I am called the Magus of Power. Welcome to my realm, which is that of the eternal and infinite. It is in my nature to seek ultimate truth and ultimate reality. This is my quest. I dare to wonder, to contemplate and to search for the ultimate truth of the nature of being. Others are content with second-hand beliefs and doctrines which bring comfort, but my quest is more direct and cannot be assuaged through words alone. I seek to know what is true that I may honour and tend to it like a precious gift, for no gift is more precious than naked truth. Others are appeased with ideas of truth but I seek to know truth face to face. My desire for truth is great and all-consuming. It galvanizes my will so that all actions are subsumed into my quest. No man may stop me or stand in my way for it is my divine right to exercise my will in the cause of my choice. I seek wisdom with understanding and understanding with wisdom, yet my knowledge is silent. For others tread another way and would prevent my journey if they knew but how. Yet what I have seen and learned and understood will not be lost but encoded and left as clue and cypher for those who want to follow in my footsteps. I am the Magus of Power.

INTERNALIZATION – THE 12TH PATH: BINAH–KETHER

Construct the Temple of Binah in the creative imagination. Find yourself standing beside the door of the Magician. The Archangel Tzaphkiel draws back the tapestry curtain so that you may pass.

You emerge into the brilliant blaze of an unearthly yellow light. This is not a familiar place and you wonder what you will encounter here so far away from home. You begin to explore this strange world. Ahead, not too far away, you see a table standing in a bower of flowers set with objects. You draw closer. There is no one around, so you have a chance to look without being interrupted. You see a sword, a rod, a chalice and a disk inscribed with a pentagram. Though there is a strong temptation to handle the objects, you overcome this desire and continue to look instead. The edge of the table is inscribed with astrological symbols. Roses and lilies intertwine in abundance at the foot of the table and more roses hang like a living curtain above it. The air is filled with a wonderful scent.

Suddenly you have the feeling that you are being watched. You feel the intensity of an unseen gaze and hear the sound of a soft footfall. You are not alone. Now a gentle hand touches your shoulder with a reassuring and welcoming gesture. You immediately turn to see the face of a young man smiling at you. Now he walks around to the far side of the table so that you are opposite each other. You have the opportunity to look at him more closely. He wears two robes, an inner one of white and an outer one of red. Around his waist he wears a jewelled serpent girdle of glistening blue stones. You have come to know that this is the Wise Serpent of the Mysteries. Its tail is in its mouth as a sign of silence; its renewing habit is a sign of rebirth and endless becoming. You look into the face of the figure opposite. His face combines the freshness of youth with the wisdom of the ages. It is a striking and rare combination. He wears a plain circlet of shining metal as a simple crown. So far he has stood relaxed and composed as you have taken your time to study him, but now he raises his right hand in a gesture of power and authority. You see that he holds a short staff tapered identically at each end. He holds the rod above each of the four items in turn, repeating a short phrase which you cannot hear. Now he partially raises his other hand and with deliberation points a finger downwards. Like a lightning conductor he stands bridging the Great Above and the Great Below. He has moved deep into a private meditation which your presence does not disturb. As he continues, it seems to you that a point of light forms above his head. You watch it, mesmerized. At first it is a mere point of brilliance that has emerged from nowhere, but it begins to spread and take on a shape of its own – a lemniscate, a figure of eight. Finally the shape stabilizes.

Points of brilliance continue to flash and sparkle like spinning jewels as the figure is lost deep in potent thought. At last he opens his eyes and relaxes the intensity of his thinking. He lowers the staff and smiles. 'My work is done but yours is just beginning.' With that, he turns his back and walks away into the distance, until he simply disappears from view.

When you are ready, leave and return to the temple. When you are ready, leave through the doorway. Finally, dissolve all images and return to ordinary consciousness.

EXERCITIA SPIRITUALIA

Take the Following as Subjects for Meditation:
- The Magus of Power
- The Four Elements
- The Four Magical Injunctions
- The Four Fixed signs of the zodiac
- Beth
- Mercury
- The Intelligence of Transparency
- 'As Above, So Below'

Make Notes on:
- Tarot Trump I, The Magician

Visualize the Following and Record your Experiences:
- The Temple of Binah including the Archangel Tzaphkiel
- The Journey of the 12th Path

CHAPTER 32

Chockmah – Wisdom

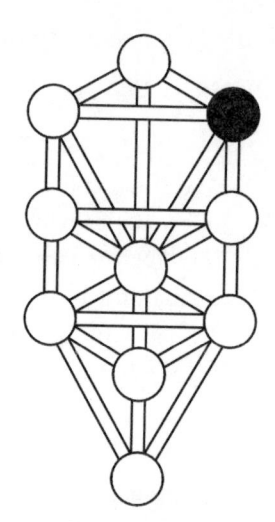

FIGURE 41 THE SEPHIRAH CHOCKMAH

TABLE OF CORRESPONDENCES

God-Name: Jehovah or Jah – eternal
Archangel: Ratziel
Order of Angels: Auphanim – Wheels
Magical Image: A bearded male figure
Virtue: Devotion
Vice: None
Titles: Power of Yetzirah, Ab, Abba, The
   Supernal Father, Tetragrammaton,
   Yod of Tetragrammaton
Spiritual Experience: The Vision of God
   Face to Face
Mundane Chakra: The Zodiac
Personal Chakra: The Ajna Chakra
Colour in Atziluth: Pure soft Blue
Colour in Briah: Grey

Colour in Yetzirah: Pearl Grey iridescence
Colour in Assiah: White flecked Red Blue
   Yellow
Symbols: The Lingham, The Phallus, The
   Inner Robe of Glory, The Standing Stone,
   The Uplifted Rod of Power, The Straight
   Line
Tarot Cards: The Four Twos
Two of Wands: Dominion
Two of Cups: Love
Two of Swords: Peace Restored
Two of Pentacles: Harmonious Change

COMMENTARY

The Second Path is called the Illuminating Intelligence.
It is the Crown of Creation, the Splendour of Unity,
equalling it. It is exalted above every head and it is named
by Kabbalists the Second Glory.

Chockmah, meaning Wisdom, is the second Sephirah. It emanates directly from Kether. As part of the Supernal Triangle, Chockmah is in relationship with both Kether and Binah. It is emanated from Kether and is in a polarized relationship with Binah. Chockmah forms the head of the Pillar of Mercy as Binah forms the head of the Pillar of Severity. Chockmah is called the Supernal Father. Binah is called the Supernal Mother.

The Holy Name of God

> Most importantly is the final realization: *All that is formed and all that is spoken is one name.* The initiate not only knows this intellectually, but he can actually visualize and see that all creation is nothing more than one Name, the Tetragrammaton.

Rabbi Aryeh Kaplan, *Sepher Yetzirah*

The creation account in Genesis contains 32 names of God. Each represents a different creative function. With its predilection for profound wordplay and encodement, Kabbalah is able to enshrine subtle nuances of meaning and differentiation. Each of the Sephiroth is assigned a different divine name. Chockmah is assigned the name Yah, meaning Eternal. The first letter Yod of this word alone designates Wisdom, but it is completed by the addition of a second letter, Heh, which designates Understanding as the feminine principle. This single word therefore instantly unites Wisdom with Understanding. Wisdom is seen as a unified quality which cannot be apprehended until Understanding provides separation. Wisdom is likened to water, an undifferentiated and undivided state which waits upon the intervention of a structured analysis through Understanding.

The letter Heh is even written in two distinct parts to indicate that the process of separation begins with understanding. The letter Yod has a numerical value of 10, indicating that all the Sephiroth are included in its

Wisdom. The letter Heh has a numerical value of 5, alluding to the five fingers of the hand representing Understanding as the hand that holds Wisdom and brings separation and differentiation through the fingers. When placed at the beginning of a word the prefix Heh means 'the', but at the end of a word it indicates the feminine possessive, 'her'. This is because Understanding is the domain of the feminine essence. These linguistic subtleties point directly to the wider relationship between Binah and Chockmah as the archetypal male and female principles.

Chockmah is called Tetragrammaton or simply Yod of Tetragrammaton, the most Holy Name of God. The four letters which form this name are rich in meaning and association. This is an entire philosophy of creation expressed in a name. The Tetragrammaton is said to be rooted in the Mother Letters Aleph, Mem and Shin. The letter Yod is derived from Mem. The letter Heh is derived from Shin and the letter Vau is derived from Aleph. 'The Mother Letters come first. *And from them are born fathers.*'

A secular alphabet provides no hint of the philosophical heights possible through a sacred alphabet. The symbolic divisions given to the Foundation Letters permit an extraordinary range of conceptual notions to be formed. The 22 letters are divided into five phonetic families which determine where the sounds are produced – from throat, palate, tongue, teeth or lips. Alphabetically, three letters – Yod, Heh and Vau – are the first of the Simple Letters, one of which is assigned to each of the first three phonetic families – gutturals, labials and palatals. The Heh is pronounced from the throat, the Vau is pronounced with the lips, and the Yod is pronounced from the palette. The four letters of the Tetragrammaton represent the four elements and the four worlds, and express either a masculine or feminine nature.

Letter	Polarity	Element	World
Yod	Masculine	Fire	Atzliluth
Heh	Feminine	Water	Briah
Vau	Masculine	Air	Yetzirah
Heh	Feminine	Earth	Assiah

The Tetragrammaton encapsulates the process of creation – from elemental Fire, the Big Bang, to manifestation, the element of Earth. Creation commences with elemental Fire, which also represents spirit. The letter Yod resembles a sperm in shape. It has a small tail and a leading head. It represents a dynamic outpouring of life force. The letter Yod is also symbolized by the open hand of a man and implies power, direction, skill and dexterity. The second letter, Heh, resembles a container waiting to be filled. It represents the feminine principle. The enclosing shape of this letter is designed to hold and consolidate. Additionally, it symbolizes a window. It channels the first breath of Kether which passes through the window into creation and forms an opening through which light may pour. The third letter, Vau, symbolizes a nail in addition to elemental Air. The seemingly disparate aspects of creation are invisibly united, nailed together invisibly by elemental Air, which is also prana, the universal life force. Finally, elemental Earth, expressed by the letter Heh, is the feminine pole in relation to the originating Yod.

Additionally, the same letters can be used as suffixes. Yod means 'me', Heh means 'her', and Vau means 'him'. There are only two letters in the alphabet to which these can be joined – the letters Lamed and Beth, which spell out the Hebrew word for heart. Here, used in combination with the letter Lamed, the same suffixes become 'to me', 'to her', 'to him'. When combined with the letter Beth, the same suffixes become 'in me', 'in her' and 'in him'. This extraordinary linguistic versatility gives the Tetragrammaton a vast range of meaning, both personal and cosmic. Chockmah is also called Yod of Tetragrammaton. The letter Yod has a numerical value of 10. The sum of the first four letters, 10, is the sum of the numbers 1, 2, 3 and 4. The following numbers, 5 and 6, are assigned to Heh and Vau respectively. The intricacies and minutiae to be found in the relationships between letters and numbers are astonishing and almost endless. Their purpose is to awaken consciousness.

As Above, So Below

> It is astonishing that an expanding universe, whose
> starting point is so simple that it can be specified by just
> a few numbers, can evolve into our intricately
> structured cosmos.

Martin Rees, *Just Six Numbers*

If Kether can be likened to the explosive moment of the Big Bang, then Chockmah can be likened to the succeeding phase of dynamic activity. Chockmah means Wisdom. Derived from the root *chakak*, meaning to engrave, the word *chock* means 'rule' and decree. Chockmah meaning Wisdom carries the implication that it contains rules or primal laws. Chockmah represents a state of primal rule. As part of the Supernal Triangle,

Chockmah represents the forces which underpin the progression of creation. It is curious that current scientific thinking supports the Kabalistic insight that numbers in relationship express a creative power:

> Mathematical laws underpin the fabric of our universe – not just atoms, but galaxies, stars and people. The properties of atoms – their size, and masses, how many different kinds there are, and the forces linking them together – determine the chemistry of our everyday world; the very existence of atoms depends on forces and particles deep inside them.[1]

It now seems that six numbers play a crucial role in the distinctive development of our universe.

> Two of them relate to the basic forces; two fix the size and overall 'texture' of our universe and determine whether it will continue for ever; and two more fix the properties of space itself:

- The cosmos is so vast because there is one crucially important huge number N in nature, equal to 1,000,000,000,000,000,000,000,000,000, 000, 000,000,000. This number measures the strength of the electrical forces that hold atoms together, divided by the force of gravity between them. If N had less zeros, only a short-lived miniature universe could exist …

- Another number, ε, whose value is 0.007, defines how firmly atomic nuclei bind together and how all the atoms on Earth were made … If ε were 0.006 or 0.008, we could not exist.

- The cosmic number Ω (omega) measures the amount of material in our universe – galaxies, diffuse gas, and 'dark matter'. Ω tells us the relative importance of gravity and expansion energy in the universe …

- Measuring the fourth number, λ (lambda), was the biggest scientific news of 1998. An unsuspected new force – a cosmic 'antigravity' – controls the expansion of our universe, even though it has no discernible effect on scales less than a billion light-years …

- … The fabric of our universe depends on one number, Q, which represents the ratio of two fundamental energies and is about 1/100,000 in value. If Q were even smaller, the universe would be inert and structureless; if Q were much larger, it would be a violent place, in which no stars or solar systems could survive, dominated by vast black holes.

- The sixth crucial number has been known for centuries, although it's now viewed in a new perspective. It is the number of spatial dimensions in our world, **D**, and equals three. Life couldn't exist if **D** were two or four.[2]

According to Martin Rees, 'These six numbers constitute a "recipe" for a universe. Moreover, the outcome is sensitive to their values; if any one of them were "untuned" there would be no stars and no life. Is this tuning just a brute fact, a coincidence, or is it providence of a benign Creator?'[3] The answer to this rhetorical question is really a projection of personal preference. In truth, it is a question without an answer.

What is beyond doubt however is the extraordinary exactitude of the imbedded dynamics. Kabbalah supports the view that such exactitude is purposeful:

Ten Sephiroth of Nothingess

Their end is imbedded in their beginning

and their beginning in their end

like a flame burning in a coal.

The Sepher Yetzirah

Malkuth is implicit in Kether as Kether is implicit in Malkuth. Martin Rees even extends the horizons of continuous creation to seriously suggest the idea of the multiverse, an infinity of other universes built upon differing imbedded numbers and therefore a different evolutionary pattern. The idea may border on speculative fantasy, but since Martin Rees has been described as 'the most brilliant and visionary living cosmologist' he is well qualified to speculate in this area.

The Starry Wisdom

Abraham had a great astrology in his heart and all the

kings of the east and west arose early at his door.

A Talmudic text

Kether is called the Crown; Chockmah is called the Crown of Creation, which is sometimes translated as the 'circle of creation'. 'The Second Path is called the Illuminating Intelligence. It is the Crown of Creation, the Splendour of Unity, equalling it. It is exalted above every head and it is named by Kabalists the Second Glory.' This second glory, the circle or crown of creation, is none other than the zodiac, called in Hebrew *Masloth*, which is the mundane chakra assigned to Chockmah. This is a powerful and important correspondence which embraces the zodiac within a spiritual philosophy. The zodiac brings a practical wisdom, namely astrology.

Astrology has enjoyed a long history, and was significant in Mesopotamia, Egypt, Greece, Rome, India, China and the Arab empire. It was often closely associated with astronomy, because both systems arose from watching the heavens. The dark sky has much to teach as stars and planets appear to move with a cyclic precision which speaks of a natural cosmic order.

However, as Christianity developed its own belief system, it began to put a distance between itself and astrology, which was closely identified with the pagan wisdom of the ancient world. Though a dilemma was felt, the solution was not always cut and dried. The Neo-Platonic current which had flowed into the Age of Scholasticism retained Pythagorean correspondences in a new Christian guise. In the 13th century Thomas Aquinas defined a distinction between judicial and natural astrology. In a solution which itself exemplifies the separation of spirit and body, the human body was ruled by the stars but the soul was ruled by God. Natural astrology, including medical, agricultural and branches that might cover mundane astrology, remained acceptable. Horary, natal and electional astrology were seen to interfere with God's will and were deemed incompatible with a Christian perspective.

The Renaissance gave a great impetus to astrology, not just philosophically as part of a general rediscovery of ancient ideas, but also practically as printing permitted the spread of almanacs and general information. At the beginning of the 21st century, in the renewing spirit of a holistic philosophy, astrology is once again seen as a spiritual science which unites the cosmic with the local, the personal with the transpersonal. It connects the heavens to the earth, the cosmic to the individual, the Macroprosopus to the Microprosopus, 'As Above, So Below'. Here is a source of nourishment, insight and revelation. This is the Path of the Illuminating Intelligence. Illumination brings light to areas of darkness through clarity and insight. Like enlightenment, which draws upon the same metaphor, illuminating wisdom brings a direct seeing into the ultimate and true nature of things. The crown or circle of creation which is 'exalted above every head' is a unifying image without equal. The 'Splendour of Unity' is equal to it. In an age of territorial disputes, ethnic cleansing and racial tension, an image of unity is much needed. This is the 'Second Glory'.

The original singular event of the Big Bang, the first point of creation, is a unity beyond individual significance, but the zodiac is an image of unity of personal significance. It is the Crown of Creation. It is exalted above every head and it is named by Kabalists the Second Glory. 'Symbolised by the zodiac, wisdom is shown as an entire encompassment of all things from every point.'[4] This is a fitting mundane chakra for the Sephirah Chockmah, which is Wisdom.

The Archangel assigned to Chockmah is Ratziel, whose names mean 'the herald' or 'one sent forth from God'. He is said to stand every day and proclaim his secret to the world in a voice which reverberates around the whole planet. When Adam was expelled from the Garden of Eden he was befriended by Ratziel, who gave him a book cut on sapphire. Adam passed it to Noah, whence it descended to Abraham, Jacob, Levi, Joshua and Solomon. The book is said to hold the secrets of the stars, giving information about the cycles of the heavenly bodies, the destiny of individuals and the collective. The pointers towards astrology as a spiritual science could not be clearer or more positive.

The order of angels assigned here is the Auphanim, meaning wheels. This provides an image of momentum and forward motion which characterize the potency of this Sephirah. The wheel as a turning circle points to the repetition of time cycles, whether seasonal or cosmic. It is a riposte to the model of a linear creation.

The Marriage of Heaven and Earth

> Wherever creation is thought of as a continuous process
> rather than a once-and-for-all event, the
> correspondences between microcosm and macrocosm,
> visible and invisible, become deeper and more complex.
>
> David Maclagan, *Creation Myths*

The prime story which sets any belief system in motion is of crucial significance. Its elements become themes and motifs which are played out on the stage of the real world as society develops institutions, forms and ideas to reflect their chosen prime model more perfectly. The characteristics given to the first man and woman, the relationship between them and the reciprocal relationship with the creator, prove to be crucially significant patterns on which society models itself. In Christianity the figures of Adam and Eve have become deeply engraved blueprints. The idea of Original Sin is derived from the Fall, and woman is but a helpmate. She is derived from the male but not directly created. The account in this creation myth is a linear one. It provides a particular model in which God's handiwork is completed in six days; on the seventh day the creator rests. This has even become the pattern for the week in the Judeo-Christian world. Creation is completed as a once and for all event. When parallel processes give birth to the cosmos and simultaneously generate organic life within it, a holistic value system emerges from the cosmic egg which links the individual into the whole. Where the primal story establishes correspondences between the creation of humanity and the wider cosmological setting, the sense of unity remains unbroken. Where the prime story lacks these cross-correspondences, a linear and polarized value system stands ready as creation is metaphorically set adrift from the hand of the creator. In the face of a primal split, succeeding ideas and formalized institutions have no option but to recreate, reflect and elaborate this primal schism into a theology of separation. The primal story from which a society takes its bearings is of profound influence. Its power is silent and invisible. The view that we hold of ourselves both individually and collectively is another determining model. It shapes the role that we take in the world. It determines our sense of purpose and meaning. It colours our search for identity and purpose. It sets limits on where we may not tread. The view of self is derived from the view of creation.

Chockmah is the realm of the Supernal Father, but this is partnered by the realm of the Supernal Mother in Binah. The symbols assigned here are the *lingham*, the phallus, the standing stone, the tower and the uplifted rod of power. These are symbols of unashamed sexual potency, virile masculinity and creative power, not images normally linked to a Western conception of God at all. But this is the language of symbol and metaphor which is designed to expand the mind. Each of these symbols has its counterpart in the symbolism attributed to Binah. The lingham is matched by the *yoni*, the Inner Robe of Glory by the Outer Robe of Concealment, the straight line by the vesica, and the standing stone, the tower and rod of power by the cup and chalice. Together these are images of polarity which cannot be understood without reference to the qualities of the other. The powers of Binah cannot be understood without referring to the powers of Chockmah. This concept is foreign to the Western mind but quite familiar in an Eastern setting. In Hinduism the complementary balance of creative powers is upheld through the dynamic pairs of gods and goddesses. This duality is found in the symbolism of the *Ajna* Chakra which can be correlated to Binah and Chockmah jointly as the consciousness of the left and right hemispheres of the brain. The *Ajna* centre combines the duality of the two brains but simultaneously also transcends this division by representing a state of undifferentiated cosmic awareness. The chakra is depicted with two petals which resemble wings set around a central sphere. This is an image of both duality and unity. In the Eastern symbol system, the deity assigned here is composite – half male, half female – Ardhanarishvar, an aspect of Shiva. The male half has camphor-blue skin and holds a trident representing the three aspects of cognition. The female half is coloured pink and wears a sari. She is decorated with shining ornaments and holds a golden lotus. Shiva too has a third eye, the *sva-netra*, and the Ajna Chakra is located at the traditional site of the third eye.

THE INNER THRONE

Imagine yourself in a palatial throne room. On a raised dais there are two thrones side by side. On the right-hand throne sits a queen of mature years. Beside her, sitting on the left-hand throne, is a king, likewise mature in years. You approach them and kneel. They then stand and hold hands. The queen places her left hand on your shoulder and the king places his right hand on your shoulder. They both place their other hand on the crown of your head in a joint blessing.

Use this time to contemplate your relationship to the archetypal cosmic parents. Stand when you are ready and depart peacefully.

It is refreshing to look to an unfamiliar creation myth to gain a different perspective. An Indian creation myth begins before time and space existed.

Brahma the creator slept peacefully within his golden lotus. As the lotus bloomed Brahma began the work of creation. First he created the *prajapatis*, the fathers of creation, and instructed them to go forth and multiply. 'How?' they asked, and Brahma himself was not sure. Suddenly he heard a divine voice speaking. At that instant Ardhanaranari came into being: the left half was female and the right half was male. Brahma realized he had made a mistake. He had produced just one half of creation. Now he created the first woman. She was Ushas. With her appearance desire arose. As she fled from Brahma's embrace she changed herself into a succession of animal forms and thereby all animal life was created. But Brahma continued the chase until from his own brow there appeared an archer who with a single shot pinned him to the sky. The archer was Shiva, a new form of Ardhanaranari. Brahma, much chastened, continued the work of creation with Ushas, now called Sarasvati. Shiva, who also emerged during this cycle of creation, went on to assume the characteristics of a cosmic creative power. His symbol *par excellence* is the *lingham*, the upright symbol of virility at all levels of creation. The axis of the revolving cosmos is the great lingham which came into being when Shiva stood one-footed for thousands of years. According to *linga purana*, Vishnu and Brahma came across a fiery pillar that seemed to stretch across the whole cosmos; from it emanated the sound of Aum. Taking the form of a swan, Brahma rode up and tried to find its summit. Vishnu gnawed into the earth trying to reach its base. Neither were successful for the great pillar, the cosmic lingham, has neither beginning nor end but stretches into infinity. Curiously, the pillar, or cloud, is also a biblical symbol of Jehovah's power and a symbol of Chockmah.

EVOCATION

Welcome to my kingdom. I am called Wisdom. I hold the rules by which your reality is created. If you seek wisdom come in search of them. Search in my kingdom and you will discover the Illuminating Intelligence. My realm is eternal for the future is written in the seeds of the present as the present was imprinted in the seeds of the beginning.

Though I am called The Supernal Father I reach out to The Supernal Mother who reaches out to me. Together we are Wisdom and Understanding. We cannot be separated. To seek Wisdom is to find Understanding; to seek Understanding is to find Wisdom.

I am the Yod of Tetragrammaton, the first impulse of creation set spinning into activity. I am part of a great mystery. I encompass vistas and timescales beyond your comprehension – stars and galaxies, planets and wonders beyond imagination. These are my children. I hold them all for I am called the Supernal Father.

INTERNALIZATION – THE TEMPLE
OF CHOCKMAH

Construct the Temple of Chockmah in the creative imagination and include
the Archangel Ratziel. Make your way to the summit of the ziggurat. As you
make the last turn, you see that a figure already stands there. Dressed in a
long flowing garment, he greets you as if you were expected. He holds a
long staff in one hand and wears a belt decorated with shining stones set in
patterns like the starry sky. He conveys an air of authority; you feel that he
is the High Priest here. Now you both stand alone on the flattened summit
of this great constructed mountain. In the centre there is a miniature ziggurat
no higher than your own height. It holds a fire which burns red against the
darkening sky and it is flanked by four fine shafts of glinting metal which
reach upwards like lightning conductors.

Now that you have arrived, there is a great sense of anticipation. The
sky above you has darkened with the unnatural cover of a storm. The air is
warm yet dry. Somewhere in the distance you hear the rumble of thunder.
Suddenly lightning breaks through the sky with a ferocious crack and tears
the air with savage speed. The High Priest wields his rod; like a baton
pointing to the distant horizon, like a conductor orchestrating a cosmic
dance. From the darkened mass of the heavens, a tentacle of whirling
darkness drops like a tail. It is a tornado. Wondrous and terrifying, it roams
along the horizon, probing all with its long finger. Everywhere the storm
rages. The High Priest is exultant. He and the storm are one. Every crack
of lightning seems to reverberate through him and his body jolts in perfect
and spontaneous unison. Time passes and eventually the sky becomes quiet.
With the passing of the storm, the High Priest tends the altar flame. In
offering, he throws oil onto the fire, which answers at the instant with
towering flames. He is engaged in his work and you begin the long path of
descent back to terra firma.

When you are ready, leave this inner landscape. Finally, dissolve all images
and return to ordinary consciousness.

EXERCITIA SPIRITUALIA

Take the Following as Subjects for Meditation:

- Jehovah or Jah
- Auphanim – Wheels
- A bearded male figure
- The Illuminating Intelligence
- The Vision of God Face to Face
- The Supernal Father
- The Tetragrammaton
- The Zodiac
- The Lingham, The Phallus, The Inner Robe of Glory, The Standing Stone, The Uplifted Rod of Power, The Straight Line

Contemplate the Following Questions and Record your Responses:

- How does the quality of Devotion operate in your life?
- How does the nature of Chockmah relate to the Brow Chakra?
- What other correspondences can you relate to Chockmah?
- How do the four Tarot cards relate to Chockmah?

Visualize the Following and Record your Experiences:

- The Temple of Chockmah including the Archangel, Ratziel
- The Journey to the Temple of Chockmah

CHAPTER 33

The Eleventh Path: Chockmah–Kether

FIGURE 42 THE 11ᵀᴴ PATH:

CHOCKMAH–KETHER

TAROT TRUMP 0,

THE FOOL

TABLE OF CORRESPONDENCES

Journey: The Fool, Spirit of Aethyr
Key: Aleph, meaning an Ox
Mother Letter: The Element of Air
Spiritual Significance: Air
Colour in Atziluth: Bright pale Yellow
Colour in Briah: Sky Blue
Colour in Yetzirah: Blue
Colour in Assiah: Emerald flecked Gold
Text: The Scintillating Intelligence

COMMENTARY

The Eleventh Path is the Scintillating Intelligence, because it is the essence of that curtain which is placed close to the order of the disposition, and this is a special dignity given to it, that it may be able to stand before the Face of the Cause of Causes.

The 11th Path connects the first Sephirah, Kether, the Crown, with the second Sephirah, Chockmah, Wisdom, which is the head of the Pillar of Force. The 11th Path carries the impulse of Kether towards manifestation. As the numbers 1–10 are assigned to the Sephiroth, the 11th Path is the first of the Paths or Stages. Whereas the Sephiroth represent objective states of being, the Paths represent the subjective experiences which connect one state with another. However, as the 11th Path belongs to the Supernal Triangle, this is a journey of cosmic dimension, not of everyday personal experience. Though in theory all Paths are to be trod from both directions, from both the viewpoint of Ascent and Descent, it is difficult to view this as anything other than a Path of Descent as life force surges forwards with all the power of the first moment of creation behind it. This Path, along with the 12th and 14th, interlaces the Supernal Triangle of Kether, Chockmah and Binah, the Crown, Wisdom and Understanding.

The First Step

The most popular current theory of the origin of the fields of nature, the superstring theory, proposes the existence of a primal unified field in ten dimensions, nine of space and one of time.

Rupert Sheldrake, *The Rebirth of Nature*

The journey towards Malkuth commences here upon the 11th Path. This Path is one of beginnings as creation explodes into being and begins its long series of evolutionary transformations. The 11th Path travels between Kether and Chockmah carrying the imprinted patterns for evolution like an encoded memory. The 11th Path is assigned to Tarot Trump 0, which is most often called The Fool. The Trump shows a figure standing precariously close to the edge of a mountain outcrop.

Dressed as the archetypal traveller setting out on a journey, carrying few worldly possessions, the Fool steps out in carefree mood into the unknown future. Drawn from folklore, myth and legend, the character of the Fool combines an innocent naïveté with a knowing wisdom. The Fool often serves as the single voice of truth when human deceit and guile are in full play. Folly has the power to act as a catalyst; candour can be disarming. The character representing the first step on the outward journey towards physical manifestation conveys a childlike simplicity and spontaneous ease. As the precipice approaches, the Fool pays no heed. With another step the Fool will be plunged from the heights to the depths: 'As Above, So Below', says the Hermetic Maxim. In the background a white sun shines. This is a representation of Kether, which is also called the White Head. Assigned to the zero, the 11th Path presents the paradox at the heart of being, emptiness which is form. This is the void from which all emerges; it is the Gnostic Pleroma, the Buddhist Shunyata and the Kabbalistic crown.

When interviewed and asked 'Does emptiness also mean fullness?' His Holiness the Dalai Lama answered, 'It seems so. I explain that emptiness is like a zero. A zero is nothing but without a zero you cannot count anything; therefore a zero is something, yet zero.'[1] This is the Path of the zero which signifies place value and brings increases. Creation began some 15 billion years ago with the Big Bang. But the creation of atoms, molecules and matter itself did not take place until much later. Life itself did not evolve for millions of years. If Kether can be seen to represent the state of the Big Bang, then the 11th Path might be seen as the first wave of life-giving potential to emerge from it.

This Path is assigned to the Scintillating Intelligence; it enjoys a 'special dignity' in that it may be able to stand before the Face of the Cause of Causes. The Scintillating Intelligence suggests a radiant brilliance and an effervescent quality of light. It is described as the 'essence of that curtain which is placed close to the order of the disposition'. In other words, since this Path emerges from Kether, like a veil over a doorway to a realm of shimmering light, the Scintillating Intelligence sparkles with light from the Crown of Creation. When applied to the quality of mind it conjures images of sparkling energy and dynamic movement. Prana is said to shine and shimmer. The character of the Fool is also known as the Spirit of Aethyr which, like prana, represents the life force itself.

This Path connects Kether with Chockmah. It connects the Hidden

Intelligence assigned to Kether with the Illuminating Intelligence assigned to Chockmah. This journey carries 'the impulse to be' towards the endless transformations and processes of evolution. The Fool's belt is that of the zodiac which is assigned to Chockmah. In the background there are snow-capped peaks. Snow, which is frozen water, represents the quality of memory as an aspect of the non-verbal unified consciousness of Chockmah, Wisdom. Here on the journey of the 11th Path, Spirit begins its descent through the planes. Called 'Soul' by the Sepher Yetzirah, and the Spirit of Aethyr by the Tarot, this is the evolving journey of the indefinable quality of life con-sciousness. Physical creation eventually arises and human consciousness appears, as the original thermonuclear event of the Big Bang undergoes endless transformation. It remains wondrous that the laws and forces imprinted some 15 billion years ago were primed to permit life and con-sciousness to arise. Was this an accident, sheer random chance, or perhaps deliberate? Was this the work of a benign creator God or an extraordinary testament to nature as a creative and evolutionary power? If only slightly different values had pertained, the laws of nature might have produced an entirely different universe. In some inexplicable way the first step on the road to being contains the seeds essential to becoming.

The 11th Path represents that first translation towards matter. The Fool as an image of innocence and simplicity represents the journey into endless transformation. The Fool wears both black and white garments, signifying the union of opposite powers. The white inner garment signifies the pris-tine quality of Akasa or Aethyr and the undivided eternal present; the black outer robe signifies the opposing pull towards incarnation, manifestation and the dark power of forgetfulness. Black is the colour assigned to the earth quadrant of the elemental mandala at Malkuth. The remaining colours – citrine, russet and olive – are also to be found in the Fool's garments. The Fool's robe shows the Sephiroth in disarray awaiting organ-ization. It is clear that the Fool is destined for Malkuth. The Fool's crown of laurel and a red feather will become the decorated ovoid enclosure of the Tarot Trump XXI, The World. The red feather becomes the ribbons which both decorate and bind the garland at top and bottom. The feather repre-sents the element of Air and all the connections to the Great Above. Its red colour however is that of the incarnate world of the physical passions and the Great Below. The Fool is destined to take material form through a long series of transformations. The descent has begun. There can be no turning back until these forces find expression in form. Just as all the forces of cre-ation were already present within the maelstrom of the Big Bang, Malkuth, the Kingdom, is already held in latent potentiality within Kether. The universe was bound to arise from the Big Bang; Malkuth, the Kingdom will arise from Kether, the Crown.

The Breath of Life

> Ten Sephiroth of Nothingness
> One is the Breath of the Living God
> Blessed and benedicted is the name
> of the Life of Worlds
> The voice of breath and speech
> And this is the Holy breath.

The Sepher Yetzirah

The word breath is translated as *ruach*, which is also the word for wind and air. It also means spirit. In general ruach indicates motion and communication. It is the vital life force, prana or chi. Air also signifies the mind, invisible yet omnipresent. These abstract, invisible and ineffable forces will become immersed in the infinite variety of the material world. The letter Aleph assigned to this Path symbolizes both the element of Air and an ox. This curious paradox between Aleph as the breath of life and the beast of burden once again defines the marriage of heaven and earth, the invisible spirit and earthly substance. Like air, spirit is invisible and undetectable except through movement. By analogy the divine breath moves to create the Sephiroth, which are sometimes described as vessels; as the glassblower breathes out, applying pressure to molten glass, so the vessel takes shape. The first breath from Kether is called the Direct Light. The first breath denotes the beginning of independent life. This is a Path of beginnings. The Midrash says, 'Breath gave birth to Wisdom'. Kether gives rise to Chockmah. The letter Aleph signifies the element of Air since it is the initial letter of Avir, meaning air. Like the air and the quality of spirit which it also represents, the sound of Aleph is undetectable. It is a silent letter.

It should be clear that wordplay is a Kabbalistic delight. Aleph is the first letter of the alphabet and one of the three Mother Letters. The second Mother Letter is Mem, which is the middle letter of the alphabet, and Shin is the penultimate letter. The final letter Tau is a Double Letter. The three Mother Letters assume a deep significance. Together they represent the constellation of associations and correspondences assigned to the elements of

Air, Water and Fire as the creative powers of cause, effect and synthesis. Apart from representing the Sephiroth in a pre-organized state, the Fool's robe includes the letter Shin encircled at his heart.

Three mothers: Aleph, Mem and Shin

a great, mystical secret

The Sepher Yetzirah

Both the letters Aleph and Shin are found on Tarot Trump 0 as depictions of the primal causative powers. The letter Mem, representing water as symbolic of matter, is represented elsewhere. This is a Path of beginning and becoming.

Endless Transformation

All nature is evolutionary, the cosmos is like a great developing organism and evolutionary creativity is inherent in nature herself.

Rupert Sheldrake, *The Rebirth of Nature*

Theories and models of nature have existed since thinking men have pondered on the world around them. Such models have ranged from the purely mechanistic to the mystical. Greek philosophers saw the world of nature as a living being endowed with a world soul. Descartes saw the world as a mechanistic machine. The attempt to penetrate and understand nature's mystery has a long heritage. There have been many versions of an animating principle within nature. It has taken different forms, in both scientific and metaphysical guise. Vitalism, entelechy, animating souls, universal ether and, most recently, the theory of morphic fields – all seek to explain how matter takes on so many different forms. Currently we are in the grip of a revisionary scientific revolution whose effects and ramifications have hardly begun to alter social views and values. Yet there is an intimate relationship between a core model of reality and the shape of society that derives from it. In the West, scientific models of reality have exercised enormous power but these are also subject to the process of transformation. We are living through a transition period; the old scientific certainties are dissolving but a new model is still in its infancy. Rupert Sheldrake and Matthew Fox summarize the implications of these two models in *Natural Grace*.

Mechanistic Universe	Living Universe
Machine	Developing organism
Inanimate	Fields
Purposeless	Attractors
Inert atoms	Structures of activity
Earth dead	Gaia
Determinate	Indeterminate, chaotic
Knowable	Dark matter
Disembodied knowledge	Participatory knowing
Uncreative	Creative evolution
Eternal Laws	Habits [2]

Taken together, these changes lead to a tremendous shift in world view. But we are not going back to the pre-mechanistic kind of animism. We are now in a post-mechanistic state, a higher turn of the spiral if you like. The new animism differs from the old animism in that living nature is now seen as developing and full of creativity. The pre-mechanistic view was of the universe as a mature organism, even as an ageing and decadent organism. We now see it as an organism still growing and developing. This new view of living nature requires a new approach to theology.[3]

But this is a time of transition and change so deep that it has been referred to as a paradigm shift. The old views still hold, side by side with the new.

Each of these views can be elaborated intellectually, each can be defended on rational grounds and each is held with deep conviction by many people. In the end we have to choose between them on the basis of intuition. Our choice is influenced by our acknowledgement of mystery, and in turn affects our tolerance of it. Those with the lowest mystery-tolerance threshold are drawn to a mechanistic-atheistic world view, which as a matter of principle denies the existence of mysterious entities like souls and God and portrays a disenchanted, unmagical reality proceeding entirely mechanically. Those who acknowledge the life of evolutionary nature admit the mystery of life and creativity.[4]

The Fool is an image of transformation. The potency of the 11th Path surges outwards from the Cause of Causes, towards the organizing principles of Chockmah, Binah and all the changes that will transform this singular energy into a myriad of forms and expressions. The one becomes the many through an endless series of transformations. The Fool's knapsack is emblazoned with the sign of the eagle, representing the astrological sign of Scorpio. With its two signs of scorpion and eagle, Scorpio represents transformation from one state into another. On the Path of Ascent, the earthly nature of the scorpion is transformed into the high-flying eagle. On the Path of Descent, the high-flying eagle takes on the nature of the earthly scorpion. Though seemingly different, eagle and scorpion are part of a single unity expressed in different forms. As the Fool steps out from the place of unity, multiple transformations lie ahead. The eighth sign of the zodiac, Scorpio, is a water sign in its fixed form. Scorpio therefore represents the penetrative and dissolving powers of water as a means of breakdown and absorption. Scorpio brings the need to penetrate life's mysteries to the core. This is the essential drive towards self-realization. It is an upwelling, insistent call from the depths of being which is never satisfied with half-truths and complacent answers. Often aligned with metaphysical or religious interests, Scorpio represents the questing mind intent on fundamental answers and in-depth questions. Emerging here from Kether, the instinct for self-realization is carried like a seed on the Path of Descent towards Malkuth, where it becomes the driving passion for the conscious Path of Ascent. Although the eagle and the scorpion are ultimately inseparable, on the Path of Descent where material appearance comes to dominate, the high-flying eagle and the earth-bound scorpion become separated.

The 11th Path expresses the unified state which will become polarized into its natural oppositions. The figure of the Fool is neither male nor female but combines elements of both. The seeds of duality, the twin poles of opposition which enable momentum and dynamic growth, are born here in the image of the Fool as hermaphrodite. From unity comes duality, from duality a myriad of forms becomes possible. From the one comes the many. Like the white sun which represents the source of all that shall arise, the Fool carries the white rose. Like the lotus, this is another expression of creation and unfoldment. The whiteness of the rose expresses a primal unity which has the power to give rise to a multiplicity. As white light contains the hidden rainbow, the white rose holds many possible evolutionary futures. It signifies the primal seed of the vast kingdom of plant and vegetative life which is as yet to be unfolded. Whiteness symbolizes the state of purity and innocence, unmarked by experience, untrammelled by adventure. This is the mode of the 11th Path, pristine potentiality and evolutionary impetus. As the prime bearer of Kether's creative energy, the Fool carries all that is

THE CYCLE OF TRANSFORMATION

Imagine yourself in the form of an eagle soaring easily over the landscape. Your eye is sharp. You are the unrivalled king of the air. One day in flight you spot a valley that is new to you. Your curiosity is aroused, you want to explore and investigate. You begin to fly in your usual manner. As you fly, the land itself seems to magnetize you so that you begin to descend with an impelling inevitability. As you descend, you observe changes in your capabilities. Your eye is not so keen; your strength seems to be failing; the effort demanded for flight is becoming onerous. You are tiring. Finally, you land in the place which has drawn you to it with such compulsion. But you have undergone a deep and inexplicable change. Your wings have gone. Instead you have the hard carapace of a scorpion. Close to the ground you scuttle for cover. Before you have time to register regret at your choice, already forgetfulness has filled your mind.

Imagine yourself in the form of a scorpion. Your world view is limited to what lies beneath your feet. Though small, your scorpion nature means that you are well equipped to defend your existence. Other creatures mark this power with proper caution. But, unusually, strange dreams of sky and open expanses lie deep in your scorpion nature. One day a whirlwind arises and sweeps you off your feet into the air. The suddenness of it alarms you but the ferocity of the wind carries you up into new realms. Time seems to stand still. For the first time new horizons appear; the land is far beneath you and now you see a panoramic vista and the sweep of the landscape below. Your sight has an unusual clarity and you have no desire to return to earth. Observing yourself, you find that you now glide effortlessly on two feathered wings. Before you have a moment to wonder at your new condition, forgetfulness prevails.

to be. As a single cell divides to create another, so unity replicates itself over and over again incurring evolution, adaptation and transformation. Yet despite the appearance of diversity and multiplicity, unity remains. It is too easy to lose sight of the one in the face of the many. Contemporary physics is still in search of its own Holy Grail, a unified theory of being. Embracing paradox opens the door to wisdom. This is the Path of the Scintillating Intelligence, the awakened and alive mind which seeks to lightly hold the one and the many, the distant and the present, the moment and the eternal, the human and the cosmic, for these are the elements on the journey of becoming. This is the Path of the Spirit of Aethyr which is life universal, present always and everywhere. This first Path expresses the essential puzzle between spirit and matter, life force and form, energy and field. It remains the most fundamental question of all. Philosophers once mused on the nature of reality, but scientists are now directly engaged in the worlds within the world. This is a Path of beginnings. It is a good time to face such questions in a new spirit.

EVOCATION

Welcome to this kingdom if your mind seeks out the path of wisdom. Attune yourself if you can to the ineffable and the invisible, to the extraordinary and the wonderful. Attune yourself to the mystery within creation. I am creation commencing its own journey. I am all beginnings at all times. I am the alpha and omega of transformation. I am the unfolding universe imprinted with all that can be. Do not relegate me to a historical past. I belong in the eternal present. Creation is continuous and I am continuously present in it. I am spirit imbedded in matter. I am scintillating life. I am the energy which gives rise to form. I hold a multiplicity of forms and unlimited evolutionary possibility. I am vastness beyond imagining and variety beyond comprehension. I bring the impetus 'to be'. I carry the seeds of what might be as I descend from places unknown towards more familiar possibilities. See me in all things both great and small. I am the Spirit of Aethyr, the spark of life itself. I am ever the hidden seed of the future veiled in the present. Can you contemplate my nature? This is my realm, that of endless becoming and eternal transformation. See me in the endless dance of creation for I am the world dancer poised at the axis of creation. Look for my dance in all transformations through time. I spin future possibilities. As the present was imbedded in the past, so the future is imbedded in the present. I am the world within the world, energy within form, emptiness within fullness. This is your realm too, for we are both becoming and changing without ceasing.

INTERNALIZATION – THE 11TH
PATH: CHOCKMAH–KETHER

Construct the Temple of Chockmah in the creative imagination. Stand beside the door of the Fool. The Archangel Ratziel draws back the tapestry curtain so that you may pass.

You emerge onto a mountain path. The air is thin but the light has an extraordinary brilliance and clarity. Looking back down the mountain, you already seem to have journeyed far. Looking ahead, you see the summit is in view. You set out. As you walk, you begin to think about the significance of the mountain. Stories of the sacred mountain abound in every tradition. The mountain exemplifies the journey of the soul. Its physical tests are those of the spirit too. In the high places away from the familiarity of routine life, otherworldly encounters happen. Like many travellers, you too are seeking a peak moment of transcendent experience here amid the physical peaks and summits of the world. As you muse on such things, you continue on your journey. Soon you reach your goal at the summit.

Standing here allow your imagination to become identified with the possibilities of the sacred mountain, with the solitary splendour of its place just below the clouds, far away from the world of men and strife. Feel the quality of the air in this place. See sunlight glinting on white snow. Refracted by the rarefied air, everything seems to shine and scintillate with a brilliance that can be found nowhere else. Everything is pristine; yours is the first footfall, yours is the first breath. You rest for a while and fall into a state of contemplative reverie. Here time seems to stand still. There is no compulsion to do anything other than enter into the fullness of this moment. Your outer senses are suspended but your inner senses awaken.

In the silence of this timeless place, you hear your name being called. You are startled by the possibility of another being in this place. Your name is called again with such clarity that it is undeniable. You know that you have entered the in-between world of sacred space and time. Terrified lest you break the visionary moment and shatter the momentum of spiritual possibility, you make an answer. As if in response you hear a dog bark somewhere close by. The earthy familiar sound is reassuring and you feel certain that another traveller much like yourself is close to hand.

As you look up into brilliant sunshine, the outline of a figure is momentarily etched against the skyline. Framed before the sun, the figure seems transfixed between heaven and earth. Light seems to emanate like a bright halo as sunlight peers from behind this unexpected presence. Somewhat dazed by the brilliant light, you try to get a better view by shifting your gaze, but light still streams around this new face and streamers of diamond brilliance shine. Finally, you simply close your eyes and allow your inner senses to guide your vision. In your mind's eye you see the archetypal wanderer. Clad in simple but unworldly clothing, you realize that this traveller does not inhabit the physical world where the four elements rule. You somehow know that this traveller is untouched by the constraints of the world. The traveller carries everything in a knapsack and you cannot help but wonder what it holds. As if in answer to your unspoken question, you hear the single word 'All' ring out in your mind.

As you watch with the eye of the mind, the traveller whose name you do not know begins to dance. The steps soon turn into a spin and the spinning becomes faster and faster. Colours flash before your eyes as the spinning increases in its momentum. The rod that was once carried to support the knapsack now stands as a central axis about which all spins. Now, like a child's spinning top, all colours have merged into bands of fleeting patterns as dynamic movement establishes its own momentum. Form and figure have quite vanished in the whirling propulsion of spinning motion. Even the dog has been absorbed into the vortex of energy; its whiteness has become a band of spinning light. As the vortex continues to gather speed, spinning faster and faster on its own axis, sparks flash and fly and you feel unexpected radiant heat. Now the vortex has become a globe of spinning and shining energy. Driven by its own momentum, the sphere rises and simply descends over the edge of the rocky abyss; only the rose is left. You pick it up.

When you are ready, return the way you came to the temple. When you are ready, leave through the doorway. Finally, dissolve all images and return to ordinary consciousness.

EXERCITIA SPIRITUALIA

Take the Following as Subjects for Meditation:
- The Spirit of Aethyr
- Aleph
- The Element of Air
- The Scintillating Intelligence

Make Notes on:
- Tarot Trump 0, The Fool

Visualize the Following and Record your Experiences:
- The Temple of Chockmah including the Archangel Ratziel
- The Journey of the 11th Path

CHAPTER 34

Kether – The Crown

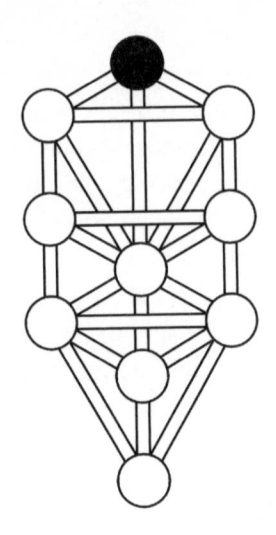

FIGURE 43 THE SEPHIRAH KETHER

TABLE OF CORRESPONDENCES

God-Name: Eheieh – I am that I am

Archangel: Metatron

Order of Angels: Chaioth He Qadesh – Holy Living Creatures

Magical Image: An ancient bearded king in profile

Spiritual Experience: Union with God

Virtue: Attainment, Completion of the Great Work

Vice: None

Titles: Existence of Existences, Concealed of the Concealed, Ancient of Ancients, Ancient of Days, The Smooth Point, The Primordial Point, The Point within the Circle, The Most High, The White Head, The Head which is Not, The Vast Countenance, The Macroprosopus, Lux Occulta

Mundane Chakra: Primum Mobile – The First Swirlings

Personal Chakra: Sahasrara – the Thousand-Petalled Lotus, the Crown Chakra

Colour in Atziluth: Brilliance

Colour in Briah: Pure White Brilliance

Colour in Yetzirah: Pure White Brilliance

Colour in Assiah: White flecked Gold

Symbols: The Point, The Point within a Circle, The Crown, The Svastika

Tarot Cards: The Four Aces

Ace of Wands: The Roots of the Powers of Fire

Ace of Cups: The Roots of the Powers of Water

Ace of Swords: The Roots of the Powers of Air

Ace of Pentacles: The Roots of the Powers of Earth

COMMENTARY

*The First Path is called the Admirable or Hidden
Intelligence because it is the Light-giving power of
comprehension of the First Principle, which hath no
beginning. And it is the Primal Glory, because no created
being can attain to its essence.*

Kether is the first Sephirah from which all others emanate. It alone constitutes the Archetypal World of Atziluth which gives rise to the increasingly
denser worlds of Creation, Formation and Action. Kether, the Crown,
represents the source and destination of all existence. The Hebrew word for
Crown is derived from the root *Katar* meaning 'to surround'. Kether not
only gives rise to creation but surrounds all that is within it through the
dimensions of time and space.

In The Beginning

In the beginning when God created the heavens and the
earth, the earth was a formless void and darkness
covered the face of the deep, while a wind from God
swept over the face of the waters. Then God said, 'Let
there be light'; and there was light. And God saw that
the light was good; and God separated the light from
the darkness.

Genesis 1: 1–4

Kether means crown. As the birthing baby is said to crown at the first
appearance of the head, so creation itself is crowned as it emerges from a
state of non-existence, as if from nowhere. How the world came into being
has tantalized every culture, civilization and thinking person. This is the
question that every child asks with an innocent simplicity. 'The world *is; it*
is irresistibly present; how do we account for its existence? Working
backwards through evolution, hauling in the chain of cause and effect, we
arrive at the notion of an original "something"; but what lies behind that

primordial presence? A blank, an emptiness; the absence of nothing.'[1] But the answer to the question is far from simple. Those who become mesmerized by the intensity of the question turn either to science or to religion for an answer – sometimes, though more rarely, to both. Ironically, science and religion start with the same question. Both fields of human enquiry are concerned with the fundamental nature of reality. The 20th-century mystic, Sri Aurobindo, speaks of creation in the following way:

> At the origin of things we are faced with an infinite containing a mass of unexplained finites; an indivisible full of endless divisions, an immutable teeming with mutations and differentiations, a cosmic paradox is at the beginning of all things. This paradox can only be explained as One, but this is an infinite Oneness which can contain the hundred and the thousand and the million and the billion and the trillion. This does not mean that the One is plural, or can be limited or described as the sum of the many. On the contrary, it can contain the infinite many because it exceeds all limitation or description by multiplicity and exceeds at the same time all limitation by finite, conceptual oneness.[2]

In an age of quantum physics, the question is perhaps more tantalizing than ever. But without the advantage of particle accelerators, radio telescopes and all the paraphernalia of advanced computer technology, Kabbalah puts forward a unique and intelligent view of creation.

Kether is the first Sephirah or Emanation of the Tree of Life. The imagery attributed to Kether is rich and sophisticated. This is not the usual fare of the creation myth but an allegorical and metaphorical synthesis of ideas and symbols which do not rest with simplistic explanations. Kether is the source for all that unfolds through the remaining Sephiroth. It symbolizes the point from which all creation springs. It is called the Smooth Point and the Primordial Point. The moment of creation is 'the vanishing point with which we are faced when we trace *everything-that-is* back to *something-that-was* and, reaching beyond that, to *nothing-that-was-not*.'[3] This is Kether: it gives rise to everything-that-is, it represents something-that–was and it reaches back into nothing-that-was-not. Can you imagine a time before anything including time? 'Before one, what do you count?' asks the Sepher Yetzirah. Can you imagine a state of nothingness? It is impossible. Can you imagine the interface between a state of nothingness and the moment that science describes as the Big Bang when everything that ever was, is or shall be, came into existence?

The magical image ascribed to Kether is of an ancient, bearded king in profile. Like the far side of the moon, one side of his face is always hidden. It cannot be seen, known, recognized or identified except as hidden and concealed. This image points to the great mystery which is the creative moment. This is action of the Hidden Intelligence. The Egyptian god Amen was also a hidden presence. His name was taken from a root word meaning 'what is hidden' or 'what cannot be seen'. Later it was connected with the word *men*, meaning 'to abide' and 'to be permanent'. Kether is assigned the God-Name Eheieh, which means 'I am that I am'. It too implies a statement of permanent being or eternal abiding.

Hebrew offers three words which are similar in meaning. *Bara* means to create something from nothing, *Yatzar* means to form something from a substance that already exists, and *Asah* has the connotation of the completion of an action. These subtle differences in meaning underlie the concept of the four creative worlds or stages in creation. *Atziluth* is often referred to as 'nothingness'. From nothingness itself comes the power to create something from nothing. From what is generated through the power to create something from nothing comes the power to form something. From what is begun in form, there arises the power to complete in actuality. This fourfold image runs through Kabbalistic thinking as a recurring theme. Each of the Sephiroth can be defined at the four levels; the Tree as a whole can be divided into these four stages and any processes which find a correlation on the Tree can also be viewed in this way.

Creation myths from around the world from different cultures and times revolve around very similar themes. From non-being comes being, from chaos comes order, from undifferentiated potential comes a hierarchy of states. From nothing comes something. This state prior to the moment of creation is perhaps even more difficult to grasp. The appearance of something from nothing is quite in accordance with current scientific understanding. Where the statistics of the Big Bang provide some kind of narrative, the energy of negative existence is difficult to conceptualize. A state of non-manifestation, a locus of non-being, is virtually impossible to grasp. Yet both contemporary physics and the Kabbalah suggest that the first point of manifestation draws energy from a state of latent energy which has no material form. Kabbalah describes this state as Negative Existence. The word for 'nothingnesss' is *Beli-mah*, which can also be translated to mean closed, abstract, absolute or ineffable. It is derived from two words: *Beli*, meaning 'without' and *Mah* meaning 'what' or 'anything'. *Beli-mah* then means without anything.[4] Negative existence, the state of abstract or absolute nothingness, is itself described as having three states of varying density, referred to as the Veils of Negative Existence: *Ain, Ain Soph* and *Ain Soph Aur*. These terms are difficult to translate. Most often Ain is translated to mean Negativity; Ain Soph, the Limitless or Infinite Being; and Ain Soph Aur, the Limitless Light. Kether is called The Point or The Point Within a Circle. This image conveys the idea of pressure converging at the centre of a circle until explosive power bursts through, carrying the energy of the Unmanifest with it. Like a black hole in reverse, the first point of manifestation spews out light and existence. *Sof* is derived from the root *Safah*, meaning 'to cease to exist'. As a figure of speech, the Ain Soph is a double negative which, through inversion, means even in non-existence there is existence. Kether is described as 'the Light-giving power of comprehension of the First Principle, which hath no beginning'. In other words, the light which is Kether gives the power of comprehension to a state which has no beginning.

The Big Bang

> We are made of stardust because we are a natural consequence of the existence of stars, and from this perspective it is impossible to believe that we are alone in the universe.
>
> **John Gribben, *Stardust***

The scientific story of creation begins at time zero when suddenly the forces of manifestation appear, seemingly from nowhere at all, in a manner beyond our wildest imaginings, on a scale beyond our ability to conceive and with a speed that defies explanation. In a thermonuclear explosion beyond description some 15 billion years ago, everything that was to be came into existence. It truly was the Big Bang. Creation began with fire. In just one hundred-thousandth of a second after time zero, elementary particles, protons, electrons and neutrons smashed into one another in a wild frenzy of convulsive ferocity. After just one second the temperature reached 10 billion degrees. Briefly, the entire universe was no more than the size of an apple. 'If we backtrack to 10–32 seconds, the moment when the inflationary era finished, we find that it is valid to use the standard Big Bang model and the equations of general relativity. These tell us that the now observable universe was then no more than 10 centimetres across, about as big as a nice apple.'[5] The body of the emergent universe was composed not of matter but of radiation. At 10 seconds, the cosmos-to-be was both expanding and cooling. At a mere few billion degrees, radiation became less energetic and deuterium was created from the collision of neutrons and protons. After only three minutes, the mass creation of deuterium had already peaked, to be followed by the mass creation of helium 3 (one deuterium nucleus and one proton) and helium 4 (two deuterium nuclei), and next by the appearance of lithium (formed from three protons and four neutrons) in smaller quantities. The temperature continued to fall. At about 15 minutes, the temperature had dropped to a few hundred million degrees and nuclear reactions ceased. Creation now consisted of a vast cosmic soup – three quarters protons, one quarter helium, with some deuterium and a trace of lithium. A state of local thermal equilibrium prevailed between the forces of electromagnetic radiation and the electrons and various nuclei forming a high-temperature, intensely bright plasma. While the temperature of the particle-radiation mix continued to drop, expansion continued, producing a less brilliant plasma. After this first phase, time now passed slowly without radical change. At an age of about 300,000 years the temperature dropped sufficiently for the first atoms to form. Matter and radiation began to separate. Radiation began to lose its dominance as gravitational forces supported the expansion of matter, even if only in a pre-material state.

Tens of millions of years passed. After 10 million years, the temperature reached 20 degrees centigrade. But after 100 million years it had plunged to 200 degrees centigrade below freezing. Regions that were slightly more dense exerted a stronger gravitational pull, breaking up the huge sheets of gas, hydrogen and helium to make galaxy-forming walls and sheets which stretched across the universe. Within those galaxies, smaller clouds of gas collapsed under the influence of gravity to form stars. A new phase of creation commenced with far-reaching consequences for us. Life on earth today is intimately connected to this evolutionary phase because planetary life begins with the process of star formation. When a star reached the end of a cycle as the nuclear fuel was exhausted, a final death throe scattered the elements of life into space with explosive power. The death of stars gave birth to the heavier elements which came to form the planetary bodies. Earth with its iron core could not have existed until the first stars had run their life cycle. Our sun was formed some 4.5 billion years ago from material that had already been partially processed inside two or more generations of preceding stars. Everything in the solar system except primordial helium and hydrogen has been manufactured inside another star. We are indeed star stuff.

Despite the vastness of creation which is beyond human conception, creation myths invariably accord a special place to the role of humanity. Kabbalah firmly connects humanity to the cosmos by the holism implicit in the figure of Adam Kadmon; biblical text states God made man in his own image. The Hermetic tradition states 'As Above, So Below'. Kabbalah directly connects Kether, the creative fountainhead, and Malkuth, the physical realm, through a number of correspondences. Later Kabbalists called the first Breath of Kether the Direct Light, but the second Breath is associated with Malkuth and called the Reflected Light. The Direct Light from Kether is causal; it results in the Reflected Light of Malkuth. The Sephirah Kether is signified by the magical image of a bearded king. Malkuth is the Kingdom. Kether is the Crown. The crown belongs to the regalia of kings. It designates kingship and a kingdom which is to be found in the world of Assiah at Malkuth. The symbol of the crown connects Kether with Malkuth very directly and conveys an intimate and close relationship. The Hebrew word used for 'dominates' in the phrase 'He dominates them all' is *Melekh*, meaning a king who interacts with his subjects, as opposed to *Moshel* a tyrannical ruler. The image of kingship so common in Kabbalah and also in Tarot is intimately related to the idea of rule as natural law. When natural law itself becomes the blueprint for living, the pitfalls of a man-made belief system might at last be avoided.

The Mundane Chakra assigned to Kether is called the *Primum Mobile* or the First Swirlings. How well this conveys a sense of chaotic activity and movement which characterises the first epochs of creation. It may be merely a metaphor but prior to any scientific understanding, it is a metaphor which stands up surprisingly well. Additionally, Kether is assigned to the sign of the *svastika*. This has nothing whatsoever to do with the Nazi swastika but represents activity in motion. Its four arms are generated from the central point. This is an image of dynamic movement as energy bursts out from the Primordial Point which is Kether. In an age of changing science, four fundamental laws still are recognized as supporting scaffolding of manifestation. It was Newton who formulated the law of gravity at the end of the 17th century. His law served well until the 20th century when it was superseded by Einstein's General Relativity Theory. The electromagnetic interaction was discovered in the 19th century when James Clerk Maxwell unified electrical and magnetic phenomena into a single theory. The strong nuclear reaction was discovered in the 1930s and explains how protons of the nucleus stick together despite their electrical repulsion. In the 20th century, Enrico Fermi formulated a theory of weak interaction which was able to explain beta radioactivity and prepared the way for recognition of the first neutrino in 1956. Curiously, the order of angels assigned to Kether is that of the four Holy Living Creatures, *Chaioth He Qadesh*. The correspondence between contemporary physics and Kabbalistic concepts is not lost on modern commentators. Rabbi Aryeh Kaplan notes:

> In the simplest physical terms, 'water' represents matter, 'fire' is energy, and 'air' is the space that allows the two to interact. 'Fire' is the electromagnetic force, through which all matter interacts. This is the 'strong nuclear' or pionic force, which binds the nucleus together, represented by water. On the other hand, even within each elementary particle, there is a need for a cohesive force to counteract the electromagnetic force within the particle itself. This is the 'air' which represents the weak nuclear force. The fourth force, gravity, corresponds to 'earth'. Earth, however, is not a basis element but a confluence of the other three. These three elements also relate to the experiential. Here, fire represents the radiation of energy, while water represents the absorption of energy. These are thesis and antithesis, giving and receiving, which themselves are manifestations of cause and effect. Air, which represents the transmission of energy, is then the synthesis linking the two.[6]

It can only be a matter of great wonder that the fine-tuning within the basic laws of creation perfectly permits the evolution of life and consciousness.

IN THE BEGINNING
Be bold! Write your own mythical account of creation.

The Book of Creation

Ten Sephiroth of Nothingness
  Their measure is ten
  which have no end
A depth of beginning
  A depth of end
A depth of good
  A depth of evil
A depth of above
  A depth of below
A depth of east
  A depth of west
A depth of north
  A depth of south
The singular master
  God faithful King
dominates over them all
  from His holy dwelling
  until eternity of eternities.

The Sepher Yetzirah

The richness and complexity of the Kabbalistic model of creation cannot be conveyed briefly. The attempt would be an insult to a marvellously intricate, sophisticated and profound philosophy which far outstrips the more common allegories of creation. Uniquely, letters and numbers take on instrumental roles as creative powers, which incidentally paves the way for the later Kabbalistic passion of *gematria*. In this unique view of creation, Foundation letters serve as instruments of creation. Using these powers, the singular master seals the universe in six directions, simultaneously creating a dimension of time and space with the addition of a spiritual or moral continuum. This image of creation takes a cube as its model. Creation begins with the concept of unity, from which duality arises. Plurality and multiplicity may next proceed, but unity is never eclipsed. The Hebrew word for 'singular' here is *Yachid*, indicating a complete or absolute unity. Always affirming the unity of the spiritual and the physical, the Sepher Yetzirah says, 'if one wishes to know the wisdom of the holy unification, let him look at the flame rising from a burning coal or from a kindled lamp. The flame cannot rise unless it is unified with something physical.' In Kabbalistic style, even this simple metaphor contains another level of meaning. The Hebrew word for coal, *gachelet*, has a numerical value of 441, the same value as that for *emet*, meaning 'truth'.

Here is a holistic philosophy *par excellence* which invites participation in the interior journey. Through a complex system of correspondences each letter is related to numbers, qualities of being and specific locations in the physical body. In this way the macrocosm and microcosm become bound together. For instance:

> He made the letter Alef king over Breath
>> And He bound a crown to it
>> And He combined them one with another
> And with them he formed
>> Air in the universe
>> The temperate in the Year
>> And the chest in the Soul

The Sepher Yetzirah

This extracts invites meditation and contemplation on the letter Aleph. The Sepher Yetzirah is simultaneously an account of creation and an instruction manual which invites participation and involvement. The processes of creation mirror the stages of meditative practice. First of all is chaos. The mind is filled with confused and transient images. The Sephiroth are first perceived only as disconnected and separate images, 'like lightning running and returning'. Next comes the process of rectification as the Sephiroth and Paths are connected to assume the human-like pattern which represents the structure and organization within creation. From chaos comes order; from nothing comes something.

It is no wonder that the extraordinary work of creation is ascribed to the divine. It is difficult, if not impossible, for the human mind to conceive of a beginning that is not begun by an outside force; to the creator is ascribed the work of creation. In this mindset, the primal causative first principle assumes the most powerful nature that the human mind can conceive; only an infinite being is capable of creating infinite worlds and infinite life. On the other hand, perhaps nature includes and contains the first creative principle as an imbedded and implicit force. It is at this point that a primal divide arises between ascribing creation to a creator or to nature. If an intelligence is at work, is it to be found transcendentally outside the vastness of creation or implicitly imbedded in the laws of nature? Einstein himself had a deep reverence for nature. In a telegram sent to a newspaper in 1929 he stated, 'I believe in Spinoza's God who reveals himself in the harmony of all that exists, but not in a God who concerns himself with the fate and action of men'. Spinoza took the view that God and the material world were indistinguishable.

The urge to describe the unknowable events of creation has never diminished. From speculation to science, our questions have remained the same. The age, extent, and nature of creation are timeless issues which fascinate and awe the human mind with dimension, proportion and infinite possibility. Our knowledge will always be partial, but our sense of wonder need never be dimmed. Scientific understanding does not diminish our admiration for the creative processes which underpin universal life. Science has now provided a creation narrative and the laws which yield creation can be expressed as a formula: $E = mc^2$ – the law of all creation. Yet there are no answers for the most tantalizing question of all. Why? Kether expresses this mystery. It is both the Admirable and the Hidden Intelligence. Unlike previous generations our cosmic horizons have increased through technological prowess and scientific insight. We now know for certain that the level of fine-tuning within the basic creative forces is astonishing. Some scientists now seriously entertain the idea of a multiverse in which an infinite number of universes simultaneously exist based on different parameters. This concept takes creation into an area beyond imagination. Yet the creator – ever hidden, ever invisible – eludes our direct gaze. But whether concealed within every particle of creation itself as an immanent creative power or transcendent outside creation in some unknown and mysterious way, this remains a mystery beyond solving.

EVOCATION

Welcome to my kingdom which is the central mystery. In my beginning is your beginning. I am beyond your conception and beyond your imagination. I am the one without name. I am the one without qualities. I am that

I am. I bring the wholeness into being. I bring every particle into being. All of creation is my domain. I am being and becoming, transformation and exchange. I am the unknowable. I am the one whose face is not seen. I am the hidden one. I am the first cause. I am the unbegotten and the self-made. I am the Ancient of Ancients. I am the Existence of Existences. I am that I am. It is I who give you birth for I bring all worlds into being. I encompass dimensions as yet unrevealed. I create wonders as yet unknown. I create possibilities as yet unexplored. My realm is infinite. I am called the Macroprosopus, the great world. Reflected in me you are the Microprosopus, the lesser world. I am alpha and omega, the beginning and the end.

INTERNALIZATION – KETHER, THE CROWN

This imagined voyage towards an understanding of the realm represented by Kether is perhaps one of the most difficult to envisage. In truth its scope is far beyond human understanding. The scope and scale of the statistics involved in the mathematics of creation are quite beyond our ability to comprehend. Nevertheless, it is these towering statistics which inspire awe and wonder at the vastness and majesty of creation. Our very inability to envisage the height, depth and limits of creation should be a source of inspiration and wonder.

The route to generating feelings about the realm of Kether is through the night sky. This is the doorway into the infinite and the transcendent. It provides our glimpse into the distant past, for we only see what light years permit. What we see as we look up into the heavens is an image of the past created by the time it has taken for light to reach us. What we see in the sky is but a fraction of the possible. What we cannot see is even more mysterious – quasars, pulsars, black holes and dark matter all have a reality. Science is no longer the irreconcilable foe of religion. It is not the enemy of the spiritual but its constant companion.

No meditative exercise is provided for Kether; it is not possible to provide any single framework which might successfully capture the essence of this Sephirah. Rather, look up to the heavens and let awe and wonder be your guide.

EXERCITIA SPIRITUALIA

Take the Following as Subjects for Meditation:

- Eheieh
- The Archangel Metatron
- Chaioth He Qadesh – Holy Living Creatures
- An ancient, bearded king in profile
- The Admirable or Hidden intelligence
- The Primum Mobile – The First Swirlings
- Existence of Existences, Concealed of the Concealed, Ancient of Ancients, Ancient of Days, The Smooth Point, The Primordial Point, The Point within the Circle, The Most High, The White Head, The Head which is Not, The Vast Countenance, The Macroprosopus, Lux Occulta

Contemplate the Following Questions and Record your Responses:

- How do the qualities of Attainment, Completion of the Great Work and Union with God operate in your life?
- How does the nature of Kether relate to the Crown Chakra?
- What other correspondences can you relate to Kether?
- How do the four Tarot cards relate to Kether?

Visualize the Following and Record your Experience:

- The Temple of Kether on a clear and starry night

AT JOURNEY'S END

- Draw the Tree of Life, placing the cards of the Major Arcana on the paths and the Minor Arcana on the Sephiroth. Use this as a glyph for your own meditation.

- Draw the Tree of Life, placing the Lesser, Greater and Supreme Mysteries on it. Use this as a glyph for your own meditation.

Postscript

As I write the closing pages, I am highly delighted to unpack a copy of *Holistic Revolution*. I see within it the same components that I have drawn upon to weave the Aquarian Initiation upon the Kabbalist Tree of Life – new science, psychology, Gaia, holistic health, feminism, the magical traditions and mysticism. In its pages I find contributions from the same voices that I too have valued – Carl Jung, Roberto Assagioli, Danah Zohar, Dion Fortune, Margot Anand, Alice Bailey, Evelyn Underhill and, of course, others who also speak for the ongoing spiritual revolution. In this new book I see another reflection of the Aquarian Initiation and I welcome its message, which I feel is exactly right for the time in which we live.

Despite the fact that the 21st century is already mired in conflict, I still see signs of hopefulness and positive change in the appearance and spread of radical new ideas which at their heart express the unity of the material and the spiritual. It remains my belief that ideas have the power to change the world. A vision brings inspiration and empowerment. The Tree of Life is an inspiring and brilliant vision of relationships, possibilities and connections. We need the power of vision. This book brings a new vision by placing our contemporary needs upon an initiatory structure. But though the journey on the Tree is solitary and its initiation is personal, this is not an isolated journey but a mass initiation being undertaken in unlimited ways. Written in the middle of the 20th century, Alice Bailey's vision of the New Age, doubtless inspired by the mind of the Tibetan, is a testament to the power of spiritual gifts of vision and prophecy which flower upon the rootstock of a highly developed consciousness. It provides an appropriate closing to the Aquarian Initiation. Her words carry the ring of truth, now just as then: 'Today, in the world, another great moment of crisis has arrived. I refer not to the present world condition, but to the state of human consciousness.'[1] Yet even while conflict and struggle dominated events, Alice Bailey envisaged the birth of a new possibility which she chose to call *The New Group of World Servers*. Writing well before New Age ideas had appeared in any recognizable form, Alice Bailey noted, 'The slow and careful formation of the New Group of World Servers is indicative of the crisis, they are overseeing or ushering in the New Age and are present in the birth pangs of the new civilization, and the coming into manifestation of a new race and a new world outlook.'[2] These words may initially have sounded hollow, but the passage of time has provided substance and meaning. She spoke of a silent, hidden, grass-roots movement assembling itself without external direction or organization. 'On the physical plane without exoteric organization, ceremonial or outer form, there is integrating silently, steadily and powerfully – a group of men and women.'[3] This is the hallmark of the Aquarian way. Whereas the Age of Pisces was dominated by religious stricture and hierarchical authority, the Aquarian style is quite the reverse – autonomous and self-directing. Her vision, to be found in *A Treatise on White Magic*, is Aquarian in every respect:

> They are being gathered out of every nation by the power of their response to spiritual opportunity, tide and note ... They are of all races, they speak all languages, they embrace all religions, all sciences and all philosophies. Their characteristics are synthesis, inclusiveness, intellectuality and fine mental development. They own no creed save the creed of brotherhood based on the one life. They recognize no authority save that of their own souls and no master save the group they seek to serve and humanity whom they deeply love. They have no barriers set up around themselves but are governed by a wide tolerance, a sane mentality and a sense of proportion. It does not matter if their terminology differs, their interpretation of symbols and scriptures vary or their words are few or many. ...[4]

> This group gives the word 'spiritual' a wide significance, they believe it to mean an inclusive endeavour towards human betterment, uplift and understanding. They give it the connotation of tolerance, international synthetic communion, religious inclusiveness and all the trends of thought which concern the esoteric development of the human being. ...[5]

> The members of this group will impose no enforced dogmas of any kind and will lay no emphasis on any doctrines or authorities. ...[6]

> Little groups will spring up here and there whose members respond to the new note. ...[7]

These groups will demonstrate no sense of separateness; they will be unaware of personal or group ambition. They will recognize their unity with all that exists. ...[8]

They are not interested in dogmas or doctrines. Their outstanding characteristics will be individual and group freedom from a critical spirit. This non-criticism will grow out of an inability to see error or failure to measure up to an idea.[9]

This is the hallmark of the Aquarian spirit. As a meditation grows from a seed thought, so the new group of world servers grows from the ten Seed Groups of the New Age.

THE SEED GROUPS OF THE NEW AGE

1. The Telepathic Communicators

These are custodians of group purpose – receptive to impressions from each other and from the Inner Planes. This group is closely related to all other groups.

2. The Trained Observers

By means of a cultivated and highly developed intuition, these individuals have a special ability to see clearly through all events, even through space and time.

3. The Magnetic Healers

These individuals work with the vital forces of the etheric body to bring mental, emotional and physical healing and an integration of being.

4. The Educators

These individuals work to bring in a new line of culture through a new type of education. Their emphasis will be upon the building of the antakarana and upon the use of the mind in meditation.

5. The Political Organizers

These individuals work in the world of human government dealing with the problems of civilization and with the relationship existing between nations in order to bring about international understanding.

6. Workers in the Field of Religion

These individuals work to formulate a universal platform, a loving synthesis, emphasizing the unity and fellowship of the spirit.

7. The Scientific Servers

These individuals work to reveal the spirituality of scientific work and to relate religion and science.

8. The Psychologists

These individuals work to relate soul and personality in a new paradigm of being.

9. The Financiers and Economists

These individuals work with the energies expressed through exchange and commerce to share and redistribute abundance.

10. The Creative Workers

These individuals work largely philosophically to provide ideas to blend life and form creatively. They are concerned with relating the other nine groups together to bring about a synthesis.[10]

These ten groups can be variously aligned to the ten Sephiroth of the Tree of Life. Moreover, it is now possible to measure this model against the unfolding Aquarian current to date and gauge its effectiveness as a blueprint. It is possible to see varying degrees of development in the visible manifestation of each of these groups. All of these seed groups can be identified in the newly emergent holistic spirituality.

This is still a time of transition and change. The old and the new are in direct conflict; like continental plates they slide across one another with grating impact. Alice Bailey points out the current challenge:

Know each of you for yourselves whether you stand for the new position, the new attitude towards work, and for the subjective method. Decide once and for all whether you prefer to work in the old exoteric ambitious manner, building and vitalizing an organization, and so producing all the mechanisms which go with such a method of work.

Should the new mode of work appeal to you, see to it that personality is subordinated, that the life of meditation is kept paramount in importance, that sensitivity to the subjective realms is cultivated, and any necessary outer activities are handled from within outwards.[11]

These prophetic words can be seen reflected in the changes that have taken place since they were written. Meditation in one form or another has become the mainstay of the spiritual renaissance now in progress. The new position, the new attitude and the subjective method are initiating a revolution in the world of ideas. A new vision is on the horizon. It is the Aquarian Initiation.

Notes

Chapter 1 Introduction and Overview

1. Jung, *Structure and Dynamics*, 71.
2. Ibid, 73.
3. Assagioli, *Psychosynthesis*, 21.
4. Ibid, 22.
5. Ibid.
6. Ibid.
7. Ibid.
8. Jung, *Structure and Dynamics*, 79.
9. Assagioli, *Psychosynthesis*, 21.
10. Jung, *Structure and Dynamics*, 48.
11. Ibid, 25.
12. Fortune, *Mystical Qabalah*, 21.
13. Ibid, 14.
14. Ibid, 25.
15. Ibid, 20.
16. Jung, *Archetypes*, 38.
17. Wang, *Kaballistic Tarot*, 1.
18. Fortune, *Mystical Qabalah*, 18.
19. Ibid, 25.
20 Gray, *Ladder of Lights*, 10.

Chapter 2 Malkuth – The Kingdom

1. Fortune, *Mystical Qabalah*, 266.
2. Ibid, 270.

Chapter 3 The Thirty-Second Path

1. Jung, *Archetypes*, 49.
2. Devdutti, *Shiva*, 120.
3. Capra, *Tao of Physics*, 259.
4. Zimmer, *Myths and Symbols in Indian Art*, 155.

Chapter 4 Yesod – The Foundation

1. Fortune, *Mystical Qabalah*, 254.
2. Jung, *Archetypes*, 24.
3. Ibid, 16.
4. Ibid, 18.
5. Ibid, 20.

6. Ibid, 279.
7. Fortune, *Mystical Qabalah*, 253.
8. *Sat-Cakra-Nirupana, the Description of the Chakras*, was translated by Sir John Woodroffe and included with other key Tantric texts in *The Serpent Power*.
9. Talbot, *The Holographic Universe*, 174–8.

Chapter 5 The Thirty-First Path

1. Jung, *Structure and Dynamics*, 215.
2. Thich Nhat Hanh, *Miracle of Mindfulness*, 27.
3. Ibid, 28.
4. Æ, *Candle of Vision*, 82.
5. Bailey, *Treatise on White Magic*, 40.

Chapter 6 The Thirtieth Path

1. *The Kabbalah Experience* has chosen to follow the translation offered by Robert Wang in *Kaballistic Tarot*. An alternative interpretation is: The Thirtieth Path is called the Collective Intelligence, so called because astrologers deduce from it the judgement of the Stars and the celestial signs, and the perfection of their science is according to the rules of the motion of the stars.
2. *Ad Herrenium III*, xx, 11.
3. Yates, *Art of Memory*, 134.
4. Ibid, 149.
5. Cade and Coxhead, *Awakened Mind*, 129.
6. Kaplan, *Sepher Yetzirah*, 45.
7. Graves, *Mammon and the Black Goddess*, 44.
8. Houston, *Search for the Beloved*, 104.
9. Ibid, 34.
10. Yates, *Art of Memory*, 174.
11. *Ad Herrenium III*, xxiv, 40.

Chapter 7 Hod – Glory

1. Bleakley, *Fruits of the Moon Tree*, 24.
2. Scott (ed.), *Hermetica*, 34.
3. Ibid, 50.

Chapter 8 The Twenty-Ninth Path

1. Jung, *Structure and Dynamics*, 115.
2. Ibid, 116.
3. Anand, *Art of Everyday Ecstasy*, 3.
4. Ibid, 2.
5. Ray, quoted in Anand, *Art of Everyday Ecstasy*, 21.
6. Harding, *Woman's Mysteries*, 38.
7. Ibid, 8.
8. Ibid, 235.
9. Ibid, 240.

Chapter 9 The Twenty-Eighth Path

1. Gadon, *Once and Future Goddess*, xv.

Chapter 10 Netzach – Victory

1. Jung, *Structure and Dynamics*, 117.
2. Ibid, 118.
3. Fortune, *Mystical Qabalah*, 226.
4. Æ, *Candle of Vision*, preface.
5. Ibid, 4.
6. Ibid, 100, 101.
7. Emerson, *Selected Essays*, 38–9.
8. Harding, *Woman's Mysteries*, 34.
9. Ibid, 38.
10. Æ, *Candle of Vision*, 19.

Chapter 11 The Twenty-Seventh Path

1. Harding, *Woman's Mysteries*, 208.
2. Ibid, 208.
3. Knight, *Qabalistic Symbolism*, 67.
4. Carter and Russell, *Workout for a Balanced Brain*, 8.
5. Cade and Coxhead, *Awakened Mind*, 123.
6. Æ, *Candle of Vision*, 81.
7. Carter and Russell, *Workout for a Balanced Brain*.

Chapter 12 The Twenty-Sixth Path

1. Zweig and Wolf, *Romancing the Shadow*, 4.
2. Jung, *Aion*, 8.
3. Zweig and Wolf, *Romancing the Shadow*, 39–42.
4. Ibid, 56.

Chapter 13 The Twenty-Fifth Path

1. Jung, *Mysterium Coniunctionis*, xvii.
2. Ibid, 272.
3. Bailey, *Ponder on This*, 319.
4. Happold, *Mysticism*, 58.
5. Ibid, 57.
6. Underhill, *Mysticism*, 385.
7. Ibid, 383.

Chapter 14 The Twenty-Fourth Path

1. Jung, *Archetypes*, 130
2. Ibid, 129.
3. Ibid, 117.
4. Bailey, *Ponder on This*, 64.
5. Lama Sherab Gyaltsen Amipa, *The Opening of the Lotus*, 17.
6. Assagioli, *Psychosynthesis*, 192.
7. Ibid, 197.
8. Ibid, 198.

Chapter 15 Tiphareth – Beauty

1. Underhill, *Mysticism*, 18.
2. Happold, *Mysticism*, 140.
3. Underhill, *Mysticism*, 17.
4. Happold, *Mysticism*, 55.
5. Ibid, 46.
6. Fortune, *Mystical Qabalah*, 189.
7. Ibid, 194.
8. James, *Varieties of Religious Experience*, 54.
9. Bailey, *Treatise on White Magic*, 197.

Chapter 16 The Twenty-Third Path

1. Lama Sherab Gyaltsen Amipa, *Opening of the Lotus*, 66.
2. Ibid, 67.
3. *Dalai Lama at Harvard*, 162.
4. Ibid, 83.
5. Ibid.
6. Lama Sherab Gyaltsen Amipa, *Opening of the Lotus*, 76.
7. Jung, *Archetypes*, 22.
8. *Dalai Lama at Harvard*, 54.
9. Geshe Rabten, *Treasury of Dharma*, 195.

Chapter 17 The Twenty-Second Path

1. *Dalai Lama at Harvard*, 134.
2. Motoyama, *Karma and Reincarnation*, 4–7.
3. Ibid, 51.
4. Ibid, 43.
5. Ibid, 28.
6. Ibid, 127.
7. Gould and Richardson, *Discovery, Recognition, Enthronement of the 14th Dalai Lama*, 20.
8. Motoyama, *Karma and Reincarnation*, 136.
9. *Dalai Lama at Harvard*, 42.
10. Motoyama, *Karma and Reincarnation*, 2.

Chapter 18 Geburah – Severity

1. Bailey, *Ponder on This*, 232.
2. Motoyama, *Karma and Reincarnation*, 61.
3. Dalai Lama, *Opening the Eye of New Awareness*, 11.
4. Ibid, 16–17.
5. Bailey and Daws, *United Nations*, 33.
6. Ibid, 115.
7. Fortune, *Mystical Qabalah*, 178.
8. Ibid, 174.
9. Ibid, 178.

Chapter 19 The Twenty-First Path

1. Jung, *Memories, Dreams*, 277–9.
2. Mackenzie, *Cave in the Snow*, 45.
3. Mackenzie, *Reincarnation*, 100.
4. Ibid, 135.
5. Ibid, 180.

Chapter 20 The Twentieth Path

1. Mackenzie, *Cave in the Snow*, 10.
2. Ibid, 119.
3. Ibid, 124.
4. Geshe Rabten, *Treasury of Dharma*, 212.
5. Ibid, 212.
6. Ibid, 219.

Chapter 21 Chesed – Mercy

1. Fortune, *Mystical Qabalah*, 165.
2. Chogyam Trungpa, *Journey Without Goal*, 97.

Chapter 22 The Nineteenth Path

1. Kerserling, *Travel Diary of a Philosopher*, 255–6.
2. Ibid, 124–5.
3. Jung, *Psychology of Kundalini Yoga*, xxii.
4. Krishna, *Kundalini*, 13.
5. Ibid, 233.
6. Ibid, 241.
7. Ibid, 243.
8. Ibid, 250.

Chapter 23 The Eighteenth Path

1. Bailey, *Treatise on White Magic*, 190.
2. Ibid, 189.
3. Motoyama, *Karma and Reincarnation*, 99.
4. Bailey, *Treatise on White Magic*, 287.

Chapter 24 The Seventeenth Path

1. Jung, *Psychology of Kundalini Yoga*, 94.
2. White (ed.), *Kundalini, Evolution and Enlightenment*, 408.
3. Ibid, 411.
4. Sannella, *Kundalini Experience*, 18.
5. Ibid, 18.
6. Jung and J.W. Hauer, *Kundalini Yoga*, unpublished manuscript.
7. Polkinghorne, *Faith in the Living God*, 95
8. White (ed.), *Kundalini, Evolution and Enlightenment*, 411
9. Krishna, *Kundalini*, 90

Chapter 25 Binah - Understanding

1. Scott (ed.), *Hermetica*, 181.
2. Knight, *Qabalistic Symbolism*, 97.
3. Lawlor, *Sacred Geometry*, 35.
4. Sheldrake and Fox, *Natural Grace*, 36.
5. Graves, *Mammon and the Black Goddess*, 164.
6. Ibid.
7. Begg, *Cult of the Black Virgin*, 133.
8. Ibid, 134.
9. Engelsman, *The Feminine Dimension of the Divine*, 156.

Chapter 26 The Sixteenth Path

1. Houston, *Passion of Isis and Osiris*, 127.
2. Ibid, 127.
3. Jung, *Archetypes*, 229.
4. Versluis, *Egyptian Mysteries*, 144.
5. Ibid, 144.
6. Ibid, 146.
7. Ibid, 145.

Chapter 27 The Fifteenth Path

1. Capra, *Tao of Physics*, 9.
2. Ibid, 10.
3. Jung, *Mysterium Coniunctionis*, 258.
4. Zohar, *Quantum Society*, 16.
5. Ibid, 2.
6. Ibid.

7. Ibid, 20.
8. Jung, *Undiscovered Self*, 44.

Chapter 28 The Fourteenth Path

1. Sheldrake, *Rebirth of Nature*, 164.
2. Kaplan, *Sepher Yetzirah*, 98.
3. Gadon, *Once and Future Goddess*, xii.
4. Sheldrake and Fox, *Natural Grace*, 46.
5. Lovelock, *Healing Gaia*, 11.
6. Ibid, 27.
7. Maclagan, *Creation Myths*, 7.

Chapter 29 The Thirteenth Path

1 Harding, *Woman's Mysteries*, 30.
2. Ibid, 8.
3. Ibid, 17.
4. Ibid.
5. Ibid, 124.
6. Ibid, 202.
7. Ibid.
8. Motoyama, *Theories of the Chakras*, 236.

Chapter 30 Daath – The Invisible Sephirah

1. Knight, *Qabalistic Symbolism*, 106.
2. Zohar, *Quantum Society*, 14.
3. Knight, *Qabalistic Symbolism*, 106.
4. Ibid, 106.
5. Ibid, 108.
6. Ibid, 109.

Chapter 31 The Twelfth Path

1. McNulty, *Freemasonry*, 89.

Chapter 32 Chokmah – Wisdom

1. Rees, *Just Six Numbers*, 1.
2. Ibid, 2–3.
3. Ibid, 4.
4. Gray, *Ladder of Lights*, 181.

Chapter 33 The Eleventh Path

1. *Dalai Lama at Harvard*, 194.
2. Sheldrake and Fox, *Natural Grace*, 19.
3. Ibid, 22.
4. Sheldrake, *Rebirth of Nature*, 171.

Chapter 34 Kether – The Crown

1. Maclagan, *Creation Myths*, 12.
2. Sri Aurobindo, *Life Divine*, 21.
3. Maclagan, *Creation Myths*, 5.
4. Kaplan, *Sepher Yetzirah*, 25.
5. Heidmann, *Cosmic Odyssey*, 136.
6. Kaplan, *Sepher Yetzirah*, 147.

Postscript

1. Bailey, *Treatise on White Magic*, 399.
2. Bailey, *Ponder on This*, 289.
3. Bailey, *Treatise on White Magic*, 399.
4. Ibid, 400.
5. Ibid, 414.
6. Ibid, 419.
7. Ibid, 426.
8. Ibid, 414.
9. Ibid, 426.
10. Sinclair, *Alice Bailey Inheritance*, 112–13.
11. Bailey, *Treatise on White Magic*, 425.

Drawing The Tree of Life

1. You will need a sheet of paper, a ruler and a pair of compasses.

2. Draw base line AD down the middle of the paper.

3. With your ruler mark the point B midway between A and D.

4. Draw a circle with B as its centre and its radius a quarter of AD. Draw two further circles of the same radius, with their centres at the points where the circumference of the first circle cuts the line AD.

5. Draw a half-circle with A as its centre to cut the uppermost circle at points 1 and 4.

6. Join points 1 and 4, 2 and 5, 3 and 6, 1 and 3, 4 and 6. Then draw in the diagonals.

   These are your construction lines.

7. Smaller circles to represent the Sephiroth may now be drawn with their centres at A, B, C and D, and points 1–6. The Paths may be broadened by drawing a second parallel line.

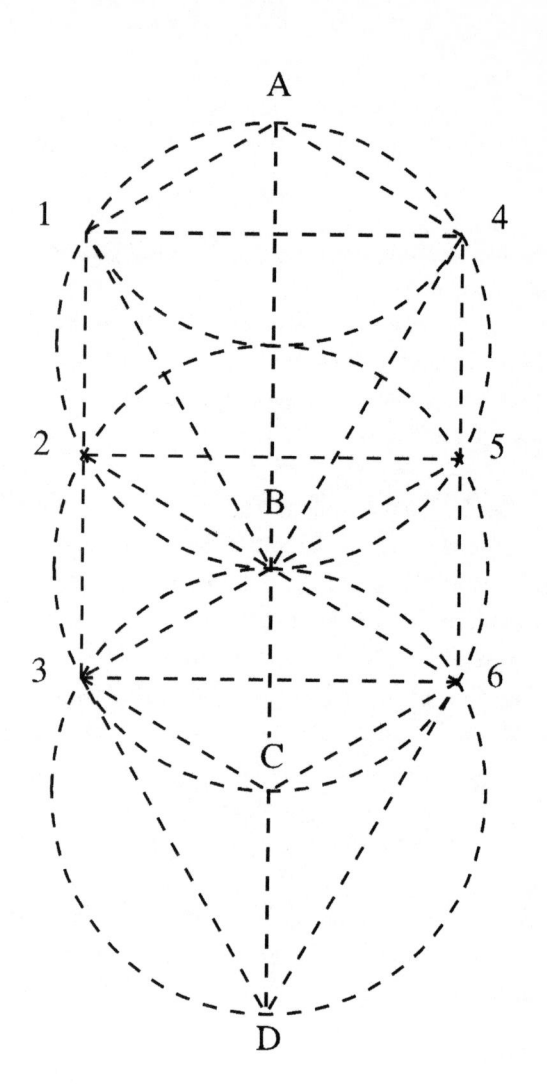

FIGURE 44 THE TREE OF LIFE

The Inner Temples of the Tree of Life

The Sephiroth are visualized as temples. This convention recognizes their sacred significance and immediately sets the tone in which transpersonal symbols have a rightful place. As part of the whole landscape, the Sephiroth as temples provide important intersections where the paths come together. Like stations on a motorway network, these locations provide an interchange before the traveller sets out again. Each temple symbolically expresses the nature of the individual Sephirah and also represents its place on the Tree in relation to the whole. Each temple is visualized with a number of doorways which lead out onto the paths. Each doorway is covered by a tapestry curtain depicting the relevant Tarot Trump. All journeys begin by passing through the doorway which leads directly onto the path. In *The Kabbalah Experience*, all journeys finish by returning to the temple. At the final closing, it is important to dissolve all mental images. This affirms the individual as the creative instigator of the process. The Archangel representing the organizing intelligence of the Sephirah acts as companion by being present at the opening of the journey and, if desired, at the closing too. The relationship with the presiding Archangel can be further developed through dialogue and meditation. The various Sephiroth as internal locations can be used beyond and above the prescribed journeys which serve to establish the basic structure and nature of the temple. This is an infinite and personal journey. When the inner landscape has been internalized, the journey will become your own.

General instructions

1. Visualize the inner temple with as much vividness and clarity as possible. To return from a journey, re-emerge into the body of the temple through the relevant doorway.

2. Spend some time in meditative reflection before finally exiting

through the main doorway once more. This threshold represents the return to everyday consciousness. Only leave the inner space of the temple when you are thoroughly prepared to do so.

3. Before leaving this subjective space, gather all the thoughts and realizations that you want to hold.

4. Always dissolve the inner landscape at the close of the session.

The Temple of Malkuth

Construct the Temple of Malkuth in the creative imagination. Find yourself standing before a doorway. Above it, there is a circle subdivided into the four colours of the subelements: citrine, olive, russet and black. Arranged around the circle in gold letters you see the phrase 'Know Thyself'. Pause and reflect upon these words before proceeding. When you are ready to proceed, just turn the handle and the doors will open.

You now stand in a ten-sided chamber with a floor of paved black and white squares. In the centre stands the Altar of the Double Cube draped with a white cloth. Ten columns stand around the circumference. In the East there are two pillars, one black and one white.

There are three doorways here, each covered by a tapestry curtain. Facing into the Tree, directly ahead, you see the door of the World leading to Yesod via the 32nd Path. At the left you see the door of Judgement leading to Hod via the 31st Path At the right, you see the door of the Moon leading to Netzach via the 29th Path.

This temple is under the aegis of the Archangel Sandalphon, who can be seen as a friendly and helpful guide wearing a lapel badge of planet earth or more traditionally visualized as an angelic being robed in the colours of citrine, russet, olive and black.

Apart from using the Temple of Malkuth to undertake the prescribed journey, use this as a space in which to reflect and find guidance on all matters relating to the physical world. Meditate within the Temple of Malkuth if you wish to offer earth service, whether great or small. All matters relating to physical well-being can be contemplated here.

The Temple of Yesod

Construct the Temple of Yesod in the creative imagination. Find yourself standing before a single door of shimmering silver, set with a lunar crescent as a door knocker. You knock upon the door and the crescent moon sends out a high vibrating note that hangs in the air. The door swings open and you enter. You are standing in a nine-sided chamber. The marbled floor of deep midnight blue is set with the four phases of the moon marked out in silver. You see the bright full moon, the dark new moon and the two crescents, one waxing and one waning. The nine walls are mirrored. In the centre of the chamber there is a nine-sided altar with mirrored sides. It is inset with a circular mirror in a silvered frame. Beside it there is a statuette of a naked male figure holding up the world. You are reminded of Atlas. A silvered lamp hangs low over the altar. Its flickering light is also mirrored in strange and fantastic shapes upon the walls.

There are four doorways here, each covered by a tapestry curtain. Facing into the Tree, directly ahead, you see the doorway of Temperance leading to Tiphareth via the 25th Path. On the right, you see the doorway of the Star leading to Netzach via the 28th Path. On the left, you see the doorway of the Sun leading to Hod via the 30th Path. Behind, you see the door of the World which opens onto the 32nd Path and leads to Malkuth.

This temple is under the aegis of the Archangel Gabriel, who can be seen as a caretaker wearing a lapel badge of the moon or more traditionally visualized as an angelic being robed in iridescent peacock colours of blue and green.

Apart from using the Temple of Yesod to undertake the prescribed journey, use this as a space in which to reflect and find guidance on all matters relating to the fluid and subjective world of living energy. Meditate within the Temple of Yesod when you are seeking to understand the past or be released by it, to recall far memory or incubate a dream. Seek guidance here when you seek self-understanding. All matters relating to psychological well-being can be contemplated here.

The Temple of Hod

Construct the Temple of Hod in the creative imagination. Find yourself standing before a plain door to a study. Knock simply and it will be opened. When you enter, you see that the Temple of Hod is an eight-sided chamber with a domed and transparent ceiling. In the centre of the hall is a circular pool of still water. In the centre of the pool a small pyramid of stone is set on a block of glinting granite. A flame burns at its summit. This is the altar in the Temple of Hod. Signs and symbols are carved around the rim of the pool. Here are astrological symbols, geometric forms, Hebrew letters and pictograms, hieroglyphs and patterns.

There are five doorways here, each covered by a tapestry curtain. Facing into the Tree, directly ahead, you see the door of the Hanged Man leading to Geburah via the 23rd Path. On your right, you will see four doorways in succession. The first is the door of the Devil leading to Tiphareth via the 26th Path. Next, you see the door of the Tower leading to Netzach via the 27th Path. Next, comes the door of the Sun leading to Yesod via the 30th Path. Finally you see the door of Judgement which leads back to Malkuth via the 31st Path.

This temple is under the direction of Mr Michael, who may be seen as a Director of Studies wearing a lapel badge in the form of the astrological symbol for Mercury, or more traditionally visualized as an angelic being swathed in fiery colours.

Apart from using the Temple of Hod to undertake the prescribed journey, use this as a space in which to reflect and find guidance on all matters relating to your own learning, research, investigation, project planning and mental organization. Meditate within the Temple of Hod when you are seeking to develop your mental abilities such as memory or concentration. Seek guidance in the Temple of Hod when you wish to improve your mental abilities. All matters relating to mental development can be contemplated here.

The Temple of Netzach

Construct the Temple of Netzach in the creative imagination. Find yourself standing outside a pair of doors softly greened by a covering of aged copper. Beside the door hangs a tasselled bell rope of green. The doors will open when you pull upon it. You enter and step into a chamber of seven sides where the walls are hung with your favourite pieces of art. As you commune with these works you recall the lives of their creators and remember the sacrifices they were prepared to make for beauty. Here are as many pictures as you desire to see. Here are all the artistic endeavours that you cherish. Music often plays in the background. Netzach holds your cultural and artistic inheritance. Netzach also holds a secret underground chamber.

This temple has five doors, each covered by a tapestry curtain. Facing into the Tree directly ahead, you see the door of the Wheel of Fortune leading to Chesed via the 21st Path. To your left you see four doors. The first of these is the door of Death leading to Tiphareth via the 24th Path. Next, you see the door of the Tower leading to Hod via the 27th Path. Next, you see the door of the Star leading to Yesod via the 28th Path. Finally, you see the door of the Moon leading to Malkuth via the 29th Path.

This temple is in the care of Lady Haniel who can be seen as a vivacious and artistic woman wearing a lapel badge in the form of the astrological sign for Venus, or more traditionally visualized as an angel swathed in green and surrounded by a halo of soft rose light.

Apart from using the Temple of Netzach to undertake the prescribed journey, use this as a space in which to reflect and find guidance on all matters relating to the development of the imagination in art and culture. Meditate within the Temple of Netzach when you are seeking to develop qualities of emotional sensitivity, spontaneity, openness, receptivity or imagination. Seek guidance here when you wish to develop your creative abilities, no matter how small. All matters relating to emotional development can be contemplated here.

The Temple of Tiphareth

Construct the Temple of Tiphareth in the creative imagination. Find yourself standing outside a door of modest proportions which shines with a veneer of fine gold leaf. You reach out and turn the handle. This small doorway opens out into a vast vaulted space which has the familiar air of a great cathedral. However, this space is built upon the form of a six-sided figure. Stained-glass windows set high in the walls reflect delicate images down onto the stone floors. A single window shows a lamen, the rose-cross, the cavalry cross, a truncated pyramid and a cube. Another window depicts a huge radiant sun. A glorious golden light fills the interior.

There are eight doorways here, each hung with a tapestry curtain. Moving mentally in a clockwise sweep, facing into the Tree directly ahead, you see the door of the High Priestess leading to Kether via the 13th Path. To the right of this, you see the door of the Emperor leading to Chockmah via the 15th Path. Next, you see the door of the Hermit leading to Chesed via the 20th Path. Next, you see the door of Death leading to Netzach via the 24th Path. Next, you see the door of Temperance leading to Yesod via the 25th Path. Next, you see the door of the Devil leading to Hod via the 26th Path. Next, you see the door of Justice leading to Geburah via the 22nd Path. Finally, you see the door of the Lovers leading to Binah via the 17th Path.

This temple is looked after by Mr Raphael, who can be seen as a friendly priestly figure and mystical friend identified by a lapel badge bearing the sun, or more traditionally visualized as an angelic form wearing robes coloured like the dawning sun.

Apart from using the Temple of Tiphareth to undertake the prescribed journey, use this as a space in which to reflect and find guidance on all matters relating to mystic or unified perception. Meditate within the Temple of Tiphareth when you seek to express the loving qualities of the heart and to be in communion with the harmony resonating in creation. Seek guidance here in all matters relating to the unfoldment of the soul. All matters relating to spiritual development can be contemplated here.

The Temple of Geburah

Construct the Temple of Geburah in the creative imagination. You stand outside a contemporary door which seems to be part of a modern complex. A light flashes above the door and it swings open. You enter into a large auditorium shaped as a pentagon. An aisle punctuates blocks of seats. The flags of the nations hang suspended from vantage points. In the centre is an open area shaped once more as a five-sided space. At its centre stands a broad open brazier where a flame burns continuously.

There are four doorways here, each covered by a tapestry curtain. Facing into the Tree, moving clockwise, directly ahead you see the door of the Chariot leading to Binah via the 18th Path. Next, you see the door of Strength leading to Chesed via the 19th Path. Next, you see the door of Justice leading to Tiphareth via the 22nd Path. Finally, behind you see the door of the Hanged Man leading to Hod via the 23rd Path.

This temple is in the care of Officer Khamael, who may be seen as a contemporary commander dressed in a scarlet uniform, or more tradition-ally visualized as an angelic being in flowing robes of red.

Apart from using the Temple of Geburah to undertake the prescribed journey, use this as a space in which to reflect and find guidance on all matters relating to conflict in the world of political understanding. Meditate here when you seek to understand the affairs of men and of nations. Seek guidance here in all matters relating to the emergence of conflict, hostility and national anger.

The Temple of Chesed

Construct the Temple of Chesed in the creative imagination. Find yourself standing outside a door. It has the sign of a square etched into the wood. You knock simply with your knuckles and enter into a large square chamber. In the centre is a round table, segmented and painted with heraldic signs. The centre of the table is defined by a painted gold circlet filled with the symbols of kingship – wand, orb, sceptre and crown. This seems like a place of assembly and meeting.

There are four doorways here, each hung with a tapestry curtain. Facing into the Tree, moving anti-clockwise, directly ahead and centrally placed, you see the door of the Hierophant leading to Chockmah via the 16th Path. Next, to your left and centrally placed, you see the door of Strength leading to Geburah via the 19th Path. Next, you see and the door of the Hermit leading to Tiphareth via the 20th Path. Finally, behind and centrally placed, you see the door of the Wheel of Fortune leading to Netzach via the 21st Path. Apart from the doorways the walls are entirely curtained in deep blue.

This temple is in the care of Frater Tzadkiel, who may be seen as a warm and humorous figure dressed in blue robes reminiscent of a monastic order. He wears a small pin resembling both the astrological sign for Jupiter and the number 4. Or traditionally he can be visualized as an angelic being robed in blue.

Apart from using the Temple of Chesed to undertake the prescribed journey, use this as a space in which to reflect and find guidance on all matters relating to the shared and central issues facing humanity. Meditate here to find your role in the wider human family.

The Temple of Binah

Construct the Temple of Binah in the creative imagination. Find yourself standing in the courtyard of a low circular building entered by a small opening covered by a dark veil. There are no windows other than narrow slits set high up in the walls at regular intervals. You stoop slightly to enter, pushing aside the veil as you do so.

Here the four doorways are set into the curved walls of the temple. Facing into the Tree, moving clockwise, you see there are four doorways, each covered by a tapestry curtain. First, you see door of the Magician leading to Kether via the 12th Path. Next, you see the door of the Empress leading to Chockmah via the 14th Path. Next, you see the door of the Lovers leading to Tiphareth via the 17th Path. Finally, you see the door of the Chariot leading to Geburah via the 18th Path

This Temple is in the care of the Archangel Tzaphkiel, who may be seen as a Mother Superior figure in dark robes relieved only by a small pin in the shape of the astrological sign for Saturn, or more traditionally visualized as a comforting and compassionate angelic figure in dark robes.

Apart from using the Temple of Binah to undertake the prescribed journey, use this as a space in which to reflect and find guidance on all matters relating to spiritual sensitivity and empathy for all life. Meditate within the Temple of Binah when you seek to be attuned to life with all its many dimensions of both joy and sorrow. Seek guidance in the Temple of Binah in all matters of great heart and universal communion.

The Temple of Chockmah

Construct the Temple of Chockmah in the creative imagination. Find yourself standing in an open plain beside a great wall of stone blocks that towers above you. Looking up, you know that this structure also climbs up into the sky. Running your hand over the joints between the blocks you marvel at the precision and skills demonstrated here. You know that without doubt you are standing beside one of humanity's monumental and inexplicable structures, a mountain cut from blocks of stone. This is not a pyramid however, but its predecessor, the ziggurat – a stairway to heaven.

You walk towards the stairway and begin to climb. As you ascend, the earth seems to become far away. You feel as if you are entering the sky. You continue climbing until you reach the summit, where an ancient priestly figure greets you and tells you how to align the ziggurat with the Tree. Deep within the ziggurat is a secret chamber with false doors painted on its walls in the tradition of spirit travel. Imagine yourself in this space. Moving anticlockwise, you see the doorway of the Fool leading to Kether via the 11th Path. Next, you see the door of Strength leading to Binah via the 14th Path. Next, you see the door of the Emperor leading to Tiphareth via the 15th Path. Finally, you see the door of the Hierophant leading to Chesed via the 16th Path.

This Temple is in the domain of the Archangel Ratziel, who may be seen as an ancient High Priest wearing a flowing robe and a belt of stars, or more traditionally visualized as an angelic being in sky-blue robes.

Apart from using the Temple of Chockmah to undertake the prescribed journey, use this as a space in which to reflect and find guidance on all matters concerning nature's raw power. Meditate within the Temple of Chockmah when you seek to reflect on the spiritual and practical relationship arising from our use and understanding of nature's own power. Seek guidance here when you wish to consider matters of dynamic growth, evolutionary leaps, universal power and radical discovery.

The Temple of Kether

The Temple of Kether is ever present. Go out into the night sky and gaze upwards!

Glossary

Abhiseka an initiatory transmission in Vajrayana Buddhism

Adeptus Exemptus the esoteric grade assigned to Chesed in the Western Mystery Tradition

Adonai ha Aretz Lord of Earth, the God-Name assigned to Malkuth

Ain, **Ain Soph** and **Ain Soph Aur** the Three Veils of Negative Existence

   Ain negativity

   Ain Soph the Limitless or Infinite Being

   Ain Soph Aur the Limitless Light

Ajna Chakra the Brow Chakra

Akasa spirit

Anahata the Heart Chakra

Antakarana the refined vehicle of consciousness commonly called the Rainbow Bridge

Aralim Thrones, the order of angels assigned to Binah

Ardhanarishivar 'the Lord who is half woman', androgynous aspect of Shiva

Arik Anpin the Vast Countenance

Ashim Souls of Fire, the order of Angels assigned to Malkuth

Auphanim Wheels, the order of Angels assigned to Chockmah

Autiot (in the singular, Aut) the letters of the Hebrew alphabet

Bardo the intermediary state between life and death

Beni Elohim Sons of God, the order of Angels assigned to Hod

Binah Understanding, the third Sephirah

Bodhicitta the thoughts of enlightenment, the determination to achieve enlightenment for the benefit of others

Bodhisattva one who is entirely dedicated to the achievement of complete enlightenment in order to support all living beings

Buddha one who has attained full enlightenment

Buddhi Enlightenment awakening to Buddhahood

Chaioth he Qadesh Holy Living Creatures, Order of Angels assigned to Kether

Chasmalim The Brilliant Ones, the order of Angels assigned to Chesed

Chazchazit Seership

Chesed (also called Gedulah) the fourth Sephirah, meaning Mercy

chi the universal life force

Chockmah Wisdom, the second Sephirah

Cholem ha Yesodeth The Sphere of the Elements, the mundane chakra assigned to Malkuth

Citta Mind in its total collective sense

Dharma the Buddhist doctrine of what is right and truthful

Eheieh the God-Name assigned to Kether, meaning 'I am that I am'

El Lord the God-Name assigned to Chesed

Elohim Gods, the order of Angels assigned to Netzach

Elohim Tzabaoth God of Hosts, the God-Name assigned to Hod

Geburah (also called Pachad) Severity, the fifth Sephirah

Haniel the Archangel assigned to Netzach

Hinayana the Lesser Vehicle, one of the three major paths of Buddhism

Hod Glory, the eighth Sephirah

Ida the lunar current

Jehovah or **Jah Eternal** the God-Name assigned to Chockmah

Jehovah Aloah va Daath God made manifest in the sphere of the mind, the God-Name assigned to Daath

Jehovah Elohim God and Goddess, the God-Name assigned to Binah

Jehovah Tzabaoth Lord of Hosts, the God-Name assigned to Netzach

Jin Shin Jyutsu physio-philosophy

Kalpa Tree the Wish Fulfilling Tree assigned to the Heart Chakra
karma the law of cause and effect
Kerubim the Strong, the angelic order assigned to Yesod
Kether the Crown, the first Sephirah

Lam Rim the graduated path to enlightenment

Macroprosopus the Greater Countenance
Mahat Universal Consciousness
Mahayana the Greater Vehicle, one of the three main paths in Buddhism
Major Arcana the 22 Tarot Trumps
Malachim Kings, the order of Angels assigned to Tiphareth
Malkuth the Kingdom, the tenth Sephirah
mandala a symbolic representation of unity and diversity in the form of
    a circle
Manipura the Solar Plexus Chakra
Marga the Path or Way towards enlightenment in Yoga
Metatron the Archangel assigned to Kether
Microprosopus the Lesser Countenance
Minor Arcana the 56 Tarot cards of the four suits
mudra a symbolic gesture formed with the hands

nadis psychic channels through which the life force moves
Nataraja Shiva as Lord of the Dance, from natya (dance) and nataka
    (theatre)
Netzach Victory, the seventh Sephirah

Pingala the solar current
prana universal life force
pranayama the science of breath control

Qbl Kabbalah, meaning 'from mouth to ear' or 'that which is received'
Qesheth the rainbow, symbol of hope and of promise

Raphael the Archangel assigned to Tiphareth
Ratziel the Archangel assigned to Chockmah
Ruach breath, wind and air, the universal life force

Sahasrara thousandfold, the Crown Chakra
samadi a state of deep concentration and awareness
samsara the round of rebirths fuelled by karma
Sat-Cakra-Nirupana description or knowledge of the chakras
Sephar number
Sepher a book
Sepher Yetzirah The Book of Creation
Sephirah emanation
Shaddai el Chai The Almighty, the God-Name assigned to Yesod
Siddhartha Gautama the man who became Buddha, the enlightened one
Sippur communication
Sunyata the non-self existent nature of the ego and all phenomena
Sushumna central nadir rising vertically through the spine
Swadistana the Sacral Chakra

Tetragrammaton the Holy Name of God
Tiphareth Beauty, the sixth Sephirah
Tong-len the practice of giving happiness in exchange for the suffering of others
Tzadkiel the Archangel assigned to Chesed
Tzaphkiel the Archangel assigned to Binah

Vajrayana the Adamantine Vehicle, one of the three major paths of Buddhism
Veil of Paroketh the first abyss before Tiphareth
Vesica Piscis the interface formed where two circles overlap
Vishnu Granthi the psychic knot within the Heart Chakra
Vishuddi the Throat Chakra

Yesod the ninth Sephirah, meaning Foundation

Zaur Anpin the Lesser Countenance

Bibliography

Æ, *The Candle of Vision, Inner World of the Imagination*, Prism Press, 1990

Anand, M., *The Art of Everyday Ecstasy*, Piaktus, 1988

Ashcroft-Nowicki D., *The Shining Paths,* Aquarian Press, 1983

Assagioli, R., *Psychosynthesis*, Turnstone Press, 1965

Avalon, A. (Sir John Woodroffe), *The Serpent Power*, Dover, 1974

Bailey, A., *Consciousness of the Atom*, Lucis Press, 1950

— *Ponder on This*, Lucis Press, 1971

— *The Soul, The Quality of Life*, Lucis Press, 1979

— *A Treatise on White Magic*, Lucis Press, 1969

Bailey, S., and Daws, S., *The United Nations, a Concise Political Guide*, Macmillan, 1995

Bancroft, A., *Modern Mystics and Sages,* Paladin, 1976

Barrow, J.D., *The World Within the World*, Oxford University Press, 1988

Begg, E., *The Cult of the Black Virgin*, Arkana, 1985

Bleakley, A., *Fruits of the Moon Tree*, Gateway Books, 1984

Brennan, B., *Hands of Light, Bantam New Age Books*, 1988

— *Light Emerging*, Bantam New Age Books, 1994

Bucke, R.M., *Cosmic Consciousness – A Study in Evolution of the Human Mind*, Citadel Press, 1977

Butler, W.E., *Apprenticed to Magic*, Aquarian Press, 1990

— *The Magican, his Training and Work*, Wilshire Book Company, 1976

Buzan, T., *Head First*, Thorsons, 2000

Cade, M., and Coxhead, N., *The Awakened Mind*, Wildwood House, 1973

Campion, N., *An Introduction to the History of Astrology*, The Institute for the Study of Cycles in World Affairs, 1982

Cannon Reed, E., *The Witches Qabalah*, Foulsham, 1986

Capra, F., *The Tao of Physics*, Wildwood house, 1975

Carter, P., and Russel, K., *Workout for a Balanced Brain*, Quarto Books, 2000

Chogyam Trungpa, *Journey Without Goal*, Shambhala, 1985

Chopra, D., *How to know God, The Soul's Journey into the Mystery of Mysteries*, Rider, 2000

Clarke, L., *The Chymical Wedding*, Jonathan Cape, 1990

Cobb, P. (ed.), *Walsingham*, White Tree Books, 1990

Crowley, A., *The Book of Thoth*, Samuel Weiser, 1982

Dalai Lama, His Holiness The, *Opening The Eye of New Awareness*, Wisdom Publications, 1985

— *The Dalai Lama at Harvard*, Jeffrey Hopkins (ed.), Snow Lion, 1988

— *Kindness, Clarity and Insight*, Snow Lion Paperbacks, 1984

Denning, M., and Phillips, O., *Magical States of Consciousness*, Llewellyn Books, 1985

Devdutti, P., *Shiva, an Introduction*, Valkis Feffer & Simons, 1997

Emerson, R.W., *Selected Essays*, Penguin Books, 1985

Engelsman, J., *The Feminine Dimension of the Divine*, Chiron Publications, 1987

Feuerstein, G., *The Shambhala Guide to Yoga*, Boston Press, 1996

Fortune, D., *Through the Gates of Death*, Aquarian Press, 1985

— *The Mystical Qabalah*, Benn, 1976

Fox, M. See Sheldrake, R., and Fox, M.

Gadon, E., *The Once and Future Goddess*, Harper & Row, 1989

Geshe Rabten, *Treasury of Dharma*, Tharpa Publications, 1988

Gould, Sir Basil J., and Richardson, H., *Discovery, Recognition and Enthronement of the 14th Dalai Lama, a collection of accounts by Khemey Sonam Wangdu*, Library of Tibetan Works and Archives, 2000

Graves, R., *Mammon and the Black Goddess,* Cassell, 1965

Gray, W.G., *The Ladder of Lights*, Helios, 1975

Grof, S., and Bennet H. Z., *The Holotrophic Mind – The Three Levels of Human Consciousness and How They Shape our Lives*, Harper, 1993

Happold, F.C., *Mysticism, Study and Anthology*, Penguin Books, 1963

Harding, E., *Woman's Mysteries*, Rider, 1971

Heidmann, J., *Cosmic Odyssey*, Cambridge University Press, 1986

Hoffman, E. (ed.), *Opening the Gates – New Paths in Kabbalah and Psychology*, Shambhala, 1995

Houston, J., *A Passion for the Possible*, Thorsons, 1997

— *Life Force*, Quest Books, 1993

— *A Mythic Life*, Harper, San Francisco, 1996

— *The Passion of Isis and Osiris, a Gateway to Transcendent Love*, Ballantyne Books, 1995

— *Search for the Beloved, Journeys in Sacred Psychology*, Tarcher, 1987

James, W., *The Varieties of Religious Experience*, Fontana, 1971

Johari, H., Chakras – *Energy Centres of Transformation*, Rochester Destiny Books, 1987

— *Tools for Tantra,* Inner Traditions, India, 1986

Johnson, B., *Lady of the Beasts, Ancient Images of the Goddess and her Sacred Animals*, Harper & Row, 1981

Johnston, W., *Arise My Love – Mysticism for a New Era*, Orbis Books, 2000

Jung, C.G., *Aion*, Princeton University Press, 1959

— *The Archetypes and the Collective Unconscious*, Princeton University Press, 1959

— *Dreams*, Ark Paperbacks, 1982

— *Mysterium Coniunctionis*, Princeton University Press, 1963

— *The Psychology of Kundalini Yoga*, Sonu Shamdasani (ed.), Bollingen, 1996

— *The Structure and Dynamics of the Psyche*, Routledge Kegan Paul, 1960

— *The Undiscovered Self*, Routledge, 1993

Kaplan, A., *Sepher Yetzirah*, Samuel Weiser, 1990

Knight, G., *Experience of the Inner Worlds*, Helios Books, 1975

— *A Practical Guide to Qabalistic Symbolism*, Samuel Weiser, 1978

— *The Rose Cross and the Goddess*, Aquarian Press, 1985

Krishna, G., *Kundalini – The Evolutionary Energy in Man*, Shambhala, 1985

— *Three Perspectives on Kundalini*, UBSPD, 1994

Lama Anagarika Govinda, *Foundations of Tibetan Mysticism*, Rider, 1973

Lama Sherab Gyaltsen Amipa, *The Opening of the Lotus*, Wisdom Publications, 1987

Lati, Rinbochay and Hopkins, J., *Death – Intermediate State and Rebirth in Tibetan Buddhism*, Snow Lion, 1979

Lawlor, R., *Sacred Geometry, Philosophy and Practice*, Thames & Hudson, 1982

Loftus, M., *Spiritual Approach to Astrology*, CRCS Publications, 1983

Lovelock, J., *Healing Gaia*, Harmony Books, 1991

Mackenzie, V., *Cave in the Snow*, Bloomsbury, 1999

— *Reincarnation*, Bloomsbury, 1989

Maclagan, D., *Creation Myths*, Thames & Hudson, 1977

Mandelbrot, B.B., *The Fractal Geometry of Nature*, San Francisco, 1982

Matthews, C., Sophia, *Goddess of Wisdom*, Mandala, 1991

Mcdonagh, S., *To Care for the Earth – a Call to a New Theology*, A Geoffrey Chapman Book, 1986

McIntosh, C., *The Rosy Cross Unveiled*, Aquarian Press, 1980

McNulty, W, Kirk, *Freemasonry, A Journey through Ritual and Symbol*, Thames & Hudson, 1991

Mookerjee, A., and Khanna M., *The Tantric Way*, Thames & Hudson, 1977

Motoyama, H., *Karma and Reincarnation*, Piaktus, 1992

— *Theories of the Chakras*, Quest Books, 1981

Mullin, G., *Death and Dying in the Tibetan Tradition*, Arkana, 1986

Myss, C., *The Anatomy of the Spirit*, Banyam Press, 1977

Osho, *The Buddha, The Emptiness of the Heart,* The Rebel Publishing House, 1989

— *Meditation, The Art of Ecstasy*, Harper & Row, 1976

Ozaniec, N., *First Directions – Chakras*, Thorsons, 2001

— *Initiation into Tarot*, Watkins, 2002

— *Teach Yourself Meditation*, Hodder & Stoughton, 1997

— *Teach Yourself Tarot*, Hodder & Stoughton, 1998

Parfitt, W., *The Living Qabalah*, Element Books, 1988

Polkinghorne, J., and Welker, M., *Faith in the Living God, A Dialogue*, SPCK, 2001

Radha Sivanandha, *Kundalini Yoga for the West*, Timeless Books, 1978

Ranke-Heinemann U., *Eunuchs for Heaven*, Andre Deutsch, 1990

Rees, M., *Just Six Numbers*, Weidenfield and Nicholson, 1999

Sannella, L., *The Kundalini Experience*, Integral Publishing, 1987

Scott, W. (ed., trans.), *Hermetica*, Solos Press, 1992

Sheldrake, R., *The Presence of the Past*, Collins, 1988

— *The Rebirth of Nature*, Century, 1990

— and Fox, M., *Natural Grace – Dialogues on Science and Spirituality*, Bloomsbury, 1996

Silburn, L., *Kundalini, Energy of the Depths*, State University of New York Press, 1988

Sills, F., *The Polarity Process – Energy as a Healing Art*, Element Books, 1989

Sinclair, J., *The Alice Bailey Inheritance*, Turnstone Press, 1984

Sogyal Rinpoche, *The Tibetan Art of Living and Dying*, Rider, 1992

Talbot, M., *The Holographic Universe*, Grafton Books, 1991

Tansley, D., *Subtle Body, Essence and Shadow*, Thames & Hudson, 1977

Thich Nhat Hanh, *The Miracle of Mindfulness*, Beacon Press, 1976

Torjesen, K, J., *When Women were Priests*, HarperCollins, 1993

Underhill, E., *Mysticism – The Nature and Development of Spiritual Consciousness*, Oneworld, 1993

Versluis, A., *The Egyptian Mysteries*, Arkana, 1988

Wang, R., *Kaballistic Tarot*, Samuel Weiser, 1983

White J., (ed.), *Kundalini, Evolution and Enlightenment*, Paragon House, 1990

Woodroffe, J., *Shakti and Shakta*, Dover Publications, 1978

Yates, F, A., *The Art of Memory*, Pimlico, 1992

Zimmer, H., *Myths and Symbols in Indian Art*, Princeton University Press, 1972

Zohar, D., *The Quantum Self*, Flamingo, 1991

— *Spiritual Intelligence*, Bloomsbury, 2000

— and Marshall, I., *The Quantum Society*, Flamingo, 1994

Zweig, C., and Wolf, S., *Romancing the Shadow*, Ballantyne Books, 1997

Index